MODERN CATECHETICS

MODERN
CATECHETICS

Message and Method in

Religious Formation

EDITED BY

Gerard S. Sloyan

THE MACMILLAN COMPANY, NEW YORK

COLLIER-MACMILLAN LTD., LONDON

Nihil obstat:
    Robert P. Mohan, **S.S.**
    Censor Deputatus

Imprimatur:
    ✠ Patrick A. O'Boyle
    Archbishop of Washington
    May 26, 1962

Fourth Printing, 1966

The Macmillan Company, New York
Collier-Macmillan Canada Ltd., Toronto, Ontario

Library of Congress catalog card number: 63-12401

Printed in the United States of America

ACKNOWLEDGMENTS

The author gratefully acknowledges permission from the following publishers and individuals to reprint excerpts from copyrighted material:

Desclée Co., Inc., New York, for an excerpt from *Introduction to Spirituality* by Louis Bouyer. Dover Publications, Inc., New York, for an excerpt from *The Art of the Story-teller* by Marie L. Shedlock. Fides Publications, Notre Dame, Indiana, for an excerpt from "An Awareness of Mystery" by Bernard Murchland, C.S.C., in *Apostolic Perspectives*, October–November 1958. Raymond B. Fullam, S.J., for an excerpt from his book, *The Popes on Youth,*

CONTENTS

INTRODUCTION

MODERN CATECHETICS means a variety of things to a variety of people. To the eminent philosophical thinker Etienne Gilson it means an increased rationalizing spirit in matters of faith, coupled with a regrettable departure from the intellectual character that justified the catechism of his youth. In his recent memoir *The Philosopher and Theology* (New York: Random House, 1962) he makes a case against contemporary catechetics without indicating much familiarity with the best developments in the field. We single out the views of this admirable Christian because he discusses at some length a modern phenomenon in the life of the Church without seeming to have acquired many solid data on the question. He possesses instead some damning information on another question, the contemporary bad catechism.

The present volume has come into being to lighten the burden of those who need to have a view on catechetical change, and at the moment have a poor view of it. Inadequate possession of the theoretical elements of the problem are the more usual reason for this, though a genuine critical faculty in some allied field such as scholastic theology helps to explain a spirit of *malaise* with the modern catechetical renewal. It may never be forgotten that theology is a science in the service of faith, faith in God's living Word. God is the proper object of theology, both in Himself and as He addresses a Word of eternal love to us. The transmission of His Word is the catechist's task, not any particular analysis of it that has proved useful to Christians in other times and places. Indeed, "usefulness" is the chief criterion that catechetics enjoins upon theology, whether positive or speculative. Does it throw light on the Word? Does it do so for these adults or children in this hemisphere and age? It may be undeniable that certain formulations or conclusions of theology are true, but this fact may equally be irrelevant to the task at hand. How do these theological statements pertain to *these listeners,* how can they be made *true for them?* That is the question catechetics asks of theology, knowing that the more profound the inquiry made by theology into the meaning of the Message, the more and better help this science can give to the catechist.

A book on modern catechetics does not need justification for the many readers for whom the field is already lively, and theoretical treatments of its problems all too few in number. They not only know that a renewal in the work of religious formation is in progress, they are helping to achieve it. These educators—bishops, parents, teachers in schools and Confraternity of Christian Doctrine classes—are well acquainted with the basic notion that content and method are sisters. Neither of the two overmasters the other, although the former gently takes the lead because she is the very Word of God. These educators know that sacred Scripture and the holy Liturgy are the chief sources of the mystery of faith, whence the householder—who is Christ living in His Church —brings forth from His store both the new and the old. They are also aware that the members of Christ's Body must constantly examine those truths that are the clear and unequivocal possession of Christ the Head, lest there be confusion in the Church over the mystery of faith and all it implies for Christian life.

Yet even these teachers, convinced as they are that catechizing must be an initiation into Christian life rather than an instruction about it, may need specific help. Realizing that their teaching must be fully biblical and sacramental in spirit, they may still be mystified as to how catechizing came to be anything but that in the past. They have a sound instinct for the need the Church has always experienced for a clear formulation of her conscious faith, yet at the same time wonder if the language of polemic, or of the Schoolmen, or of an abstraction proper to intellectually keen adulthood, are the only means of clear formulation available to the catechist.

All these and other questions the chapters in this book pose and try to answer. Its scheme is suited to immediate pedagogical needs. First comes an exploration of the ways in which God's Word comes to us in the Church, namely the biblical revelation, liturgical celebration, and the formal affirmations of faith made in creed, council, and catechism. Next comes an inquiry into how the type of catechism familiar to most Christians came into being and came to receive such high sanction. Then, step by step, an approach is made to the child, the adolescent, and the young adult, that is based on a sure knowledge of the Message that has come to us, coupled with utter fidelity to its mode of transmission.

The paradox at the heart of the catechetical question is that we of the Church, although deeply concerned about fidelity to the *substance* of divine tradition, are so casual about passing it along in the way in which it first came to us and comes to us now in the sacramental life of the Church. If these pages do no more than put in their proper relation Message and method in religious formation, they will have served their purpose.

The editor should like to express gratitude to his fellow theologians in the department he is associated with at the Catholic University of America for any merit this work may have, and to the numerous doctoral candidates of the last five years in a special way. Fitting into neither category are his sister Virginia M. Sloyan, Mrs. Inez M. Williams, and Sister Mary Pierce Butler, M.S.B.T., all of whom lent invaluable aid.

Gerard S. Sloyan

MODERN CATECHETICS

1 THE USE OF THE BIBLE IN TEACHING THE CHURCH'S FAITH

Joseph Colomb, P.S.S.

THERE IS only one catechesis in the Church, but it can be viewed in three different ways:

1. *historical catechesis* first announces, then explains, a past event in which God has spoken to make manifest His salvation. The role of this form of catechesis is to testify to the real, objective, and positive character of the Word of God;

2. *theological catechesis* derives from the revealed facts a knowledge based on faith which is the work of human reason. Its special contribution is to point out the intelligibility of the Word of God, to specify its various elements, and if necessary to defend it;

3. *liturgical catechesis* tries to explain the action of the liturgy and point out its significance in everyday life. Its contribution is to show the *present* significance of the Word of God continually being addressed to us through the liturgical act.

It will readily be understood that none of these three forms is ever realized in a pure state. All of the Church's catechesis must simultaneously witness to the objectivity, the intelligibility,

1

and the contemporaneousness of the Word of God. Any narration of an event constitutes a kind of explanation. A theological explanation must in turn rest on revealed data. And these data, plus their theological elaboration, are always present in the liturgical act.

Religion lessons may emphasize at different times now one aspect, the historical, now another, the theological or the liturgical. Moreover, there may be many forms of presentation intermediary to the three distinguished clearly above. Thus, a historical-type religion lesson may wish to establish an exact succession of events. Or, neglecting the historical aspect entirely, the lesson may render the event present in terms of theological or liturgical faith in a few swift strokes.

Not only is the distinction between these forms of catechesis necessary, but it also points to some genuinely diverse and complementary functions of catechizing. The distinction is especially useful today because the Bible is being employed in a slightly different way than in the centuries or even decades immediately preceding. This raises problems, according as one or another of the various forms of instruction is being utilized.

Our procedure in this essay seems laid out for us. We shall give, in outline form, three samples of catechetical presentation. After each, we shall consider some problems in theory which they raise.

AN EXAMPLE OF
HISTORICAL PRESENTATION

As an instance of historical catechesis, let us propose a lesson on Israel's crossing of the Red Sea. The text that needs explaining is the fourteenth chapter of Exodus. It is a problem to know the different readings of this text that can be employed with different age groups, but that can conveniently be left to one side for now. The general assumption is that, at a given time in a catechetical program which deals with the *mirabilia Dei*, this text will be used. Children of about ten to twelve years are contemplated in the presentation that follows.

Outline of the Lesson

The plan will be first to situate the event by means of historical and geographical details geared to the age and mentality of the children; then to present the biblical text itself, with emphasis on the words and expressions best suited to convey the religious drama enacted in the event:

(a) the Israelites are seized with fear; they cry out against Moses. Their words show a lack of confidence in their leader and in their God, who is the Lord. Moses answers: "See the *salvation* which Yahweh will grant us this day." Yahweh says to Moses: "Stretch forth your hand over the sea and I shall *manifest my glory.*" As Moses extends his hand, Yahweh turns back the sea by a strong east wind which blows all night, thus converting the sea into dry land. As the account continues, little stress is placed on this prodigy. The Israelites pass over; the Egyptians pursue them. The wind ceases, the sea flows back again, and the Egyptians are drowned. Israel is saved.

On that day Yahweh *delivered* Israel from the hand of the Egyptians. Israel saw the powerful hand of the Lord and began to *fear* Him. This people then *believed* in Him and in Moses his servant. All began to sing this canticle: "I will sing to the Lord for he is gloriously triumphant. Horse and chariot he has cast into the sea. My strength and my courage is the Lord, for he has been my savior" (Ex 15, lf.);

(b) throughout their history of many centuries, the Israelites remembered this day when God delivered them from the slavery of the Pharaoh. The event became for them the type or symbol of what God was still doing to save them. When they were in danger, they cried out to God who had saved them from the Egyptians.

The teacher should then read (or have someone read to the class) Psalm 135 [136];

(c) when we Christians read this account, as the Church asks us to do, we too think of all that God has done for us. We recall the *great deliverance* which He has accomplished in our regard, and still accomplishes. God continues to be the One who saves us, who delivers us. Now, however, it has become a matter of our sins and our weaknesses. We cannot on our own overcome the obstacle placed by our sins, and thereby achieve or maintain friendship with God. God has sent His Son, therefore, who died and rose for us. Jesus intercedes for us now in heaven. By His prayer we are pardoned. We can pass through temptations—which are considerably weakened in their power over us—and live like children of God.

When we read the account of the crossing of the Red Sea, the power of God which enables us to overcome temptations strikes us forcibly. When we sing Psalm 135 [136], we include in our prayer our gratitude for all God has done for us.[1] (At this point in the lesson the last few verses of the psalm should be repeated: "Who remembered us in our abjection, for His mercy endures forever . . . Give thanks to the God of heaven, for His mercy endures forever," vv. 23–26).

Commentary on the Lesson

A few reflections on the lesson just outlined would include the following:

(a) first, why should this text be chosen? Because it is written in the epic genre? No, that can't be it. It is rather a case of its being chosen in spite of certain characteristics which provide many difficulties. The text of Exodus is introduced into the lesson for its importance in the history of the Word of God, for its religious value. Because it holds such an important place in the thought and liturgy of the Church, we must attend to it. Thus, in the very choice of the text a certain view of the faith the catechist brings to it enters in. This view is provided by the Church; it is, in fact, *traditional* in the Church (after preparation by the whole Jewish tradition).[2] This gives us the first rule for the use of stories from the

---

[1] The crossing of the Red Sea could also be considered a figure of baptism, according to the text of I Cor 10, 1–4.

[2] It is not always easy, we know, to distinguish between *tradition* and traditions. The biblical texts have often received an "accommodated" sense. Biblical and theological studies help us to discover the deepest religious sense of the texts and determine their importance.

Bible: we have to choose texts which are religious in essence, that is to say texts which express an essential aspect of the mystery of faith;

(b) after the text has been chosen we must take it and interpret it in the light of faith. The intellect is the faculty which penetrates deeply into what is studied. That means that we must first read, then evaluate, understand, and explain the text as we find it.[3] We must try to convey the full meaning of the words, the images, and the important expressions, in keeping with the aim of the lesson. The explanation we give is a reading *in faith*, but above all it is a reading. Our explanations are not juxtaposed with the text, that is to say put on a plane with the sacred writing. They bring out its meaning and shed light on it, nothing more.

The essential aim of the religion lesson, therefore, is to bring out the religious sense of the text. It is the Word of God that must be heard. All else is symbol, meant to convey it. The human elements of the text must be taken into consideration, of course. It is necessary for the teacher to know and respect the type of writing (literary genre) that is being used. He must also situate, both historically and geographically, the event related.

It is always useful to note what a given text teaches us about the mentality of the Hebrew people. But in catechetics all this is necessary only in the measure in which it contributes to making the very Word of God objective, living, and concrete in the eyes of students. Not only should we not destroy the religious message which the text conveys by an excessive insistence on details and a too scientific preoccupation with them,[4] but also we should see to it that even these explanations are geared to orienting the atten-

---

[3] This does not mean that we may not omit passages or modify expressions; but these are problems in pedagogy. Whatever solution is adopted, it must always respect the religious sense of the text.

[4] In the example cited above one can draw attention solely to the element of marvel in the story, or on the contrary to a scientific explanation which confines the story to its historical dimension. An earlier temptation was to neglect these historical, geographical, and literary data; now certain catechists risk allowing their solicitude for the scientific reading to supersede the religious reading.

tion of students toward a better understanding of faith. Knowing
how to channel the interest children have in the human aspect of
a story toward eliciting an act of faith is one of the catechist's
major problems.

If our reading of a past historical event is to lead to better
understanding of mystery and elicit an act of faith, then the event
or rather the mystery it contains must be made present to the
hearer. Indeed, no teacher truly catechizes children unless they
recognize through his teaching an actual personal call from God.
They must be inspired by the event or exposition which claims
their attention to a greater confidence in God or a deeper gratitude
to Him. Otherwise they have not been well taught.

For this reason the explanation of the text of the crossing of
the Red Sea was given a new dimension by the search for the
narrative's spiritual sense (which was indeed the sense it had for
the inspired author). Crossing over the Red Sea is a fact out of
the past, but the mystery it expresses is something present. The
event of Moses' time is but the first and (if we may so speak)
carnal realization of the salvific action of God. It will culminate in
the liberation from sin which God assures us in Jesus Christ. Thus
it is undoubtedly the text itself that is being explained and not
some private or subjective elaboration of it; what we do is place
it in a broader context which should yield its total meaning. The
passage is being read in light of the faith we have in Jesus Christ.

However, the explication of the spiritual sense presents a problem: on the one hand it may not be absolutely necessary to do
things this way; on the other, such a treatment of the text may
prove inadequate. In other words, this is perhaps not the only way
nor even the principal way of rendering present the Word of
God which is heard through narratives from the past.
An Objection

In the use of the historical form of catechesis we encounter, at
least when dealing with twelve-year-olds, a rather widespread
objection which must be faced squarely. The Bible speaks to us of
the past. It relates events which have very little intrinsic interest.
It is true that in the presentation of a psalm the religious senti-

ments expressed have a certain timeless character,[5] making it relatively easy to disengage states of soul comparable to those of the present from the circumstances in which the psalms were written. When we deal with a historical narrative, however, the case is not the same. By definition this narrative presents a fact which is not repeated and which is located at a given point in the past, between preceding and subsequent events.

Moreover, in presenting these past events we exceed the religious possibilities of the children. They do not have a historical sense: their present faith cannot, in a word, be nourished by the historical presentation of past events.[6]

The answer to this objection requires consideration of the following facts:

1. we are not here concerned with the teaching of history as such;

2. the process of making a past event a present reality is achieved by attending to certain factors of human psychology;

3. on the catechetical plane this making real of the past is accomplished essentially by the act of faith itself.

1. It is quite true that for a child, even of ten or eleven years, the account of a past event is not, properly speaking, a historical narrative. The event is not situated exactly with relation to those which precede and follow it, nor is the completest connection possible made with the human agents who control it. It is this care in situating the event in the midst of other events, and in explaining it in terms of human agents, that constitutes the historical outlook. Let us be quick to admit, then, that we do not appeal to the historical sense properly so called. The form of our catechesis is never totally historical.

A catechesis which, while presenting a succession of Old Testa-

[5] The imperfection of certain sentiments, of expressions proper to the ancient world in a Semitic milieu, must be taken into account.

[6] It should be noted that this objection is almost equally valid for the events of the New Testament.

ment events, would consider the very succession the proper and prime object of its teaching would undoubtedly exceed the ability of the children and risk not conveying the present significance of the events in the light of faith. But of course the latter is what the biblical author intended the narrative to achieve.

Two observations are in order on the historical sense of a child of ten or twelve, and on the interest he has in past events. For the example chosen above, it is sufficient that the child be interested in concrete and fairly brief sequences (e.g., the parts of a biography or a happening), and be able to comprehend these parts as a whole. Psychologists have noticed this possibility in certain children whose interest in the past takes shape at nine or ten, and in the succession of events in an individual life, in certain children, toward the age of ten.[7]

The historical outlook should not be represented as something at first nonexistent which then appears in adolescence fully formed. Actually this function develops progressively from childhood to adulthood. In order to reach full development by the end of adolescence the child's consciousness must utilize many facts which from the viewpoint of the historical function become increasingly valuable to him. It is important that they should be supplied to him much earlier, and at the same time be given an inchoate temporal dimension.[8] One would be quite wrong in denying too readily that a child of eleven can be interested in the past.

2. It is not sufficient, however, for the child to be interested in the past. He must be able to consider the past events as present, that is to say as useful with regard to his present conduct. The question is, then, how can the past event be made to have present value for him?[9]

[7] A. Godin, "The Historical Function. For a Religious Education of the Christian in Time," *Lumen Vitae*, 14 (June 1959), 248.

[8] *Ibid.*, p. 250.

[9] It is not a question of making present the past event; this would be contradictory. It is a matter of showing how the past event can have an influence on the present; of seeing by what mediatory function it possesses this influence; finally, of determining the relationship between the past and the present so as to establish a unity between the two.

The first explanation is based on certain factors of human psychology. Even for the two- or three-year-old a story from the past can be made effectively present by the storyteller. There is soon added to this work of mediation an emotional and volitional identification with the characters in the story. One needs only to employ gestures, words, sentiments, persons which correspond to the affectivity of the hearer.

The capacity for affective participation undoubtedly lessens at ten or twelve years. Rather, it is changed. Children of this essentially active age identify themselves with active characters who can overcome difficulties. Undoubtedly, however, they would identify more with a past event that appears *bound* to a present activity. That is why it is advisable for history teachers to connect the past with whatever traces of it remain today, e.g., the study of ancient monuments, visits to museums, etc.

This practical connection is easily established, it seems, in a presentation of historical facts closely joined to the *liturgical* type of religion lesson or catechetical experience. Recalling the past is linked to the present in preparing for the liturgical feast of the following Sunday, and even more in celebration of the feasts themselves. The epistle and gospel which are read out in church narrate past events, but they do so in a context of the present action of the community. These readings are joined to the offertory and the communion, likewise activities of the present. The continuity of the liturgical act assures the continuity of past and present. In this sense, the crossing of the Red Sea can be integrated into the general preparation for Christmas, i.e., thought of in connection with *Advent* rather than with history. The objection we spoke of above loses force immediately when historical catechesis is combined with liturgical.

3. We could continue pointing out elements of the psychology of the preadolescent and adolescent which give him a certain empathy with historical figures, but we must move to another level. Up until now we have been employing natural elements in the catechizing process to connect past events with the present: a nascent historical sense, or participation by affective involvement, the

activity principle. In order to go deeper, a more fundamental answer drawn directly from the nature of catechesis and faith must be
added to what has already been noted.

In considering the Church's act of faith in which the catechist
participates and wishes to make his students participate, we see
that it binds the individual directly to the Father through the
glorified Christ, both subjectively and objectively. No one can believe in Christ glorified, however, who does not identify Him with
the Christ who was born, suffered, and died for us; for what I
affirm in His resurrection is the divinity of *this Man* which has
shone forth. The union of the historical Christ and the glorified
Christ is perceptible to both senses and spirit in the act of faith.
This being the case, narratives from the life of Christ are made
present in faith more directly than incidents of the Old Testament,
since the focal point of both is Christ.

In the realm of history and what is perceptible to the senses
there can only be a question of degree between the meaningfulness
of events out of the Old Testament and the New. The Old Testament, joined historically to the New, will participate in the present
significance of New Testament events.[10]

This linking of Old Testament events to Christ need not be made
on the explicitly historical level. Such would presuppose that the
child had a historical sense; it would oblige him to follow the unfolding of events from Abraham to Christ. The link is made by the
strength of that *act of faith* which made Abraham believe in Christ,
even though he could but vaguely foresee His coming, on the
historical plane. Let us put it this way: our faith in Christ unites
us, more or less objectively and historically, but by the path of
faith immediately and unequivocally, to all that partakes of Christ,
whether it prepares for Him or extends His influence.

It matters little then that on the level of human psychology past
actions are linked to present without any succession being clearly
perceived. On the level of faith, by the bond which faith provides,
they are present to the act of faith. Actually we are not transported

[10] The characters we present are remote in the measure in which they
are remote from the faith of the child, and remote from Christ.

back into Israel's past, from which we would have to return to the present. This might be the procedure if our outlook were purely scientific, but in the act of faith things go in the opposite direction. The past event is made the possession of the individual in his present faith. The procedure that is valid for the acquisition of all knowledge is valid *a fortiori* for the act of faith.

To conclude: when the catechist explains that the crossing of the Red Sea is a figure of the saving action of God in Christ, the past event is made present more explicitly on the objective plane. It can become a present reality to the child antecedent to the catechist's explanation, provided that the child has elicited an authentic act of faith. God was declared Savior, the individual's Savior, in the narration of the past from the moment he first read the account (or had it read to him) in the spirit of the Church's faith. From the time of baptism, when Christians are first in communion with the spirit of Christ which contains all and in which all is present, they have possessed the meaning of the Exodus event seminally. A catechist's explanation can certainly assist the act of faith, but it can only do so by lending support to what the act of faith has already accomplished aided by the effective and active participation of the child.[11] Inversely, the catechist's explanation would undoubtedly have been fruitless had he not made every effort in his lesson to bring the child to the plane of faith.

It appears, then, that what is of primary importance is that all catechizing should be carried on in an atmosphere of faith. The catechist must speak with a faith that suffuses all his words; it must penetrate to the marrow of his students, so real will it be. The children need to have enough spirit of faith already to hear this past event proclaimed in terms of faith. Basically, the question to be asked by anyone undertaking a historical catechesis is:

[11] It is understood, of course, that the narrative does not become a present reality by the mere spelling out of practical applications nor by suggesting resolutions to be made. On the contrary, only in the measure that the narrative is made present by faith can these applications be evoked. After a while it will cease being necessary to do this for the child. Once the approach to religion and a spirit of faith are assured, the catechist will urge the child to move toward God as One who is constantly saving us.

"Do my children have faith enough to hear this account with the faith of the Church, or must I first endeavor to strengthen the spirit of faith in them by other means? Have *I* enough spirit of faith to speak of this event as a present reality, one that I believe in?"

None of the above-proposed is alien to the practice of the Church in her liturgy, which speaks to young and old alike. Neither does it go against the practice of Christian parents who share with their children many historical narratives in teaching them within the family circle. Yet we must not overlook the possibility of presenting to children a catechesis in which the historical form would be so emphasized that it would inevitably impose the study of the historical succession of events. One can only agree with Grelot when he rejects a program that would require for three years (even for one year or four months, one might add), a study of the succession of revealed events as the core of a catechetical program.[12] The historical form employed at this age can be emphasized only slightly, in the sense that when the catechist is dealing with the Old Testament he must appeal to the narratives most filled with spiritual sense. These must then be linked to the mysteries of faith in the present. This brings out the fact that catechesis must use the theological and liturgical forms as well, and of these we shall now speak.

AN EXAMPLE OF
THEOLOGICAL-LITURGICAL
PRESENTATION

Let us propose a lesson on the mystery of the holy Trinity for children of eleven and twelve years.

In the preceding example a scriptural text was considered, read

[12] Two more observations on this point: (a) it is possible that through the study of profane history or by a certain critical sense awakened by it, individual children may be scrupulous about the historical reality of the ancient narratives used. In such case we must answer the need by setting the narrative in the context of profane history; (b) it is quite possible that children will have great difficulty in seeing past events in the light of the present. Here it is the spirit of faith that is lacking; there is no escaping the work of educating in faith, to which a good presentation of biblical narratives can then be joined.

in light of the Church's faith. In what follows, a doctrinal formula will be presented: the mystery of the Trinity or one God in three Persons. The problem is to present a doctrinal lesson or series of lessons on the Trinity which will at the same time assign to Scripture its rightful place.

The reader is asked to be indulgent in what follows. It is the only way the writer knows of presenting catechesis on the Trinity which is both within the grasp of children and can elicit their "conversion" and a better attitude toward the three Persons.

We presuppose here that the religious formation leading up to this lesson has taught the children to turn to the Father, following the example of the Son, in docility to the Holy Spirit. Further, it is presumed that the notion of the Trinity has implicitly dominated the whole catechetical program. At this point in the year the sequence on the life of Christ has reached Pentecost. Having listened to Christ's words on the Father and the Holy Spirit, the students turn their attention to the Father, Son, and Holy Spirit as they are revealed to us in the passion-resurrection mystery.

Outline of the Lesson or Unit

There are two possible approaches to this catechesis. In the *first*, (a) the words of Jesus concerning His relations with His Father are recalled: "The Father and I are one" (Jn 10, 30); "I am in the Father and the Father is in me" (Jn 14, 11); "All that is mine is yours, and yours is mine" (Jn 17, 10; cf. Jn 10, 22f., 26). Jesus' words on the Holy Spirit are likewise recalled: "But the Advocate, the Holy Spirit, whom the Father will send in my name, will teach you everything, and refresh your memory on everything I have told you" (Jn 14, 26);

(b) in addition to these texts (and others, e.g., from St. Paul) the thinking of the Church on the subject of the mystery of the three Persons is considered. It has ever been her teaching that the Son, the image of the Father, has the same power and intellect as the Father and is equally God along with Him, and that together with the Father and the Son, and co-equal with them, is the Holy Spirit who gives unity and love to the Trinity.

This mystery of the life of God is beyond our understanding. Indeed, all human words do not begin to convey the reality. Yet the Church tells us: "Only one God, but three Persons in God. This is the mystery of the Trinity." What we know, however, is sufficient to make us adore: "Glory be to the Father," etc.;

(c) once again the words of Jesus concerning His Father, Himself, and the Spirit of Truth are recalled: "Anyone who loves me will treasure my message, and my Father will love him, and we shall visit him and make our home with him" (Jn 14, 23). The Trinity is not far from us; it is in the center of our beings. It is in us. The Father is in us as the goal of our life. All that we do is done for Him. The Son is in us as our priestly model. All that we do is in imitation of the Son. The Spirit is in us as the love which makes us act. All that we do is done under the influence of the Spirit. We do all, "In the name of the Father and of the Son and of the Holy Ghost."

A French Carmelite who died in 1906, Sister Elizabeth of the Trinity, understood her life with the Trinity so well that she found all her joy in speaking interiorly to the Father, Son, and Holy Spirit. "I have found my heaven on earth, for heaven is God and God is in my soul," she said.

Once understood, these truths will lead to an attitude of adoration of the Three who dwell within us.

A *second* approach to this catechesis will emphasize the following points:

(a) the liturgy of baptism, i.e., the sign of the cross, texts of the exorcisms, the profession of faith, is used in this type of catechesis. We are baptized in the name of the Father and of the Son and of the Holy Spirit. The prayer of Sister Elizabeth of the Trinity could once again be used, for she lived in continual awareness of the Three in her soul;

(b) the question that needs to be asked is: What does it mean to live in union with the Trinity? Within the life of God, the Father gives himself completely to His Son, just as the Son communicates with the Father (Jn 17, 10). The Holy Spirit who unites the Father and the Son is the very love of the Father for the Son

and of the Son for the Father—a love so great that Father, Son, and Holy Spirit are one. We say something similar (not the same, but similar) when two friends love each other very much. We say they are "as one";

(c) now you have some understanding of what it means to live in company with the Trinity; as a child of God; like Jesus; in the Trinity. It is to love as the Father loves the Son and as the Son loves us. It is to love the Father and all men as the Son loves the Father and all men, namely to lead them to the Father. It is to allow oneself to be led by the Holy Spirit, by the love of the Father. All who love God and their brothers have within them the love of God, the Father, the Son, and the Spirit in whom they live (cf. I Jn 4, 11–14);

(d) "Beloved, now we are children of God [i.e., now we live with the Trinity]. And what we shall be have not yet been manifested. We know that when he appears . . . we shall see Him just as He is" (1 Jn 3, 2). Following this, there should come the sign of the cross made carefully and thoughtfully, or else the "Glory be to the Father."

Commentary

This has not been an attempt to give a model lesson on the Trinity but only to show what place Scripture must have in a theologically oriented catechesis, and to furnish a background for the following remarks:

(a) in this form of catechesis we are not obliged to begin with a biblical text. The second of the two approaches above began with a concrete fact of Christian life (in this case, phrased in the words of Sister Elizabeth of the Trinity). Liturgical texts from the sacrament of baptism or from the feast of the holy Trinity may also be used. A sense of trinitarian life, which is the goal of this lesson, is one of the effects of the living Word resounding in the Church. In order to assure a good foundation for this presentation, establishing contact with this trinitarian sense at any one point will suffice.

The role of tradition (theologically understood), important in any catechesis, is much more in evidence here. It is interwoven with the biblical text. Determining the precise role of the Bible in catechetics involves determining the relationship between Scripture and apostolic tradition;

(b) Pierre Grelot has already offered a solution to this problem by distinguishing between the living Word and its crystallization in the written Word.[13]

Whether we are dealing with the Old Testament or the New, there is first the living Word of God which creates, illumines, and guides the Israelite or Christian community, which in fact raises up the prophets, Christ, and the apostles. This mystery of the creative and illumining Word of God was at a certain time in the past expressed in writing under the inspiration of the Spirit. Since then the Word of God has been present in a privileged way in Scripture.

By the time of the death of the last apostle the Church, the unique witness to Christ, had expressed in the Scriptures the knowledge she had of the mystery of Christ in its essential elements. Henceforth, those in the Church who write will no longer be "witnessess" of a Master whom they have known, with whom they have lived in redemptive mystery "from the baptism to the resurrection" (Ac 1, 22). Their speech will no longer be the Word of God springing forth fresh. There will be no further revelation, properly so called. "Constitutive" tradition is an accomplished fact.

Writings will no longer have the function of crystallizing what is essential in the living Word. Henceforth, Scripture will serve as a rule for the Church, a norm of her faith and practice. Obviously the living Word cannot contradict the written Word. Nothing really new can be added to the living Word which is Christ; Scripture has incorporated Him into its unchanging texts.

The life of the Church continues beyond the New Testament

---

[13] Other helpful discussions of this problem include that of J. R. Geiselmann, "Scripture, Tradition and the Church: An Ecumenical Problem," in *Christianity Divided*, ed. Callahan, Oberman, O'Hanlon (New York: Sheed and Ward, 1962), pp. 39–62; Jean Daniélou, "The God of the Church," in *God and the Ways of Knowing* (New York: Meridian Books, 1957), pp. 174–214.

period. As a living community she knows herself to be ruled and judged by the written Word of God and also, interiorly, by the Spirit of Christ. Scripture and the Spirit are both in her, and she is in them. Both serve as rule for her. In the course of the centuries, as she continues to encounter new problems, she turns to Scripture and to the light of the Spirit who is in her. Her growing "memory" continually adds to the richness of interpretation she gives to the written Word that is in her, in light of the living Word.

There are times when the Church must set down her interpretation, her own view of herself according to the norm of Scripture, in formulas akin to the Scriptures (such as the creed), or in formulas treated abstractly, to achieve theological understanding (e.g., a definition of the Trinity or the eucharist).

These formulations are often defensive in tone and come about by way of reaction; they may likewise result from a need for intellectual comprehension. All of them are the expression of the thought of the living community which is the Church. She contemplates herself as she exists under the rule of Scripture; when she speaks it is the magisterium that is her voice of expression;

(c) it is clear then that all catechesis, in whatever form, has as its starting point the living Word at work in the Church in the present, made manifest in the various forms of her life: sacraments, commandments, formulas of faith. It is a Word that has been partially expressed in Scripture.

A given religion lesson may, therefore, have the task of either announcing or explaining a text of Scripture, or a doctrinal fact, or a text from extrascriptural tradition: sacraments, creed, lives of the saints, etc.

But if the catechist is to proclaim the written Word by dealing directly with a scriptural text, he must do it with a *consciousness* of all tradition and in the Spirit who speaks the living Word in the Church today. His explanations must partake of those of the Church. They are particularly akin to the formulas of the Church in the measure that these formulas are catechetical, that is to say framed for proclamation, with an eye to religious pedagogy. There must be no "biblicism," or catechesis that would limit itself to the

written Word. We have seen that such an attitude is impossible
from the start, since the very choice of the text to be explained has
already been made by tradition.

If the catechist happens to be dealing with a liturgical rite,
which is also an event of tradition described by the Church in her
living utterance, he may not forget that this rite and this event
have not been incorporated into tradition without first having been
compared with Scripture and judged by it, in the Spirit. For
this reason his catechesis, too, must refer this rite and this event
to Scripture. In the preceding lesson on the Trinity we discovered
in Scripture an expression of the belief of the Church contained
in the trinitarian formula. If presenting confirmation were the
problem, we would be in a position to "judge" this rite by means
of the words of Jesus on the Holy Spirit and the account of Pentecost. Were we to discuss the life of a saint, a comparison of his
acts with the words of Jesus would provide the assurance needed
that these acts are the fruit of the Spirit of Christ. Thus, whatever
procedure is followed, in a complete catechesis the relation between Scripture and tradition must always be respected;

(d) but there is a function which Scripture plays in religious
instruction that we would do well to insist on.

In the first outline developed above, we encountered the theological formula for the mystery of the Trinity in the course of the
presentation. The prescribed catechism manual might propose it
as a datum to be explained, as so many of them do. If it is thought
to be a point of departure there will be the strong temptation to
stop there—to call a halt to all discussion.

This, however, would be to succumb to a temptation. We have
seen how normal it is to come upon a theological formula or precise
expression of the living consciousness the Church has of the three
Persons in God. We memorize this formula so as to provide the
desired precision to our faith. But the purpose of the catechesis is
anything but the possession of a formula. It is concerned with
living faith, and the dialogue to be established with the Three.
That is why our development does not end when it first strikes the
formula, but only when it succeeds in conveying to the students a
sense of the presence of the Trinity.

Scripture continually calls our attention to the purpose of the catechetical process, namely to bring us face to face with the Three. They speak to us, challenge us, ask us to respond to Them in faith. Scripture places us before Christ and the Spirit, not before mere ideas. The Three know that the words used in Scripture, often symbolic in character, engage the *totality* of our humanity. Throughout our presentation we must be faithful to this direct, person-to-person attitude which Scripture provides—unless, of course, we are to substitute for the catechetical outlook a specifically theological one. Maintaining this fidelity will be greatly facilitated if our rational presentation is guided by Scripture and keeps close contact with it.[14]

The liturgy invites us, moreover (see the second outline above), to the same attitude of personal faith as Scripture does, but especially to a faith that is relevant here and now. It is evident there is no proper beginning simply with a formula that requires explanation. The attitude that must be inculcated is one of living faith in the Trinity proper to Christians in the Church. This attitude is manifested by baptism; by the feast of the holy Trinity; in the mystical life of a Sister Elizabeth of the Trinity. A living faith has been crystallized in our theological formula. It now remains for us to see, in a more detailed way, the liturgical form of catechesis and the place the Bible holds in it.

AN EXAMPLE OF LITURGICAL CATECHESIS

We shall take as our example a lesson on the feast of Christ the King.

Outline

(a) A point of departure here is the fact of the feast of Christ the King. We begin with a present reality within the Church. Its

[14] The union of the catechist with the living Church (e.g., through the communion of saints who live by the Trinity, through the celebration of the sacraments and feasts) places him in a relation with the Trinity which must assure a living, personal, kerygmatic character in his catechesis. The Trinity speaks to us today through Scripture and through the total living Word in the Church.

catechetical value depends on the importance placed on the feast by the faith and practice of the Christian community in which the children live;

(b) first the meaning of the word "king" is explained briefly: the symbolism of power, glory; the possession of a kingdom;

(c) Jesus was announced as a king:
> Isaia 9
> Psalm 71 [72]
> the angel of Luke 1
> the procession with palms: Luke 19, 38;

(d) but not a king like other kings:
> Zacharia 9, 9
> after the multiplication of the loaves: John 6, 15
> before Pilate: John 18, 33–8;

(e) the royalty of Jesus is explained through the text of:
> Philippians 2, 8–11
> Romans 1, 3.

This kingly status is connected with the teaching of Pope Pius XI in the encyclical on the kingship of Christ, *Quas Primas:* "Jesus is king of minds, wills and hearts in the faith."

One day He will be king more totally with the elect in heaven. (Cf. Apocalypse 5, 12—Introit of the Mass.)

Here and now, in company with the whole community of Christians, we recognize Him as our King and praise Him.

Commentary

(a) In a liturgical catechesis it is to be expected that numerous biblical texts will be used. The liturgy is to a large extent composed of such texts. However, it should be pointed out that, from the pedagogical point of view, undoubtedly too many texts have been introduced into the above outline. The multiplication serves to emphasize the possiblities which Holy Scripture offers, in light of the general theme of this essay.

We should try to realize that a liturgical catechesis can easily provide a synthesis of the various uses of Scripture, i.e., the four functions of biblical texts: historical, doctrinal, and prophetical wisdom, and prayer texts. All these are used according to the dialectics of liturgy. Historical events such as those of Palm Sunday, the multiplication of the loaves, or the trial before Pilate are of significance here, not insofar as they are historical, but "prophetical" or indicative of the true kingship of Christ. Since we are considering a lesson on the feast of Christ the King, in a liturgical framework that is close to the act of prayer, it is to be expected that texts will be used in which Christ is addressed as a king;

(b) it should be pointed out that when the lesson is liturgical in character the qualities of biblical texts appear in sharper relief.

On the one hand, liturgical catechesis spontaneously uses certain symbolic concepts fraught with human sentiment which will insure the concrete, affective, personal character of the lesson even when it is theological in form. Here the symbol used is that of a king. Children, who have perhaps only seen pictures of royal weddings, still find this symbol meaningful. The symbolism can be used rather effectively in the service of the Word of God. Generally speaking, the choice made of biblical symbols by the liturgy will help us in the use of the most important symbols of our faith.

Moreover, the liturgy will lead us to give to the texts of the New Testament their full importance in relation to the texts of the Old. The latter evoke an earlier, more carnal realization of the former, while the New Testament must remain at the center of our catechesis. It should be remarked that the texts of the Old Testament do no more than prepare for the texts of the New, especially one such as Philippians 2, 8–11, which places us squarely in the passion-resurrection mystery. In uniting catechetics and liturgy we are kept from limiting the history of salvation to the Old Testament or even to the ascension of Christ, for the perspective of the return of Christ, the *parousia,* is always present in the liturgical outlook, just as it is in Scripture.

Finally, and we hope this has been underscored sufficiently, catechizing in the liturgical form makes present all those historical events it brings to mind. We have begun not with the Bible but with an action of the Christian community; not only a "formula" but a feast. The Bible has been situated in the feast as the written

Word of God in that living Word of God that establishes and regulates the feast.

At the end of the lesson we return to the Church's present which we have never really left. It is *now* that Christ is our king. Next Sunday all Christians will unite to celebrate His kingship, to glorify Him, and to proclaim that He is for each of us way, truth and life. Now we can sing the hymn which the whole community will sing on Sunday.

The Word of God, under its living form of the tradition of the Church in the Spirit, is ever-present. Catechesis continually proclaims this Word. The Word of God in its written form is likewise ever-present, serving unfailingly as guide to tradition and hence to all religious instruction. The latter, according as it takes the historical, theological, or liturgical form, will carefully blend Scripture texts, the contemporary teachings of the Church, and the discursive language of reason. But the balanced relation between these diverse elements will always remain the same.

Scripture texts will be chosen according as they are appropriate to the aim of the lesson, that is, to assure the certitude of divine facts, the intelligibility of faith, or the present reality of the Christian mystery. The texts of the New Testament will always be given first place, those of the Old Testament being read in light of the New.

The few remarks proffered above certainly do not give the solution to all the theological and pedagogical problems involved in the use of biblical texts. They may however serve to sketch in outline what a chapter in a catechism aimed at being faithful to history, theology, and liturgy should be like, for after all, these three comprise the living, creative Word of the Church.

2 THE LITURGY

AND CATECHETICS

Mary Perkins Ryan

"And this is everlasting life, that they may know You . . ."

IF, some Sunday morning, you were to ask a number of Catholics why they were going to Mass, at least six out of ten probably would say "Because we have to" or "The Church tells us to," and one or two probably would add "To get grace" or even "Because it makes me feel good." Contrast this with the answers given by the African martyrs of Abitene: "We cannot live without the Mass; . . . it is Christians who make the Mass and the Mass that makes Christians, in such a way that one cannot exist without the other."[1]

This still largely prevalent attitude implies that the Mass and the whole sacramental life of which it is the "crowning act"[2] are *ancillary* to life. They are thought to be means—even though "means of grace"—of which one must use at least a minimum: means to each individual's being saved from eternal unhappiness and earning

[1] J. P. Migne, PL 8, 711–12; quoted more fully in J. Hofinger, ed., *Worship: the Life of the Missions* (Notre Dame, Ind.: University of Notre Dame Press, 1958), p. 9.
[2] Encyclical *Mediator Dei*, n. 66 (the numbers used are those of the NCWC and America Press editions).

eternal happiness hereafter; means to his happiness here and now if he is religiously inclined. The earlier attitude expressed by the martyrs of Abitene implies that the Mass and the whole sacramental life of which it is the vital core are focal in life, *are* life at its deepest, both in relation to the individual Christian and to the Christian community.

Doctrine and Worship Integrated: A Restoration

The ancillary attitude has certainly been predominant in the Western Church in recent centuries.[3] But the ferment of a return to the older attitude has been working in the Church for several decades—notably since the time of St. Pius X.[4] Movements in the fields of Scripture, theology, liturgy, pastoral practice, catechetics, have been gathering momentum, with the approval and guidance of the highest authorities of the Church, and these are now converging to indicate the focal attitude as being the more fully traditional, the more fully Catholic. The attainment of this attitude, then, its becoming the one taken for granted by all the children of the Church today, is seen to be not a mere return to something older and simpler but rather a further stage, enriched by all the Christian thinking and living of all the centuries and of our own times, in our "growing up in all things in Him who is the Head, Christ" (Eph 4, 15).

Obviously, such a change cannot be a matter of formal instruction alone, if only because the whole way in which the Christian

[3] This is owing, in great part, to a onesided emphasis on the causality of the sacraments at the expense of their characteristic as signs—though this emphasis itself is the result of a great many other historic factors. In "Two Approaches to Understanding the Sacraments," *Education and the Liturgy,* Proceedings of the 1957 North American Liturgical Week, also published in *Come, Let Us Worship* (Baltimore: Helicon, 1961), Godfrey Diekmann, O.S.B., points out that the *Summa Theologiae* of St. Thomas contains the principles and the elements of a balanced approach—but that these were largely ignored in the centuries after him.

[4] In the last six chapters of *The Whole Christ* (Milwaukee: Bruce, 1938), Emile Mersch, S.J., indicates the historical development in recent centuries of many of the elements of the present trend.

life is conceived and lived is what finally determines the spirit, the orientation, the emphases of the whole educational process and of the religious instruction which is one part of it. The educator (priest, teacher, parent), then, first needs to work toward a personal realization of what this focal nature of the sacramental life means in itself and in his or her own life; next, toward its implications for his particular work; and finally, toward how to make it the center of all. This chapter is an attempt to point out various lines for the reader's own study and meditation.

Right Thinking about the Sacraments

Many people have already begun to discover the place of the sacraments in their own lives from today's renewed emphasis on the sacraments as *acts of Christ*, the privileged, authenticated "meeting-places between the action of God and the response of man . . . encounters, personal encounters, between man and God."[5] Realized as such, it is obvious that they somehow must be focal in our personal spiritual life. To consider them as merely ancillary would be rather as if the devoted wife of a great man were to think of the events of their engagement and marriage, and the moments of his actual presence and activity in his home, as more or less essential formalities, seeking for real communication with him by reading books and articles about him, and talking to other people about his work.

Many more people, perhaps, have already discovered something of the place of the sacraments in the life of the Church as a community from the aspect of *social worship*, centering in the holy eucharist ("the culmination and center, as it were, of the Christian religion")[6]—social worship seen as the focus of Christian lives dedicated, in one way or another, to the work of justice and peace, pre-

[5] Charles Davis, *Liturgy and Doctrine* (New York: Sheed and Ward, 1960), p. 107. See also A. M. Roguet, O.P., *Christ Acts Through Sacraments* (Collegeville, Minn.: The Liturgical Press, 1954); A. G. Martimort, *The Signs of the New Covenant* (Collegeville, Minn.: The Liturgical Press, 1963), esp. chap. 6.
[6] *Mediator Dei*, n. 66.

paring for the fulfillment of Christ's prayer, "that all may be one" (Jn 17, 21).[7]

But these discoveries open out into a far deeper and wider realization. The sacramental life is focal in the life of the Church and of each of her members by the very nature of God's self-revelation and self-giving to us in Christ, by the very essence of the "plan of His heart" for the salvation of mankind. For—as modern Scripture studies, liturgical research, biblical, liturgical, moral, and "spiritual" theology all converge to bring out—it is precisely in and through this sacramental life that God takes hold of us where and as we are, to unite us, as he wants us to become, with Himself.

The Way God Deals with Men

Our age is characterized by depersonalization, dehumanization. But today in the Church, the discoveries and rediscoveries of modern times are bringing out more and more clearly the personal and interpersonal values, the human qualities of God's dealing with mankind, with each of us. We begin to see that God gives us His life here on earth in such a way—a sacramental way, effecting what it signifies—that it can leaven and transform our ordinary human lives from within, enlisting our whole human cooperation with His gift; that the life He invites us to lead with Him here and hereafter is the abounding fullness of human life raised to the dimension of the Spirit.[8]

Nor does this mean any anthropomorphizing, of which thoughtful men today are becoming more and more suspicious, or that often blasphemous "chumminess" ("Somebody up there likes me" . . . "Remember me to God"), which is perhaps actually the rather pathetic recourse of those ignorant of truly sacramental religion. On the contrary, we begin to see that it is precisely because God is

---

[7] See Cyprian Vagaggini, O.S.B., *Theological Dimensions of the Liturgy*, Vol. I (Collegeville, Minn.: The Liturgical Press, 1959), pp. 153–65; John H. Miller, C.S.C., *Fundamentals of the Liturgy* (Notre Dame: Fides Publishers Association, 1960), pp. 347–53; J. A. Jungmann, S.J., *Public Worship* (Collegeville, Minn.: The Liturgical Press, 1957), pp. 1–7.

[8] See, for example, F. X. Durrwell, *The Resurrection* (New York: Sheed and Ward, 1960), esp. chap. 6–8.

so transcendent, so infinitely "other" in His infinitely generous love, that He makes Himself so "human" in His dealings with His human creatures.[9]

Judaism and Christianity are unique in that they are religions based not on man's search for God, but on God's search for man. His speaking to man, His actively intervening in human history—and in *our* history—are always primary, initiating and making possible human response. But God speaks to men and acts among men precisely in order to set up communication, personal communication, between Himself and them. His whole effort, if we may put it so, is to arouse us, vivify us, enable us to know Him as He knows us.[10]

This living communication is to take place, with an immediacy beyond human hope, in the very life of interpersonal relationships which is the inner life of God.

At the heart of the Christian mystery is the divine love or *agápe*. There is a twofold movement of that love, a movement of descent and ascent, or of outgoing and return. The divine love of God the Father is communicated to us through Christ and in the Holy Spirit, and that divine love, present and active in us by the gift of the Spirit, draws us back through Christ to the Father, where we rest as His sons in Christ, and share the inner life of the Godhead.[11]

Such a life of "knowing God" must of its nature ultimately engage our whole freedom, all our power of knowing and loving, our whole being. So, when Adam's sin had enclosed mankind in its own limitations and enslaved it to the powers of evil, God did not

[9] See Hans Urs von Balthasar, *Science, Religion and Christianity* (Westminster, Md.: The Newman Press, 1959), pp. 97–103.

[10] See L. Bouyer, *Introduction to Spirituality* (New York: Desclée, 1961), chap. 1, esp. pp. 6–17. Also chapter 11, pp. 264 ff., in which the biblical and Christian meaning of "the knowledge of God" is discussed. The author points out that this knowledge implies conformity to and union with its Object; it is a dynamic knowledge, and is cognate with the term "to know" used in the Bible for the union of marriage.

[11] Davis, *op. cit*, p. 30.

save us from ourselves by some purely divine decree, but by the sacred history that centers in the Incarnation. In Christ our human nature which had turned away from God completely responds to God's love with the filial obedience of the eternal Son. By His "going to the Father" in that human nature through death itself, He became fully "the Lord," the Son of God in His glorious manhood. Now completely "with" the Father in His humanity, as eternally in His divinity, He sends us the Holy Spirit, making us in turn sons of God, responsive to the Father's love.[12]

Following Christ in the Spirit

Thus it is not as disembodied "souls," but as complete human persons that the Father makes us "sons in the Son" in the Spirit. Our Lord was "born of a woman, born under the Law . . . tried as we are in all things save sin" (Gal 4, 4; Heb 4, 15). He took on our whole human nature in its condition of "flesh"—that is, the "human condition" which is the effect of sin—so that, by living and dying *in* this nature, by dying to the life of the "flesh," in loving obedience to the Father, He might raise our whole human nature to the condition of "spirit" that God meant for it from the beginning. Our risen Lord, body and soul wholly "enspirited" by the Holy Spirit, is the "final man," the exemplar and cause of what God wants us all to become in Him.[13]

Moreover, we are to reach this goal by following Christ in the most deeply literal sense—"I *am* the Way" (Jn 14, 6). At baptism, our most intimate life-process was, as it were, stamped and formed to the act of Christ's "*transitus*," His going from this world to the Father, His dying to the life of the "flesh" and rising to the life of the Spirit. All our personal human development is to be leavened, reoriented, transfigured, by this process, to which every sacramental encounter with Christ adds a special impetus and force, and

[12] See E. Schillebeeckx, O.P., "Ascension and Pentecost," in *Worship,* 35 (May 1961), esp. pp. 349–63.
[13] See L. Bouyer, *The Meaning of Sacred Scripture* (Notre Dame: University of Notre Dame Press, 1958), pp. 174–82; Durrwell, pp. 287–90.

with which we cooperate by our own efforts at self-discipline and self-sacrificing love. With Christ we are to "die daily" to the life of the "flesh" in order to live and act more completely in the life of the Spirit.

Here our age adds an insight perhaps peculiarly its own to the "humanness" of the Christian life. Modern psychology sees human development toward true maturity as necessarily taking place through a series of "deaths." The child must leave behind, "die to" his childish satisfactions and privileges, the adolescent to his, in order fully to attain the next stage of human life, and so on. More than this, in order to overcome the greater or lesser handicaps which life brings to all of us, we must accept them for what they are, "die" to what we have lost and accept that death in order to go on, to continue to live and grow as persons.[14]

All the Deaths Till Death

In this light, what might otherwise seem the most inhuman if not antihuman aspect of Christianity shines out as God's most loving adaptation of His plan to the needs of human nature as it has made itself through sin. Suffering, frustration, death itself are the effects of sin. But if we go *with Christ* through all the partial "dyings" of our lives, we shall attain not only human but Christian maturity. If we strive to accept them with Christ's acceptance of His death, to unite ourselves with His obedience and love, we can make of all these painful necessities, even of physical death, a free-will offering to the Father in the Spirit of love. Thus united with Christ's redeeming work, all these dyings can become creative, not only of a fuller degree of true life in us, but in our fellow men (see Col 1, 24: "filling up what is wanting to the sufferings of Christ, for His body, the Church.").[15]

The divine life that Christ gives us in the Church, consequently, is not conferred on us in the way that fictional animals or robots

[14] See, for example, Thomas J. Carroll, *Blindness, What It Is, What It Does, and How to Live with It* (Boston: Little, Brown, 1961), chap. 1.
[15] See Bouyer, *Introduction to Spirituality*, chap. 7, esp. pp. 175 f.

are suddenly endowed with human life and powers, and then act as fully human beings.

The characterizing of grace as created was taken as a pretext for representing it as a second nature, a "supernature" super-imposed on our original nature. . . . Nothing would be more contrary to the profound thought of St. Thomas. . . . While grace is supernatural in the basic sense that it is superior to any created nature or to any that could be created, it is in no way a "supernature." It is as it were a new "accident" inserted into the substance of the soul, fitting it as a soul to live the very life of God, wholly divine.[16]

Openness, One to Another

Moreover, it is *not as isolated human beings* that God wants us to come to Him and live with Him. He created us as members of one human family, dependent on one another, meant for personal relationships with one another, for fruitful cooperation and union with one another in the society of the family and the wider societies of the community and mankind itself. But sin and the effects of sin separate and isolate us from one another, shut us up each in our own selves, cause us to try to possess one another as things, rather than to communicate with one another as persons. Psychologists measure a person's emotional maturity by the extent to which he can break out of this cell of his own self-interest, so as to love other persons for their own sakes. It is because we are fallen children of Adam that so few of us become emotionally mature.

Christ's redeeming work gives us the possibility of loving in a mature way, taken up into the divine dimensions of the Spirit of love. We are commanded to love one another not only as we love ourselves but as Christ loves us; His gift of the Spirit enables us to do so. Our Lord's prayer "that all may be one, as you, Father, in me, and I in you" (Jn 17, 21) shows us what we are meant, in Christ, to become *to one another*.

And so He speaks to us and gives us His life through the various "ministries" of the Church, making our fellow men living signs of

16 Bouyer, *Introduction to Spirituality*, p. 153.

His own presence and activity to us, and us to them. Even our ministering to one another's human needs becomes a way in which we can lay down our lives for one another—the final test of our "knowledge of Christ" and our fitness for heaven.

God's Work in Time: History and Symbol

Finally, God's salvation is human in being *historical*. Biblical studies today are bringing out more and more clearly the extent to which, in the Old Testament and the New, God's revelation and intervention were adapted to and even conditioned by human customs, ways of thought, and expression.[17] Research in the development of doctrine, liturgy, and spirituality indicates the same thing in the history of the Church. God means us to receive His salvation *as members of the human race, participants in the whole "human adventure" through the centuries,* the human adventure to which sacred history gives meaning, structure, and purpose.

For the stages of sacred history are all summed up in Christ; in Him each stage illumines the others. God's wonderful works for His people of old prepared for and foreshadowed the saving work of Christ—the work extended to mankind here and now through the Church—which will reach perfection in the "life of the world to come."

Thus the wonderful works of the Old Testament and of Christ's earthly life, communicated to us by the Church in the inspired words of Scripture, become God's words to us *here and now,* telling us about the invisible wonderful works He is accomplishing in us through the sacraments, giving us His commands as to our cooperation with these works and His promises of the final work to be accomplished at the Lord's return in glory and the life with Him it will inaugurate.[18]

[17] See H. Urs von Balthasar, "God Has Spoken in Human Language," in A. G. Martimort, *et al., The Liturgy and the Word of God* (Collegeville, Minn.: The Liturgical Press, 1959).

[18] See J. Daniélou, "The Sacraments and the History of Salvation," in *The Liturgy and the Word of God,* and by the same author, *The Bible and the Liturgy* (Notre Dame: University of Notre Dame Press, 1956) and *From Shadows to Reality* (Westminster, Md.: Newman Press, 1961).

So in the Church, our own personal history is made and is discovered to be an organic part of sacred history. As Bouyer says,[19] the law ruling the development of organic life, that ontogenesis must reproduce phylogenesis, applies here also. Our personal "spiritual" development is to follow the pattern of the development of the People of God through the ages, the development patterned on the "*exodus*" of Christ from this world to the Father. We are to become fully *ourselves* by being taken up into, by freely participating in, the organic growth of the body of Christ.

And so we discover the continuity, together with the character of being continually created, of history—of sacred history, that is to say of the history in which it is God Who acts. We see also that sacred history is not an extraordinary history which has taken place in a little corner with no organic connection either in itself or with the rest of human progress. We understand that it is the history of God little by little taking possession of the history of all mankind, as of the history of each man. In it, we discover how, beginning from this lost center of Palestine, the God who speaks and whose Word is all-powerful act, is taking hold of all peoples in order to form of them one people, taking hold of all men in order to make of them one man, the heavenly Adam. In this final Mass, all the children of God whom sin has scattered are to be gathered to form one body. Finally, the whole world, gravitating around this center in which the Word of God has resounded, will emerge from the second chaos in which Adam had plunged it, to come forth into the unshadowed light.[20]

The sacramental life of the Church, therefore, is focal by the very nature of God's plan to bring us to Himself in a way that is at once fully divine and fully human. It is here that God speaks and gives Himself to men through Christ; that Christ adapts and re-adapts men to the requirements of His life; that He builds up His body in the Spirit; that He enables men to respond to the Father's love with His own response; that He enables men to take part in

19 Bouyer, *Introduction to Spirituality*, p. 34.
20 Bouyer, *The Meaning of Sacred Scripture*, pp. 231 f.

His work of redemption, by joining in His sacrifice and by all their "prayers, works, and sufferings." Here human lives are incorporated into the history of salvation, so that their human acts may extend that salvation in human history, "until He comes."

What We Mean by Christian Worship

The sacramental life of the Church, strictly so-called, is made up of the celebration of the eucharist and the celebration of the other sacraments (in one way or another ordered toward or flowing from the eucharist in which "the work of our redemption is renewed"); the prayer of the Church, again radiating from the eucharistic celebration; and other rites and prayers in some way related to it. All this is laid out in human time, the dynamic context of the liturgical year, so that through these celebrations, in which the Church already anticipates the life of heaven by communion with the Risen Lord, she progresses, as if by an ascending spiral, toward the Day of His return.

Thus all the liturgical year is a life *drawn out of* the mysteries of Christ's life as the revelation of the Trinity. . . . Over against the "neutral" time of the clock, there is liturgical time, which is time endowed with a value of which we find the deepest meaning in the parousia or Christ's return. *We* do not make this time; the holy liturgical time makes us, if we *live with* the sacred events of the Church's liturgy in faith and love and allow ourselves to be carried into the meaningful reality of the great feasts of the liturgy celebrated in the course of each year.[21]

How Teaching Serves the Life of Worship

Obviously, carrying on this life of worship and sanctification is not the *whole* of the Church's work on earth. Yet *toward* it is oriented all her missionary work of preaching the good news of salvation. For this "heralding" conveys God's message to men precisely to arouse their initial response of *faith*—faith in God reveal-

[21] Schillebeeckx, *loc. cit.*, p. 363.

ing Himself to men through Christ. And this faith, itself God's gift, is meant to lead to the Church, to baptism and participation in the sacramental life.

Similarly, *around* the sacramental life is organized all the Church's work of instructing and forming her children, her work of guiding and leading them, her work to remove the obstacles to her life and to Christian living which "the world"[22] is always setting up afresh. All this work is ultimately intended to enable her children more fully to be formed by, more fully to take part in her sacramental life, and to live the Christian lives that should radiate from it.

All the Church's works of loving care and concern for the human needs of men, her corporal and spiritual works of mercy, are but the *radiation* of her sacramental life, communicating the love which she receives from God therein. The work of this love is to aid the human persons whom it reaches, to free and strengthen them to hear and respond to God's call. Thus, in one sense, all such work is to "make straight the path" for the heralding of the good news; in another—because love seeks the good of each person in the mystery of his human freedom and God's dealings with him as a person—it is more directly ordered toward the final communication of each person with God in the community of the redeemed in heaven.

Sacramentalizing All of Life

Similarly, taking part in the sacramental life of the Church, strictly so-called, cannot be the *whole* life of any Christian, nor is it meant to be. But his life will be the more fully Christian the more his sacramental life is its focus: the more, that is, his prayer centers in and is formed by the Church's prayer, above all the Mass; the more completely he *offers* and commits himself, his sufferings and his activities, to the Father's love in and with Christ's eucharistic

----

[22] In St. John's sense: the world is still ruled by Satan, its "prince," as it is organized in active opposition to "the Lord and His Christ" (see Jn 12 31; 14, 30; 16, 11).

sacrifice; the more fully he gives himself in *communion* to the life of Christ's body, to work of God's love in himself and in the world.[23]

Thus each Christian's life is meant to become increasingly "sacramentalized" and "sacramental"—but not in the sense that he necessarily spends more and more time participating in the sacramental life of the Church. How much time he spends in communal and personal prayer depends, of course, on his particular vocation and circumstances (though he must spend *some* time daily and weekly if he is to lead a Christian life in any positive sense). But the whole point of God's plan, if one can put it so, is precisely that we can carry it out in and through ordinary human ways of life *if* we take *His* way of doing it. Communicating with God in a prayer centered in the sacramental life, coming to know Christ and our fellow Christians in this life, dying to the life of the "flesh" and living the life of the Spirit given us in this life, we become increasingly able to find and serve Christ in the "sacrament of the neighbor,"[24] through all created things. Becoming more wholly "Christian," we become more clearly living "signs" of the love of God given us in Christ. And thus our whole life becomes increasingly oriented to communication with God, and to the communication of all men with God, here and hereafter.

THE CHURCH'S SIGNS
AT WORK AMONG US

But Christ does not act through the sacraments in some magical or mechanical way to bring all this about in our lives. He acts through "sacred signs that effect what they signify" precisely so that His gift and our response may engage our whole being. The *ex opere operato* effects of the sacraments affect our being at a

[23] See H. Urs von Balthasar, *Prayer* (New York: Sheed and Ward, 1961), pp. 88–103. On the role of each sacrament in the Christian life, see, for example, A. G. Martimort, *The Signs of the New Covenant* (Collegeville, Minn.: The Liturgical Press, 1963), chaps. 2–7; Vagaggini, *op. cit.*, pp. 43–54.

[24] See Urs von Balthasar, *Science, Religion and Christianity*, pp. 142–55.

level beyond the range of our consciousness; the sacramental signs extend these effects to the conscious levels of our minds and "hearts" (in the biblical sense of the center of our whole volitional life)—and even to the levels below consciousness, so that we may be wholly formed by them and may cooperate with them freely as human persons.

The sign constituting each sacrament, therefore, is seen to be made up of persons, things, and actions, and the "word" that makes the sacramental sign intelligible. The meaning of the seven particular signs is brought out, again, by the biblical-liturgical context of rites and prayers. And this whole "sign" in turn illumines and is illumined by the signs of the liturgical year, of the whole sacramental life. All these signs are not human inventions; they are communications of God's Word, entrusted by Christ to His Church and given to us in the Church. They are essentially biblical signs— in their form, their spirit, and their content[25]—signs through which God today gives us His message spoken once and for all to all men in Christ, and His life which is Christ in us.

Thus the sacramental signs have what might be called four dimensions: they are seen as *demonstrating* the present invisible realities which they signify; as *commemorating* the past history of salvation; as *obligating* the life of the Christian; and as *anticipating* the realities of the world to come.

Consequently, it is what is actually given and signified in the sacraments that is studied in its various aspects in the separate sacred sciences: Scripture, doctrinal, moral, and ascetical theology, etc.—the study of each separate discipline thus in turn enriching our understanding of the sacramental signs and of the Christian life which they communicate and signify.

Further, since the sacraments involve us in—to use the beautiful phrase of a contemporary French theologian—"the common experience of God and mankind," our understanding of their meaning can be still further enriched by all fields of human knowledge. This

[25] See P. Jounel, "The Bible in the Liturgy" in *The Liturgy and the Word of God*, pp. 1–20.

fact is abundantly indicated by the contemporary progress of biblical studies, but it can and should be true of each Christian's personal advance in human knowledge, skill, and experience.

More immediately and more urgently, our own experience of Christian living, our own efforts to be doers of the word which we hear in the sacramental signs, are absolutely necessary if we are to "know" Christ through them. "In only hearing God's commands, they were not enlightened, but in doing them" (St. Gregory, Homily · for Easter Monday).

The sacramental signs, then, are not an arbitrary code: they are a language, but far more than a language in the ordinary sense of that term. They are essentially Christ's revelation and communication of Himself in the human terms that He Himself has chosen, chosen to affect our whole being, to form us to live His life.

They affect us only to the extent to which we actively consent to be affected. To receive the *ex opere operato* effects of the sacraments we must, if we have the use of reason, at least consent to do so with some rudimentary awareness of what we are consenting to. And to be fully formed by Christ in the sacramental life, we must open out our minds and hearts; we must actively cooperate with Him; we must strive to "sacramentalize" our lives, to "die daily" and live in the Spirit.

Sacraments a True Revelation of God

But the sacramental signs are not self-evident. Precisely because they are not a code or a mere "language" but the communication of the "unsearchable riches of Christ" to human persons, they are meant to be opened out to us by the Church in which Christ is present and active. It is the Church, in fact, to which Christ has entrusted the celebration of the sacraments and the continuation of the history of salvation. It is she who, through the ages, has built up the whole complex sign of her sacramental life. It is she who can adapt it to the changing needs of her children—in accordance with the different cultures of ages and peoples, but always along the lines laid down by Christ Himself—to make it more fully His communication to us and our living response to the Father in Him.[26]

It is the Church which opens out the sacramental signs by her whole living tradition of the past and present, by her teaching and by her life. The immediate *locus* of this opening-out has always been the homily which is an integral part of the complete Mass celebration. Here the representative of Christ, sent to a particular congregation by the bishop, himself sent to his flock by Christ as Christ was sent by the Father, opens out God's message in this particular Mass to this particular congregation—helping them to enter into its full relevance to their own personal and communal life. This same purpose is to be served by the instructions which, as commanded by the Council of Trent, the priest is to give before and/or after the administration of the sacraments.[27]

Sacramental Initiation by Word and Act

More widely, it is normal that the individual Christian and the community should receive from their pastors, week by week and season by season, year by year, a continual "initiation" into the sacramental signs.[28] For neither the persons nor the community nor the Church as a whole is static; we are all meant to grow up together as members of the Church, under the guidance of those whom Christ has set over His flock, "to the mature age of the fullness of Christ" (Eph 4, 13).

But such "initiating" will be fruitful only to the extent to which it awakens persons to *fully active participation* in the sacramental

[26] This is the reason for the liturgical "renewals" and reforms of the last decades—and the reason why we may hope and pray for others to come. See H. A. Reinhold, *Bringing the Mass to the People* (Baltimore: Helicon Press, 1960) and G. Ellard, *The Mass in Transition* (Milwaukee: Bruce, 1956).

[27] *Rituale Romanum*, Titulus I—Caput Unicum, n. 10: "In Sacramentorum administrationem eorum virtutem, usum ac utilitatem, et caeremoniorum significationes, ut Concilium Tridentinum praecipit, ex Sanctorum Patrum et Catechismi Romani doctrina, ubi commode fieri potest, diligenter explicabit."

[28] A fact not known to the pastor who groaned, after a pre-Lenten clergy conference, "Do I have to go into all that Red Sea stuff again this year?"

life, in the complete and more intimately personal sense outlined above. The importance of outward "active participation" by attitudes, speaking and singing, is precisely to express, form, and foster full inner participation.[29]

Our greatest need today is, consequently, a growing awareness of what "participation" really means—not a passing series of outward acts, but the slow opening out of each person, under the formative action of the Spirit and with his own cooperation—to receive God's communication more and more fully *by* receiving it and responding to it in the Church. Participation is the slow interweaving of the experience—the life-experience—of each person with the experience of the People of God, the experience of Christ; the slow conformation of each person to Christ by participating in His worship and in His work, in the sacramental life and in the Christian life which flows from it, toward the perfect life of worship in joy where there will be no need of sacraments and God will be "all in all."

THE LITURGY AND EDUCATION

Implications for Christian education as a whole and for religious education in particular do not need to be blueprinted here. But some few, perhaps, may be indicated. First, if the sacramental life is focal in the life of the Church and is meant to be so in each Christian's life, it must certainly be focal in religious instruction (an essential part of religious education). This is so in two senses: (1) the basic objective of religious instruction must be God's own objective: to form "worshippers of the Father in spirit and in truth"; hence, all religious instruction must be basically oriented toward active participation in the fullest sense—toward the awakening of each person to receive Christ's word and gift and increasingly to respond to it *all* his life and with his *whole* life; and (2) the basic means of working toward this objective must follow the lines laid down by God Himself: all religious instruction must in some way be oriented toward or flow from sacramental life.

[29] *Instruction* of September 3, 1958 on Sacred Music and the Liturgy.

In the ancient Church, the catechumens were first instructed in the history of salvation and, on the basis of God's commands and promises as revealed in that history, were shown the elementary requirements of Christian living. Then they were baptized, confirmed, and admitted to participation in the Eucharist. Only then, on the basis of this actual experience of the visible, audible, tangible sacramental signs, was the meaning of these signs unfolded, in direct reference to the Christian life the newly baptized were henceforth to lead.[30]

The same pattern is always psychologically valid, even though carried out in different ways. The study of the history of salvation flows *toward* participation in the sacramental life. *From* this participation, *from* the sacred signs which produce their effects in the context of sacred history, flow formulations of doctrine and of the commitments of Christian living.

Some Specific Applications

On elementary levels, this pattern should be, so far as possible, that of each unit of instruction, and as closely related as possible to actual celebrations: the Sunday Masses, the liturgical feasts and seasons. On the secondary level, where wider opening out of the dimensions of the sacred signs in separate courses may be advisable, everything should still be ordered around *actual existential* sacramental life and the Christian living that should flow from that life—the course (or units of each course) directly concerned with the sacramental life as such being integrative on *this whole level* of instruction.

On the college level, students thus prepared may be ready for "pre-theology," that is, for some initiation into the various sacred sciences as such. But, here again, continuing initiation into the sacramental life itself and into the Christian life that should flow therefrom must, in one way or another, be made focal. Otherwise the actual life of the student will inevitably be formed *away from* sacramental living.

[30] See Martimort, *The Signs of the New Covenant,* Introduction.

Second, we must abandon the attempt to give students of any age a short cut to understanding the invisible realities of the faith by means of abstract definitions, prescinding from the biblical-liturgical signs in which God has chosen to express these realities. Certainly, abstract definitions of doctrines are necessary; but they must be used only to summarize for purposes of correlation and the avoidance of error, not as in themselves communicating truth as God wishes to communicate it.[31]

Equally, we must give up trying to make doctrines seem interesting and relevant by making up our own analogies without reference to God's. *Only* He, and the Church in her whole tradition as guided by His Spirit, can express what He wishes to say to men in human terms so as to bring men to "know" Him as He wishes to be known. To describe grace as "juice in the wires," prayer as "broadcasting," in order to appeal to young people is to falsify grace and prayer.

This sort of thing did seem to be called for when abstract definitions were considered to be the only means available of conveying revealed truth, with Scripture thought of as a kind of illustrative appendage to doctrinal formulations. It was a well-meant attempt to play the role of God's own inspired and inspiring Word. But there is no place for it, now that the nature of God's communication to us in the Church is more clearly realized.

Our task is not to *substitute* for God's own Word, but to make God's own analogies, His signs, fully *available* to students at various levels. And the key here is above all the *identity of human experience* through the ages. It is true that God's inspired Word is composed in terms of civilizations, customs, ways of thought, landscapes, and material creatures not necessarily familiar to us. But we can enter, and cause others to enter, into the *experiences* of the People of God, which made up the "common experience of God and mankind" in the past, and so aid Christians of today to continue that experience.

[31] See G. S. Sloyan, "The Experience of Mystery: Requisite for Theology," in *Catholic Educational Review*, 55 (May 1957), 289–99.

We may not eat homemade bread, we may drink Coca-Cola rather than wine, but we do eat and drink. We may not use olive oil for health or beauty purposes, but we do use similar substances for the same purposes. We may not flee to rock caves, but we have all fled from terrors to some safe refuge. This identity of experience is equally (and more obviously) true on higher, deeper, and wider levels. So we can help our students, by indicating this identity (and appealing also to their wide vicarious experience through TV, magazines, movies, etc.), to receive God's communication of realities which are in themselves beyond the range of earthly experience, and to "incarnate" them in their own lives.[32]

Thirdly, the sacramental life is by its very nature formative, "educational" in the deepest and widest sense. It cannot be otherwise while we are still *in via*. God's purpose in all His dealings with us must be to bring us to the final goal—the life of glory.[33]

But Christian worship "in spirit and in truth" is an end in itself, subordinate only to the final union of redeemed mankind with God in heaven. We cannot *use* the Mass, the sacraments, prayer to educate people—let alone for any other purpose. In this sense, we cannot make participation in the Mass and Christian prayer *part of* the educational process as such. As personal and communal intercourse with God in Christ, these remain above and beyond our educational purposes. Our instruction is to be focused *toward* them and flow *from* them, but it cannot *contain* them. And this means that they must be given their rightful and focal place in the *life* of the educational community—class, school, parish—so that the student takes part in them as *life*, not as "instruction."

The Sign as Threat to Underlying Reality

It should, perhaps, also be noted that it is not the sacramental *rites* themselves which are focal, but the personal and communal worship which they signify, effect, and form us to. This is why the "colorful-rites-of-the-ancient-Church" approach is, to say the least,

[32] See M. P. Ryan, "The Psychology of Worship: Another Approach," *Worship*, 34 (June–July 1960), 380–86.
[33] See Vagaggini, pp. 68–83.

misleading.[34] Archeologism, rubricism, academicism of any kind is to be avoided here. So too is sentimentality—the fostering of emotion for its own sake. Christ came to give us life. If our instruction presents that life as desiccated, dusty (even though the dust be well lacquered over), it will be worse than useless.[35]

Again, the "mystery" of Christian worship does not lie in any mysteriousness of the sacramental rites, but in the Mystery of Christ,[36] which they effect and signify.[37] Hence, for one thing, the fact that modern man can no longer feel anything "sacral" about water, fire, etc., should not be taken as an obstacle to participation in sacramental life. It is not the things and actions in themselves, it is their use by God in sacred history and their present use by Christ in the sacraments that make them sacred. The very ordinariness of the material things and of many of the actions (washing, eating, and drinking, putting on salve or perfume) involved in the sacramental signs indicates how *ordinary* life is to be taken up into the Mystery of Christ, and made sacred *in Him*, not in its own right.[38]

On the other hand, the very way in which the Mass, the sacraments, Christian prayer, are carried out should—above all by its dignity, simplicity, clarity—be as transparent a "sign" as possible of the Mystery being celebrated, allowing the sacramental signs to express themselves with their own clarity and beauty.

[34] There is, in a sense, no soberer judgment passed on modern sacramental life than the journalistic lead sentence used consistently on the occasion of a bishop's consecration: "In the centuries-old pageantry of the Roman Catholic Church. . . ."

[35] This obviously applies very forcefully to all the "signs" we may use in education or in Christian living—architecture, art, music, visual aids, etc. These must follow the laws of the sacramental signs, be prolongations of them, lead back to them—and, above all, point beyond themselves to the invisible realities of Christ's life in us. A misleading sign is worse than no sign at all.

[36] See Reinhold, *op. cit.*, Appendix 3.

[37] On the Christian sense of the word "mystery," see L. Bouyer, "Mysterion," in *Mystery and Mysticism* (New York: Philosophical Library, 1955), also R. E. Brown, "The Pre-Christian Semitic Concept of 'Mystery,' *Catholic Biblical Quarterly*, 20 (October 1958), 417–43; "The Semitic Background of the New Testament *Mysterion*," *Biblica*, 39 (1958), 426–48; 40 (1959), 70–87.

[38] See Martimort, *op. cit.*, chap. 1, art. 1.

The special difficulty facing religious educators today is in quite another sphere. The general attitude of students seems to be peculiarly passive—"teach me if you can"—and peculiarly utilitarian—getting marks for a diploma or degree, for the sake of a well-paying job, for the sake of security. And this attitude runs directly counter to the whole idea of the Christian life.

One of the greatest problems of religious education is, consequently, how to lift religious instruction out of this whole context of passive and "interested" education—how to show that the Christian life is essentially vital, dynamic, "liberal" in the fullest sense—opening out to Truth itself, to self-giving love of neighbor in the love of God.

Here the problems of religious instruction are interwoven with the problems of Christian education itself. For if it is truly to be Christian, it must, however gradually and painfully, be re-formed and vitalized by this same spirit, this same orientation. And this in turn broadens out into the still wider problems of family, parochial, and Catholic life generally; it is the task of "re-establishing all things in Christ."

But at least—in this age in which, as Pius XI said, "No one is allowed to be mediocre"—the lines along which the religious educator should be working seem now clearly to be indicated: to strive, in his own life and in the lives of all those whom he influences, toward that full active participation in the worship and life of the Church which forms Christians to the knowledge of God and the charity of Christ, in the Spirit who "renews the face of the earth."

3

THE FAITH OF THE CHURCH AND FORMAL DOCTRINAL INSTRUCTION

Franz Schreibmayr
OF THE ORATORY, MUNICH

THE faith of the Church comes to the child in three ways: through the religious life of the family and the parish, primarily the liturgy; through the words of Holy Scripture; and by way of the systematic teaching provided in catechism instruction.[1] Each of these forms has its peculiar structure and function with respect to the child's life of faith and his religious development.[2] In the school of the Scriptures he hears God's inspired Word, especially the words of our Lord and the accounts of His first witnesses—in the context of

[1] Cf. "Program of the Catechetical Apostolate," in Johannes Hofinger, S.J. and Clifford Howell, S.J. (eds.), *Teaching All Nations* (New York: Herder and Herder, 1961), pp. 398 f.

[2] *Ibid.*, pp. 407 f.

the history of redemption. In the liturgy the mysteries of faith are not only proclaimed in the scriptural passages but also expressed in prayer and song and realized in the cultic commemoration. Do we need for children, in addition to the formation provided by the Scripture, liturgy, and the Christian life, a systematic—and that seems to mean "logical-conceptual"—presentation of faith as well? Many modern catechists are prone to put this question.

Inquiry into the fundamentals of faith shows us that formal doctrinal instruction also has its unique function in the work of catechizing. Yet it must be remembered that the formulations and modes of presenting doctrine originate not only in the Church's creeds and magisterial definitions but also in the witness of faith provided by the primitive Church, and are found in their living form primarily in Scripture and Christian worship. This essay will attempt to establish clearly the relation between Bible and liturgy on the one hand, and formal doctrinal instruction on the other, with a view to developing the most fruitful catechesis possible. At the same time it hopes to provide an important service to the catechist, namely that of giving him a total picture, based on the scriptural and liturgical proclamation made by the Church, of those matters he must convey in his teaching. Whoever pursues patiently the relationship that obtains among the three modes of instruction will observe what rich fruit accrues to his catechetical efforts.[3]

I

Proclamation and Teaching

The basic task not only of preaching but also of catechizing is to herald the good tidings of God.[4] For that Christ was "sent" (Mk 1, 38; Lk 4, 43). As the ambassador of His Father He announced the event the prophets had foretold which would fundamentally change and decisively determine the destiny of the world. As "herald" He *proclaimed* or *announced* the imminence of the un-

[3] A detailed study of the cited scriptural passages is especially recommended.

[4] Cf. *Teaching All Nations*, p. 394, "Our Aim."

veiled, grace-infused kingdom of God that had its prototype in the theocracy of the Old Covenant. Through Christ's powerful proclamation, through His holy death and glorification, this kingdom has already begun to take effect. The apostles, as their very name indicates (*apo* + *stellein*, send out), were sent into the cities and towns of Israel and subsequently the whole world, to announce the kingdom of God by testifying to what they had seen and heard as disciples of the Lord, from His baptism in the Jordan to His raising up by God and the outpouring of the promised Spirit (cf. Ac 1, 22). This living message, filled with divine reality, reached men in their innermost beings. It forced them to make a radical about-face and espouse a new life, in light of the coming kingdom of God and the power of Christ's love (cf. Mk 1, 14; Ac 2, 38 ff.; Gal 2, 20).

But it is also reported of the Lord Himself, as well as of the rabbis, that He "taught." He taught in synagogues in accord with traditional custom (cf. Lk 4, 15–21). Or again, "When he saw the crowds he ascended the mountain, seated himself and drew his disciples toward him; then opening his mouth he began to teach them" (Mt 5, 1 f.). Despite external similarity His teaching was radically different from that of the scribes and Pharisees. He did not merely offer interpretation of the Old Testament. In His instructive discourses and conversations He unfolded the joyful message of the kingdom of God. He led His disciples ever deeper into the mysteries of the kingdom. Basing Himself on the Scriptures, He spoke about a new holiness (*tsedaka, iustitia*). Moreover He always spoke "with authority" (Mt 7, 29; Mk 1, 27; Lk 4, 32). His teaching was an expansion of His message and again and again returned to the direct proclamation: "Today this Scripture is fulfilled in your hearing" (Lk 4, 21). Through Christ the work of teaching, indeed the very word, acquired a new sense. It came to mean something thoroughly alive and at the same time absolute, corresponding to the new situation of God's plan of salvation (cf. Mt 23, 8; 28, 18).[5]

[5] Cf. on this point the synonymous use of *kēryssein* and *didaskein* in the summary Mt 9, 35, and especially the mutually parallel places, Mt 4, 23 = Mk 1, 39 = Lk 4, 44.

In the primitive Church, similarly, no sharp distinction was drawn among the activities of proclaiming, teaching, and instructing (*katēchein*), although there was a difference of stress. In any case the words "proclamation" and "message" (*euaggélion; kērygma*) were not limited to missionary preaching in the strict sense. Again and again it is the believer to whom the joyous message is announced, chiefly in the "Liturgy of the Word," in the Mass of the Catechumens (cf. Rom 1, 13 ff.).[6] Conversely, the first proclamation is often enough designated as "teaching" or "catechesis," which by the way corresponds to the original meaning of the word *katēchein* (cf. Lk 1, 4; Ac 5, 28; 11, 26; 15, 35; 18, 11; 20, 20; Col 1, 28; 2, 7; Eph 4, 20).[7]

As might be expected, in the enumeration of charismatic offices the various concepts are more sharply differentiated. 1 Cor 12, 28 names teachers immediately after apostles and prophets as those whose charism has fundamental meaning for the whole Church. Eph 4, 11 names in addition evangelists. The apostles, sent forth by the risen Jesus and filled with the Spirit, lay the foundation by their witness and continue to remain the senior teachers of the community. To the prophets, who in general are not firsthand witnesses, has been given, as to the apostles, the gift of inspired speech which relies on special insight into the internal connection among the redemptive events, on an understanding of the Scriptures, and on a recognition of the mystery of salvation. Evangelists and teachers, however, whom Gal 6, 6 designates "catechists," have the charism and insight of the apostles and prophets to carry further the message of faith. To this the evangelists dedicate themselves

[6] The gospels were composed, so far as we can discover, for the use of believers in the "assembly" (*ekklēsia*).

[7] The contrasted juxtaposition *kērygma*—first proclamation, and *katēchēsis*—instruction of the already converted, seems to us to be exegetically incorrect and misleading. *Kērysso/kērygma* (in an active sense) like their synonyms *euaggelizomai/euaggélion*, denote in the NT the proclamation, the announcement of the good tidings which also repeatedly occurs in community preaching, eucharistic celebration, and catechesis. Cf. G. Friedrich in Kittel, *Theologisches Wörterbuch zum Neuen Testament* (Stuttgart: W. Kohlhammer Verlag, 1935), II, 715, lines 31 ff.; 717, lines 13–19; III (1938), 702, lines 21 ff.

not only in *missionary preaching* to unbelievers but also in *community preaching* to the established congregation (2 Tim 4, 5). The word "teacher" is likewise used interchangeably both within and outside the community of believers.

A primary task of the teacher therefore was (and is) the coherent presentation of the *kērygma*. Connected with it from the early period, particularly in divine service, was the continuous reading of Holy Scripture (*lectio continua*) and the explanation customarily given (cf. 1 Tim 4, 13).

Origin and Significance of Credal Formulas

From the beginning, in proclamation and teaching both, certain especially important points emerged which were soon summarized into kerygmatic formulations and creeds. Christ Himself in His proclamation of the kingdom of God, building on the hope of salvation of the former covenant, expounded the theme and the ultimate meaning of sacred history and His place in it (cf. Mt 4, 17–23; 9, 35; Mk 1, 15; Lk 16, 16). He charged those whom He sent out with proclaiming this message of the kingdom (Mt 10, 7; Lk 9, 2; Ac 1, 3). It is faithfully handed down by the Church, as the gospels show (cf. Mt 24, 14). The preaching and teaching of the apostles is nothing other in content than a progressive unfolding of the joyful message of the kingdom of God (cf. Ac 8, 12; 19, 8; 20, 25; 28, 23–31).

The way in which God carried His plan through in the public life and the death, resurrection, and exaltation of the Lord, and likewise in the outpouring of the Spirit, was formulated in the sermons recorded in the Acts of the Apostles. In all of them a primitive Christian pattern of proclamation shines through. There likewise originated in the primitive community the formula recalled to mind by Paul in 1 Cor 15, 3 ff. which gives the "core" of the *kērygma:* death, burial, and resurrection of the Lord. Its formulation is already familiar to us. Again, the pre-Pauline hymn to Christ in Phil 2, 5–11 traces the way of Christ, beginning from the eternal existence and incarnation of the Son (cf. also 1 Tim 3, 16).

In addition to summaries of the redemptive events, often by way of conclusions, there are to be found creeds in the stricter sense: the ancient traditional profession of faith in the one true God, for example, but now filled with deeper meaning (cf. Mt 4, 10; 23, 9; Jn 17, 3; Rom 11, 36; Jas 2, 19). With special frequency there occurs a confession of faith in Christ under a variety of forms (cf. Mt 16, 16; Jn 20, 28. 31; Ac 2, 36; 9, 22; Phil 2, 11; Rom 10, 9; 1 Cor 12, 3; 1 Jn 2, 22). We find such single-membered formulas very often, those confessions to Christ which are decisive for Christian belief. A gentile milieu produced two-membered confessions, expressing belief in one true God and in one Lord Jesus Christ (cf. 1 Cor 8, 6; 1 Thess 1, 9 f.; 1 Tim 2, 5; 6, 13; Jn 17, 3). Side by side with these there existed from earliest times, chiefly in Paul, formulas with three members in which the Holy Spirit and His gifts are named (cf. Mt 28, 19; 1 Cor 12, 3–6; 2 Cor 13, 13; Eph 1, 3–14). These are, as it were, the concluding summary of the message of Christ and of the redemptive and saving occurrences, simultaneously illumined by the trinitarian mystery. We might mention in conclusion that multimembered credal formulas also occur.[8]

Formulas as Old as the Gospel

The examples cited show at a glance that formulas of proclamation and of profession are found in the Scriptures themselves. Indeed, historical research into the origins of the Apostles' Creed establishes that they originated in the earliest preaching even before the writing of the New Testament.[9] The faith of the Church, as even non-Catholic research scholars stress, is dogmatic from the

---

[8] Cf. J. A. Jungmann, *Handing On the Faith* (New York: Herder and Herder, 1959), p. 379.

[9] Cf. J. de Ghellinck, S.J., *Patristique et Moyen âge, I, Les recherches sur les origines du symbole des apôtres* (2 ed.; Gembloux: J. Duculot, 1949); J. N. D. Kelly, *Early Christian Creeds* (London: Longmans, 1950); *ibid.*, Rufinus, *A Commentary on the Apostles' Creed*, "Ancient Christian Writers," 20 (Westminster, Md.: Newman, 1955); Josef A. Jungmann, *Handing On the Faith*, pp. 377–86; Pierre Benoit, O.P., "Les origines du symbole des apôtres dans le Nouveau Testament," in *Exégèse et Théologie* (Paris: Cerf, 1961), II, 193–211, reprinted from *Lumière et Vie*, No. 2 (1952), 39–60.

beginning. Before the message of the New Testament was fixed in written form, Cullmann says, the early Church experienced an increased need for short summaries of Christian belief. After the New Testament writings arose in a rich profusion, summary formulas were found embedded there.[10] The credal formularies grew out of the primitive preaching and are to be found scattered through the New Testament writings "like crystals in a mass of amorphous stone,"[11] perfectly clear in one place, obscure in another, occasionally as citations, again as more or less free renderings. Discovering them in their context and studying them is most profitable for the catechist and profoundly stimulating for his catechetical practice.

The occasions which led to the framing of these formulas have already been indicated in part. The formulas were summaries of apostolic proclamation and were the basis of both missionary preaching and preaching within the Christian community. We find them in the liturgy as cultic acclamations or as responses in praise or thanksgiving to the proclamation of the mighty acts of God. They play an important role in the preparation for baptism and its administration, and equally so in the fuller instruction provided after baptism. The creeds were formulated in the crisis-hour of martyrdom and in opposition to heresy; consequently they received a particular coloration.[12] The existential milieu in which the credal formulas arose therefore comes into our purview. They are seen to be documents of a living faith, filled with the power of primitive preaching, permeated with the spirit of prayer, and sanctified by the blood of martyrs.

It is evident from all this that long before Christian belief came into contact with philosophy and with philosophical systems there was an orderly presentation of faith whereby the message of Jesus and His apostles was further spread. This followed a definite

[10] Cf. O. Cullmann, *Die ersten christlichen Glaubensbekentnisse* (Zürich: Evangelischer Verlag, 1943), pp. 6 f. This has been translated as *The Earliest Christian Confessions* (London: Lutterworth Press, 1949).
[11] E. Stauffer, *New Testament Theology* (London: SCM Press, 1955), p. 238.
[12] Cf. Cullmann, *op. cit.*, pp. 13 ff.; de Ghellinck, *op. cit.*, pp. 263 ff.

pattern, summarized in credal formulas yet always remaining a spiritual, living message adapted to the hearer. This mode of presentation lived on in the doctrinal instruction of the Church—whence important practical consequences flow.

Our teaching must be a continuation of the teaching of Jesus and His apostles; therefore, it cannot confine itself to a notional explanation of credal formulas and definitions of the Church. Like primitive Christian teaching itself, it must mediate that total view of the message of Christ which the Holy Spirit revealed to the apostles and prophets and which the Church ever since has unfolded and guarded against misconception. In practice this means that formal doctrinal instruction must be fed by both the Bible and the liturgy, and especially by those passages which promote the essential and all-encompassing outlook found there. Only thus can it convey not only knowledge but also spiritual understanding leading to a personal *credo* and a faith that is lived.

II

In this second part we shall briefly examine some of the more important formulations of faith proclaimed by the Church and try to point out what assistance the Scriptures and the liturgy can render with respect to them.

The Christian View of God

Christian preaching and Christian faith derive, as we have seen, from the joyful tidings of the kingdom of God which Jesus, our Master and Lord, announced in the land of Israel and among its people. It has been claimed, and quite correctly, that the message and the Word itself of the kingdom of God should have a predominant place in doctrinal catechesis.[13] The kingdom of God is the theme of the preaching of Jesus which is encountered again and

---

[13] Cf. Theodor Filthaut, *Das Reich Gottes in der katechetischen Unterweisung* (Freiburg: Herder Verlag, 1958), pp. 203 f.: "The kingdom of God is the comprehensive matrix, Christ the central figure, in catechetical instruction." This book provides a rich literature on the point. Cf. a notice of it in *Theological Studies*, 20 (September 1959), 487.

again when the gospel is read during the "service of the Word." It is later echoed in the "Our Father." In this message the true future of man and the world "which has already begun in Christ" is revealed. The message is the answer to man's anguished question on the meaning of his existence. The end is neither the atomic destruction of all life on this planet nor utter chaos, but the everlasting kingdom of God our Father, holy and impregnated with grace. This kingdom is already powerfully at work in the world; it has taken root in our very midst even though in a hidden manner (cf. Mt 12, 28).

The picture of God we find in the gospels is derived from this message. The God and Father revealed by our Lord is not the God of deism who has finished His work and lets things run their course because He can do no more beyond that which He already has done. He is the sovereign, living God whose judgment, love, and power extend far beyond all human thoughts and actions (cf. Mt 22, 29). He is emerging, so to say, from His overwhelming mysteriousness to conclude a compact of undying love with us and to celebrate the wedding feast He has prepared from the foundation of the world. He is the thrice-holy Lord of heaven and earth. To Him we owe our undivided worship. He deserves to be loved with our whole heart and soul and strength, for He is the all-knowing and solicitous Father who is ever near to us. To Him should we confide all our faults, on Him cast all daily concerns.

This living message from God is proclaimed to us continually in the sacred liturgy. It must be "in our hearts and on our lips" when we speak about God, our Father and Lord, in our catechesis. In other words, when we teach about God the gospel must lie open before us. If it does, the instruction we give and all our endeavors will bear fruit.

Behind the message of the Lord lie the revelation and faith of the former Covenant. The same transcendent yet intimate God appeared to Moses in the burning bush, ordering him to announce to the people the coming deliverance from Egypt. With His mighty arm He rescued from slavery the people He had chosen. Clothed in glory He transmitted to the people on Sinai His Law, and con-

cluded with them His Covenant. He led His people and lived as
"the Holy One" in their midst. His name, His faithfulness to His
word, His power, His righteous wrath and anxious care for His
people, were not mere concepts for them. They were experiences
of faith which our catechesis must bring alive again. To confess
Him daily was not to enunciate a proposition but to renew devoted
thanks to a covenanted Lord.

As time was fulfilled the living God further revealed Himself—
not only in word but also in mighty deeds which the first witnesses, filled with the Spirit, saw and proclaimed. He it is, Peter
tells us, who gives testimony to Jesus through powerful signs. The
consummation of His holy design is brought about in the death of
Jesus. God frees Him from the bonds of death, raises Him up at
His right hand, and through Him pours out the promised Spirit in
whom the new alliance is sealed.

Far more wonderfully than in the history of Joseph in Egypt is
the providence of God seen in Jesus' path from utter abandonment
to exaltation as Lord and Savior of the entire world. Nowhere is
God's mysterious wisdom and His victorious power more gloriously
revealed than in the cross and resurrection of the Lord (cf. 1 Cor
1, 18). The love of God is nowhere better disclosed to us than in
His sending His own Son into the world and giving Him up for us
(cf. Jn 3, 16; 1 Jn 4, 9). When Paul extols "God the Father of our
Lord Jesus Christ" he has in mind the fullness of grace and mercy
God has blessed us with in His beloved Son (cf. Eph 1, 1ff.; 2 Cor
1, 3 ff.). He recalls the work of creation God accomplished in the
heart of this apostle when He revealed the Son to Paul (2 Cor 4, 6;
Gal 1, 15 f.).

If the Church praises and acknowledges God with such venerable words of tradition as the "Lord," the "holy Father," the "almighty everlasting God," it is because ever before her are the great
and wonderful deeds He performed and continues to perform
through and in His Son. And in the Spirit we the faithful see ourselves with the redeemed of every age and nation already gathered
before the face of Him "who sits on the throne" and whose glory
fills heaven and earth (cf. Apoc 4, 1 ff.; 21, 5.22). All that—we sug-

gest—lies behind the Church's confession, "I believe in God the Father, the almighty sovereign," i.e., *pantokratora* (*omnipotentem*). (Cf. *Symboli apostolici forma occidentalis antiquior*, Denz. 2). This is what must come to life in our catechesis of faith.

The phrase "Creator of heaven and earth," historically an unfolding enlargement of the first article (cf. Denz. 6), turns the mind's eye back to the first of the mighty works of God. The words of this phrase are of decisive importance for understanding the world of nature and man's relation to created things. They undergo further development in the teaching on creation, the pristine condition of man and nature, and original sin. It is very important to observe that the first chapters of Genesis do not serve as the only biblical basis for teaching about God the Creator. Of eminent importance in this connection also are the psalms and prayers which extol God as the wise, powerful, and loving Creator and Lord of the universe. (Cf. Pss 8; 18; 32; 94; 103; 145; 148; 2 Mc 1, 24; 7, 28 and important statements by the prophets, chiefly Isaia 40, 12. 26.28; 44, 24; 45, 18; 48, 13.)

In the liturgy of the Easter Vigil the account of creation serves as powerful background for the new creation realized in the resurrection of Christ and its gateway baptism (cf. Is 65, 17 f.). The belief that God is the Creator of heaven and earth was of foremost importance in the encounter of Israel and later the Church with the pagan world. The God who chose Israel as His own and whom the Church professes as her Lord is the sovereign master of heaven and earth; He gives the breath of life to all being and witness to Himself in the longings of the nations (cf. Ac 17, 24–27).

In missionary areas and in secularized milieu, therefore, catechesis will often start with creation and the natural knowledge of God. St. Thomas Aquinas in his *Summa contra Gentes*, for example, does not begin his treatment of God in the light of *sacra doctrina* but of *sapientia* because, as he says, he "must have recourse to natural reason which all can agree on."[14]

The child of believing parents on the other hand surely comes to

[14] *SCG* 1, 2.

know God first as the heavenly Father who loves us, sees us, and cares for us. He is someone we shall live with eternally. It seems that the vivid image of God found in Scripture often appeals most directly by its simple truth even to the adult mind in search, especially when it is encountered in a genuine witness to the faith.

The Profession of Faith in Christ

Jesus' primary task was to proclaim God's message, to make a revelation of the Father. This remains the basic theme of the gospel (cf. Jn 17, 6). But the authority with which our Lord spoke, the signs that accompanied His preaching, the holiness of His ministry brought to maturity in His disciples an awareness which Peter formulated at Caesarea Philippi as spokesman for his fellows in the name of the embryonic Church. Peter's profession of faith grew out of what the disciples heard and saw. All this has been recorded in the gospel and is brought to life for us again in the liturgy or in meditative reading and listening. Our catechesis on Christ must be tied in with this experience if it is to lead to an interior knowledge of Him and a profession of living faith.

The knowledge of the apostles was deepened and suffused with new light by the events of the death and the glorification of Christ. His career, the work He came to do, the secret of His innermost self, were all more profoundly disclosed to them by the risen Lord and His Spirit (cf. Jn 20, 28.31; Ac 2, 36; 9, 20.22; 1 Cor 12, 3; Rom 10, 9; 1 Jn 4, 2; 5, 1). The profession of faith in Jesus, the Christ (Messia), the Kyrios at the right hand of the Father, the Son of God sent into the world and delivered up for us, forms the core of the preaching and writing of the apostles. It is taken up in the prayer of the Church, in the homage paid to the Lord by the assembled community in its cry of "Kyrie" and the words of the Gloria, "You alone are holy, you alone are Lord, you alone are most high, O Jesus Christ." All this is summarized in the confession of the Church's faith: "I believe . . . in Jesus Christ, His only Son, our Lord."

Thus Christian proclamation does not proceed either deductively or analytically. As the preaching of Pentecost shows particularly, the confession of faith in Christ is a summary of those things revealed to the first witnesses and thereby to us and our catechumens in the events of the life, death, and glorification of the Lord which shed light upon His mission and person. Any attempt to discuss this confession, therefore, must keep in view the concrete circumstances that resulted in the formulation. Only in this way can the full force of the testimony be effective for the child.

The profession of faith in Christ—as is evident from as early as Caesarea Philippi—is the kernel, the cardinal point of the creed. Whoever believes in Christ believes also that the kingdom of God is near at hand and that in Christ salvation is achieved for us. He likewise declares himself ready to follow Christ and take up His cross after Him (cf. Mk 8, 34 ff.).

Around A.D. 200 a relative clause was added to the profession of faith in Christ which expanded and substantiated the second article. This addition bears a resemblance to an old Christ-kerygma cited by St. Paul (1 Cor 15, 3).[15] It consists of two parts, as the questions of the baptismal rite show more clearly: the one concerning the mystery of the incarnation and the other the passion and glorification of the Lord. This makes it possible to tie in closely this part of our teaching of faith with the feasts of Christ's incarnation (the annunciation, nativity) and those of his passion, resurrection, and ascension. In any case we can at this point in the catechesis bring in the corresponding texts: the prefaces, hymns (e.g., the *Exsultet*), songs, and of course the scriptural readings. We may not dwell exclusively on accounts of the infancy or on the passion and resurrection accounts, but must bring to light those passages of the Old and New Testaments which provide spiritual insights into the ways of God in Christ, for example the song of the Servant of the Lord (Is 53; the origin of the phrase *pro nobis* is to be found here), the hymn to Christ in the letter to the Philippians (2, 6–11), and other such New Testament summaries (e.g., Ac 2, 22 ff.; Gal 4, 4–7; 1 Tim 3, 16). Thus it will become clear to us that in Scripture and the liturgy the redemption is not simply a work of the Son; it

[15] Cf. H. Denzinger *et al., Enchiridion Symbolorum.* 30 ed.; Freiburg: Herder, 1950. N. 2; Jungmann, *op. cit.,* p. 380.

is primarily the mighty deed of the Father, whom we answer in words of praise and thanksgiving.

The main point is that a catechesis oriented toward Scripture and liturgy will not remain fixed in the abstract or the purely historical. It will continually find expression in a living confession to Christ our Lord seated at the right hand of the Father. Like the apostles, evangelists, and martyrs, like the Church herself at worship, catechists and pupils must conceive themselves as before the face of the living Lord of the Church whose Word they hear, whose love they experience, to whose Spirit they are enabled to give living testimony. Also, when we gather in the classroom Christ is in our midst. Everything said about His life, death, and glorification should serve the purpose of drawing us closer to Him and making us await more ardently His coming. Just as the kerygma on Christ in the creed concludes with the Lord's return, so must our catechesis keep alive a yearning for the day of Christ. From this lives the faith and prayer of the Church, His Bride. When He appears to judge all mankind and turn the redeemed world over to His Father, only then will we fully apprehend who He is and all that He means to us.

Thus does the image of the Lord of power take its place at the beginning and end of the teaching on Christ. This not only corresponds to the experience and the kerygma of the apostles; it is also of decisive importance for the conscious faith of the children we instruct.

The Holy Ghost, Holy Church, and New Life

After the Lord had ascended into heaven and left to His disciples who remained behind His promise to return, He sent the Holy Spirit down upon them from the Father. The Spirit had hovered low over Him, the "Anointed," at His baptism in the Jordan (cf. Lk 3, 22; 4, 14.18). Now, as the prophets had foretold, the Spirit was to be poured out on all flesh. Through the Holy Ghost the company of disciples whom the Lord had called by His Word and consecrated by His death was made manifest as the new people of God unto life everlasting. Filled with the Spirit the Church went forth, gathered around the apostles, with Peter proclaiming the message of the arrival of the time of salvation, and of the life, death, and glorification of the Lord. Peter called on Jews and gentiles alike to be converted; by holy baptism some three thousand shared that day in the remission of sins and the gift of the Holy Spirit.

The fruits of the Spirit manifested themselves in the living faith, in the powerful witness given to the faith, in prayer filled with the Spirit, but most of all in an active brotherly love. The focal point of the new life was the "assembly" in which "bread was broken" with gladness and simplicity of heart in union with the Lord and in expectation of His coming (Ac 2, 46).

The third part of the creed also, which discusses the "gifts of Redemption"[16] has its foundation in the process of our salvation, especially in the Pentecostal events, which continually are reenacted and working in the Church (cf. Ac 4, 31; 1 Cor 12, 4 ff.). Any catechesis about it not only must refer to the evidence provided in the gospel concerning the Holy Spirit, the nascent Church, and the redemptive gifts. It also must make use of the vital reports in the Acts of the Apostles; concern itself with the apostolic letters on the work of the Spirit and the life of the early communities; analyze the liturgical texts of the feasts of Easter and Pentecost. In that way the inner connection between the teaching on the Holy Ghost, on grace, and on the Church and her life will become clearer. The tongues of fire descend upon each of the disciples singly—a distinguishing feature of the New Covenant—but as they are assembled. The gifts of the Spirit are given to each for his salvation not only as an individual but also as a member of the Church. Put another way, the gift of the Holy Spirit is love. At the same time, in the perspective of Scripture and the liturgy, an isolated conception of any sort is avoided. Through the Spirit and His gifts of grace the Lord works in the Church, which is His body (cf. 1 Cor 12, 5; 2 Cor 3, 17 f.). It is the living God, however, who is supreme over everything, "who works all things in all" (1 Cor 12, 6; cf. Rom 11, 36).

The teaching on the gifts of redemption must not remain at the

[16] Jungmann, *op. cit.*, p. 382.

halfway mark. As early as Peter and John we see a "proclaiming in the case of Jesus of resurrection from the dead" (Ac 4, 2). Paul too names the resurrection and takes his stand on it as the central teaching of faith (Ac 23, 6; 1 Cor 15, 12 ff.). The Spirit is given to us as a "first installment," or pledge of eternal glory (cf. Eph 1, 14; 2 Cor 1, 22). Through the Holy Spirit who dwells in us God will bring to life our mortal bodies, that Spirit who lets us groan inwardly as we wait for adoption as sons and the redemption of our bodies and of all creation (cf. Rom 8, 11.23). The Church is the beginning of a people of God that will be unending. Its eucharistic celebration is the pledge and foreshadowing of the heavenly wedding feast. The life given us in baptism is the beginning of eternal life; the love implanted in our hearts by the Holy Spirit is the form of life of the world to come, shown to us in the great visions of the Apocalypse. The first thing we will recognize in the new creation is what that salvation is with which Christ has endowed us.

Profession of Faith in the Trinity

Thus does the Church, filled with the Holy Spirit, speak to her catechumens: not only of the kingdom of God and of Jesus Christ (cf. Ac 8, 12) but also of the redemptive gifts which they come to share at baptism. She does not merely speak of "the one true God and Him whom thou hast sent, Jesus Christ" (Jn 17, 3) but also of the Holy Ghost, the Counsellor who teaches us all things and "prompts" us regarding all that Christ has said. Very early,[17] a comprehensive, threefold baptismal creed, in which the results of the baptismal catechesis were summarized, preceded the act of baptism. The events of our salvation proclaimed by the Church to the baptismal candidates provided the living background for this: the approach of the kingdom of God, our redemption through Christ the Lord, and the sending of the Holy Spirit. It likewise expressed the deepest mystery of faith revealed to us in the course of salvation history, one which the Church celebrates immediately after the feast of Pentecost: the mystery of the most holy Trinity. Faith in the Trinity has been solemnly professed by the godparents

---

[17] Around the year 100 A.D. Cf. Jungmann, *Handing On the Faith*, p. 380.

in baptism and voiced by the children when they first make the sign of the cross.

It is constantly renewed in prayer and in participation in the liturgy. Formal doctrinal instruction of the young must so bring knowledge of this mystery to children that they recognize its profound relation to the work of their salvation and are led to thoughts of adoration and gratitude.

We have examined the most important themes of the proclamation of faith in their inner connection, seeing in the process how deeply rooted doctrinal instruction is in Scripture and the liturgy. We have called attention to the most important sources of discovery in order to stimulate the catechist to derive the propositions of doctrinal instruction from the Bible and the texts of the liturgy much more than has been customary heretofore. In the course of this inquiry the specific function of doctrinal instruction has come to light more clearly. It is *unfolded proclamation.* The catechist tells of the coming of the kingdom of God, of the events in Christ's life, and what happens to us through His Spirit, thus bringing us to a living awareness of God the Father and Christ our Savior, and to a more intimate familiarity with the Holy Ghost. Doctrinal instruction does not bring with it the fullness of detail, the discourse, of the accounts found in Holy Scripture. It accentuates the great words of revelation, the basic events, the predominant ideas that convey life and understanding, the important truths and demands, all with a view to their inner coherence. For that reason, here just as in the liturgy the New Testament revelation centering on Christ is always to the fore, the Old Testament revelation and redemptive events of the Old Testament always in the background.

The presentation is, therefore, more directly concentrated on Christ than in biblical catechesis. From the very first article He is the Teacher and Master of faith. Also, as we saw, in the sequence of great themes, doctrinal instruction follows the Master. It develops according to the relation in which the themes have been revealed in Christ. It follows the catechesis which God "presented" once for all time through His Son and later charged His Church with carrying on everywhere. Its "system" is by no means that of human logic but one that derives from the Word made flesh, the Logos in whose life, death, and glorification all truth and grace have been made to shine on us.

From the earliest period doctrinal instruction drew upon the prayers and hymns of the liturgy; the rule of faith has always been the rule of prayer. It can, as in soteriology, be in contact with the liturgy in its sequence, that is, with the seasons which emphasize more the single events of our redemption while remaining distinct from it in its essence. Sacramental commemoration, as every Sunday shows, essentially contains the entire mystery of our salvation.[18] Cult is more than proclamation of the Word and catechesis. What is one in a living act of liturgy must be developed in various themes in doctrinal teaching. This is oriented toward the creeds of the Church which have their roots in the earliest Christian proclamation and have been unfolded and explained by the Church's magisterium. The purpose of cult is not sterile knowledge but spiritual insight into the "ways" and the "depths" of God (Ac 18, 25 f.; Rom 11, 33; 1 Cor 2, 10). It should make those who receive catechetical instruction capable of living by faith; of facing the world as mature Christians, and of talking about the things of God and our salvation to those who search and ask.

We shall achieve that best if we continually lead them to the sources and the basic monuments of faith. They must learn, even in catechism instruction, continually to dig into the "documents" of faith so as to experience the pristine force of the words and events of our salvation. They must gain the impression that in instruction class just as in liturgical participation, they "have fellowship" with the Lord's disciples, with the confessors and martyrs of apostolic times—and thereby a share in the joy which has come into the world through the message of the Lord (cf. 1 Jn 1, 1–4).

[18] Cf. Jungmann, *Public Worship* (Collegeville, Minn.: Liturgical Press, 1957), pp. 178 f., for the origin, character, and (limited) meaning of the Church Year in the Liturgy. Unfortunately we are not able to trace here the consequences of this reference for catechetical instruction.

4 THE RELATION OF THE CATECHISM TO THE WORK OF RELIGIOUS FORMATION

Gerard S. Sloyan

In October 1950, an international catechetical congress was held at Rome, summoned by the Sacred Congregation of the Council in conjunction with the Holy Year of Jubilee. The proceedings were published in 1953. In them one can find recorded (among other things) an important resolution on catechism textbooks.[1] The Roman meeting resulted in the publication of the following recommendations:

1. Uniformity of wording should be achieved to express religious truths, especially in common formulas, so that the same words will be used to convey the same truths. 2. Insofar as possible, one catechism text should be issued for all the chil-

[1] *Acta Congressus Catechistici Internationalis MCML* (Roma: Typis Polyglottis Vaticanis, 1953), pp. 175 ff.

dren [*pueris,* normally distinguished from *pueruli*] of a given country, constructed along modern lines [*hodierna methodo compositus*]; it should be graded or in cycles, should be rooted [*adhaerens*] in Holy Scripture, have brief and pointed responses, embrace all the truths of faith and practice that need to be known, and at the same time include [*referens*] liturgical concepts and the principles of Catholic social teaching.

The resolutions which follow ask in turn for editions of the Bible in every tongue, for the spread of the knowledge of the liturgy, "so that it will teach the faithful the truth of God by its rites, and lend optimum assistance in catechetical instruction," and for aid books suited to today's mentality, for the use of teachers, principals, directors of study clubs, and the educated. The remaining suggestions contain no surprises. Catechetical libraries, periodicals, films, pictures, and radio are all recommended as means to achieve an effective catechesis.

One wonders what to think of that national *textus unicus catechismi* which comes in for such praise. Canon Beckers, inspector of primary schools in the Archdiocese of Mechelen (now Brussels-Mechelen) in Belgium, pointed out during the same congress that in a pastoral letter dated February 2, 1947, Cardinal van Roey had praised the national catechism ("this summary of Christian doctrine") as clear, substantial, brief, and comprehensive of all necessary knowledge. "For it contains the core [*medullam*] of sacred theology, presented in formulas calculated to reach the minds of children, but also spur adults to heed it and mull it over."[2] The book that will achieve this result, the Canon continues, is in four parts: (1) truths to be believed; (2) the Christian life; (3) the commandments; (4) aids to salvation.

ONE CATECHISM
FOR THE WHOLE CHURCH?

Not much has been heard in recent times about a uniform catechism for the Church, a project last aired seriously in the

[2] Ludovicus Beckers, "De institutione religiosa in scholiis primariis," *ibid.,* p. 46. The Cardinal was describing a work produced under his aegis.

pontificate of Pope Pius X and less effectively by Benedict XV in 1917. In 1870 Pope Pius IX submitted a brief schema to the Vatican Council suggesting that he himself should edit a new Latin manual patterned on St. Robert Bellarmine's *Dottrina Cristiana breve* (1597), which Pope Clement VIII had put out in 1598 with the expressed wish that it be universally adopted. Pope Benedict XIV reiterated this hope in a special constitution of February 7, 1742, and Pope Leo XIII praised the catechism of the Jesuit cardinal in a new edition of December 3, 1901, as "sanctioned by centuries of use by bishops and learned men of the Church." Pope Clement XIII (July 14, 1761) reedited the Catechism of Trent and asked all bishops to see that it be used by those charged with the work of religious formation.

To return to Pius IX, that pontiff desired to eliminate the great variety of catechisms in use which, he said, confused many. He had in mind not a manual for priests but rather a small handbook adapted to the needs of the most simple and unlettered: "a token of faith, as it were, and pledge of the heavenly joy promised to those who live by faith." Debate lasted from February 10 to 22, 1870. Those who opposed the plan were led by Bishop Dupanloup of Orléans, but most of the fathers of the Council favored it (notably Sola of Nice and Vérot, then of Savannah), and it appeared that the project would pass. After it went out in committee a reformed schema was distributed on April 25, and by the end of the renewed debate of April 27–30 it contained numerous emendations. A final report was made on May 13 by Bishop Marilley of Lausanne. The vote was 491 in favor, 56 opposed, with 44 casting conditional ballots. As Mangenot says in his article on the events, because of the suspension (of the Council), "The question was not taken up again by the Council; the decree was not promulgated; and the Holy See to which the matter was referred never published the universal catechism."[3]

[3] E. Mangenot, "Catéchisme," *Dictionnaire de Théologie Catholique* (Paris: Letouzey et Ané, 1928), 2, 1963; in the matters of Trent, the Vatican Council, and Pope Pius X, cf. Domenico Grasso, S.J., " 'Pour' ou 'Contre' un Catéchisme Universel," *Catéchèse*, No. 5 (October 1961), 483–93. Grasso's opinion, after weighing the advantages of such a book *pro pueris et indoctis* (unity, orthodoxy, concern for mobile populations) and disadvan-

Heirs to the mantle have not been wanting. A catechism was prepared by Pope St. Pius X (1905; reissued in final form in 1912) with a similar hope in mind. It was adopted for use in the dioceses of Italy, but as a thing of the universal Church it came to nothing.[4] This catechism has 433 questions and answers and is in three parts: the principal truths of faith, Christian morality (commandments and virtues), and the means of grace, namely sacraments and prayer.

Even less success in this direction was enjoyed by the *Catechismus Catholicus* of Peter Cardinal Gasparri, though it has been by no means devoid of success.[5] The Cardinal includes Pio Nono's previous inconclusive schema but cheerfully omits the date or any mention of the outcome.[6] His work is at three distinct levels: the first in 26 questions for first communicants; a second composed of ten brief chapters with 240 questions, for children; and the third (595 questions) for adults. Gasparri's order of treatment is as follows: (1) the sign of the cross, (2) the apostles' creed, (3) the commandments of God, (4) the precepts of the Church, (5) grace, (6) prayer [the Lord's prayer and Hail Mary], (7) sacraments, (8) virtues, (9) sins, and (10) last things. The order is not unlike that of Bellarmine's smaller catechism.

THE INFLUENCE OF BELLARMINE

Whereas Cardinal Bellarmine in a brief introductory note to his *Dottrina Cristiana breve* praises the 370-page, prose-style

---

tages (lack of adaption to cultures and to the hearers' age, characteristics, customs, and circumstances) is that it is quite understandable why the last three popes never mentioned the project despite their keen interest in religious education and the missions.

[4] *Compendio della Dottrina Cristiana,* Pubblicato per Ordine di S.S. Papa Pio X (Roma: Typis Polyglottis Vaticanis, 1905). Despite its distinguished sponsorship, it is a volume in no way distinguished from a host of others.

[5] Peter Cardinal Gasparri, *The Catholic Catechism,* Hugh Pope, O.P., trans. (New York: P. J. Kenedy and Sons, 1932), from *Catechismus Catholicus* (Roma: Typis Polyglottis Vaticanis, 1931); 5a ed.

[6] *Ibid.,* pp. 265 ff.

Catechismus Romanus (1566) commissioned by the Council of Trent to be written for the use of parish priests, the little book itself was more in the medieval form of lists of things to be memorized than of a consistent exposition of the mysteries of Christianity. The subtitle indicates how much memorization was part of Bellarmine's plan: *perchè si possa imparare a mente.*

The fourfold division of Trent's manual for clergy had been: (1) faith and the creed, (2) the sacraments, (3) the decalogue and the laws of God, and (4) prayer and its necessity [chiefly the Lord's prayer].[7] Its order of treatment is noteworthy in that it deals with the sacraments as part of the plan or mystery of Christ, not as aids in adhering to precepts. In no sense could its long and thoughtful developments be construed as an arsenal of religious facts. It had no questions and answers; its whole spirit was humanistic, in the fashion of Hosius, Colet,[8] and Erasmus.[9] Although

---

[7] *Catechismus ex Decreto Concilii Tridentini ad Parochos Pii V Pontificis Maximi et deinde Clementis Iussu Editus* (Roma: Typis Sacrae Congregationis de Propaganda Fide, 1844).

[8] On Cardinal Hosius, cf. n. 61 below. John Colet (1466–1519) was Dean of St. Paul's and founder of its school, on the front of which was inscribed in Latin, "for the catechizing of youth in the faith of Christ Most High, and in humane letters. In the year of Christ 1510." Colet was a Platonist and anti-Aristotelian, a great lover of the New Testament and despiser of what he thought to be the non-Christian subtleties of Aquinas, Scotus, and the other Schoolmen. His Christocentric humanism ran deep; one gleans something of it in his brief *Cathecyzon* which was bound in with the articles of admission to St. Paul's School and extracts from his Latin grammar (*Coleti Aeditio*). [It is published in J. H. Lupton, D.D., *A Life of John Colet, D.D.* (London: George Bell, 1887; reprinted Hamden, Conn.: The Shoe String Press, 1961), pp. 285–92.] The language is a most elegant English. It remains a catalogue of prayers and doctrines, but its spirit is one of freshness and a firm grasp on the nature of the redemptive mystery. On the title page is inscribed in Latin Gal 5, 6: "For in Christ Jesus [neither circumcision] is of any avail [nor uncircumcision], but faith which works through charity." The brief treatment is in three sections, "The Articles of Faith" (the creed in twelve articles with a few phrases expanded), "The Seven Sacraments" (order and matrimony first, the remaining five in usual order, all with an explanatory phrase about the relation of this particular sacrament to grace and sonship), and "Charyte." The child must love, honor, and serve "god—the fader almyhty that made me . . . jesus Chryst that redemed me, and the holy ghost—that always inspyreth me"—with all his

cited approvingly by many others since Bellarmine's time, the Catechism of Trent had no real follow-up in the realm of catechisms for the simple, a fact which is essential to the understanding of subsequent catechetical history. It was a kind of sport in nature, and some of its nearest of kin died with the twofold stigma of

"herte, mynde, & strength, & fere god alonely & put my trust in hym alonely." Love for self and neighbor must equally be "to godwarde." It includes, first, abstaining from the "synnes deedly," then frequent prayer, fasting, making amends for wrongs committed, loving fellow pupils, obeying teachers, and helping parents. There appear, after the three major sections, one sentence each on "Penaunce, Howselinge" (communicating), conducting oneself in "sekeness" (penance and eucharist!) and "deth (enealed, and so armed in god)"; and finally 49 "Preceptes of Lyuyng." The pupil must love and fear God; love all men; believe and trust in Christ Jesus, worship Him and His mother Mary; meditate on death; use confession; fear God's judgment but trust in His mercy. The Apostles Creed, Pater, and Ave follow in Latin, then two Latin prayers presumably by Colet, the longer one to Christ with reference to His boyhood—still recited at St. Paul's School. Cf. Ernest William Hunt, *Dean Colet and His Theology* (London: S.P.C.K., 1956), pp. 1–17.

[9] The chief catechetical works of Erasmus (1469?–1536) were two, of which the shorter is his *Christiani hominis institutum* (ca. 1514), a piece of Latin poetry containing the rudiments of faith done "in the simplest style" while he was in England, at the request of his friend Colet; in it the sacraments are in the same order as in Colet, coming after the creed and before the love of God, vices, and precepts. The second is a more professedly catechetical work entitled *Dilucida et pia explanatio Symboli quod Apostolorum dicitur . . . Decalogi praeceptorum, et Dominicae praecationis* (1533), or simply "Catechism," as it is often termed. The first-mentioned is to be found in Erasmus' *Opera Omnia* (Leiden: P. Vander Aa, 1703–06), 5, 1357–60; the second in *ibid.*, cols. 1133–96. The catechism is in the form of a conversation between Catechist and Catechumen. The latter is seeking Catholic faith, not a theological formation. His youth is stressed frequently, though Erasmus later said in a heated letter against Luther that if he had meant to address "*idiotis*" he would have used German, not Latin. The treatise is meant for teachers rather than children: parents, godparents, and pastors. Actually its lofty language and use of Scripture and the Fathers confine it rather severely to the learned classes. Luther could not absorb the notion of classic forms serving as the framework of the gospel (man before the fall, *protasis;* the Cross, *epitasis;* the glorious change of man's fortune that came with Christ's resurrection, *katastrophē*). The first catechesis deals with faith as the doorway to the Church, with Holy Scripture and the creed; the second, the articles of the creed on God the Father; the third, the incarnation; the fourth, Christ's death and resurrection; the fifth, the communion of saints, the sacraments,

humanism and heresy attached, unjustly in the latter case.

The successive brief chapters of Bellarmine's shorter catechism are on: (1) the essential faith of the Christian and the Sign of the Cross, and (2) the creed—both to be studied in the first class; (3) the Lord's prayer and the Hail Mary, for the second class; (4) the commandments of God, (5) the precepts of the Church and the counsels, and (6) the sacraments—all in the third class; (7) the theological and cardinal virtues, (8) the gifts of the Holy Ghost, (9) the works of mercy, (10) sins, (11) the four last things and the mysteries of the rosary—the latter five headings to be taken in the fourth class. There is an appendix on the most commonly recited prayers and hymns, and three separate instructions to prepare candidates for confirmation, penance, and the Eucharist; also the responses at Mass.[10] The articles of the creed receive one question each ("Explain the first," "Explain the second," etc.); so too do the sacraments ("What is the effect of Chrism?" "of Holy Oil," etc.). A significant difference between this brief summary and the *Fuller Exposition of Christian Doctrine* written one year later is that in the smaller book the teacher is the questioner and the pupil the respondent, whereas in the larger things go in reverse. This indicates

and the concluding portion of the creed; the sixth and last, the decalogue according to the twofold commandment of Christ, and the Lord's prayer. The answers are very moving in their evangelical simplicity and concentration on true faith in the great mysteries of Christianity. If the work has a fault it is mistrust of reason, by which Erasmus means chiefly mere human opinion, *tumida mundi philosophia*. Extended quotations are given in Latin and German translation in Rudolf Padberg, *Erasmus als Katechet* (Freiburg: Herder, 1956), pp. 69–124, and it exists in English as *A playne and godly exposytion or declaration of the commune crede . . . and of the .X. commaundements of Goddes law* (London: Robert Redman, 1533: reissued 1720), pp. 178.

[10] Roberti Bellarmini *Opera Omnia*, XII (Paris: Vivès, 1874), 261–82. The *Dichiarazione più copiosa* (1598), follows in this edition, pp. 283–332. Cf. James Brodrick, S.J., *Life and Work of Blessed Robert Bellarmine* (London: Burns Oates and Washbourne, 1928), I, 389–99; *ibid.*, *Robert Bellarmine* (Westminster, Md.: Newman, 1961), pp. 152–55. An English translation of the *Dottrina breve*, entitled *Summary of the Christian Doctrine* was done by the Reverend N. Simon, Pastor of St. Francis de Sales Church, New Orleans (from which it was published), 1875. It runs to twenty-six small pages.

that in the second book Bellarmine intended a teacher's manual and did not have memorization in view. Several of the expositions are a few hundred words long, e.g., the responses in Chapter 13 to the question "What do the gifts of the Holy Ghost help us achieve?" This longer book has twenty-two chapters, the most extensive of which is on the commandments of God. Its order of treatment is the same as that of the *breve,* and it concludes with an instruction on the reception of the eucharist, plus the acts of faith, hope, love, and contrition.

Bellarmine indicates that his framework is basically that of Augustine,[11] namely: those things a Christian must believe (the articles of the creed), must hope for (the petitions of the Lord's prayer), and must do to prove his love (the commandments, precepts, counsels).[12] After he has dealt with these he proceeds to the sacraments, "by means of which the grace of God is acquired."[13] These "four principal parts of doctrine" concluded, Bellarmine goes on to "some things which help greatly in living in conformity

[11] The fundamental catechetical idea of Augustine is chiefly developed in his treatise on *Faith, Hope and Charity* (as he himself called it), sometimes entitled Enchiridion or "handbook." It is contained in Migne, PL40, 231–90; an English translation is that of Louis A. Arand, No. 3 of "Ancient Christian Writers" (Westminster, Md.: Newman Bookshop, 1947). Henry Paolucci recently produced an inexpensive edition (Chicago: Regnery, 1961). Augustine wrote around the year 421, acceding to the request of a certain Laurentius. He says that God is to be worshipped by faith, hope, and charity (3), that no better summaries of faith and hope, easily committed to memory, exist than the creed and the Lord's prayer (6–8), and that all the divine commandments hark back to charity (121). The importance of this treatise for all catechetical history in the West cannot be minimized. Aquinas used it as the basis of his *Compendium theologiae.* The threefold scheme is the spine of all medieval catechetical treatments. It must be recognized as a departure from the more primitive credal scheme of a trinitarian-redemptive confession followed by the "works of the Spirit" or *bona redemptionis.* Augustine never meant to separate the response of Christian life from the revelation of Christian mystery —least of all by prayer as the wedge—but this is precisely what happened.

[12] Bellarmine, *op. cit.*, pp. 263, 264.

[13] "Resta che noi trattiamo de santi Sacramenti, per mezzo de' quali s'acquista la grazia di Dio; dite dunque quanti sono i Sacramenti?" *op. cit.*, p. 265.

with the will of God."[14] The phrase is broad enough to cover the virtues, the gifts, and the spiritual and corporal works of mercy ("concerning which we shall be asked in particular on judgment day"). Sin is next, chiefly because the topic has not occurred yet. ("Now, coming to sin, what kinds are there?") The saint achieves an integration of his work somewhat in reverse by asking at the end of his booklet, "What are the last things for man, called in Scripture *novissimi*, which can make him abstain from sin if he thinks well on them?" It is typical of the medieval catechesis which this represents that the notion of Christ's return in glory at the end has no place in it. Even in the *Dichiarazione* the primary notion is man's judgment and the importance of its outcome which will be declared before all the world by a *giudice supremo*.[15]

Bellarmine initially did his catechizing and wrote his summary of doctrine for the simple brothers of his Society of Jesus. Others, lay people, asked permission to attend and were granted it.[16] It is important to recall this. His early learners not only possessed faith but were vowed to a life of perfection. Consequently no effort was required to beget faith in them. But this is the chief catechetical problem in dealing with the young. In the adolescent period the allegiance of faith must be won anew because of the emotional and intellectual changes that mark the period.

Bellarmine says he is sensitive to the problems of vocabulary and complexity of ideas, as instanced by his prefatory explanation that he had omitted the beatitudes and the fruits of the Holy Spirit because they were hard to remember. "Even the learned get confused in recalling their order," he says charmingly. Yet the fourth and fifth answers in his manual for the unlettered are as follows:

"[The Unity and Trinity of God] means that in God there is one sole Divinity, that is to say one essence and divine nature which is in three divine persons who are called the Father, the Son, and the Holy Ghost"; "[There are three divine persons because] the

[14] *Ibid.*, p. 266.
[15] *Ibid.*, p. 335.
[16] Brodrick, *Life*, I, 390.

Father has no principle and does not proceed from any other person; the Son proceeds from the Father; and the Holy Ghost from the Father and the Son."

THE FUNCTION
OF A CHILD'S CATECHISM

Bellarmine's catechism, in a word, was meant for adult Christians who had fully conscious faith and who needed knowledge. Children's catechisms, conversely, must help the young acquire conscious faith, a part of which is knowledge. They possess the virtue radically from the time of their baptism; in these early years it must come to life. The question is whether knowledge of the Christian mysteries in verbal formulas such as those used by the saintly catechist have any proved record of contributing to the genesis of a living faith. There is no doubt that they may provide the teacher with the opportunity of awakening faith in the child through a careful exposition of their meaning. The question facing all catechists is, however, do they provide the *best* opportunity? Would other formulations provide a better one? Do those of the medieval period culminating in a Bellarmine or Canisius perhaps provide a very limited opportunity to awaken faith, a virtue which must come to birth through intimations of the reality of God that are quite different in character?

The answers to these questions must be left open until more evidence is assembled in the following pages. Meanwhile, it seems right to set aside as an argument of any cogency the great success of Bellarmine's catechism. It was printed, it is true, in 58 languages and exists in thousands of editions. What this establishes mainly is that it correlated highly with the clerical education of the times and with prevailing pedagogic practice. It is not a fair conclusion to draw that parents or children were deeply attracted by it. The work deserves all praise as a providential response to a crisis in the life of the Church. A serious balancing of the ledger, however, requires that it be assigned its measure of responsibility for the quality of Mediterranean Catholicity, for the modern temper of the Church's life in all parts of the globe, and for the sobering record of Catholic mission progress over the last three centuries. It is unrealistic to account the leading summaries of faith solely a factor in stemming the tide of the Reform when they are inextricably a part of the direction taken by the Church as well.

THE WORK OF CANISIUS

St. Peter Canisius, the other catechetical giant of the latter sixteenth century, produced three handbooks of the Catholic faith: a *maior* in 1555 (Vienna); a *minimus* bound in with a grammar in 1556 (Ingolstadt); and a *parvus* or *minor catechismus* (Cologne) in 1558.[17] The smallest is called a *Summa Doctrinae Christianae per quaestiones tradita et ad captum rudiorum accommodata;* it is composed of 59 questions. All of Canisius' catechetical works were done in Latin first, then German. This does not prove that they were not meant for children. The Latin was necessary, first to make them available to the limited number of boys who pursued an education, but also to all learned adults in multilingual Europe. Six main headings comprise the *Summa Doctrinae:* faith and the creed, hope and the Lord's prayer, charity and the decalogue, the sacraments, sins to be avoided, and goods to be sought after. That this formulation comprised no radical departure is evident.

Canisius' middle-sized catechism (*Capita Doctrinae Christianae compendio tradita ut sit veluti Parvus Catechismus catholicorum*) had 124 questions and two appendices. One of the latter was composed of Scripture texts against heretics; the other was a quotation from Augustine on remaining steadfast in faith. The division of this catechism (for the middle and upper grades, we would say) was fivefold, the first four chapters being entitled as in the *minimus* above. The last chapter, "On the Duties of Christian Holiness," listed sins, virtues, works of the flesh and the spirit, the beatitudes, counsels, and last things. It is evident once more that this section was a catch-all for matters unattended to after "the four principal parts of doctrine" had been dealt with. An important feature of the

---

[17] S. Petri Canisii Doctoris Ecclesiae *Catechismi Latini et Germanici* ed. crit. curavit Fridericus Streicher, S.I. (2 tomi; Monachii: Officinae Salesianae, 1933–36).

most popular, or middle-sized, catechism was added to the third
German edition (Dillingen, 1564), namely an appendix of prayers
for all occasions derived in good part from the writings of the
medieval mystics.

Each of the above was in the nature of an abstract from the
larger volume which Canisius had written first.[18] This book had
103 leaves in all (numbered on one side). In a large-sized modern
book it covers 73 pages of two columns. The title is *Summa doctrinae Christianae. Per quaestiones tradita, et in usum Christianae
pueritiae nunc primum edita.* Canisius' name was omitted, both
out of modesty and because he and King Ferdinand alike were
convinced that more authority would attach to it if it were thought
that a group of scholars had done it. He first claimed authorship in

---

[18] Most instructive in this connection is the background of the composition of the first of these three books. King Ferdinand of Austria in 1550
had asked Claude Lejay, the French Jesuit, to attempt a theological
Summa to supplant the *Liber Sententiarum* of Peter the Lombard as a seminary manual. Lejay turned the task over to Canisius, who had no taste for
it. After Lejay's death in 1552 the project was given to James Laynez who
never completed it. Canisius meanwhile wished to write a catechism for
students, youth, and the simple folk of German-speaking lands, both to
cope with the great success of Luther's catechism (printed many times in
six different editions between 1529 and 1542), and to supplant the many
complex Catholic catechisms available. He submitted a portion of his new
work to the King in early 1554. Ferdinand was pleased. At that point
Ignatius conveyed to Canisius, as the result of a letter from the King,
the idea that it might be good to do the book in two parts, one a catechism, and the other a theological manual for parish clergy. This was too
much for the beleaguered Canisius. He wrote back to Polanco, secretary
to Ignatius, that the impossible was being demanded. Was not a trilogy
in preparation? Laynez was to do the theological manual, some other
members of the Society a handbook for the parish clergy, and he himself
the humblest part, "which is offered as a kind of basis, for elaboration in
the other books." His first catechism, the *maior* for boys in classical secondary schools and universities, was ready in 1554, but did not get through
the press until the following spring. On all this, cf. J. Brodrick, *St. Peter
Canisius, S.J.* (London: Burns Oates, 1935), pp. 221–34. Petrus Busaeus,
a Dutchman like Canisius, produced with the Saint's help in 1577 a volume
called *Opus Catechisticum* which supplies the more than 4,000 references
from Scripture and the Fathers on which the answers in the *Summa Doctrinae* were based. It exists in four volumes, *Doctoris P. Canisii Summa
Doctrinae Christianae . . . Busaeo Noviomago* (Augsburg: C. Kollmann,
1833–34).

a revision of 1566, although publishers had attributed the catechism to him as early as 1559. For Canisius, Christian doctrine is
concerned with *wisdom* and *holiness;* consequently his work is in
two major parts. He quotes from Ecclesiasticus (Ben Sira), 1, 33 in
the Vulgate, to make his point: "Fili concupiscens sapientiam,
conserva iustitiam et Deus praebebit illam tibi."[19]

A woodcut of Jesus' crucifixion served as frontispiece of the first
edition. Above and below it were inscribed "Jesus Christ crucified,
Author and finisher of our Wisdom and our Holiness [Justitia]."
To be *wise,* a Christian had to know faith, hope, charity, as
Augustine taught. The sacraments made this possible. *Holiness,*
the acceptance of wisdom or "response of faith" as we would say
today, was dealt with in a second section of two parts. The four
chapters of the first part dealt with the kinds of sins to be avoided
(seven capital, nine ways of being accessory to another's sin, six
against the Holy Ghost, four crying to heaven for vengeance). Part
two had seven chapters, one each on (1) prayer, fasting, and almsgiving, (2) spiritual and corporal works of mercy, (3) cardinal
virtues, (4) gifts and fruits of the Holy Ghost, (5) beatitudes, (6)
evangelical counsels, and (7) four last things. Although his questions are brief, Canisius will at times develop his answers in five or
six hundred words, complete with quotations from Scripture and
the Fathers. The book is frankly theological at an elementary level.
Thus on the eucharist it asks: "Is this sacrament to be venerated
and adored by us?" (Yes, because here servants are in the presence
of their Master and Redeemer; if the Magi are praised by the
evangelists for adoring Christ in his mortal flesh, so much the more
should we adore him in the eucharist where he is immortal and
glorious, etc.) At other times he is quite brief. Thus, "What is sin?"
"We have Augustine's word that sin is the will to resist holiness or
seek after what it forbids, when one is free to do otherwise. Ambrose says: 'What is sin but a deceit contrary to the divine law and
disobedience to heavenly precept?'"

The phenomenal acceptance of Canisius' catechisms, especially

---

[19] "Son, desirous of wisdom as you are, make straight your ways and
God will give it to you." Cf. Sir 2, 1.6, C.C.D. translation.

the *minor*, is a matter of record, though they never outran Bellarmine's *breve* in numbers of editions.[20] He made himself responsible
for getting a German translation of the catechism ordered by
Trent through the press within a year of its appearance,[21] and said
on that occasion he would not have undertaken the labors of the
previous dozen years if he knew that it was impending. Of neither
Canisius, Bellarmine, nor the learned Dominican and secular priest
authors of the *Catechismus Romanus* is it entirely accurate to say
that their catechetical endeavors betrayed a counter-Reformation
or "siege" mentality. Indeed, one must search diligently—even in
Canisius and the *Romanus* on the nature of grace and faith—to
gain clues to the fact that Christendom was being torn asunder,
and on precisely what grounds. It is far more true to say that,
retaining the framework of an analytical theology that did not
take its shape from the biblical books in which the divine revelation is recorded, these authors heroically referred the message of
salvation thus abstracted to its biblical sources, patristic witness,
and conciliar development. Message and form remained extrinsic
to each other, however, like a suit of mail that gives shape to a man
less successfully than his own frame.

The fault was not so much in the times as in the five or eight
centuries that had preceded the times. Despite certain apparent
similarities to the *Liber Sententiarum* of Peter the Lombard,
Aquinas' *Summa Theologiae* was a real "leap in nature," accountable in terms of his genius but not adequately by any circumstances
of the period. Unfortunately catechetics and pastoral theology (for
practical purposes the same discipline) had no such figure as did
speculative theology. We have pointed out that the catechism of
Trent made a tentative break away, but the two faithful guardians
of the recent past—Canisius and Bellarmine—prevailed over a re-

---

[20] The present writer has had access to an edition of the *minor* (intermediate) Canisius, but not designated as his work, published at "Pittsburg" in 1846 by Victor Scriba, as *Katholischer Katechismus*. The title
page gives editorial credit to the Congregation of the Most Holy Redeemer,
with the approval "des Hochw. Bischofs von Pittsburg, Dr. Mich. O'Connor."

[21] Brodrick, *op. cit.*, pp. 651 f.

turn to tradition that gave the appearance of innovation. In a way, the Catholic past demanded both Bellarmine and Canisius, for if the age had been ready for a better exposition of the saving work of Christ and his Church, who can say whether the sixteenth-century tragedy would have taken place?

ENGLAND AND THE COLONIES

The highly popular work of Canisius made its way to England in 1567 through the translation and adaptation of Laurence Vaux, a Lancashire priest exiled from Manchester to Louvain, who late in life (1572) became a Canon Regular of the Lateran.[22] The Canisius model of catechism-organization then passed into the Turberville-Challoner stream, coming on to America as straight Challoner or in the form of Bishop Hay's *Abridgement of the Christian Doctrine* which Bishop John Carroll of Baltimore was influential in circulating. Vaux probably did his book at the request of Thomas Goldwell, Bishop of St. Asaph in Wales, whom he met in Rome in 1566. In it he kept to the order of faith, hope, charity, the sacraments, and *"offices* of Christian *righteousness."*

[22] Laurence Vaux, *A Catechisme of Christian doctrine necessarie for Children and ignorante people,* etc. (Manchester: Printed for the Chetham Society, New Series, 4, 1885), T. G. Law, ed. The book appeared in eight editions before 1605. St. Edmund's College, Old Hall, Ware, has a first edition (Louvain, 1567) and a third (Liège, 1583). The latter has 313 unnumbered pages, and is 3" x 4¾" in size. Cf. A. Whitehead, "Vaux His Catechism," *Clergy Review,* 42 (May 1957), 277–84; James D. Crichton, "Religious Education in England in the Penal Days," in Gerard S. Sloyan, *Shaping the Christian Message* (New York: Macmillan, 1958), pp. 71–75; Brodrick, *St. Peter Canisius,* pp. 243–48. Vaux said in a preface: "And what I have set furth in this little booke, the ground and substance I have collected & translated out of the Scripture, and general Councells, out of the bookes of D. Petrus de Soto, and D. Canisius, addinge here and there some sentences of the ancient Fathers, S. Cypriã, Athanasius, Ambrose, Hierome, Damasceen, & S. Bernard." Peter Soto, the learned Dominican confessor to Charles V, had written a Latin manual to help in preparing for the sacrament of penance. The edition the writer has had to access is entitled *Methodus confessionis seu . . . epitome* (Dillingen: Sebastianus Mayer, 1576), pp. 190, numbered on one side. The first chapter is on the creed, the second on the commandments and the eucharist, and the remaining four on the headings of sins and on dying well. A story of the gospels by Bishop Cornelius Jansen of Ghent is bound in.

Under the four marks of the Church Vaux says, "in heaven, earth or purgatory, be members of Christ his mistical body (which is the Church) and communicate and participate one with the other." His approach is adult throughout. He gives ample attention to the Church's law on marriage and the sacraments and the duties of the clergy, also a "Brief Fourme of Shrift or Confession" in three chapters. Vaux was a very influential figure but in no sense an innovator. His chief claim to the attention of Catholics and Reformers alike was that he gave England her sole catechism of the old religion between the break in Henry's time and 1604.

The Reverend Henry Turberville (ca. 1607–78), professor at the English College at Douai, produced some time before 1649 *An Abridgment of the Christian Doctrine: with Proofs of Scripture on Points Controverted, Catechistically explained by Way of Question and Answer*. Originally it had had twenty-one chapters, the last of which was on the last things. Chapters were later added on "the Substance or essence and Ceremonies of the Mass," on "the Office of our Blessed Lady," on "the Solemnities of Christ our Lord (instituted for the most part by the apostles)," and on "Some Ceremonies of the Church," making twenty-five in all. Turberville followed Bellarmine's order largely, except that the counsels (chap. 10) came after the precepts of the Church and before the sacraments. The book is far from being a mere translation and has many original features. It is marked by a strong apologetic tone and a distinguished prose style. Perhaps both points may be illustrated by a selection from the chapter on the Church. A previous response had said that if the Church erred in faith she would either be conspiring in a notorious lie and thus damn herself to posterity or "be ignorant what hath been taught her for faith by the church of the precedent age, which are both natural impossibilities."

Q. How prove you these to be impossibilities by nature?
A. By the constancy and immutability of contingent causes, whose particulars may be defective, but the universals cannot.
Q. Explain that a little.

That seems a fair enough challenge. The author answers that a man can be born defective as to an eye or an arm but nature cannot fail entirely with respect to all men at the same time; "that the whole church should so far break with the nature of man (which is reason) to conspire in such a lie, or to be so mistaken, is as impossible in nature as it is for men to be no men."[23] One hopes that this was never inflicted on children, and one has every reason to doubt that they were spared it. There are four proofs for purgatory in successive questions, answered by the citation of 1 Pet 3, 19; 1 Cor 3, 13 f.; Mt 5, 26; Mt 12, 32. Directly after them, as a tailpiece in the chapter expounding the kinds of sin, comes the list of the nine ways of cooperation in other men's sins.

"How prove you that?" is a question frequently encountered in Turberville, and his answer is usually a biblical quotation. "Is charity imputed as protestants would have it, or is it a quality truly inherent in the soul?" he asks.[24]

The eucharist is dealt with as real presence rather than as sacrifice, though with flashes of great beauty: this sacrament is prefigured in the old law "by the tree of life, the burning bush, Melchisedech's bread and wine, the Paschal Lamb, and the heavenly manna."[25] The portion on the Mass in Chapter XXII is highly allegorical. ("Why is the Host divided into three parts? To signify the division of our Savior's soul and body made on the cross, and that the body was . . . divided . . . hands, side and feet.") One might be studying in tenth-century Aachen at the palace school as well as nineteenth-century Boston, where the edition cited enjoyed considerable success after being "recommended for his diocese by the Right Rev. Benedict [Fenwick] Bishop of Boston" in 1833. Turberville's catechism is for adults, for late medievals under siege of heresy, for those who savor phrases like, "fidelity, which makes

[23] Henry Turberville, *An Abridgment of the Christian Doctrine* (New York: Edward Dunigan, 1843), p. 26. A third edition existed as early as March 1649, published at Douai and bearing the president's name, William Hyden, as censor. The title page of a London edition of 1708 says that it is "By H.T."
[24] *Ibid.*, p. 45.
[25] *Ibid.*, p. 86.

us punctual observers of our covenants and promises." One gleans from it the robustness of the faith that came out of Doway College. It is a tool well fashioned to the age that had forged it. Proof out of Scripture was amply provided to silence objectors employing Scripture on the same polemical terms.

John Lingard (1771–1851) produced a catechism in England in 1836 for Bishop Penswick, coadjutor of the Northern District. It had nine chapters and followed the order of creed, prayer, commandments, then sacraments, virtues and vices, and the Christian's rule of life. Public and private prayers came at the end in a "Christian's Daily Exercise."[26] An occasional answer familiar from the Baltimore catechism occurs, e.g., "Sin is any thought, word, deed or omission against the law of God." "What do you call the sins which we commit ourselves? Actual sins, which are either deadly or venial." "[Prayer is] the raising up of the mind and heart to God." A well-intentioned but somewhat defensive hand has improved on Dr. Lingard by saying, "Do you adopt that name [Roman Catholic]?" "We glory in our communion with the see of Rome, but call ourselves American Catholics." "Why not Roman Catholics?" "Because that name implies what we cannot admit, that a man may be a Catholic, without being in communion with the centre of Catholic unity, the see of Rome."[27]

The surer touch of the historian Lingard is evident in his two questions on the place of the creed in the life of the Church: "2. Does the creed teach all the doctrines of the Christian religion? No: those only, to which the convert was required to assent previously to his baptism. 3. What doctrines was he to learn after baptism? Those which concern the worship, the sacraments, and the government of the Church."[28] Lastly, a theological sense absent from many catechisms that are grimly theological in appearance marks certain answers, e.g., "The communion of saints means

---

26 John Lingard, D.D., *Catechistical Instructions on the Doctrines and Worship of the Catholic Church* (London: 1840, pp. 139; rev. ed. Charles Dolmen, 1844, pp. 130; New York: Patrick S. Casserly, 1841, pp. 167).

27 *Ibid.* (1841 ed.), pp. 49 f.

28 *Ibid.*, pp. 63 f.

that union of charity and brotherhood, which binds in one true body members of the Catholic Church";[29] by baptism men are "made members of the Church of Christ";[30] an indulgence is a "relaxation of temporal punishment . . . on condition of true repentance, and the performance of certain works of piety and charity . . . [having] no concern whatever with the pardon of sin."[31]

Those who might hope for something from a "liturgical catechism" of the same period as Lingard will be disappointed by Bishop Challoner's handbook of 1737.[32] It proceeds through the sacraments and sacramentals, fasting, abstinence, and a variety of devotional practices in a way that is vitiated by its apologetic concern. In response to certain slanders Challoner concedes nothing whatever, even when the attacker has a grain of truth. He is frequently uncritical, moreover, in his learned-type answers.

Dr. George Hay, the convert Bishop of Edinburgh and one-time surgeon (1729–1811), produced in 1781 a two-volume work entitled *The Sincere Christian* which went into more than twenty editions.[33] His first volume has 21 chapters, his second 28 plus an *"Inquiry* whether salvation can be had without true faith, and out of communion with the Church of Christ" (95 pages) and an *"Appendix* on communicating in Religion with those who are separated from the Church of Christ" (36 pages). Both of the latter are in straight prose style, not questions and answers. Hay's scheme of organization is elusive, there being no divisions other than chapter headings. He proceeds from God to the blessed Trinity, thence to creation and providence, the fall of angels and men, the promise of a redeemer, Christ himself and the redemptive mystery. The Holy Spirit gets only four (long) questions under "the redeemer."

[29] *Ibid.*, p. 52.
[30] *Ibid.*, p. 122.
[31] *Ibid.*, p. 144.
[32] Dr. [Richard] Challoner, *The Catholic Christian Instructed* (Baltimore: John Murphy, n.d.).
[33] *The Sincere Christian Instructed in The Faith of Christ from the Written Word,* 20th ed. (2 vols.; Dublin: Richard Coyne, 1822), pp. 427 and 396.

A chapter follows on faith in Christ and still another on the rule of faith. The latter, in the midst of an answer nearly a page in length, is defined as "the rule left us by Jesus Christ . . . *the written word as interpreted by the Church.*"[34] Chapters on the Church and the marks of the Church are followed by one on the "law of God" in general and another on her precepts (the six as we know them). There is no treatment of the decalogue whatever except a brief discussion of the biblical enumeration of verses. Evidently the bishop was for deferring all discussion of morality until his *Devout Christian* (1783), or else he might have been following Erasmus' simple catechetical principle, "In accord with right faith, let us live rightly." (Padberg, *op cit.*, p. 76.)

Next in order come sin, repentance, and grace (long chapters on actual and sanctifying, in that order). The chapter on sacraments in general has an appendix "on sacred ceremonies." The sacraments taken singly receive extended treatment. The Mass as sacrifice comes after the eucharist as real presence and as the effect of transubstantiation, the former in a chapter of 23 pages, the latter two, 44 pages. Indulgences, purgatory, and public penances are appendixes to the chapter on penance. The seventh sacrament is called "marriage." Four sections at the end of the treatment of marriage give pastoral and canonical information. An attractive feature is the concluding chapter, "On the Church Triumphant," which deals with death and hell as appendixes. Somewhat less attractive are the long and lugubrious answers on death, which feature in detail the unfortunate consequences of leaving the "carcase" of even the best-loved husband and father around the house for a few days.

The chief importance of Bishop Hay's work to us in the United States is that Bishop Carroll put out an abridgment of it, and many of the questions and answers found their way into the catechism of the Third Baltimore Council.[35] Thus, from the first chapter, "God

[34] *Ibid.,* I, 149.

[35] *An Abridgment of the Christian Doctrine* by Bishop Hay (Philadelphia: Matthew Carey, 1803), p. 143. This pocket-sized volume has 45 chapters in the same general order as those of *The Sincere Christian* and contains reading references to it.

is a spirit, infinitely perfect; the creator and sovereign Lord of all things." "[We do not see God] because he is a spirit, which having no body, cannot be seen with bodily eyes." "He [sees and knows all things], even our most secret thoughts." There is explicit treatment of the commandments of God in this abridgment. An interesting device is the inclusion of material from the medieval "lists" under the commandments, e.g., the spiritual and corporal works of mercy under the fifth commandment, the sins "crying to heaven for vengeance" under the seventh. Overall, however, the literary parentage of the best-known United States catechism is not to be found directly in Bishop Hay's *Abridgment*.

THE ROOTS OF THE BALTIMORE CATECHISM

The clearest claimant to that title seems to be a volume of unacknowledged origins, also entitled "An Abridgment of Christian Doctrine," which was widely available before 1860. A publisher's preface dated February of that year speaks of "the small catechism" and "Collot's Catechism" for learners as if they might be identical.[36] In any case, the queries and responses of the former work serve as the basis for 82 fairly jejune instructions, full of proof-texts and defenses. The order is clearly that of creed, commandments, sacraments, and "lists" (virtues, vices, works of mercy, etc.). An appendix in two chapters gives the Christian's "Daily Exercise," a rigorous program of personal piety. The present writer can only say of this *Abridgment* that the great bulk of its text is identical in form to the catechism of the Baltimore Council he memorized in the 'twenties and 'thirties. This fact tends to heighten the ambiguity of the celebration of 1960, when a catechism presumably only 75 years old was being hailed by the national office of the Confraternity of Christian Doctrine.

Before passing on to the catechism of Baltimore, brief mention

[36] John Perry, *A Full Course of Instructions for the Use of Catechists* (New York: D. & J. Sadlier, 1885), p. 1. Perry provided extensive commentary on the material of this *Abridgment*. As to the probable source of this abridgment, cf. the account of Bishop Butler's catechism, n. 50 below.

should be made of Josef Deharbe's catechism (*Katholischer Kate-chismus oder Lehrbegriff*, Regensburg, 1847), which appeared, both in its large and small forms, in many American editions before 1882 (creed, commandments, means of grace).

The Christian Doctrine was a bilingual catechism compiled by the Archbishop of Tuam, John MacHale, and his suffragans (Dublin: C. M. Warren, 1865), in roughly the same order as Deharbe but with the material of the "lists" somewhat elusive (in general, after commandments and before sacraments). The present writer's paternal grandfather studied this little book in Irish in MacHale's diocese. He trusts that gives him the right to point out the delightful Hibernian syllogism, "By what names are liars denominated? They are called children of the Devil. Why so? Because the Devil is the father of lies."

A more serious matter is the unexplained reversal of the treatment of commandments and sacraments from Trent's order (the sacraments appearing second in Trent, third in MacHale), followed by the bald misstatement on page 22, "By what authority do you divide the catechism into these four parts? By the authority, and after the example of the best and most explanatory Catechism that has ever been compiled . . . The Catechism of the Council of Trent."[37]

[37] On the question of the "ordering of parts" in the catechism, cf. Johannes Hofinger, "De apta Divisione Materiae Catecheticae. Tentamen Historico-criticum," *Collectanea Commissionis Synodalis*, Peking Vol. 13 (1940), 583–99; 729–49; 845–59; 950–65, condensed as, "The Right Ordering of Catechetical Material," *Lumen Vitae*, 2 (1947), 718–46. The essential change came in the late medieval period. The act of faith and the object of faith, i.e., the articles of the creed, had indisputably come first in the tenth-century catechisms attributed to Bruno of Würzburg (PL 142, 557–68) and Alcuin (PL 101, 1136–44). This was still true through the period of Aquinas, in his catechetical sermons on the creed and Lord's prayer (*Opuscula omnia*, ed. P. Mandonnet, 4, 349–460, Paris, 1927) and his treatise "On the two precepts of charity and ten precepts of the law" (*ibid.*, 4, 413–55). Through the fourteenth and fifteenth centuries, however, the handbooks of piety stressed the means and a way of Christian perfection that was quite divorced from the saving deeds of God as proclaimed in the creed. Examples of this are Kaplan Wolff's *Beichtspiegel* (1478), Dietrich Kolde's *Christenspiegel* (1480), and Johannes Herolt's *Discipulus de eruditione Christifidelium* (1490). The triumph of lists of

HOW THE BALTIMORE
CATECHISM ORIGINATED

With this much background of the American scene provided, it should be a fairly brief matter to expose the interesting story of the catechism "proposed and enjoined" (as its title page says) "by order of the Third Plenary Council of Baltimore."[38] Archbishop Gibbons of Baltimore, in a statement dated April 6, 1885, and printed on the facing page of the first edition, wrote, "The Catechism ordered by the Third Plenary Council of Baltimore, having been diligently compiled and examined, is hereby approved." A modicum of research establishes that this was as much approbation as the volume ever got, for once the Council was dissolved the archbishops of the country as a national body never attended to it further except to hear a chorus of complaint against it in their annual meeting of 1895.[39]

---

things to know and do is complete, and because preparation for the annual confession (*Beicht*) was the formal object of many of them, the commandments dislodged the creed in primary importance. The latter became not the framework of salvation history but something there were twelve of. Cf. Padberg, *op. cit.*, "Katechetische Situation . . . beim Ausgang des Mittelalters," pp. 22–44.

[38] *A Catechism of Christian Doctrine* (Baltimore: J. Murphy, 1885), 72 pp. There are 421 questions and answers in 37 chapters, in the order creed, sacraments (gifts, fruits, and beatitudes after confirmation), prayer, commandments, and last things. Sin is dealt with as part of the fall, directly after creation.

[39] John K. Sharp, "How the Baltimore Catechism Originated," *Ecclesiastical Review*, 81 (December 1929), 581, quotes a letter written to him by John Cardinal Glennon dated December 13, 1928, who had the minutes of the 1895 meeting before him and quoted: "In its present form it seems unpopular." The archbishops agreed on this occasion to consult their suffragans. At the 1896 meeting "a majority recommended a revision." Gibbons suggested a revision committee of priest-catechists under the chairmanship of Archbishop Kain of St. Louis. Writes Glennon: "After this . . . (there is) no record of definite action . . . Kain called several meetings . . . had submitted to him outlines of an improved Catechism . . . but (there has been) no action . . . then, nor . . . since then." Work was hindered by news reports of a universal catechism after Pope St. Pius X came to the throne in 1903, the year in which Kain died. Gibbons had to write to Propaganda on December 24, 1903, explaining the delay in revision. Cf. Joseph A. Newman, letter to *ER*, 94 (May

It did, however, enjoy tacit acceptance and widespread use, and became the national catechism of English-speaking Catholics in fact, if not in the usual sense of formal adoption by an entire national hierarchy.[40] Many bishops have used other catechisms from then until now, as they are quite free to do in virtue of their apostolic office.

On August 25, 1884, Archbishop Gibbons sent a circular letter to the country's archbishops, saying that a request for a unified catechism had come to him from Archbishop Feehan of Chicago and Bishops Kain of Wheeling, and Janssens of Natchez.[41] He ap-

---

1936), 517 f., in which he proposes that the word "enjoined" be deleted from the title page since the Council merely ordered it, and did not formally enjoin for use any catechism that might have been produced as a result. In fact, it laid down a condition that was never fulfilled: "Opus suum ita perfectum, ad coetum Reverendissimorum Archiepiscoporum remittere, qui denuo catechismum recognoscent." [*Acta et Decreta Conc. Balt.* (Baltimore: John Murphy, 1886), Tit. 7, No. 219]. Dom Francis Augustine Walsh, O.S.B., first national director of the Confraternity of Christian Doctrine, had maintained that Gibbons' approval in his role as apostolic delegate was a sufficient follow-up of the then dissolved council [*ER*, 94 (April 1936), 414 f]. That he had approved it in this capacity would doubtless have come as a surprise to Gibbons. His role as presiding officer of the council and archbishop ordinary of the historically first see would have kept the question from occurring to him. The title page bears the inscription, "Copyright, 1885, J. L. Spalding. All rights reserved," and this explains the status of the book as much as anything. Bishop Spalding of Peoria was the leading episcopal figure in preparing the volume, and he quite naturally brought the completed work to Gibbons.

40 The revision committee evidently became conscious of this problem, and whereas the first edition bore no attempt at authorization other than Gibbons' name, that of 1949 (No. 3) carries the statement in its back cover, "*A Catechism of Christian Doctrine No. 2* is the complete revision of the *Baltimore Catechism*. This revision, begun in 1935 [completd 1941] was examined by the Catechetical Section of the Sacred Congregation of the Council, to which the revised text was submitted by the American Hierarchy. All directions given by the special Commission appointed by the Sacred Congregation to examine the text have been followed, and all the changes suggested have been incorporated in *Catechism No. 2*. This text should be used, under Diocesan direction, to complete the religious instruction in grade schools."

41 For what follows, cf. Sharp, *op. cit.*, pp. 573–86.

pointed a committee composed of Archbishop Alemany of San Francisco as chairman and Bishops Goesbriand (Burlington), Ryan (Buffalo), Dwenger (Fort Wayne), Spalding (Peoria), Kain (Wheeling), and Janssens (Natchez). They were to report "at or before the council" on "the expediency of adopting a uniform catechism . . . naming the Catechism which they prefer to be sanctioned" and to decide whether "Germans, Slavonians, Italians, Spaniards and French" should have a translation of the one chosen or some other approved. At the private congregation of the council, held November 11, 1884, the committee asked leave to report at once (long before their turn on the *Schema Decretorum*). They did so, and the whole matter was referred back to them, their numbers being enlarged by bishops and priests, appointed by Gibbons, whose names the minutes do not contain. Some of the committee members strongly favored adopting the catechism of Bishop Butler of Cashel (1775), recently approved by the Synod of Maynooth, with adaptations. More, however, stood for the production of a new one. Certain changes in the original *schema* were suggested by the committee in a meeting of the private congregation, November 29, 1884. At the final such meeting, December 6, 1884, a draft of a new catechism was submitted to the assembled bishops on galley proofs, with a view to getting suggestions for changes. Because the days of the council were growing short, it was suggested that all suggestions be forwarded to Bishop Spalding of Peoria *who would make a full report to the next conference of archbishops*. After they approved it in final form it was to go to Spalding for publication.

Archbishop Messmer of Milwaukee, who had been at the Council, took the pains subsequently to make this memorandum: "To several objections raised at the last meeting that the proposed Catechism was very imperfect, in fact inferior, answer was made that the uniformity was more important, and that quite evidently many improvements were to be made in the course of time as experience would show the present deficiencies. But in the end the 'Baltimore Catechism' would attain all the perfection that could be reasonably demanded of a uniform Catechism for a large and mixed population like that of the United States."[42]

Messmer recalled with a "faint recollection" that the actual making of the new catechism was placed in the hands of Msgr. Jannarius de Concilio, rector of St. Michael's Church, Jersey City. De Concilio, a former professor of theology at Seton Hall Seminary, attended as theologian to Bishop O'Connor, vicar apostolic of Nebraska, and was one of the twelve priest theologians assigned to the Deputation of the Chapter on Christian Doctrine, made up of six bishops under Archbishop Elder of Cincinnati. Further testimony on the point comes from an anonymous correspondent who wrote Sharp that, as he understood it, "Dr. Moes of Cleveland Seminary put some serious work upon it during the closing days of the Plenary Council. Bishop O'Connor gathered up his manuscripts and committed the finishing of it to Monsignor de Concilio."[43] His informant was Msgr. (later Bishop) John Hagan at a meeting of school superintendents in Detroit in 1927.

Archbishop Schrembs likewise "was told positively . . . back in 1889 that de Concilio had been the final author, Moes having been in on preliminary discussions of it."[44] Another man who was chancellor to Spalding and his companion for fourteen years had the impression that "Bishop Spalding did most of the work."[45] Spalding hurried the preparation of the catechism, according to Thomas McMillan, C.S.P. "It never went out to teachers."[46] He stayed in New York City as guest of the Paulist Fathers from early December to at least January 25, 1885, working with de Concilio on the Catechism.[47]

Archbishop Elder, President of the Chapter on Christian Doctrine, wrote to Gibbons sometime before Septuagesima Sunday to

[42] Sharp, *op. cit.*, pp. 575 f.
[43] "Presbyter Septuagenarius" to Sharp, December 20, 1928, *ibid.*, p. 578.
[44] Schrembs to Sharp, July 17, 1929, *ibid.*, p. 579.
[45] F. J. O'Reilly, rector of St. Patrick's Church, Danville, Ill., *ibid.*, pp. 579 f.
[46] *Ibid.*, p. 580.
[47] *Ibid.*

ask if Spalding "would make the final revision on his own authority, and would the new catechism be obligatory?"[48] That is no small uncertainty for one who had been directly charged with the matter at the Council, to be expressed two months before the book "prepared and enjoined" by the Council appeared.

According to one witness, Bishop Gilmour of Cleveland said in Rome on July 18, 1885, that de Concilio had provided the text of a catechism in a week when the committee said it could not be ready sooner.[49] Messmer, McMillan, and Sharp, the patient compiler of all these data, go on the supposition that the chief influence on de Concilio was the catechism of Bellarmine he had studied in his youth in Italy. Internal criticism indicates that this is not the case, except insofar as the *Dottrina breve* played a role as forbear of the entire *genre*. It could be, of course, that the text produced at high speed and presented at the December 6 congregation was such a Bellarmine-influenced product.

The final result of Spalding's *coup* underlines the truth that although the pen is mightier than the sword, the scissors is mightier than both. Textual comparison of the wording and the order establishes that the work is basically that of Butler, with emendations from a popular manual done by the Christian Brothers.[50] Other

[48] *Ibid.*, p. 583.

[49] This suspiciously accurate memory after forty-four years belonged to M. A. Lambing of Scottdale, Pa., in a letter of December 7, 1929 to John K. Sharp quoted in "The Origin of the Baltimore Catechism," *ER*, 83 (December 1930), 621 f. Lambing said he was able to date Gilmour's visit to the North American College, and to recall clearly matters he had no previous information on which hence were not liable to confusion.

[50] So Michael V. Kelly, C.S.B., who did such a comparison; cf. Sharp, *ibid*. The present writer must concur. The copy of Butler available to him has 457 questions in 31 lessons. Its general order is creed, commandments, sacraments, though sin and purgatory come after the creed; grace is done in six questions embedded in the chapter on sin, prayer follows the precepts of the Church, and the last things fittingly conclude the whole. Perhaps Butler had the order of the Apostles' Creed in mind as his schema (like the authors of *Katholischer Katechismus*). In such case the lengthy treatment of the commandments would describe the terms of membership in the Church, while the sacraments would be (as traditionally) the *communio sanctorum*. Cf. *Catechism of the Diocese of Limerick*, being the Most Rev. Dr. James Butler's Catechism Revised (Cork: Guy and Co.,

influences observable are the Carroll *Abridgment of Christian
Doctrine* of 1772, approved by a committee named by the First
Plenary Council (1852), and McCaffrey's catechism (President of
Mt. St. Mary's Seminary, Emmitsburg), recommended to the Second Plenary Council (1866) by Archbishop Martin J. Spalding of
Baltimore.[51] James Veale of Brooklyn wrote to Sharp to press the
claim of the Sulpician Augustin Vérot who became first bishop of
St. Augustine in 1870, having served as Florida's vicar apostolic
since 1857 and bishop of Savannah from 1861–70.[52] During his
time at St. Mary's Seminary, Baltimore (1830–57), he produced a
catechism which remarkably resembled that of the Council in
sequence and phrasing. Sixty of the 187 questions in Vérot's
abridgment occur in identical phrasing in the Baltimore Catechism sixteen years later. Vérot leaned on Butler considerably, it
appears.

One would think that the actual producer of this American land-
mark would have shortly been to the fore, but this was not the
case. The man most closely associated with the diamond jubilee
event of 1960 had proved so modest that he disclaimed parentage
of the product outright, somewhat in the manner of Jerome and the
deuterocanonical books translated "in one night." Monsignor de
Concilio had evidently heard enough comment on the catechism,
according to one witness, to wish to dissociate himself from it

---

n.d.), pp. 115. Butler was Archbishop of Cashel 1774–91 and produced
his catechism in 1775. A Synod of Maynooth in 1875 ordered its revision
and in 1882 a revision appeared which claimed this authorization. For a
good insight into the mental processes of the "born catechism-maker" cf.
Patrick Walsh, *William J. Walsh, Archbishop of Dublin* (Dublin: Talbot
Press, 1928), pp. 379–86.

[51] Cf. Raymond J. O'Brien, "The History of Our English Catechism,"
Petit Séminaire (Quigley Preparatory Seminary, Chicago: June 1920), pp.
253 ff.

[52] Sharp, "The Origin . . . ," p. 621. Available to the present writer is
a copy of Vérot's larger work entitled: *General Catechism of the Christian
Doctrine* (Augusta: S. T. Paterson, 1864), and also (through the kindness
of the Reverend Michael V. Gannon of the University of Florida at Gaines-
ville) an abridgment entitled *Short Catechism of the Christian Doctrine,
on the Basis Adopted by the First Plenary Council of Baltimore* (Baltimore:
John Murphy, 1879), 32 pp.

actively.[53] If he had known how much attention it was going to receive, he would have given it more time and his best efforts, etc. There is no record that Bishop Spalding was any more anxious for the title of leading spirit.

It is quite a different matter with the Confraternity revision of 1941, a lengthened version of 1885 (creed, commandments, sacraments, and prayer). It is scarcely distinguishable in spirit from the earlier work, and comprises a retrogression in its ordering of material.[54] Francis J. Connell, C.SS.R., has not hesitated to admit his considerable part in this editorial task, which also included the production of a much-expanded catechism for adults (No. 3). It is extremely interesting to see the use made of the Sharp researches on the earlier catechism.[55]

THE RELATION OF
CATECHETICS TO THEOLOGY

With the above data as background, there seems to be recommended a discussion of the relation of the catechisms in widespread general use to the important work of the religious education of children in the next fifty or one hundred years.

In the first place, the stylized query and response is a device that so lends itself to memorization that casting children's books in this form will almost inevitably have the result of enforcing memory

[53] So Mark J. Moesslein, C.P., who writes that he gave a mission in St. Michael's shortly after these events, and heard Msgr. de Concilio make this disclaimer. *ER*, 93 (December 1935), 613.

[54] Francis J. Connell, C.SS.R., "Is the Baltimore Catechism Outmoded?" in *AER*, 97 (January 1960), 1–9. "It was only in 1941 that the present order was adopted—at a time when, according to Father Hofinger, the best catechists were accepting what we then rejected. Moreover, Dom Augustine Walsh, an outstanding catechist in our land, after an investigation to find some link between the Baltimore Catechism and previous works of the same character, admitted that he could not find any particular one which served as the basis of the Baltimore Catechism." Cf. Walsh, *AER*, 95 (September 1936), 279. As to order (the only solid contribution of 1885) this statement can be defended; as to the outlook and phrasing of the catechism, it means very little. Cf. n. 38 above.

[55] Cf. Francis J. Connell, "Catechism Revision," in *The Confraternity Comes of Age* (Paterson: Confraternity Publications, 1956), pp. 189–201.

work. This is not a matter to be opposed in principle. Several conditions need to be met, however: (1) the questions asked must individually be such as to voice difficulties that the students might be expected to have in their present condition; otherwise the technique is a sham and a potentially harmful one;[56] (2) the responses given must genuinely satisfy the desire for knowledge that, hopefully, has been induced (though it is unreal to assume that the same desire to know can be brought to birth in all students of a given condition at the same time); (3) the books produced for children should never be couched in the form of successive questions and answers, since no child experiences concern about the things of God in that rapid-succession pattern; (4) the question-and-answer is a wholly respectable means to make secure those learnings which have slowly been built up in the learner's mind; therefore it has a place at the end of a developed lesson but none whatever as the starting-point for lessons which proceed to analyze the terms or content of the queries; (5) from what has just been said, it follows that questions and answers should flow from the development made concerning the God-man relation, and not vice versa; in other words, no good teacher starts by writing a catechism in question and answer form, though he may end by writing a book for children in which questions and answers have a place; (6) since the process of bringing God and the child into an intimate relation is the essence of religious education, and since memorized for-

---

[56] This raises the question of the root ambiguity of catechisms, which must be terminated if they are to have any efficacy whatever. The lists for memorization were devised for the adult penitent; handbooks like Bellarmine's for unlettered adults; Canisius' basic book for the relatively small student population that was getting training in letters during late adolescence; and the manual prescribed by Trent, for the guidance of the clergy. The device of asterisks to indicate questions proper to the very young is especially harmful because it puts on young minds the burden of seeing the same panorama of faith the adult sees but aided by fewer landmarks of the same type. To employ the same or similarly phrased answers for ages six and sixteen is to fly in the face of all we know about the development of the human mind and personality. Here it is not a question merely of simplified phrasing (important though this might be to the child) but of a whole way of thinking foreign to him.

mulas give very little evidence that this had been done, no sound educator who is not the child's catechist will ever directly ask for the memorized answer to a question. He will discuss sacred matters with the child, and if a memorized answer is volunteered will know immediately whether it testifies to a true understanding. If it does, the child will use it in context, whereas if it does not he will employ it badly and help to prove the case against memorization as contributory to his mental structure of faith.

These simple rules of thumb are so obvious that they scarcely need setting down. Their obviousness has escaped many, however, whose zeal for the work of religious education is beyond question. Why should this be? Why should approaches to learning be thought to have a peculiar efficacy in the sacred sphere which they do not possess in any other? The question all but answers itself: the proponents of this view tend to think it equally valid in all areas of pedagogy, a field they have normally been too busy to examine.

The handbook of faith in dialogue form, it should be remembered, emerged from an era that was largely illiterate. This was also a period in which pedagogy was not a developed art. The world has since changed considerably in its whole approach to learning, but forms and customs closely associated with a changeless faith are very slow to change.

Secondly, there is an irrational fear of "heresy" within the Catholic body, which does not mean heresy at all but only the mild theological inexactness scarcely escapable if one is to speak of incomprehensible mysteries. In fact, most catechisms are marked by considerable imprecision, despite valiant efforts to achieve exactness. The difficulty is that these efforts preclude any counterbalancing merits in the realm of evangelical expression. The plain language of every day is eminently suited to express the mysteries by which God means His sons to live. Credal formulas are sometimes marked by subtlety or philosophical allusion, while the definitions of councils inevitably are; this is because of the subtlety or equivocation of heretics who need to be answered. The results have been what we might expect. The modern child sings (or says) of God the Son that He is "Light of Light" without knowing why it was once thought essential for the Catholic to say so; the case is the same when He is declared "of one substance with the Father." When the modern child says that Christ is "really, truly, and substantially present in the eucharist" he is theologically right; he is quite wrong however if, moments later, he affirms in the speech proper to his country and his time that "Jesus Christ is substantially present in the eucharist." For as any user of English speech knows, the word has come to mean "in the main, by and large."

The point in all this is that philosophical and credal language need not be used for the child's Catholic faith to be kept pure. Admittedly, this speech can keep it from being impure but it can also keep it from being faith. No, the point is that while the mysteries of faith are unchanging, the human language that couches them—even in solemn ecumenical council—can change in important particulars from age to age; and often this language does not speak to the child in any age. This is merely to say (what chills the unreflective Catholic heart) that the truth of Jesus Christ can not be captured firmly and forever in verbal formulas. It can however be conveyed in a great variety of verbal formulas suited to the young and old, the East and the West, the first century and the thirty-first century, the poetically inclined (which is most of us) and the philosophically inclined (which is very few of us, and not many below twelve).

A matter of great importance follows from the above, though it may not seem to. It is this. Not only is the Church obliged to make her faith explicit from age to age, especially in response to denial, but she has a quasi-responsibility to have a theology, lest the purity of her faith be insufficiently guarded. She will always, in fact, have a variety of theologies, given the kinds of minds from different parts of the globe that come to believe in her. The matter of importance is not—what is so often said—that since theology has one purpose and catechetics another, the chief sin of catechisms is that they are distillations of theological *summae* or of manuals done by pedestrian minds. It is that catechetics and theology are so intimately related that we will get the catechisms we deserve only after we have developed the theology of proclamation we require.

The variance of purpose between theology and catechetics is sometimes proposed as the chief reason why catechisms written by theologians often miss the mark. It is an attractive solution, and it possesses a grain of truth. But the reasons for the sad estate of most catechisms go wider and deeper.

In the first place no one but a theologian can write a catechism. The writer need not be a male, nor a seminary graduate, nor the holder of a theological degree: but to be a theologian is essential. The chief reason why theologians do not make good catechism authors seems to be that they are not good enough theologians. If they were, they would immediately recognize the difference on the one hand, between theology and catechesis, and on the other the close interrelation of theology and catechesis. Often they tend to think of their science in its framework and phrasing as having a necessary place at the heart of catechesis. The truly skilled theologian, however, never takes handmaid for mistress nor human explication for saving message. He is a skilled theologian when he knows the limitations of his science, its historical adventures, and the superiority of the gospel to any paraphrase that may be made of it. This is another way of saying that men who are prisoners of their time theologically have never been fully equipped to do the catechetical job needed, however saintly they may have been or esteemed as theologians.

THE "TRADITIONAL METHOD" AND ITS ORIGINS

Modern catechetical activity, to be seen in its proper context, must be recognized not as part of a continuum (though the faith on which it is based is surely that) so much as a return to a pattern that prevailed only until the break-up of the catechumenate (sixth–seventh centuries). One should not hesitate to characterize the intervening centuries between then and the pre-Reformation period as a catechetical vacuum.[57] The admonitions in the form of legislation addressed to clergy, parents, and godparents was occasional and not widely effective. Authors differ on the state of reli-

[57] Padberg, *op. cit.*, pp. 24–27.

gious illiteracy in late medieval Europe, but they are unanimous that it was widespread.[58] The attempts by Catholics to return to the traditional catechesis of the patristic period which was cast in a salvation-history framework were interrupted by the fateful events of the early sixteenth century. The reformers were, if anything, less interested than the Catholics in a humanistic telling of God's mighty deeds done out of love,[59] though their desire to spread a knowledge of the Scriptures was genuine. The catechetical battleground they chose was the late-medieval one, and counter-Reformation Catholics chose it perforce. The matter was further complicated by the fact that the great figures of the counter-Reform like Canisius and Bellarmine were schoolmen who doubtless would have been equally unhappy in the face of any catecheses that departed too far from accepted categories.[60] The effort of men like Cardinal Hosius[61] of Ermland or Bishops Nausea

[58] Cf. Albert Hauck, *Kirchengeschichte Deutschlands*, Vol. 4 (Leipzig: J. C. Hinrichs, 1903), 38: "The later Church failed in an objective that the ancient Church had achieved. Proposing to parents and godparents that they had the obligation of initiating children into Christian belief was an inadequate substitute for this goal." A similar poor view of medieval preparation for confession is taken by Peter Browe, S.J., "Beichtunterricht im Mittelalter," *Theologie und Glaube*, 26 (1934), 427–42; cf. the Lambeth canon of 1281 which indicts strongly the ignorance of clergy who by their preaching diffuse more darkness than light, J. D. Mansi, *Sacrorum conciliorum collectio*, Vol. 24 (Paris: H. Welter, 1903, reproduced from A. Zatta, Venice, 1780), 410.

[59] Luther's impatience with Erasmus is well-known: "I hate Erasmus vehemently and from the heart," *Tischreden* (Weimar: 1912–21), I, 818; "I hold Erasmus for the greatest enemy of Christ; such a one has not been seen in a thousand years," *ibid.*, I, 837; "I cannot endure his catechism in which nothing is taught for certain; he confuses everything and calls it into doubt, wishing to create a state of doubt in the young," *ibid.*, 3, 3302b. Luther's passion for "certitude," well known from his spiritual history, is reflected in his total view of the catechetical problem. There are two human ways of thought in question here, rather than a heretical view versus a Catholic view.

[60] Cf. Brodrick, *Canisius*, p. 458, for the saint's adverse judgment on Erasmus, though his admiration for the *Catechismus Romanus* is a matter of record.

[61] Stanislaus Hozjusz, *Confessio catholicae fidei christiana: vel potius explicatio quaedam confessionis* (Viennae, M. Zimmermann, 1561); Friedrich Nausea, *In catholicum Catechismum Libri sex* (Coloniae, 1543).

of Vienna and Grodziecki of Olmitz to present the message of Christ in a primarily biblical and patristic mold they did not duplicate. This is by no means to say that Scripture or the Fathers meant little to them. No one familiar with the works of the two Jesuit saints can maintain that for a moment. Their shortsightedness lay in letting the reformers choose the weapons and the field of debate, namely a fragmented theology (and hence catechetics) to which both the Word of God and the traditional understanding of it expressed by the Fathers were adventitious. Their misfortune was not that they were theologians—for as we have indicated only a theologian is equipped to write a catechism—nor that they were schoolmen, but that they were schoolmen living in the period they happened to.

The works of Göbl,[62] and Bahlmann[63] establish sufficiently against the claims of Protestant scholars like Burckhardt[64] and Geffcken[65] that Catholic catechisms and manuals of piety existed in great numbers before the Reformation. Unfortunately, this is taken for a victory.

The directions given to pastors by the Synod of Lambeth (1281) instructed them to teach their people four times annually, on feast days, "without any fantastic weaving of subtle adornment, the fourteen articles of faith, ten commandments of the decalogue, the precepts of the gospel, namely the two concerned with charity, seven works of mercy, seven capital sins and their progeny, seven principal virtues, and seven sacraments of grace."[66] There follows a brief summary of Christian doctrine according to this scheme. Seven articles of the creed pertain to the mystery of the Trinity

[62] P. Göbl, *Geschichte der Katechese im Abendland vom Verfall des Katechumenates bis zum Ende des Mittelalters* (Kempten: Josef Kösel, 1880).

[63] Paul Bahlmann, *Deutschlands katholische Katechismen bis zum Ende des sechzehnten Jahrhunderts* (Münster: Regensberg Buchhandlung, 1894), 83 pp.

[64] Hieronymus Burckhardt, *Biblia, Das ist: Die gantze Heil. Schrift, Alten und Neuen Testaments* (Basel, 1753).

[65] Johannes Geffcken, *Der Bildercatechismus des fünfzehnten Jahrhunderts . . . bis auf Luther* (Leipzig, 1855).

[66] Mansi, *loc. cit.*

and seven to the humanity of Christ. Of the former, four pertain
to matters intrinsic to the deity (belief in one God and in each of
the three persons) and three to things that result from Him, "effectus divinitatis" (the creation of heaven and earth; the Church, grace
and sacraments, all effects of the Spirit; and the Church's confirmation through eternal glorification of body and soul and through its
opposite, damnation). The seven articles on Christ are those of the
creed. When the decalogue is dealt with, a division is immediately
made between the first three commandments (God) and the latter
seven (neighbor). After the seven corporal works of mercy, seven
impediments to lawful marriage are referred to but not listed, and
seven causes of excommunication are spelled out in detail—including what amounts to a charter of civil rights[67]

The French synod of Lavaur (1368) gives a similar but much
more complete catechesis.[68] It begins with a good summary on the
necessity of faith before it gets into the lists of sevens, and lays
a heavy charge on the clergy for the religious ignorance of the
faithful when they come to be judged. The Augustinian scheme
of things to be believed, loved, and hoped for (note the order) is
cited as the framework of the instruction to follow.[69] The things
to be believed are the fourteen articles of the creed (sic) and the
sacraments of the New Law; in the next phrase it is said that on
"sacraments and articles the whole Christian religion is based."
Virtues and opposite vices come next, and after that the gifts of
the Holy Spirit and the beatitudes which correspond to them.
Seven of the fourteen articles "pertain to the Divinity, seven others
to the humanity of Christ. Seven, therefore, have to do with God
secundum se; and seven others concern God *ratione humanitatis
assumptae.*"[70] It is evident in this medieval catechesis not only that
the lists of sevens are going strong but that the scholastic form of
distinction is introduced almost as soon as a religious "fact" has
been enunciated. As to a Christ-kerygma or a proclamation of

[67] *Ibid.*, cols. 412 f.
[68] *Ibid.*, 26, 484–93.
[69] S. Aurelii Augustini, *De Fide, Spe et Charitate,* PL 40, 232.
[70] Mansi, 26, 486.

trinitarian faith, it is an absentee. This becomes increasingly the case in the late medieval period. Earlier catechetical summaries like the *Disputatio Puerorum* attributed to Alcuin,[71] the catechism of Bruno of Würzburg,[72] and the numerous pieces of synodal legislation from the Carolingian period[73] had been solidly in the baptismal and catechumenate traditions of stress upon the Credo and Pater. Even with the addition of the decalogue under charity as a specification of "things to be done,"[74] the mysteries of faith retained their primacy as "things to be believed" and "things to hope for."[75]

The same continues to be true of late medieval handbooks of piety such as the *Fundamentum aeternae felicitatis* found with Gerson's works,[76] the *Christenspiegel* of Dietrich Kolde,[77] and Johannes Herolt's *Discipulus de eruditione Christifidelium*,[78] though the primacy of doctrine is now one of place rather than importance. Thus, Herolt devotes six pages to the Creed, three to the Our Father, and 101 to morality (commandments, deadly sins, and various moral precepts).

Padberg indicates clearly how the aspect of proclamation of faith that had marked ninth- and tenth-century catechisms is replaced by scholastic distinction and analysis even in books of popular piety like *Die Himmelstrass* and *Der Christenspiegel*[79] (cf. the "effectus divinitatis" of Lambeth, above). For the former of the two works above the Church is no longer the mystical union of biblical and especially Pauline teaching but the "community of

[71] PL 101, 1097–1144.
[72] PL 142, 557–68.
[73] Cloveshowe, A.D. 747 (Can. 10), Mansi 12, 398; Frankfurt, 794 (Can. 33), Mansi 13, 908; Arles, 813 (Can. 19), Mansi 14, 62; Mainz, 813 (Can. 45, 47), Mansi 14, 74; Leipzig, 743 (Can. 25 f.), PL 89, 822; Aachen 802 (Can. 14 f.), PL 97, 247.
[74] S. Thomae Aquinatis, "De duobus praeceptis charitatis et decem legis praeceptis," in *Opuscula omnia*, P. Mandonnet, ed. (Paris, 1927), 4, 413.
[75] *Ibid.*, p. 349.
[76] Bahlmann, *op. cit.*, p. 12.
[77] C. Drees, ed. (Werl, 1954).
[78] Bahlmann, *op. cit.*, p. 12.
[79] Padberg, pp. 38 f.

all men who profess true faith." In the Christ-mystery the soteriological emphasis on cross, resurrection, and parousia has yielded to stress upon His boyhood, His bitter passion, and the sacrament of the altar which mysteriously renews and contains Christ in that passion.

Aquinas's stress on the twofold law of charity in the gospel, which contains the whole Law, has been replaced by attention to the ten commandments almost as if they had not been fulfilled in Christ. In Gerson's *Opusculum tripertitum de praeceptis decalogi, de confessione et de arte moriendi* preparation for confession and for dying well is so much to the fore that the mysteries of faith are almost a prologue to be got through in embarrassed haste.[80] The fifteenth-century handbooks of penance and piety are plumcakes filled with beatitudes, works of mercy, evangelical counsels, fruits of the Holy Ghost, works of prayer, and almsgiving; they describe no clear and evident relation between these things and Christ and His love which give them meaning.

Certain conclusions seem to force themselves upon the reader from some of the evidence advanced in the foregoing chapter. One is that the catechisms of Canisius and Trent especially (though of these two the palm goes to the latter), despite the defects inherent in them because of the late medieval theological situation, restored a basis in doctrine to a European Catholic Christendom that had been moralizing almost apart from it for some centuries. Secondly, they succeeded—the *Romanus* more so than Canisius—in dislodging much scholastic terminology that impeded the clear message of the gospel, putting in its place a genuine if somewhat tentative proclamation of the mystery of salvation (see, for example, the introduction to the *Catechismus Romanus,* or the treatment of signification under the sacraments in general).

The catechetical effort in the United States has been on that counter-Reform plateau during the whole history of this nation, for understandable reasons. What is called the catechetical renewal

---

[80] Joannes Gerson, *Opera omnia,* I (Antwerp: Ellies du Pin, 1706), 426–50.

is predominantly a return to tradition. Like all activity in a living Church it looks forward as well as back. To see in this renewal a series of intemperate attacks on the Baltimore Catechism or a desire for novel "approaches" is to misconstrue it entirely. The clearest thing about it seems to be its impatience with novelty and its commitment to the spoken Word of a living Church that forever brings forth treasures old and new.

5 TEACHING THE

VERY YOUNG

"IN SPIRIT AND IN TRUTH"

Kindergarten, First and
Second Grades

Mother Maria de la Cruz
Aymes-Coucke, H.H.S.

SOME years ago the picture of a Sister teaching a firstgrader to make the sign of the cross was widely circulated, bearing the provocative caption, "WHAT IS WRONG WITH THIS PICTURE?" The answer expected was that the child should have been taught this Christian practice at home rather than have to wait six years to be taught it by a Sister.

Besides bringing to light a failure on the part of parents, this picture could also be used to illustrate a very common misconception on the part of many religion teachers, namely believing that a

102

child's ability to make the sign of the cross and recite certain essential prayers indicates that he "knows" his religion.

There is no doubt that when a child comes to first grade already knowing the fundamentals of his faith he most likely comes from a home in which God is not a stranger. Such a child already has made a contact with God through living in an environment that promotes the learning and practice of religion. His natural desires have led him to imitate the exterior manifestations of the faith of his parents. Even though these actions and words may be repeated mechanically at first, they have a solid foundation in the very parental faith and example. These external practices are not entirely empty of meaning even at an early age. Further instruction will strengthen the faith from which they spring. In such cases, when the child knows basic Christian practices it is a fairly good indication of his actual knowledge of religion—by knowledge being understood a comprehension of its inner meaning.

However, the (quantitatively) same signs of knowledge, hurriedly crammed into firstgraders by a teacher who wants to make up for lost time, is far from being an accurate measure of the child's religious knowledge. When some teachers are confronted with the appalling ignorance of children who come from homes where God is an unknown or perhaps even an unwelcome entity, they feel compelled to fill in, as quickly as possible, the void created by six years of neglect. They usually want to do it in a way that is immediately *evident*. The desire to do so leads them into the serious error of equating the proper teaching of religion with mere drill in external practices. This approach may fill them with a sense of accomplishment, but all too often it remains a meaningless and superficial exercise for the child.[1]

Does Memorization Serve Child or Adult?

Sometimes in watching parents and teachers instruct very young children one gets the impression that their efforts are misdirected.

[1] See Marc Oraison, *Love or Constraint?* (New York: Kenedy, 1959), pp. 9, 11.

It is not so much the child's spiritual welfare that they have in mind (even though they are convinced that they do) as their own personal satisfaction in achieving results that can be measured. Who can blame parents or teachers for the pride they feel when their children answer correctly and recite accurately? But the question still remains, *what does the child get out of all this?* Do the words he repeats evoke in his mind a true and vivid picture of God? Do they awake or stimulate in him the desire to respond to God's love by doing what He expects of him?

The child's ability to memorize should not be confused with his ability to understand. While it is true that a child can grasp the essential reality of deep mysteries of faith in a clearer and truer way than does an adult, because of his purer spiritual vision and simplicity of outlook, his lasting hold of these truths will depend largely on how they have been taught to him. To help the child learn the supernatural mysteries of faith, parents and teachers must be guided by basic teaching principles. The elders must create in the child's mind clear pictures of these truths before they force dogmatic definitions into his memory.

> We condemn neither memorization nor the question-and-answer method. But we contend that memorization should come not at the beginning but at the end of the process. . . . The teacher must first supply the necessary concrete background which the catechism answer presupposes.[2]

If this concrete approach is neglected, all the carefully worded sentences approved by the most exacting theologian can easily become distorted by being identified with untheological mental pictures. The harm done then may be irreparable. The teacher, satisfied with the external signs of apparent learning, will fail to rectify any erroneous concepts acquired by the child. The consequent danger is that in later years the adolescent is likely to question the truth and application of religion to life's realities;

[2] Rudolph G. Bandas, *Catechetical and Confraternity Methods* (St. Paul: 251 Summit Ave., 1957), p. 12.

he may end by rejecting it along with other myths, fairy-tales, and fallacies of childhood.

Retaining the Right Things for a Lifetime

A common example may serve to clarify this point. Suppose that, without concrete preparation, firstgraders are asked to repeat the answer to the basic questions, "Who is God?" or "What is grace?" The answer expected by the adult may be, "God is the Supreme Being who made all things" or "God is my Father in heaven" and "Grace is a supernatural gift of God bestowed on us for our salvation." The teacher, satisfied with hearing the little ones give the "correct" answer after a few minutes of drilling, would be shocked if she were able to see the images that these answers have created in the children's unguided imagination.

One child might easily have identified God with some brand of canned goods used at home or seen on TV . . . since both are named "Supreme" (there is even a Supreme gasoline!). Another could have pictured God as a straggly *bean*—such as the one growing in the backyard. If the term *father* was used, what a variety of images it evoked! In some cases what images of selfishness, indifference, or even downright cruelty may have flashed across the "mental screen" of the children! As for *grace*, it might easily be identified with a redheaded neighbor girl or a princess in faraway Monaco. The children are quite content with their "pictures" and will offer no protest as the teacher continues her "orthodox" lesson. "God made us—He wants us to be happy—we show our love for Him by our obedience to His will—without grace you cannot please God—if you die without grace you cannot go to heaven." Every new statement, no matter how theologically correct its wording, tends only to add to the distorted picture already conceived by the young child.

Any primary-grade teacher who has listened to the equal devotion with which a little child will sing, "Gladly, the cross I'd bear!" or "Gladly, the cross-eyed bear," or has seen the compunction with which he says, "I'm partly sorry for having defended Thee . . ."

will readily agree that we cannot take *any* knowledge for granted when teaching children in the early grades. Great care must be taken to create clear true concepts and then to prove their validity before reenforcing learning with definitions to be memorized.

Since much of a small child's awareness is in his imagination rather than in his intellectual faculties, it is far more important that our explanations produce in him a mental picture that is substantially right than that the wording of the explanation be theologically correct. In other words, the question we should ask ourselves in preparing a religion class for young children is not "Does it avoid all heresies?" but rather, "Does it create a correct picture of the truth?"

Teaching More Than the Child Can Understand

Some might argue that it is better to have the children memorize from the very beginning accurate definitions of moral and dogmatic truths *whether they understand them or not,* reasoning that later on they will come to understand them. Psychologists and pedagogues cannot agree with this point of view, and the good catechist must be something of both. A child learns through images, pictures, and personal experiences and not by the mere vocalizing of words. Images, not words, will sink deeply into his subconscious, producing a learning that will greatly influence his intellectual and moral decisions at a time of crisis in later years.

The catechism questions and answers are necessary—just as the dictionary and encyclopedia are necessary—but not for first-graders or preschool children.[3] As the child matures he will need clear, correct statements of Catholic doctrine that will crystallize for him the truths already learned and understood. Still, in these later years it is "of paramount importance that professional theologians and elementary school teachers combine their distinctive gifts in a common enterprise."[4] Even then, no matter how care-

[3] See Joseph B. Collins, S.S., *Confraternity Teachers' Guide* (Milwaukee: Bruce, 1960), pp. xii and 73.
[4] John T. Foudy, "Is There Confusion on the Catechism?" *American Ecclesiastical Review,* 143 (June 1960), 381.

fully-worded a catechism is it should never be considered the basis, much less the source, of religious knowledge.

How are we, then, to teach religion to small children? How will we create an image of God "whom no man has seen"? The answer is to be found with God Himself.

RELIGION TEACHING
BASED ON THE BIBLE

The Christian religion is a revealed religion. It is based on what God has made known to man, not on what man has discovered. The faith of the Christian rests upon the revelation which God has made of Himself as recorded in the Hebrew writings, and in and through His Son, Jesus Christ.

Our teaching from the very beginning must be based on Holy Scripture and guided by it as it has been presented to us by our Mother the Church. It is the Bible which reveals to us the fundamental outline of the Christian mystery and makes known to us the course of the economy of salvation. How, then, "can we neglect, in our work of religious education, that which is its fundamental element, and of which all the rest is but a development, an explanation or a corollary?"[5]

The Bible reveals that the teaching of religion is, by its nature, the unfolding of a story. It is evident that in teaching young children, who have not yet developed a historical sense, biblical passages must be carefully chosen and limited. The child is unable to absorb a multiplicity of details; but there is no need to compress much information into a small space in order to bring out the economy of salvation and the mystery of Christ. It can be done quite satisfactorily in a few clear, bold strokes. The child's vivid imagination will help make him react to such a presentation, and the theological virtues he possesses will awaken a response in his soul.

Bible stories, precisely because they should be presented in primary grades in summary, must be *absolutely faithful* to the

[5] Most Reverend Léon A. Elchinger, "The Bible and Catechesis," *Teaching All Nations* (New York: Herder and Herder, 1961), p. 141.

biblical spirit. Parents and teachers must exert utmost care not to teach in a literal way stories that have an allegorical or symbolic sense. Popular traditions that are too easily mixed with the sacred text have a deplorable effect, since the children will later find it very difficult to make a distinction between the revealed Word of God and the invented human additions. For instance, children who are told that the world was made "in six days"—that Adam sinned because "he ate an apple"—that "4,000 years" elapsed between the fall and redemption, and so forth, will eventually have to unlearn them, often to the great detriment of their belief. The unlearning process then will be necessarily a painful growth in faith because of the earlier, harmful teachings.

God chose to reveal Himself first by His lavish gifts to man in the orders of nature and grace. Man learned to discover in these gifts the goodness, greatness, and authority of God. Man's grateful love found its best expression in prayer—communion with God —and in a loving obedience to His will. Sin, however, came to break the harmony love had established. Chaos followed, and still . . . God continued to love man. Even the just punishments man calls on himself are tempered by a merciful love. Then comes the culmination of God's gifts in the person of His Son. Christ, the Anointed of God, comes to wrestle for our salvation. Through His death He accomplishes our redemption; He then attains to the glory of His resurrection, the pledge of our own regeneration.

From this story of salvation, which could be summarized essentially in the divine adoption of mankind in Christ Jesus, we draw the "key" notions that can best help children to receive the all-important message of God's love for us—the kērygma (presentation, proclaiming) of His deed in Christ.

A few considerations on the manner in which these key notions can be presented to young children are here offered. No two children are alike, nor do they have the same religious background; therefore, all suggested methods of presenting the message of salvation must be adapted to the needs and abilities of the children in a specific class. This adaptation is essential in all pedagogy, but especially (as Acts and the epistles of St. Paul make clear) in adopting the kerygmatic or New Testament approach.

I. Goodness and Love of God Seen in His Gifts

If the child comes to religion class without any idea of God or with a distorted one, the first step necessary is to create for him an image of goodness, greatness, and authority. With children we must proceed from the known to the unknown. Therefore, it would be helpful to evoke the image desired by telling the familiar story of a good and generous grandfather, who lives far away but who is very much aware of his grandchildren. The children learn about him from their parents—they have concrete proofs of his love and interest for them by the gifts he sends—they soon discover that grandfather reacts favorably when their good behavior is reported to him—that he is displeased when they do wrong. Their self-centered love for him gradually develops into a desire to please him, to see him, and to be with him.

The comparison finds an easy application as we subsequently speak of God. The term "grandfather" is dropped and replaced by "our Father in heaven" but the image of goodness, greatness, and authority remains. The children are prepared to see in all the beauties of nature gifts from their good Father in heaven who loves them and wants to make them happy.

From the visible gifts of nature we move to the more personal gifts of those who love us and whom we love. By recalling the warmth and security enjoyed when we are with those dear to us, the immensity of God's love is stressed: "God loves us *more* than anyone else." Then we go a step farther and speak of the gift of God's own life and love in us (without using the term "sanctifying grace"), a gift which makes us His own dear children.

II. Our Grateful Response to God in Prayer

Gradually we try to awaken in the child the desire to give thanks for all these gifts. The prayer of thanksgiving (not of petition) is the first prayer to be instilled in the heart of a child.

It is not too difficult to teach a child how to pray, but parents and teachers do not always know how to distinguish between "praying" and "saying prayers." The definition of prayer as the raising of our minds and hearts to God should be understood

properly. It means *thinking* about God and *loving* Him; not necessarily "talking" to Him. The young child, whose vocabulary is
very limited, finds it extremely hard to "say" prayers in his own
words. Those taught to him are often formulated in incomprehensible language as far as he is concerned.

The following true incident is deeply significant. A four-year-
old child who lived next door to the parish church developed the
habit, no doubt encouraged by his mother, of making frequent
visits to the church. Usually he would walk to the first bench and
sit down without any ceremony. He remained there for a short
while, quite contented and satisfied with the awareness of the
proximity of Someone who was friendly. To his mother's question,
"Where were you?" he would simply answer, "I went to church
to pray." Two years later, when he began attending religion
classes, his visits to church stopped. His surprised mother in-
quired, "Why don't you go to church any more to pray, as you did
for so long?" The child shrugged and after an embarrassed silence
admitted, "The teacher said that when we pray we must talk to
God. I don't know what to say to Him."

If a child is to learn the meaning of prayer, it is of prime importance that he be allowed to enter into personal *contact* with
God. Once this contact has been established, God becomes Someone very real and intimately present to the soul of the child. This
mystical experience, the value of which he hardly recognizes,
will remain deeply rooted in his soul even though he does not
know how to give expression to it. Then the child will know God
"in spirit and in truth"; only then will he know how to pray. This
contact cannot be *established* by parents or teachers, but as religious educators they must remove all obstacles and create the
favorable atmosphere that will facilitate and promote it.

Teaching Private Prayer

As an example of preparing the ground for the sowing of a
religious concept let us consider an effective way of leading a
preschool child to a realization of the presence of Jesus Christ
in the blessed sacrament. The mother brings the child to church,

preferably at a time when no services are being conducted. In perfect silence and reverence she kneels before the altar, her eyes fixed upon the tabernacle. No words are spoken. The child is watching the mother, who after a short while gently points to the tabernacle. Perhaps she could then close her eyes and bow her head in adoration, thinking gratefully of the mediatory office Christ is performing at the Father's right hand. After a short while, without any comment, she stands, makes a devout genuflection and leaves. Even if the child asks no questions he has already sensed that there is Someone in church who his mother thinks is important and who can make his mother happy. This is quite enough for the present.

Subsequent visits will draw the childlike question, "Who is there?" When this happens the child is ready for some explanation, which must be absolutely true in its simplicity. "Jesus is there. Jesus the Lord, God's own Son, our best friend." (*Not*, "Baby Jesus is there, living in that little house," nor "Jesus is there like a prisoner staying with us"). It will not be long before the child will want to know *how* Jesus is there. Once more the truth must be stated in a true and simple way. "Jesus stays with us from Mass to Mass under the form of Bread." Gently, without forcing on the child information that he cannot assimilate, the mother will explain that under the form of Bread Jesus offers Himself to the Father. We join Him in doing so. It is the greatest gift that anyone can give to God. We also receive Jesus as our food.

It must be remembered that what *first* impressed the child, led him to ask questions, and made these later explanations meaningful to him was the actual experience that preceded them. Similarly, the recollected and prayerful way in which parents say their prayers at home will make the child more aware of God's presence than the words they recite.

In taking firstgraders to church for a visit, the teacher will have more success in a lesson on prayer if she shows by her example the actual purpose of going to church. She should walk in front of the children and not behind them, and her whole manner should reveal respect and joy. Her attention should be given to the One who receives a holy offering in this place, not exclusively to the behavior of the children. If she has succeeded in winning their respect and admiration she will soon find them imitating her recollection and learning from her not only correct church behavior but above all how to give a living expression to their faith in the divine presence. If, on the contrary, the teacher is continually correcting the children, urging them to be quiet, to kneel up straight, not to talk or turn their heads around, her concern for externals will stand in open contradiction to her words.

The Need for Silence

It is not always easy, however, to lead the children to this awareness of God when religion is taught as a subject in a classroom and when, as is often the case, there has been no previous religious training at home. The difficulty arises from the fact that this teaching cannot be rushed. It needs silence, recollection, and leisure which unfortunately the ordinary classroom seldom provides. It is most regrettable that the religion class has fallen under the curse of our century: rush and pressure. There seems to be little time to teach in depth—"in spirit and truth." There is fear of running out of time, of not completing the course of studies, of examinations finding the children unprepared. The pressure is often too great and the teacher somehow lacks the courage to stand up against it. Naturally this feeling robs her of her peace, even if she is not aware of it. She consequently fails to create an atmosphere conducive to recollection and prayer. Real contact with God is seldom achieved. Thus it too often happens that in religion classes the mind is educated at the expense of the soul.[6]

There is need not only of courage on the part of the primary teacher in order to teach the little ones leisurely and joyfully, but also for the cooperation and understanding of pastors and principals. They must be aware of the value of leading the children into recollection and silence in order to promote learning in depth. A superficial observer might consider wasteful the time given to

6 See Joseph Goldbrunner, *Holiness Is Wholeness* (New York: Pantheon, 1955), pp. 23 ff.

train children to acquire the all but forgotten art of recollection. The value of the techniques used in the Montessori schools is gaining more recognition by American educators, but there is still a long way to go before these techniques find their rightful place in religion classes. This is especially true of those conducted by the Confraternity of Christian Doctrine. For example, the techniques of "walking on the line" and "the lesson in silence" could, if used in adapted and simplified form, contribute greatly to the creation of an atmosphere most conducive to prayer and learning. For the sake of those who might not be acquainted with them the procedures are here outlined.

Achieving Receptivity in the Child

A narrow line is traced on the floor of the corridor leading into the classroom (the use of chalk may provoke janitorial complaint unless the teacher is careful to remove it after the exercise). The firstgraders are told in a friendly way that they are going to play the game of "Walk on the Line" (not "along the line"). They are encouraged by the teacher who says, "It's fun to walk on the line! Try to stay on it." Thus, the attention of the children will be riveted on an exercise that requires the coordination of will and muscular activity. To walk on the line the children must concentrate; silence and order quietly replace noise and dissipation, without disciplinary threats that tend to make the religion class a disagreeable experience. The children are being effectively conditioned to become receptive.

This activity might be followed in the classroom by "The Lesson in Silence." The children line up along the rear wall. They may be allowed to squat, provided they remain motionless. The suggestion, "Make your feet and hands be quiet," will help them to become aware, in a practical and concrete way, that their wills must govern their bodies. As soon as they are motionless the teacher makes them notice a faraway or dim noise—the ticktock of a clock or the dropping of pins on the desk—to focus their attention on one point. The teacher, in a very low voice, then calls each child by name; the child rises and goes in silence to stand by his desk.

When all the pupils are in their places their attention may again be called to the faint noise.

By this time the children are keenly alert and expectant—silence has created in them a void which demands to be filled. Now the contact with God will take place more easily. A few words, *quietly* spoken by the teacher, will orient the children toward the awareness of the presence of God. "God our Father is here—He is in our hearts. He loves us. We love Him, too." These words may be accompanied by the gesture of crossing the arms over the breast, a gesture which the children imitate without repeating the words. There is a brief pause. "We want to give to God all we are and all we have." The teacher extends her arms upwards and so do children. The gesture confirms the sentiment just awakened. No words are said and yet prayer has taken place. Now teaching can begin. The initial contact has already been made and the silent recollection will bear fruit in the greater ability of the children to listen and think.[7]

These two activities which may at first take a maximum of five or ten minutes cannot be expected to be carried out perfectly on the first day of class; but they are worth the effort and the time spent on them. There is, in fact, a poorer use of time in trying to get the attention of children who have rushed into a classroom with dissipated minds and noisy manners. The teacher's words then are drowned in a multitude of distractions and the prayers recited will be mere verbalisms.

It is evident that the understanding of the children's emotional and physical needs cautions us against prolonging these types of activity for any period of time. But once the children are familiar with them, three to four minutes at most should produce effective degrees of concentration. When these activities are not possible, their underlying principle should not be ignored by primary-grade teachers. Young children need time, recollection, and brief periods of silence not only to achieve a "personal contact" with God but also to be able to assimilate what they learn.

[7] Hélène Lubienska de Lenval, *L'Education du sens religieux* (Paris: Editions Spes, 1946), pp. 20, 83, 104.

III. Love is Shown in Obedience

As the lessons progress and the concept of God's love in and around us become clearer, the children should come to realize that the best way to thank God for all His gifts is to please Him, doing what He wants them to do. The teacher uses a positive approach, pointing out to the children what God expects of them and trying to stimulate a desire to do His will in order to show their love for Him. This is of greater value in life than stressing what God forbids. If this positive approach is used there is greater hope that their religious and moral life will be properly oriented. There is less danger that later they will calculate how far they can go on the wrong path without mortally offending God. If genuine love for God and not merely fear of punishment is their motivation, they will try to avoid sin no matter how small the offense might be.

IV. The Ingratitude of Sin

The harmonious communion between God and man was broken by sin. The disorder it produced is already vaguely experienced by the small child, as soon as he begins to distinguish between good and bad, in the feeling of guilt (even though it is not yet "the sense of sin") which he has concerning his actions. He also has personal experience of some of the consequences of sin in the suffering that is part of his life. All this makes the child capable of acquiring in his religious lessons some idea of the evil effects produced by disobedience to God. In teaching about sin the teacher should not stress the punishment it brings but rather the ingratitude toward God it displays. The story of the fall, devoid of details that are nonessential to children, should bring out the fact that Adam and Eve wilfully *turned away* from God their loving Father. This "turning away" from the One who is the source of love and goodness is the essence of sin. If the children get an understanding of this essential point they will more readily grasp the meaning of true contrition which is a turning toward God, a "conversion."

Recognizing Wrongdoing

The formation of the conscience of a young child is one of

the religious educator's most delicate and difficult tasks. For the teacher the task is greatly complicated if the children are punished at home for mistakes they cannot avoid and, on the other hand, are hardly scolded for breaking a law of God. In these circumstances there is danger that sin will gradually be considered merely as a social convention. Its supposed relativity will bring about the dulling and hardening of the conscience.

It is necessary, therefore, for the children to be able progressively to discern the mysterious transcendence of the Person of God, infinitely distinct from parental authority, so fragile in itself. Put simply, the teacher must help the children to become aware of the absolute justice of God. She must lead them to examine their conscience, quietly and without fear, guided by the light of His law of love.

In the primary grades there is not yet need of teaching the distinction between mortal and venial sin. It is certainly regrettable that this knowledge is required in many places before first- and secondgrade children are allowed to receive holy communion. It is not that the children at this age level are incapable of memorizing the conditions necessary for a mortal sin, but simply that they are psychologically incapable of committing one.

This point bears some further discussion, and here we can but echo the opinion of esteemed theologians, psychologists, and religious educators. If a preschool or primary-grade child were to commit a crime, wanting to do it and knowing he was doing something very wrong, even if he stated that he knew at the time that it was a "mortal sin," he would never be sentenced to capital punishment. Why? Parents, teachers, psychologists would all concur in affirming that a child within his first eight or ten years is not sufficiently mature mentally and emotionally to realize the implications of his actions. They would say unanimously that he does not have the moral development needed to make him fully responsible for his action. Why then assume that such a child could be condemned to eternal punishment by His all-merciful Father?

It is very difficult to state at what age the child could have the freedom, philosophically viewed (sufficient advertence and rational deliberation), plus the psychological freedom (freedom from obstacles, pressures, and impediments which make choices difficult), to render him accountable for his actions.[8] In fact Jungmann has said, "It must be assumed that on account of insufficient insight grave sins are, as a rule, not possible before the tenth or eleventh year."[9]

All the above provides reasons in plenty why in the primary grades the emphasis should be placed on leading the children to virtue out of love for God rather than drawing their attention to distinctions and degrees of sin. The same is true of the punishment due to sin, which they are not able to grasp or will easily misunderstand. This does not by any means indicate that the ugliness and ingratitude of sin are not to be mentioned. It is this dark background that will bring out all the more the greatness of God's love for us in the gift of His Son.

Even though young children do not experience a personal need for a Savior, they do long for the happiness they were created for. They do want to be free from suffering and fear. If Christ is presented to them as the Savior who makes us free and leads us to God our Father who alone can make us happy, they will gradually learn to appreciate the gift of Jesus Christ.

V. Jesus Christ, True God and True Man

Jesus Christ—the Son of God made man for our salvation—is the core of our message. The question, "How to teach Christ?" is therefore of paramount importance.

Here we face a problem which is not easily solved, for the simple reason that it is not recognized as a problem. Sometimes parents and teachers have a lopsided devotion to the Lord Jesus which unconsciously makes them transmit to the children a distorted picture of Him. Either the divine status of the Son of God

[8] See John C. Ford, S.J., and Gerald Kelly, S.J., *Contemporary Moral Theology* (Westminster, Md.: Newman Press, 1959), pp. 211 ff. See also Oraison, *op. cit.*, p. 100.
[9] Josef Andreas Jungmann, S.J., *Handing On the Faith* (New York: Herder and Herder, 1959), p. 303. See also footnote on that page.

is obliterated by the humanity of the Savior, or else His manhood is so stressed that it is forgotten He is the eternal Son. This results in statements such as, "God is on the altar," "Jesus is watching you," or "Baby Jesus is hurt if you do this," which show a lack of correct understanding of the relations in God and His work of saving us. Again, certain statements will overemphasize an aspect of the Savior to the detriment of His whole person: they will make an overly sweet character of Him, or else someone who is continually demanding sacrifices—who cannot be pleased unless we suffer.

It is essential that religion teachers, especially those entrusted with the formation of the very young, get as clear and complete a picture of Jesus Christ, God and man, as possible. Holy Scripture reveals the qualities that make the Person of our Lord the ideal Leader whom the children have to learn to believe in, admire, and follow. It is not correct to think that little children are attracted only by the sweetness and kindness of Jesus revealed in several biblical scenes—on the contrary! Even naturally speaking they will feel far greater attraction to Him if His strength and courage are brought out. The gospels are filled with incidents that reveal not only the meekness of Christ but also His fearlessness before the enemies of God, His uncompromising struggle against the spirit of the world, His ardent zeal for the glory of His Father.

The Most Necessary Knowledge about Christ

It is Christ's love and devotedness to His Father that must be stressed above all. The mission of Christ was to reveal the Father and lead us all, as one great family, back to Him. Our teaching of Christ must have the same end: to reveal the Father and lead to Him. This will be achieved only when the personality of Our Lord as manifested in the gospels becomes familiar to the teacher. The reproach He made to Philip might well be addressed to not a few religious educators, "Have I been so long with you and you have not known me? Philip, he who sees me sees also the Father" (Jn 14, 9).

Without forcing the mention of "God our Father" in every single lesson, the whole approach should be clearly God-centered.[10] The more children advance in their religious instruction the clearer it should become to them that we are continually on our way toward God our Father, led by Christ our Lord, and strengthened by the Spirit of love. This predominant idea will bring all doctrines into an organic unity.

Children need then a strong, virile, and true idea of Jesus Christ their Lord and God. This they must get not only through the gospel stories they hear but also through the pictures they see. We are swamped commercially with pictures of Jesus which run the gamut from cheap art to art masterpieces, the latter frequently not masterpieces of sacred expression. The danger in choosing among them is that very often parents and teachers tend to follow their own tastes rather than consider the effect the pictures can have on the children.

A familiar example might be presented to point out the lack of "psychological common sense" in the selection of many pictures shown to small children. It is the case of a young mother whose husband has to go away from home for a length of time. She is anxious to keep the memory of her husband in her child. What will she do to keep before his eyes the image of one who loves him, who is strong enough to defend him, who provides for all his needs, and whose authority demands recognition? Will she look for a picture of her husband when he was six or seven years old, present it to her child, and hope to awake in him feelings of love and admiration, security and respect as she says to him, "This is your Dad?" Isn't it obvious that she will rather select the picture that best reveals his *true and actual* personality?

There is no need to press the argument any further, but how can anyone explain the purpose of those pictures of Jesus with soft, curly hair and transparent eyes that all too often invade the child's bedroom and the bulletin boards of primary-grade classrooms? What conceivable benefit does the parent or teacher hope to

[10] For the identity of the terms "God" and "God the Father," see Karl Rahner, S.J., "Theos in the New Testament," in *Theological Investigations,* I (Baltimore: Helicon Press, 1961), pp. 136–48.

achieve by crowding the imagination of a child with pictures of
Jesus sitting on the lap of His mother, cutting flowers, talking to
birds, or dressed in velvet and furs (changed like an antependium
according to the feast)?

"Hagios, Athanatos, Ischyros"

There is no Baby Jesus *now*. There is only the glorious and immortal God-man Jesus Christ, who has conquered sin and death
and is the living head of the Church, His body. Therefore a picture
of the adult Christ, revealing the plenitude of His strength, power,
and sacred manhood should be predominant in the home and in
primary grades.

It is not wrong, of course, to show pictures of the infant of
Bethlehem and the youth of Nazareth. These visual aids make the
teaching of historical events in the life of the Savior more vivid.
Such pictures can be posted during liturgical feasts which recall
the mysteries of Christ's infancy. But the children should not be
continually exposed to soft, pastel-like images of an infant Jesus.
To use the expression of Dr. Josef Goldbrunner, a respected psychologist and theologian, "These images are poison for the spiritual
life of young children."

It is a fact that these pictures may please some *adults* and be
harmless to them so far as they are aware. It is not unusual to
find in religious sisters a true devotion to the infant King, but it
must be stressed that such devotions are not to be imposed on the
children. It is a mistake to think that such pictures are helpful
to the little ones because they seem to like them. Children can be
brought to like anything their parents and favorite teachers like,
but neither parents nor teachers will be able to undo the harmful
impressions these pictures will make—unconsciously—on their receptive minds. Later on, when the adolescent is struggling against
serious temptations and look for guidance and support in his
religion, whose image is liable to surge up before him? That of a
soft Baby Jesus! Will this image be a source of courage to him,
will it motivate him to fight with loyalty and virility for a leader
who guarantees victory? The question is self-answered.

Calendar Art Yields Calendar Piety

Certainly, we should not rashly attribute all lapses of adolescent and adult Catholics to the soft religious art to which they were exposed in their childhood; but there is no denying that such pictures, unless counterbalanced by a practical life of faith nourished by prayer and frequent reception of the sacraments, can undermine the foundations of their spiritual life.

Slowly, gradually, the strong personality of our Lord and Savior must take hold of the minds and hearts of children. They must learn to know and love Him as one who is, here and now, present and living in His Church. It is not necessary to teach in the first grade all that is known about the seven sacraments to bring the children to an understanding that it is Christ who gives them the gift of God's life. He it is who makes them children of God, nourishes and strengthens the life of grace in their souls, and cleanses and heals them of sin through holy signs. As they advance into higher grades they will have the opportunity to learn more and more about how Christ acts through the sacraments and how we are all made one in Him.

VI. The Mystery of the Three Persons in God

In a true biblical spirit the teaching of the doctrine of the most blessed Trinity in first grade should come as the culmination, not as the introduction of our teaching. Only after the children have a notion of the love of God the Father, of the redemptive mission of God the Son made man for our salvation, and of the work of the Holy Spirit who sanctifies and unites us to Christ will they have the necessary background for a more accurate and solid understanding of this mystery of mysteries. Then the words that accompany the making of the sign of the cross will become more meaningful. When they are explained without any prepation there is great danger that this holy sign and these words will remain a gesture empty of meaning and devotion.

To summarize: the initiation into the mystery of Christ, even from the very first grade, should be based on Sacred Scripture. It is not enough, though, that the teacher follow the pattern set down by God; she should take care that the children are made aware that the lessons they learn are taken from the Bible. Whenever a biblical story is told, they should know it is from "God's book," the Bible. The Bible itself, even though quite beyond the reading level of primary-grade pupils, should be brought to class so that they can see and venerate it. The teacher should read suitable short passages to the class directly from the Bible. When this is done the children ought to stand out of respect for God's Word. Later on, when in second grade, they could be asked to memorize short and well-selected scriptural quotations, especially words of our Lord. For instance, "I am the good shepherd. The good shepherd lays down his life for his sheep" (Jn 10, 11). "A new commandment I give you . . . that as I have loved you, you also love one another" (Jn 13, 34).

The memorization of the Word of God is of far more importance than the memorization of definitions written by men.

After all, these are the words of God and are more precious than the words of any theologian. It is essential that certain biblical passages of special significance should be learned by heart. By means of these the children will store up in their subconscious minds considerable active reserves of power and light. Far more than catechism texts, biblical texts—our Lord's own words—can sustain the children throughout their lives both at school and afterwards.[11]

TEACHING RELIGION
IN THE SPIRIT OF LITURGY

In order to make it clear that the economy of salvation is operative here and now and to show that the sacred history of the past is continued into the present, our lessons in the primary grades should follow the liturgical year as closely as possible.

During Advent we can speak of creation, the elevation of man, sin, and the promise. Thus, the years of longing for the coming of the Savior, relived by the Church, will coincide with the child's anxious awaiting of Christmas.

[11] Elchinger, op. cit., p. 151.

Christmas, so filled with joy for children, is the ideal time to speak of the great gift God our Father has sent us in the person of His Son. During the Christmas season, the mysteries of His infancy and childhood are presented. With Septuagesima we move on to the public life, bringing out some of the miracles and parables of our Lord and gradually preparing the children for the study of His passion and death. This should be done as closely as possible to Holy Week. Easter provides a spiritual climate of incomparable value for the teaching of the glory and triumph of the resurrection. The Easter-Pentecost cycle lends itself to speaking of the gift of the Holy Spirit, the blessed Trinity, the Church, and the sacraments. The school year will end fittingly with a lesson on the second coming of Christ.[12]

The liturgy of the Church is not only a true source of doctrinal knowledge but also the means of sanctification, both personal and communal. It is a sacred "sign" that teaches truths of faith and at the same time gives the necessary grace to live according to this faith. "It is in this way that the liturgy has an eminent kerygmatic value since it enables us to participate in a divine reality at the same time it is enlightening us. In the liturgy of the Church we find the 'means of participation' in the highest form."[13]

Some Ways to Teach from the Liturgy

The religion teacher who is aware of the rich teachings found in liturgical texts will not fail to make frequent use of them, drawing from the celebration of Sundays and feastdays the doctrines they contain. The recitation of some of the prayers said during Mass, such as the *Gloria*, the Preface, *Agnus Dei*, etc., should not be restricted to actual participation during the Mass. These prayers recited in class will bring to life the significance of a lesson related to them. The short responses taken from the prayers at the foot of the altar or Preface can be used as prayers in the classroom. Excerpts from the proper of the Sunday Mass, for instance the Introit

[12] For an example of how themes can be taught following the liturgical year see *With Christ to the Father*, Teacher's Guide, Grade 1, "On Our Way" series (New York: Sadlier, 1958).

[13] Guy de Bretagne, O.M.I., *Pastorale Catéchetique* (Tournai: Desclée de Brouwer, 1953), p. 235.

and/or the Collect will train the children to pray in the spirit of the Church.

The best way to teach children about the sacraments is undoubtedly to reenact the ceremonies and study the prayers used in their administration. Even in the first grade a simplified demonstration of baptism will give children a better idea of its effects than a mere descriptive presentation.

The Church, a pedagogue par excellence, knows the importance of gestures, songs, and ceremonies in the expression of her faith. These religious activities which often deepen religious sentiments should not be neglected in the classroom. Activities of a liturgical character carried out in class, such as processions, veneration of the cross, etc., will gradually prepare the primary grade children for a better understanding of the significance of the liturgy of the Church.

The Well-Formed Catechist Teaches the Catechism

When a religion teacher has made himself familiar with the written Word of God and has learned to draw from the liturgy of the Church the teaching it contains, his task as a messenger of Christ will be greatly simplified. Drawing strength and guidance from the very source of supernatural light and life, he will be able to bring this light and life into his teaching. His religion lessons will not be mere formalities. Children will learn the catechism, but along with its definitions will come something far more precious: the love of what is being learned and the actual living by it. As an instrument and "extension" of Christ the teacher will lead the young souls entrusted to his care to the Father, and form in them "true worshipers . . . who will worship the Father in spirit and in truth" (Jn 4, 23).

6 THE RELIGIOUS FORMATION OF CHILDREN IN THE SECOND, THIRD, AND FOURTH GRADES

Eva Fleischner

INTRODUCTORY: THE AIM

One way of defining the goal of religious education is to say that it should bring about a meeting between two persons, the believer and the living God—a meeting which will result, on the part of the believer, in conscious and wholehearted commitment to God. This is only another way of describing faith in Jesus Christ, the supreme revelation of God. It is the purpose of this chapter to point out some of the principal ways in which religious educators can give the child access to this faith at the ages of seven, eight, nine, and ten.

Since our subject is the formation of children in the second, third, and fourth grades we are dealing with a period at which the child's spiritual life is still very fragile and pliable, although no longer in its most formative stage. "His experiences at the beginning of this stage have been few and brief. He is ignorant of life and its promises, difficulties, and perils. He is also pliable and eagerly responds to affectionate guidance. Now is the best time to train him for a way of life."[1] This is the time for laying foundations: developing religious attitudes and a sense of God composed of love and reverence; giving the child a taste for prayer; forming his conscience; initiating him to the sacraments and the life of the Church. These foundations must be solid and deep enough to support the entire life-edifice of the faith of the adult Christian in later years. Nothing should now be done that must later be undone. This implies a religious education which, while paying delicate attention to the child's physical, psychological, and mental development, will never at any moment be childish, or fail to do justice in vocabulary and content to the splendor and sacredness of the Christian revelation. It implies, further, that our teaching be directed at the faith and prayer life of the children rather than at their intellectual formation. It would be vain to try to give to children of seven through ten an instruction which is primarily rational and abstract. For although the second period of childhood they have now entered will see a marked strengthening of their reasoning faculty, it is still only in its beginnings. Moreover, the child's intellect does not work in isolation, but is intimately bound up with his heart and body. In our considerations on method, therefore, we shall give a prominent place to creative activities—always, however, for the sake of the goal: the meeting with the living God.

BASIC APPROACHES

Developing a Religious Sense

The desire for God lies deep in the heart of every man. But just as the life hidden in the seed will not awaken unless it is brought into contact with moisture, so too the hunger for God will make itself felt only if the child has caught a glimpse of His goodness

---

[1] Robert P. Odenwald, *Your Child's World* (New York: Random House, 1958), p. 81.

and beauty, and has somehow experienced that it is good to be with Him. It is one of the most important tasks confronting religious educators in the lower grades to awaken, or to deepen, the child's *sense of God*. Without it there is danger that Christianity will never be more for him than a moral code, a long and burdensome list of things he must not do; without it the child—and later the adult—will perhaps say that he believes, but it will be belief in a set of truths which remain at the level of abstract principles, rather than belief in the living God. Ideally, the sense of God should be fostered in the child by his parents from his earliest years. But since this is often no longer the case, the task will devolve on the religious educator much of the time. Where shall we begin?

We must cultivate in him certain attitudes which will be as it were the climate in which his sense of God can awaken and grow. Most basic among these is the *sense of reverence*. Modern children in the United States and Canada often seem to have little of it, but this is the fault of parents and educators. We may not simply shrug our shoulders indifferently and say, "Too bad, we'll have to get along without it." We cannot get along without it, for it is essential to any true religious education. Nor is the situation as hopeless as might seem at first sight. For the child has a sense of reverence by nature: he is weak and little and looks up to those who are big and strong. Mme. Lubienska de Lenval, the well-known French educator, writes: "The child has the cult of greatness and strength. His one ambition is to be big, his one pride is to be strong. . . . The piety of the child goes instinctively toward a God who is great and strong. He seeks in Him the compensation for his own weakness."[2]

We must also cultivate a *sense of wonder* and *sense of beauty*, both of which are still very much alive in children of seven or eight. "To approach life with a sense of wonder is a stepping-

[2] Hélène Lubienska de Lenval, *L'éducation du sens religieux* (Paris: Editions Spes, 1946), p. 128. This fact has implications for our teaching on Christ: the young child is drawn far more to the glorious and triumphant Christ than to a child who seems as weak and small as he himself is. See on this subject the article by François Coudreau, "Catechesis on Jesus Christ," in *Lumen Vitae*, 11 (July–September 1956), 401–26.

stone for continuous religious growth."[3] Wonder at what? At the natural goodness and beauty of creation first of all, through which are revealed the goodness and beauty of the Creator. If our school is near a park or in the country we are fortunate. But the beauties of nature are not absent even in our large modern cities. A bit of sky glimpsed through the window—a ray of light playing on the wall—the song of a bird—the snowflakes falling slowly—these and many other wonders surround us if only we have eyes to see and teach the children to see. If we are giving a lesson on creation it will help to take the children for a walk. It need not be a long one, and a few trees near the school suffice; even thirdgraders can delight in gathering and comparing handfuls of brightly colored fall leaves.

Let us not forget that our children are born in the space age. Already at the age of eight or nine they are becoming aware, both at home and in school, of science and its discoveries. We can capitalize on this to heighten their sense of God's greatness. For to look up at the night sky and its millions of stars flung in outer space is still more exciting than thinking of them as being set in the "firm vault of heaven."

The positive education of a sense of beauty must be accompanied by the negative aspect of removing, as much as is within our power, all that is ugly or untrue from the child. We shall come back to this when we discuss the importance of the environment.

Reverence and admiration, wonder and a sense of beauty—all these are already, in a way, part of the sense of God, since they find in him their highest cause and fulfillment. Once again we come back to the aim of religious education: faith in the living God. And where is this living God revealed to us above all? In the *Bible*. There is nothing like familiarity with the Bible for giving the children a sense of God. The human characteristics with which the Old Testament dares to endow Him make God as real to us as we ourselves are, while in the person of our Lord the holy, inaccessible, and invisible God takes on our very flesh and blood.

[3] Margaret Fisk Taylor, *Time for Wonder* (Philadelphia: The Christian Education Press, 1961), p. 11.

Never is the God of Judaeo-Christian revelation in danger of becoming a theological abstraction. God's "face" is revealed to us through his actions, through his intervening in human history. This is the great value of teaching the children salvation-history even at this early age.

One of the principal objects of the child's religious formation from the age of seven to ten is to make him familiar with God's loving design and His great interventions in human history. This should be done simply, by the use of loosely connected episodes and not by a strictly historical method, which will be beyond him until he reaches the age of ten or eleven.[4]

Education to Prayer

The meeting with God must be prepared for and built up gradually, over the years. It will take place in prayer, either in the spontaneous prayer of a moment, or in the more prolonged prayer of meditation. That is why prayer in one form or another should always be the culminating point of our teaching. This does not mean that we must introduce it artificially and at all costs. It should be an organic outgrowth of the lesson and an integral part of it, the natural response to the good news of God's love that has been presented. Nor should it ever become an inflexible routine. Nothing, indeed, is more harmful to sincere and genuine prayer than the regular recitation of certain fixed formulas at certain fixed times (for example, invariably at the beginning and at the end of class). It is better not to establish a fixed pattern. Sometimes the presentation of a lesson will lead to moments of intense silence and prayer; sometimes it will come at the end of class; sometimes at the beginning—but never as a means to establish external discipline and quiet, as we might be tempted to do! Prayer should not be used to create the proper atmosphere; rather, much effort on our part should go into creating an atmosphere in which prayer will be possible.

[4] Pierre Ranwez, S.J., et al., Together Toward God (Westminster, Md.: Newman, 1959), p. 103.

Children have a great facility for prayer, despite the many aspects of modern life that make it difficult (the noise and commotion, general lack of recollection, our inability to be alone with ourselves, the frenzied pace of our life, and the like). If, when we invite them to pray, they do not, it is often not because they are incapable of it but because we have placed them amid conditions which make prayer difficult or impossible.

We must pay attention first of all to the *physical setting*. Adults can on occasion succeed in making themselves independent of their environment, they can divest themselves of it. But children? They are at the stage of unfolding, of developing, of absorbing and taking into themselves their surroundings. If they do not consciously suffer from ugliness and noise, they feel it nonetheless.

We should not forget that for the child up to eight years of age at least it is a question of a kind of emotional response to the atmosphere that surrounds him—either by "direct assimilation" or by an attitude of reaction or opposition if the situation for one reason or another is intolerable.[5]

We can, it is true, hold a class in an ugly or tasteless environment; but it will not be possible under such circumstances for the teaching to take root in the soul. "The most skilful surgeon cannot succeed in a septic environment; he will only make the infection spread. If we make Demosthenes speak in a railroad station, no one will pay attention to him."[6] All that is disorderly, ugly, or dirty in the classroom will profoundly "wound" our teaching.

This does not mean that we must have all sorts of expensive equipment. If we cannot afford good art (which, incidentally, is not always the most expensive), let us have none. Better to have the walls bare than cluttered with confusion. However limited our funds may be, we can always see to it that the floor is swept, the classroom aired, the general impression one of order and simplicity. If not even a tree-top is visible through the window, we can bring nature into the classroom with a bunch of flowers (brought, per-

[5] Marc Oraison, *Love or Constraint?* (New York: Kenedy, 1959), p. 124.
[6] Lubienska de Lenval, *op. cit.*, p. 121.

haps, by one of the children). The quiet tone of our voice can help to draw the children away from the noise they have not yet wholly left behind.

If it is a case of teaching children who attend public school, we must help them, when they first arrive for class, to make the transition to the new world they are entering. We shall not begin abruptly, but shall first make them welcome, talking to individual children, making a link with their daily life. We shall try to create a congenial and warm atmosphere where the children will feel at home, so that the weekly hour of instruction will be less in danger of being completely isolated and in contradiction to their experience the rest of the week. Only after we have put them at ease will the beginning of our lesson which is technically called "preparation" follow.

The creation of the proper environment is not always easy, especially if we are using a room which is "lent" to us for our weekly hour of instruction. Maybe we don't like the sort of art that is around; maybe there are sixty immovable desks, whereas we would like to have some thirty chairs which can be arranged in different ways to suit the need of a particular lesson; maybe the focal point is a picture of the child Jesus, whereas it happens to be Eastertide or the end of the time after Pentecost, and we are telling the children that Christ now, and forever, is the risen and triumphant One. In such and similar cases we must use our ingenuity and do the best we can.[7]

In speaking of the proper atmosphere for prayer a few words must be said about the importance of silence. They will not be new to anyone familiar with the significant studies of Maria Montessori and Hélène Lubienska de Lenval. "Without silence one cannot hear God; one cannot hear oneself. Hence prayer is not possible."[8] The silence in question here is not mere absence of noise or talk

[7] In this connection the setting up of catechetical centers which is being discussed and done nowadays may turn out to be something other than a necessary evil. It would give us an unprecedented opportunity to construct and furnish buildings and rooms that could in every way be a fitting setting for our religious instruction.

[8] Lubienska de Lenval, *op. cit.*, p. 23.

imposed from without, but a positive and willed silence which is creative. The quiet way of speaking on the part of the teacher will help, as will a general state of order and peace. In addition, however, some effort will have to be made to train the children to observe complete silence and stillness from time to time. For in our world silence is seldom to be found. Not only are we afflicted by more external noise than past generations, but there is a restlessness within us which is the lack of interior silence. Since interior silence is the place where we meet God, we may not neglect it in the religious formation of our children. Physical exercises of relaxation as well as listening exercises are helpful here.[9] The following exercise was used with success during a lesson on the call of Abraham, in the fourth grade:

> God did not speak only to Abraham, he still speaks to us. But if we want to be able to hear him we must know how to listen. Let us try listening right now. Close your eyes and put your hands in front of your face, and listen to the sounds outside in the street. . . . What do you hear? . . . Now let us come inside our classroom. . . . I heart a chair creaking . . . someone's feet are moving . . . what else? . . . And now that everything is quiet around us, let us listen to ourselves, because when God speaks to us he speaks to our hearts, inside us.

By this time not a sound was to be heard, the children had grown completely still. The silence that had been established for these few moments not only carried over to the rest of the class that day, but the children remembered it the following week. Such an effort to establish silence may seem exaggerated to those of us who have come to take our large, noisy classes for granted. But anyone who has observed children trained to silence, absorbed in their work and fascinated by it, their power of concentration developed far above the average, will find it difficult to be satisfied with anything less. "If we can give to modern children some

---

[9] For Maria Montessori's "silence game" see E. M. Standing, *Maria Montessori, Her Life and Work* (Fresno: Academy Library Guild, 1957), pp. 178 f.

insight into the value of religious silence we shall be giving them
a great gift through which God may work his will. At a purely
psychological level, we may be saving them from who knows what
psychoses later in life!"[10] This religious silence is by no means to
be confused with enforced quiet for the sake of order, which begets total passivity of spirit. The silence we speak of must somehow
be elected by the child. He will be ready to express himself or to
move into action when it is required ever so much better if the
silence has been a thing of *his* doing.

To return to actual prayer. How should we pray in class with
the children—spontaneously or through formulas learned by heart,
silently or aloud? There is room, and need, for all different forms.
Spontaneous prayer can make a profound impression. The teacher
will normally be the one to pray in his own words, but gradually,
and at times, one of the children can be asked to do so; and, silently,
the entire class. For example: "Let us now be quite still for a
minute, close our eyes, and thank our heavenly Father for the
wonderful gift of his life in us." Set formulas, however, especially
the great prayers of the Christian such as the Our Father, the
sign of the cross, the Gloria Patri, and for children from the fourth
grade up, the Apostles' Creed, on occasion, must not be neglected.
We deprive the child of a precious help if we fail to teach him
these. But we must not overburden him with too heavy a load, or
with prayers which he cannot as yet understand (or worse still,
which are not "true" in content or text). Whenever we enter the
realm of the spiritual life, whether that of the child or the adult,
our axiom should be: quality, not quantity.

Litanies also have their place, and make it possible to combine
the spontaneous prayer of the catechist with the children's vocal
response. On certain occasions the children themselves can compose a litany, for example, a litany to their patron saints for the
feast of All Saints, each child invoking his patron and the whole
class responding, "Pray for us." Here is another kind of litany, one
which was prayed as entrance processional by the children of St.

[10] James D. Crichton, "Gesture and Chant in Religious Education," in
Lumen Vitae, 11 (October–December 1956), 632.

Barbara's School in Lawton, Oklahoma, at the end of Advent, during their last Mass together before Christmas; only a few typical invocations are given here:

> Let us ask our Lord to come and bring light to the world made
> dark by sin
>
>> *Response: Come to your People, O Lord!*
>
> That there may be peace in the world
> That all peoples may have the light of your truth
> To the young and the old
> To the poor and the rich
> To the sick and suffering
> To the children of this parish who worship you here

We should also acquaint the children with the great prayers of the Bible, especially with texts taken from the psalter, that inspired and most wonderful of all prayer books. While they are not yet capable of experiencing the whole gamut of emotion of the adult, every shade of which finds expression in the psalms, it is nevertheless true that the psalms are filled with those religious attitudes which are so essential to the spiritual life. A verse or two from a psalm will often make an excellent opening or closing prayer; if repeated a few times the children will easily learn it by heart, and thus we shall have equipped them with a priceless treasure for the rest of their lives. A few samples are given here; they are chosen at random and many others could be added.[11]

Ps.   83,   2   How lovely is your dwelling place, O Lord of Hosts!*

Ps.   91,   2   It is good to give thanks to the Lord, to sing praise to your name, Most High!*

Ps.   8,   2   Lord our Lord, how glorious is your name over all the earth!*

Ps.   42,   4   I will go into the altar of God, the God of my gladness and joy.*

Ps. 121,   1   I rejoiced because they said to me, "We will go up to the house of the Lord."*

[11] Music for the psalm verses marked * can be found in *Feast Day Melodies*, composed and edited by Grailville (Cincinnati: World Library of Sacred Music, 1957). To sing the psalms is better still than speaking them; see p. 150 below.

Ps. 32, 6   By the word of the Lord the heavens were made; by the breath of His mouth all their host.

Ps. 144, 16   You open your hand, and satisfy the desire of every living thing.

Ps. 146, 4   He tells the number of the stars; He calls each by name.

In teaching the children to pray, the catechist's own prayer plays an important part. Praying with them, turning with them to face the focal point of prayer, is more helpful in the long run than watching to see whether they are praying. What is true for the catechist in general is particularly true here: our own prayer must be the embodiment of our teaching on it. Moreover, we should at all times guard against giving the impression that the religion we teach is for children only and not for adults.

Initiation to the Sacraments

Initiation to the sacraments is one of the most important tasks of catechesis in the lower primary grades, perhaps indeed the most important. Technically the word "initiation" is confined to the second grade, since it is then that the children are normally prepared for first communion. However, we must not only prepare them for the sacraments they are about to receive for the first time, but also make them aware of those they have already received. For the seven-year-old this is baptism; while for eight- and nine-year-olds this will mean a deepening understanding of the eucharist and of penance (and preparation for confirmation in the fourth grade). First confession and first communion, then, must not be considered as goals in themselves; the religious attitudes awakened in the children on the occasion of this first sacramental initiation should henceforth become permanent in their lives. If the sacraments are truly the great acts of God in the life of the Christian, accompanying him all through life, strengthening and nourishing him, we may not be satisfied with an initiation geared to seven-year-olds.

Before speaking of preparation for first confession we shall consider the *formation of conscience* of the child. Only then will the sacrament of penance be seen in its proper perspective.

Too often in modern teaching . . . Christianity is confused with simple morality. Even the very rhythms of the spiritual life, the regular frequentation of the sacraments, are presented exclusively as a kind of administrative and obligatory rule of procedure. There is a way of imparting the positive instruction of the Church that is curiously akin to the regulations of the Pharisees.[12]

Such a legalistic outlook fails to do justice to the Christian message of joy and love. Christianity is something altogether different from the observance of a certain number of laws and duties. Its dynamic and formative power comes not from the imposition of the law from without, but from the new, life-giving law of love operative from within. This has been expressed very well in several articles by the Oratorian Tilmann.[13] He uses the expression "living with God" to define an attitude in which God and life with him embrace and penetrate everything. The norm here is not the punctilious observance of the ten commandments, but a joyful, spontaneous, and fresh approach to life:

If we constantly say "you must" and "you must not . . . ," if we always speak of "fulfilling religious obligations," if we make the whole of Christian life depend on the ten commandments, we disfigure God's plan of salvation. Religion will then become a burden rather than life, and we shall arouse [in the children] dislike rather than love of God. How can the child have an inkling that the spiritual life is self-development to the highest degree and deepest fulfillment of life? All religious education which does not have joy as its basis is "crooked" psychologically and theologically, and misrepresents both God and man.[14]

Doing the right thing must not be a duty imposed from without, but our free and joyful answer to the message of God's love. We

[12] Oraison, op. cit., pp. 123 f.
[13] Klemens Tilmann, "Initiation to Life with God," in Lumen Vitae, 15 (March 1960), 31–42; see also Katechetische Blätter, 85 (January 1960), 29–35; (February 1960), 71–75; (March 1960), 120–25.
[14] Tilmann, Katechetische Blätter, 85 (September 1960), 405.

must teach the children to identify what is right and good with what is beautiful, hence easy; and to see wrongdoing and evil as they really are: ugly, hence undesirable.

Preparation for first confession must be such that it will not be necessary at a later stage to unlearn what was then learned; rather, it will simply be a matter of adding to and deepening the knowledge that has already been acquired. At the same time, we must not overtax the child's capacity by asking more of him than he is capable of giving at the age of seven. For as Dr. Josef Goldbrunner points out, although confession is an eminently personal act of encounter with God and a free decision, this personal aspect will not, in the case of young children, be the dominant one.[15] What, then, should receive the main emphasis?

The most important part of confession is contrition. This presupposes that the child already has some sense of God, of His holiness and, by contrast, of his own lack of it. We must dwell on this rather than attaching too much importance to lists of sins "duly catalogued and so to speak prefabricated, taken from Mosaic law rather than from the Gospel law of Jesus."[16] Dr. Joseph Collins also warns against using the lists of sins in certain prayerbooks and texts for first confession, saying that "most of the 'offenses' listed are not sins."[17] Nor should we be greatly concerned with clear and precise formulation of his faults by the child. Expression of his faults is difficult for him because until now it has not been necessary, and because his language is still elementary. If the priest cannot make out entirely what he is saying, "he should not worry too much, provided he can discern the accent of sincerity and truth which is worth far more than all the same old stories expressed in beautiful language."[18]

[15] Josef Goldbrunner, *Teaching the Sacraments* (New York: Herder and Herder, 1961), p. 11

[16] Ranwez, "Catechesis and Liturgy," in *Lumen Vitae*, 10 (April–June, 1955), 275.

[17] Joseph B. Collins, *Teaching Religion* (Milwaukee: Bruce, 1953), p. 259.

[18] Ranwez, "Forming a Moral Conscience in the Very Young Child," in *Lumen Vitae*, 15 (March 1960), 77.

Not to insist on a ready-made list of sins does not mean, however, that we may neglect to train the child in examining his conscience. On the contrary, this should be done carefully and thoroughly. We recommend here the plan proposed by Goldbrunner.[19] Instead of the ten commandments he uses headings such as the following: Living with God; The Honor of God; Sundays and Holy Days; Parents; Neighbor; and the like. All ten headings are seen, not as commandments, but as "signposts" on our road to God.[20] On the front of each signpost is written a positive "wish" of God; for example, on the fourth: "God wants us to obey our parents and to give them joy." Once the child knows what it is that God wants of him it will not be difficult for him to see where he has fallen short of God's wishes. An entire lesson is given to the explanation of each signpost, and at the end of each the children, guided by key questions from the catechist, examine their conscience quietly and for themselves on a particular point. Little by little they are thus led to look into their hearts and to see for themselves where they have failed to respond to God's love. Each of the headings is comprehensive enough so that, as the child matures, it can be widened to include all aspects of adult life. What is at this time taught as preparation for first confession must subsequently be continued and deepened. Preparation for first confession must contain everything in germ.

The morality of the gradeschool child is a morality of obedience. This is the time for learning, for developing habits, in the spiritual life as elsewhere, and especially in regard to the sacraments.[21] We should therefore give the child a firm "scaffolding" for the external procedure (the five acts of confession), so that he will feel secure and, with its help, will more easily overcome a possible time of crisis later in life. A certain feeling of familiarity with what he must do is necessary if we are to avoid making him afraid of his first confession. Usually the cause for fear is that we over-

[19] Goldbrunner, *op. cit.*, pp.17 ff.
[20] See also Sister Maria de la Cruz, *Christ Leads the Way*, Vol. IV of "On Our Way" series (New York: Sadlier, 1960), pp. 37 f.
[21] Goldbrunner, *op. cit.*, p. 11.

emphasize the importance of the confession of sins, and that we demand feats of memorization which he is incapable of performing. "Completeness" in the confession of venial sins is not required even of adults, much less of children.

Care should of course be taken not to draw attention away from the inner reality of the sacrament to a merely outward observance. It is precisely in order to make him as free as possible for the essence of the sacrament (contrition and resolution) that the external "scaffolding" is given. A long-range progressive preparation, beginning with developing a sense of God and training of the conscience, is necessary if the child is one day to enter into a fully personal relationship with God. As to the important distinction between venial and mortal sin: we must show him the full weight of mortal sin, but we add here that young children, while they can commit objectively grave sins, cannot yet offend mortally.[22]

Preparation for first communion is at the same time preparation for a more conscious and active participation in the Mass. Here even more than elsewhere our catechesis must lay foundations for life, and must be an introduction to the mystery of the eucharist in all its breadth and depth. We must take care to develop a true eucharistic piety, not an isolated "communion piety." To treat of only one aspect of the sacrament while neglecting others would be to lay poor foundations: all aspects must be present from the beginning. In the case of young children, however, we shall stress first of all that which they can actually see, leading them only by degrees more deeply into the totality of the mystery.

The starting point for our eucharistic catechesis will be the sacramental principle itself. We shall proceed from the visible, external form to the invisible, inner reality. We must take the sacramental signs seriously. In this case they are bread and wine, and the setting is a communal meal. And so, starting with the eucharist as food and meal, beneath which the sacrifice is hidden, we shall gradually penetrate more deeply into the sacrament. Such a procedure is not only in accord with the sacramental principle and

[22] Josef A. Jungmann, S.J., *Handing On the Faith* (New York: Herder and Herder, 1959), p. 303.

the inductive method, but also with Scripture. The biblical figures of the eucharist—the manna, the paschal lamb, the water from the rock—as well as Our Lord's own words in promising the bread of life, all point in this direction.

An important part of preparation for first communion is helping the child to independent prayer immediately after he has received the eucharist. This is the moment when the personal encounter with the risen Lord should be stressed. The lesson worked out by Goldbrunner[23] suggests the procedure to be followed here: we lead the child successively to silent adoration, greeting the risen Lord, thanksgiving, and petition for himself and for others. Here also the aim is to equip him with a basic procedure which can support him later, when habit and routine will often dull the sensitivity of the soul.

We should avoid too intensive a preparation for first communion and expressions such as "the most beautiful day of your life." Not only are the latter theologically incorrect (is it really conceivable that the spiritual climax for man, who not infrequently lives to a ripe old age, should come at the age of seven?), but also using them invites trouble. Once the long prepared-for day has come and gone a natural reaction will set in. A sounder approach is to speak of this day as the first on which the child will be allowed to participate fully in the Mass, in the same way as his family and all other adults.

The chief task of eucharistic education comes after, not before first communion. For the *opus operantis*—the efforts of the recipient—have their effect only after the gift has been given, in cooperation with the grace received. Eucharistic catechesis, therefore, far from suddenly ending with first communion, must be continued in an ascending movement. What began as preparatory catechesis is now deepened. To neglect this is to neglect the most important part, and is to lend support to the idea that the sacraments work like magic. Thus eucharistic education will continue in the third and fourth grades (and in the upper grades also) as

[23] *Op. cit.*, pp. 111 ff.; see also Sister M. Noella, *Ready for Sunday* (O'Fallon, Mo.: Precious Blood Convent, 1960), p. 2.

education for the Mass. We shall encourage the children to receive holy communion frequently, but above all reverently and
with the right intention. We shall make sure that from now on
confession and communion are not indissolubly linked in their
minds. We shall also do what we can to prevent frequent reception of communion from degenerating into an external habit, as
can so easily happen. A rule which could well be followed is:
"(1) I must go: once a year. (2) I should go: every Sunday and holy
day. (3) I may go: every day."[24]

POINTS ON METHOD

Although our method must at all times be subservient to the
aim and content of religious education, this does not mean that
it is unimportant.[25] Indeed, only the best possible method is
worthy to be the "carrier" of the message God has entrusted to
us. We shall not discuss here any one particular method, for this
has been done competently elsewhere,[26] but shall give the chief
characteristics which should mark any method we use.

Our method must first of all be *psychological,* that is to say, it
must be based on the needs and capacities of the child at any
given stage. If we give too much too soon, if we want to give
spiritual food before the hunger for it is there, we run the risk
of killing the latent "appetite" before it has ever awakened. Instead of doing violence to the child, we shall follow his development and make our teaching correspond to it. We must be aware
of the laws of growth in him, if our teaching is to support rather
than hinder them. God has placed within each living thing a
power for growth, an "overwhelming power to be itself, to maintain its individual existence, to be with, one might almost say, in-

[24] *Ibid.,* pp. 121 ff.

[25] For a treatment of the relation of method to content, see Goldbrunner,
"Catechetical Method as Handmaid of Kerygma," in *Teaching All Nations*
(New York: Herder and Herder, 1961), pp. 108–33.

[26] See G. Emmett Carter, *The Modern Challenge to Religious Education*
(New York: Sadlier, 1961), pp. 271 ff.; on the Munich Method, see Jungmann,
op. cit., pp. 180–92, and Goldbrunner, "Catechetical Method . . . ," pp.
108 ff.

tense tenacity its unique self."[27] Since both the laws of growth and the desire to be "one's unique self" are given by God, we may set about our task of education with a basically optimistic outlook. We shall cultivate the child's powers and faculties and know and trust those drives in him which can become the basis for his Christian life and of which the latter is meant to be the fulfillment: his desire to develop and unfold, to accomplish and succeed, to be loved and appreciated and in turn to love and appreciate. What is demanded of the catechist is more than an optimistic outlook, however (which by itself would fail to take into account the deep wound wrought in human nature by sin); he must be rooted in the theological virtue of hope. As Louis Lochet wrote some years ago in *Lumen Vitae:*

> His love as a teacher makes him cooperate with the psychological center of each and discover the possible lines of progress. He does not judge him in a static way, from what he is, but calls forth the man he is to be. . . . To know a man is to discover his possibilities. . . . To hope is to look at someone with God's eyes; already this raises him, makes a man of him. . . . Hope engenders life. . . . The teacher's hope is like the sun, the warmth, the vivifying atmosphere, which causes good desires to germinate and good will to spring up.[28]

If our method is truly based on psychological needs, it will of its very nature be an *active* method. "Doing is basic; it includes the whole human person with all his creative powers."[29] To learn by doing is to learn on a deeper level. We still tend to identify learning too exclusively with the acquisition of intellectual knowledge. For the development of a healthy personality, "it is of the utmost significance that a proper balance be kept between emotional and intellectual growth."[30] Moreover, the child is not "differentiated," his entire being is involved in all that he does: body

[27] Oraison, *op. cit.,* p. 18.

[28] Louis Lochet, "The Christian Teacher as a Man of Hope," in *Lumen Vitae,* 9 (July–September 1954), 400 f.

[29] Romano Guardini, *Sacred Signs* (St. Louis: Pio Decimo Press, 1956), p. 12.

[30] Viktor Lowenfeld, *Creative and Mental Growth* (3d ed.; New York: Macmillan, 1960), p. 54.

and soul, emotions and will, muscles and thought. If we try to isolate his intellect from the rest we are guilty of an artificial departmentalization which will be disastrous not only to the process of learning, but to the development of a whole, balanced, and healthy human being.

Our present-day, vastly improved methods in education all originated in the secular field; in the case of religious education, they must be brought into the service of the life of faith. "Children must see, move, touch, act on objects, but they must also find God."[31] Indeed, all their activity (and ours) is for the sake of this. That is why activity for activity's sake is not enough. It is not enough even in secular education. As catechists we must constantly rethink and reevaluate our activities in the light of the goal of our catechesis: are they contributing to the child's faith, are they helping him advance toward the meeting with the living God?

Before considering those activities which are of the greatest profit to religious education, let us say a word about the principle which underlies them all: *creativity*. The child has an instinctive need to create. He will create even if we do not teach him how, for his creativity is his means of expressing himself. It will take many forms: "Children naturally express their ideas and imagination in words and melody, in paint and chalk and clay, in playing a story and in dancing. They are born to be artists, destined by Providence to be makers in (God's) image."[32] All these various forms of expression are the child's way of giving external shape and body to what is happening in the secret depths of the soul. If little or nothing is happening, there will be no external expression either. If, on the other hand, we constantly impede the external expression, for example, by insisting that he sit still, hands on desk, and listen passively to what Canon Drinkwater has graphically styled "that constant cataract of verbal unreality,"[33]

[31] Marie Fargues, *Catéchisme pour notre temps* (Paris: Editions Spes, 1951), p. 16.
[32] Sister Mary Nona, O.P., "Know You What It Is to Be a Child?" Part 1, in *The Catholic Educational Review*, 58 (April 1960), 228.
[33] F. H. Drinkwater, *Telling the Good News* (London: Macmillan, 1960), p. 223.

the interior movement of the soul too will gradually become atrophied. Man's supernatural life takes place within the total body-soul composite. "In order that he may think, believe, hope, and love, he must express it. He expresses himself because he thinks and he thinks because he expresses himself. His interior life, origin of the expression, is in turn intensified by the very fact that he is able to express it."[34] To develop his creative faculties is therefore not only valid but essential for religious education. Let us now look briefly at the various forms this creativity will take.

The most fundamental of all is *gesture*.[35] The younger the child, the more important this form of expression. It is still ideally used in the second grade, before he loses his spontaneity and unselfconsciousness.[36]

Everyone has experienced to some extent the power of gesture as language: the movement of the hand stretched out in welcome or support—the turning away of the face in contempt—the shrug of shoulders in indifference—the hiding of one's face in shame or sorrow. Why not make use of this powerful language also in the classroom? Gesture is rooted in the wholeness of man, and can in turn be a means to preserve his wholeness. Mme. Lubienska de Lenval calls gesture the most spontaneous expression of the soul. It is not only an expression of ourselves; in expressing us it creates us. The liturgy is a powerful example of this: in bowing and striking the breast we actually experience contrition; in standing erect during the proclamation of the gospel we are present with our whole being to the Word of God, and the like.

Let us teach the children a simple "alphabet of gesture": walking erect and slowly, standing, genuflecting, kneeling, raising the arms in wonder and thanksgiving, bowing profoundly in adoration. This will facilitate their liturgical participation, for "from a

34 Fargues, *op. cit.*, p. 124.
35 See on the subject of gesture the slight but excellent book by Guardini cited above.
36 For an excellent and practical treatment of creative movement for children of five, six and seven, see Taylor, *op. cit.*

human point of view, the liturgy is a highly developed art-form which needs an initiation before it can be profitably used."[37] Moreover, practicing liturgical gestures in the classroom allows us a range of expression which, during the actual celebration, is reserved to the priest alone (for example, praying the Preface responses with arms uplifted, in the ancient "Orante" posture).

Whenever possible, a short practice of these basic gestures should be followed by a visit to church. Before entering the children are reminded of the sacredness of the house of God, and that He lives there in a special way. Then they enter quietly and reverently, and the gestures which have just been practiced in class become prayer. It is best to keep such visits brief, centered on a single, common purpose. For instance: "Let us now go and thank God for the beautiful world he has given us by standing before him, very straight, raising our arms, and singing: "O Lord our Lord, how wonderful is your name in all the earth, alleluia!"[38] Many times our moments of prayer at the beginning or end of class will be more intense because the word is united to an appropriate gesture. But they should be few, simple, and meaningful, and must be repeated often enough so that the children will feel at ease in them.

Here are some simple gestures that were worked out for children in the second and third grades to accompany the praying of the Our Father:

Our Father who art in heaven	hands folded, looking upward
Hallowed be thy name . . .	
. . . as it is in heaven	slowly raising the arms
Give us this day our daily bread	putting out both hands, palms slightly cupped
And forgive us our trespasses	bowing the head and striking the breast
As we forgive those who . . .	turning to each other and bowing
And lead us . . . Amen.	folding the hands

[37] Crichton, *op. cit.*, p. 631.
[38] *Feast Day Melodies*, p. 10.

As the children grow older they begin to find expression in gesture more difficult, unless they have been trained in it when they were little. But if the teacher uses gesture spontaneously and unaffectedly, even children in the third and fourth grades will, with a little practice, follow.[39]

Art and art education also play an important role in our method.

Art education, introduced in the early years of childhood, may well mean the difference between a flexible, creative human being and *one who, in spite of all learning, will not be able to apply it and will remain an individual who lacks inner resources.* . . . Because perceiving, thinking, and feeling are equally stressed in any creative process art may well be the necessary balance for the child's intellect and his emotions.[40]

We must keep in mind, however, that art is not the same for the child as for the adult. He does not approach it as art, but only as a means of expression. This is particularly true of the child up to seven or eight, in whom the critical faculty and the tendency to compare his pictures with those of adults have not yet awakened. Nor is art to him merely a distraction. It is his means of expressing himself, of bringing to the light of day questions or difficulties of which he is often but dimly aware, and in so doing, not infrequently overcoming them. Art is therefore valuable to the child, in the first place. But it is also useful to the teacher. A drawing may reveal to him inaccuracies or gaps in his teaching. More important, as he learns to read the "language" of a child's picture it will tell him things about the child-traits in his character, his emotional state, some hidden joy or sorrow, his sense of God. The child will unconsciously express things in drawing which he cannot put into words. Here is an example: after a lesson on Moses

[39] The value of Gregorian eurhythmics (the expression of chant in bodily movement) has been strikingly revealed by the work of the late Dom Ermin Vitry. It is not being discussed here because Dom Vitry maintained that children under ten are not yet sufficiently in command of their bodies to practice eurhythmics. Gesture, singing the chant, and "pulsing" it are the normal preparation for eurhythmics with younger children.

[40] Lowenfeld, *op. cit.*, p. 2; italics added.

and the burning bush, a seven-year-old drew an enormous bush and a tiny Moses. No words could have conveyed as graphically Moses' (and the child's) awe before the greatness of God.

In speaking of drawing the greater value of free drawing over mere coloring or copying should be stressed. What is "free" is not, generally speaking, the theme, but the child's expression of what he has understood and experienced of a given theme as it was presented by the teacher. Often this presentation will be in story form, especially if the theme is taken from Scripture. (Hence the importance of being able to tell a story well; the catechist who wants to make the children draw must be a good story-teller). In listening to it the child lives the story, identifies himself with its characters, is in sympathy with them or dislikes them. When invited to draw the scene he will quite naturally do so in terms of what he has just experienced. If he does not know how to draw— or thinks he does not—it is not enough to repeat the invitation (or order!); nor is it enough to help him physically, by choosing the colors for him, suggesting the layout, and all the other "helps" we so readily proffer. What he needs is to live the story more intensely. This alone will help him overcome his shyness, awkwardness, lack of skill, fear, or whatever it is that impedes his free expression. Let us take as an example the call of Moses. It is no use simply repeating, "Draw Moses and the burning bush," if the child sits before the empty piece of paper and does not know where to begin. We must help him with questions such as these: "What would you do if you saw a bush on fire and not burning up? . . . Would you be afraid if God told you that he is hidden inside the fire? . . . How would you greet him?" etc.

Drawings of the main events and people of salvation-history made during the year can serve as an enjoyable way of review from time to time: they are pasted on a long roll of paper, in the right order; each end of the roll is attached to a pole or stick, which in turn is inserted through two holes at each end of an open cardboard box. The box is set on the teacher's desk with the open end facing the class, and the drawings are slowly unrolled, while each child tells the story of his picture. This movie-like procedure is greatly enjoyed even by fourthgraders.

The teacher of religion is not, most of the time, an art teacher; indeed, he may not be able to draw well himself. This does not matter, for our aim is not a perfect artistic product but to help the child live a religious experience. We must take his drawing seriously and receive it with respect, no matter how strange it may seem to us. A child draws as he thinks, and a seven-year-old thinks differently from the adult. If we do not understand what he has drawn, let us simply and quietly ask him to explain it to us. He will not refuse, if he senses in our request a real desire to understand.

Even though our primary concern is not with the artistic quality of the picture, we should keep in mind certain things that will help him in his task. Children from seven to nine have no difficulty in drawing *things* (because things don't move); animals are more of a problem, people nearly impossible (because they not only move but also think—and how is one to draw that?). We shall encourage them to start with the setting (e.g., the hillside and grass and "crowd" of the multiplication of loaves); once the paper is no longer despairingly empty and large they will have more courage to tackle the central figures.

Acting is another valuable form of expression, and much of what has been said with reference to drawing applies here also. Again, it is not the finished performance that matters; if we place too great emphasis on this, e.g., if all the effort goes into putting on a performance that will please the parents, the spontaneity and freshness will be lost, and with them the value of acting as the child's means of expression.[41] Elaborate costumes can be a distraction; but a few strips of colored cloth skilfully used as veils, cloaks, etc., will help the children to go out of themselves and identify themselves with the role they are to portray.

In motivating the child to act, it is again the teacher's skill in rendering the story that will be decisive. Our telling of it must be

41 Collins, *op. cit.*, pp. 235 ff.

so absorbing that the children's inhibitions will be overcome. In order that their expression may be true, they must have entered into the situation, forgetting themselves and their own personality. If their gestures lack this truth we must go back to the source, start all over with the story, make it live the more for them. Once the child is able to identify himself with his role, acting can become a powerful means for him to break through the "imprisonment of his own ego."[42]

The importance of the art of story telling has been mentioned already with reference to drawing and acting; the teacher of the lower primary grades cannot afford to be deficient in it. For "it is just at the time when the imagination is most keen, the mind being unhampered by an accumulation of facts, that stories appeal most vividly and are retained for all time."[43] Because he realizes the importance of the imagination as a means of reaching the child's intellect,

the teacher uses examples and illustrations which will bring the pupil by way of imaginative situations to the sure ground of understanding. Only by these can he—or we ourselves—see into the meaning of abstract ideas. Christ, who knew what was in man, introduced sublime truths by recourse to the imagination of His listeners. The Gospels are filled with similes and parables. . . . Every story told by Our Lord was an invitation to learn of God by the power of imagining which He had given to the men and women gathered about Him.[44]

[42] As to material for acting: while Christ's miracles and parables provide a wealth of exciting matter, care should be taken not to act them out in the same way as a play. The atmosphere and setting should be prayerful and reverent, resembling a paraliturgical celebration rather than a play. On this subject see Coudreau, *op. cit.*, p. 425.—For primary school plays, see F. H. Drinkwater, *Prophets and Kings* (London: University of London Press, 1952).

[43] Marie Shedlock, *The Art of the Story-teller* (New York: Dover, 1951), p. xvii. This book contains many useful hints on story telling, as does the work of Ruth Sawyer, *The Way of the Story-teller* (New York: Viking, 1942).

[44] Sister Mary Nona, *op. cit.*, Part 2, in *The Catholic Educational Review*, 58 (May 1960), 289.

Much of the time the stories will be taken from Scripture; lives of the saints too can be helpful, especially in making the children aware that they belong to the great family of God.[45] As to fairy tales, there is no doubt at all that children enjoy them, especially the younger ones. Should we for this reason use them in religious education? In the case of seven- and eight-year-olds, we do not think so. They are not yet able to distinguish between fact and fiction, and there is danger that they will put fairy tales on the same level as the stories from Scripture. Later, when they learn that "this isn't true at all," the truth of the Bible will be endangered. We must not allow the miracles of Christ's life, for instance, to be confused with magic. This does not mean that fairy tales have no place in religious education. As the children grow older (from the fourth grade on) they may sometimes be used with great profit, since many fairy tales point up some religious truth.

All the creative activities mentioned so far—gesture, drawing, acting—lose their attraction for children as they grow older. But there is one which will appeal to them at every stage of life: *song.* For this reason it occupies a privileged place among all the other forms of expression. "Singing is an activity involving the child's whole personality. A child spontaneously sings with his entire being. The song becomes for him a concrete reality—its total concept part of the child's thinking."[46] Moreover song, like gesture, is woven into the liturgy to the extent that there can be no full-bodied worship without it. We refer here to the work of Dom

[45] For Scripture stories, see Daniel-Rops, *The Book of Books,* and *The Book of Life* [stories from the Old and New Testament] (New York: Kenedy, 1956).—Among the many lives of the saints, here are some of the most recent ones: Daniel-Rops, *Golden Legend of Young Saints* (New York: Kenedy, 1960); the *Patron Saints Books* published by Sheed and Ward, 1959; Katharine Wood, *The Twelve Apostles,* and *The Four Evangelists* (New York: Kenedy, 1956 and 1959); and Mary Reed Newland, *The Adventures of Catherine of Siena* (New York: Kenedy, 1960). For catechism stories, see F. H. Drinkwater, *Catechism Stories* (Westminister, Md.: Newman Press, 1948).

[46] Richard H. Werder, in *Music Education,* Proceedings of the Workshop held at The Catholic University of America, June 12 to June 23, 1953, published by The Catholic University of America Press, 1954.

Ermin Vitry, in particular to his outstanding article on "Music and Prayer,"[47] and to his slogan, "singing our way to God."

Because ours is not, by and large, a singing society, it may well happen that our children have not yet experienced the beauty and joy of singing when they arrive in our classrooms. Let us give it to them by singing with them, by joining song to our prayer in gesture and word. We need not be expert musicians in order to sing with the children, but of course a good ear, sense of rhythm and pitch are helpful![48]

The Liturgy

In leaving this topic to the last we do not mean to imply that we consider it merely another point under "Method," of equal importance with the rest. On the contrary, it is in a certain sense the summing up and climax of what has been said so far. In the first place, the liturgy exemplifies all that modern psychology and pedagogy have taught us about method. It makes use of the principle of *activity*, instructing through action as much as through word. The liturgy demands of us no mere passive onlooking, but an activity involving our body and senses in a quiet alternation of standing, sitting, kneeling, walking, speaking, singing, etc.

The Church has always been aware of the importance of en-

---

[47] E. Vitry, "Music and Prayer," *Orate Fratres*, 25 (Oct.–Nov. 1951), 549–58.

[48] For simple Gregorian chants for the second and third grades, see Dom Ermin Vitry, *Praise and Song Series, Books One and Two* (O'Fallon, Mo.: 1947). The third and fourth books are available from Fides Jubilans, 3401 Arsenal St., St. Louis 18, Mo.—For psalm settings, see Joseph Gélineau, *Twenty-four Psalms and a Canticle* (Toledo: Gregorian Institute of America, 1955); for short songs taken from the texts of the liturgy, see *Feast Day Melodies* (Cincinnati: World Library of Sacred Music, 1957). Among songs in general, Negro spirituals are particularly recommended: the melodies are nearly always good, the strong rhythm makes them easy to learn, and the words are often much closer to Scripture than those of many modern songs. Spirituals can be found to suit many different occasions (e.g., "The heavens are shining . . ." for a lesson on creation). The children can act them out, clap to them, or sing them reverently as prayer. For a good and inexpensive ($.25) collection of spirituals, see *Look Away* (Delaware, Ohio: Cooperative Recreation Service, Inc., n.d.).

vironment for worship, and spares no pains to bring into the service of God all that is beautiful: light and color, movement, sound, art. "The liturgy is a symphony of action, sound, and word, all of which are symbols appealing to the whole man, and conveying divine truth and strength to man."[49] Because the liturgy appeals to the *whole man*, it succeeds in unifying him, making of body and soul the obedient instruments of the spirit.[50]

The liturgy is, moreover, a great school, even though (perhaps just because?) its primary concern is the glory of God and not the education of man. A school of doctrine, but doctrine prayed, sung, gestured, dramatized, and thus brought within the reach of the children. A school, too, of *reverence*, for the holiness of God shines through it.

If we do well to look back to the early Church for a profound understanding of the liturgy's educative and formative role in the life of the Christian,[51] we must also keep in mind that the early Church realized very well that sound instruction must precede, accompany and follow liturgical participation. If this was true at a time when the liturgical rites were still far more "transparent" than they are today and were performed with words which the congregation could hear and understand, it is still more true today. As Fr. Johannes Hofinger points out,[52] while meaningful and active participation in the Church's worship is more important than religious instruction courses in school, we may not neglect instruction. We must "unlock" the liturgy for the children, not by overwhelming them with a mass of details, but by giving them certain key concepts which will open up all the rest: the centrality of Christ—a sense of the Church (for little ones the "family of God")—baptism as our initiation into the life of God—the eucharist as a sacrificial meal—the liturgical year as the constant un-

[49] Crichton, *loc. cit.*, p. 637.
[50] Lubienska de Lenval, *Le silence à l'ombre de la parole* (Tournai: Editions Casterman, 1956), p. 50.
[51] See Jungmann, *op. cit.*, pp. 1–10.
[52] *The Art of Teaching Christian Doctrine* (Notre Dame: University of Notre Dame Press, 1962), p. 41.

folding before our eyes of the mystery of Christ. The basic attitudes mentioned in the first part of this chapter are also essential to liturgical education, and will in turn be fostered by it. The degree of participation should, whenever possible, be adapted to the capacity of the children. Of secondgraders we shall expect only the simplest Latin responses and a few easy psalm verses or short songs; only little by little shall we teach the longer prayers of the Mass.

The liturgy has rightly been called "a veritable catechetical treasure house";[53] but this does not yet constitute its highest function in religious education. In bringing this chapter to a close we revert once more to the goal stated at the outset—the meeting with the living God. It is above all in the liturgy that this meeting takes place, for it is here that "God keeps descending among men and men keep rising to God."[54] It is here that we come into direct contact with the life-giving acts of Christ. Through his death and resurrection he has won a kingdom, and of this kingdom the Church is the witness and sign.

Therefore she reflects something of the majesty and power and beauty of that kingdom . . . She is conscious of the presence in her midst of him who was dead and is now alive forevermore, of him who is the Victor King. Something of the majesty of the risen King of Glory must fill his temple . . . His presence in our worship means that the world to come, the *vitam venturi saeculi*, breaks in upon this world, and heaven comes down to earth.[55]

We can say, therefore, that the liturgy is not only the most important means at our disposal in attaining the goal, but is in a sense already the goal attained.

[53] Hofinger, *op. cit.*, p. 36.
[54] Vagaggini, *Theological Dimensions of the Liturgy* (Collegeville, Minn.: Liturgical Press, 1960), p. 53.
[55] W. O'Shea, *The Worship of the Church* (Westminster, Md.: Newman, 1958), pp. 26 f.

7 RELIGIOUS EDUCATION

IN THE INTERMEDIATE GRADES

Sister Anne Norpel, S.N.D.

THE psychological and sociological insights of our day suggest that the natural development of children in the intermediate grades provides innumerable possibilities for religious growth along certain lines. Hence, at this crucial time in the child's development it is equally important to know the subject of religious formation, the child, and the subject matter, the message of Christ. A twofold obligation rests upon every teacher of religion: first, the duty to study, to read, to perfect himself in all that relates to the science of theology; and second, to gain new insights into his pupils' needs and abilities, for since he is a catechist his primary work is to engage in a pedagogy of faith. The educator must form for himself the most complete picture possible of the interior world of the child and do so objectively. Only then can the interior world of Christian mystery—equally objective—have any meaning for the child.

The late pontiff Pius XII realized very well the gravity of the catechist's obligation in this regard. Addressing an international meeting of catechists during the Holy Year of Jubilee in 1950 he said:

154

The catechist will wholly deceive himself and err gravely if he feels that a sketchy and superficial knowledge is sufficient for the untrained mind of learners. The very contrary is true. The teacher is actually obliged by his office not only to explain all the essentials of faith, but also to accommodate them even to the level of those who are slow to understand or are lacking in educational background. He should accordingly apply himself to the study of psychology to determine accurately their intellectual ability; moreover he ought to give serious attention to their needs in order to meet them.[1]

Children in the intermediate grades are generally nine, ten, and eleven years old, with slight age extensions on both ends. In conformity with the late Holy Father's exhortation, an investigation of the psychology of the students under discussion is in order here. Because the stages of child development overlap considerably, a few initial observations will be made on the upper level of the age group treated in the previous chapter.

THE FOURTH GRADE

The nine-year-old is just beginning to emerge from self. The words "just beginning" can be underscored. According to Piaget, between the ages of eight and eleven a real evolution in the child's concept of reality takes place.[2] Three steps mark his awareness of the world outside himself. He passes *from realism to objectivity* when he distinguishes what comes from himself and what things are as they appear to others. His next step is *from realism to reciprocity*, when, after entertaining his own point of view as absolute, he comes to realize other points of view. His third advance, *from realism to relativity*, takes place when realities outside himself no longer have a claim in his mind to being totally

[1] Pope Pius XII, *Allocutio in Acta Congressus Catechistici Internationalis MCML* (Roma: Typis Polyglottis Vaticanis, 1953), p. 187. Eng. tr. in Raymond B. Fullam, S.J., *The Popes on Youth* (Buffalo: Canisius High School, 1956), p. 93.

[2] Jean Piaget, *The Child's Concept of Physical Causality* (New York: Harcourt Brace, 1930), pp. 241–53.

independent substances or attributes. At an earlier age the child has failed to see the interdependence of life and movement, but by degrees he becomes conscious of a universe of relations which replaces the universe of independent and spontaneous substances.

These three steps proceed from the social to the intellectual to the social/intellectual order. As the child becomes conscious of his "I," external reality is stripped of the subjective element, and we say that objectivity has been reached. It is the social character of life that has forced the child to become conscious of his ego. We may conclude that the egocentric tendency is on the decrease as the child becomes more and more conscious of his own subjectivity.

This course of events makes the nine-year-old no longer a mere child but one who has the capacity to assume responsibilities. He understands explanations and wants to do things well. With ideas of justice and fair play prominent, his perception of right and wrong is becoming keener. His growing reflective habits recognize both property rights and the rights of individual persons. *The development of the ethical sense makes age nine the optimal time for character development.*[3] Since children of this age are receptive to explanation, they are ready for a clearer delineation of the Christian way of life. It is time to present those motives which will be efficacious in helping the child to overcome temptations of the future.

Moral Education in a Context of Religious Education

At this age, it is apropos to discuss moral life in its social context. An education with the notion of fault and punishment dominating it may be termed moral, but certainly it is not religious.[4] One who is absorbed in an egocentric preoccupation with his own failure in a given crisis is overemphasizing a secondary matter. It is his relationship with the Other that is primary, but of

[3] Arnold Gesell and Frances Ilg, "The Child from Five to Ten," *Child Development* (New York: Harpers, 1949), pp. 188–91; 210 f.

[4] Marc Oraison, D.D., M.D., *Love or Constraint?* (New York: Kenedy, 1959), p. 97.

course this realization depends on the emotional maturity and progressive autonomy that is desirable for every human being. This stature is not arrived at all at once. The abyss between immaturity and fulfillment in all phases of life (or in any one phase) is not bridged overnight. Involved is a slow and sometimes painful development, all bound up with the learning process. Trial-and-error is one way of learning. A child seeks that which will bring him praise or be a practical good as he sees it. If he chooses a false good he must pay the penalty. Humility (which builds on humiliation) is a by-product of learning, particularly when the learning takes place by way of a fall. However, though knowledge is the fountainhead from which much good springs, in the realm of self-discipline knowledge is not power. Power is born of a personal inventory of one's strength and weakness, crowned by guidance of the will. In a real sense it takes humility and self-abnegation to recognize the weakness involved in a fall, but the aftermath should be that the weakness is better known.

The conscious subjectivity we have already mentioned as increasing should help the child of this age to evaluate objectively and in perspective his personal assets, and even beyond, help him find his first real insight into what is involved in the world of human and human-divine relationships. Real choices do take place at this age. There is the attractive but unwholesome personality, someone of a boy's own age, with whom he wishes to be friends in an association that here and now should give him "status." On the other hand there is also present, through the workings of grace, a realization that such a relationship could be an occasion of sin. The child's decision will be a step in either the integration or the disintegration of his Christian personality.

Now that the child is capable of newer and deeper insight into the problem of human relations, it is an opportune moment to apprise the boy or girl of the fact that though certain encounters will of themselves make receptive souls better members of Christ, in other meetings the child must take the initiative to bring truth, beauty, and goodness into focus.

Attitudes formulated in these fact-facing veins must surely

foster a positive outlook that leads from ego-reliance to hope in the redemption. It is well known that irreparable damage has been done to religious growth by threats far removed from New Testament morality, threats generating a moral but not a religious concept of sin. A distinction between rational and Christian morality needs to be emphasized over and over again. The goal of the catechist is not to make the child decalogue-conscious, but rather dialogue-conscious. It is not keeping the Law that is the ideal, but deepening the relationship with the God who has first loved us. What He proposes to us in the moral command is a share in His life. He awaits a definite response from each individual. Making a success of life means answering God's call, not by words, but by what we are. The moral life is not an indefinite repetition of certain stereotyped and sterile judgments; it is answering in a positive way the question put by our conscience: "What does God expect of me in this situation?" ". . . How am I to imitate Christ at this moment?" Every action is a real "self-making" into a son of the Father and a brother of Christ.[5]

Christian Behavior a Personal and Free Answer

It is of great importance, therefore, to establish those fundamental attitudes which affirm God's commandments as most reasonable and life governed by them as most beautiful.[6] Christian dogma and morals should not be taught in isolation, divorced entirely from sacred history and liturgy. A systematic teaching of morals should be integrated in a more comprehensive plan. The faithful Christian is called upon to do his part in establishing the kingdom of God on earth, to become more and more conscious of his responsibility. There are laws to regulate his collaboration. What should be his response to what God has done for his salvation? Christian behavior is the personal and free answer which has as its consequence a constantly deepening relationship with

[5] Robert Blomme, "Towards a Genuine Moral Sense," *Lumen Vitae,* 15 (October–December 1960), 652–55.

[6] John Hofinger, S.J., "On Our Way," *Lumen Vitae,* 12 (July–September 1957), 529.

Love.[7] The law was given to guide our answer, but of itself and in itself it is nothing. Sin in the Christian sense is a refusal of the Other, a flaw in the texture of love; it is a turning in upon oneself rather than an infraction of the law.[8]

It is from these perceptions that the child's first notions of self-responsibility must evolve. Since few if any children nowadays, on entering school, have much concept of self-discipline, the teacher is usually spared the task of eradicating the fears once so prevalent in children. Lest he himself create them, the teacher should avoid a pharisaic emphasis on minutiae, for they will serve no spiritual purpose. In the first years at school, discipline is more or less imposed or thought out for the child. Even from a purely pedagogic point of view it is well to remember that *the more formal and detailed are rules and regulations, the greater the stimulus to make a game of trying not to get caught in violations.* Whatever laws are imposed are to work toward God-directed self-discipline. Unless this atmosphere is sensed by the child, he will feel that persons in authority are only trying to restrict him, and possibly transfer his resentment of authority to its ultimate Source. Genuine Christian motivation will supplement the child's growing understanding that in some way rules make for good order. At the same time a continual effort to develop respect for himself and for the rights and welfare of others is part of the upbuilding of his whole personality.

Acceptance of the Cross at an Early Age

By the time the child reaches the intermediate grades, he should begin to be informed with the discipline of Christ's own teaching: "If any man will follow me let him deny himself. . . ." This denial has both positive and negative aspects. Let us emphasize the former. Kindness and solicitude toward younger children, a spirit of give and take with peers, a reverence for each member of God's

[7] Walter Croce, S.J., "Content of Catechesis: The Message of Salvation," *Lumen Vitae*, 11 (October–December 1956), 603 f.

[8] Oraison, *op. cit.*, p. 125.

family which will give birth to respect for the opinions and wishes of others even in the face of conflict, evenness of temper, manliness, are seeds of heroic virtue to be planted at this time when the child can grasp what the cross of daily living means.

Problems of life are dawning as a reality upon the child at this age. Peace, war, life, death, justice, fear, hate, and love are human concerns which are sometimes very real to children. It is not only instruction regarding the sacraments and doctrine which must be transmitted by the religion teacher, but a way of viewing all daily situations with the eyes of Christ. The first and greatest thing to teach is how to live the life of faith. Coudreau says the task is not merely instruction, but transmission of doctrine for living. The Greek word our Lord used was *mathēteúein:* "make disciples."

> We must be faithful to the precise nature of His charge. We are not professors of religion; we are masters of the Christian life. We must make disciples, teach sincerely and well—but with the objective of introducing the catechized into a new life which, once received by the child, will transform him. It must "renew" him first interiorly and then in his entirety until it works in him a "conversion" which is the condition of all Christian life.[9]

The widespread loss of faith and the giving up of religious practice that marks our times might have been mitigated if defectors had been formed in the faith during the whole period of their religious instruction, however brief it was. Coudreau does not hestitate to say this is true particularly from ages nine to twelve.[10] If catechizing meant merely teaching, then knowledge would be all that mattered. But it is perseverance in a life, the Christian life, that is the goal of catechesis. The religion lesson deals with a contact that is being established moment by moment between one person and Another. This present and real event has embodied

[9] François Coudreau, P.S.S., "Introduction to a Pedagogy of Faith," *Shaping the Christian Message,* ed. Gerard S. Sloyan (New York: Macmillan, 1958), p. 134.
[10] *Ibid.,* p. 139.

within it an appeal from God which asks a response from the whole man.

THE FIFTH GRADE

The ten-year-old in the fifth grade has wide-open mental receptivity and broad-ranging interests. His active mind has a great capacity for memorization. The ten-year-old likes to learn through pictorial material.[11] At this time, though his thoughts tend to be concrete, he is beginning to develop the power of abstraction. There is a decided withdrawal from the world of fantasy.[12] For the religious educator these characteristics of the ten-year-old present inestimable opportunities.

Naturally, turning aside from the world of make-believe will tend to focus the child's attention on the material world. At this age the competitive spirit appears. Petty stealing becomes common; there is cheating in assignments and tests. Gossiping begins and jealousy comes of age. These are all causes of great concern to parents and teachers. From the simple things that once delighted him, the ten-year-old's eyes are fixed on wrist watches, ice skates, expensive clothes, bicycles, transistor radios, and many other objects. An undue esteem for material goods makes great inroads, an esteem which may easily develop, unfortunately, into a lifelong attitude. It is surely incumbent upon the religion teacher to be on guard to help the child meet and evaluate these allurements the world proffers him. The child should be happy, but the educator's task is to guard him, showing him that vigilance is necessary to avoid becoming "fixed" on present happiness. This fixation, the result of a false concept of permanence, will never prepare him to accept life's supreme moment of liberation and "moving on," death.

Awareness of the Invisible and Retreat from Fantasy

Here, then, is the psychological moment in which to emphasize the unseen world which is more real than the world we inhabit.

[11] Gesell, Ilg, Ames, *Youth, from Ten to Sixteen* (New York: Harpers, 1956), p. 61.

[12] J. A. Jungmann, *Handing On the Faith* (New York: Herder and Herder, 1959), p. 86.

Contact with a supernatural world has already been established, but now a reverence for other-worldly realities, the foundations on which to build a sense of mystery, can be laid by the alert catechist. Sooner or later, if the child is well balanced, he will realize not everything in this life has an answer here. The religion teacher can prepare the way for this conclusion. As in all subjects in the curriculum, religion-study requires a readiness period. The awareness of mystery, with its valuable impact on the child's mentality, can be facilitated by an intelligent understanding of those symbols which are the gateway to the world of mystery. In a small book Guardini has illustrated the profound significance of twenty-four simple signs that are meant to reeducate spiritual faculties grown dry and superficial. The sign of the cross, doors, candles, God's name, and gestures here take on a new dimension.[13]

With what precision ten-year-olds can vociferate: "A sacrament is an outward sign, . . ." but is it clear to them what these seven signs of love really mean? We have long expounded the causal aspect of the sign, but the rich symbolism contained in the total picture of each sign has remained unexplored, uncommunicated. Signs are the language of the intellect; they must signify *something*.

Christian Life as Social and Personal

In addition to the explanation of the symbolism contained in each sacrament, the teacher of the ten-year-old should not miss the opportunity at this psychological moment to discuss the social nature of the sacraments. In the past much emphasis has been placed on personal preparation as well as on the external ceremony mentioned above. Needless to say these are important, but one could say of almost greater importance in the whole perspective of the Christian's life is his understanding of the social implications involved in his reception of the sacraments. In other

[13] See Romano Guardini, *Sacred Signs* (St. Louis: Pio Decimo Press, 1956).

words a positive, mystical-body presentation of sacramental doctrine will help the child discover his destiny and his place in the Church much more effectively than any other procedure.

The reality of God is unfathomable, true, but love will help to plumb the depths. Life on earth must be shown in its relativity if there is to be progressive development in the spiritual, emotional, and social life of the child. With these principles in mind, Murchland proposes a reorientation of thought in these vital areas:

> Grace, for example, will not be conceived of in terms of definitions or mechanics. Rather it will be a *quest* for identity, a progressive immersing of self into the totality of presence and meaning. Sanctity, and how familiar all of these categories are, will not be conceived of as observances and the result of gliding along the rails laid down by someone else. Rather it will be understood as a *tension*, a skillful and personal maneuver of balancing opposites. Truth itself, and how static that tends to become, will be understood, less as "something we have" than as the final framework of existence within which search always takes precedence over acquisition.[14]

These remarks are not to be construed as at odds with grace as state or truth as absolute; they are simply a plea for the introduction of the ideas of dynamism, search, and personal relation into the catechizing of the young. The word "mystery" expresses a hidden yet communicated reality. God, inaccessible in Himself, has revealed Himself to us in Christ. The saving acts of the history of the world are all ordered to Christ and dependent upon Him. Christ in what He was, in what He did, in what was fulfilled in Him is mystery in the basic sense; He is the divine reality present in history to save.[15] If this living mystery is not the dynamic power of daily life, the catechist's attempts will conclude at best in a merely moral education. A religious and further a

[14] Bernard G. Murchland, C.S.C., "An Awareness of Mystery," *Apostolic Perspectives,* 3 (October–November 1958), 23.

[15] Charles Davis, "Odo Casel and the Theology of Mysteries," *Worship,* 34 (August–September 1960), 430.

Christian education involves personal powers *motivated* by Love, a morality of the ever-growing search for communion with God and one's neighbor.[16]

Now if from the very beginning of religious instruction, God has been lovingly regarded as our heavenly Father, the implications of the Father-child relationship would be that all doctrines and practices are presented in such a way as to communicate the idea that Christians are the happiest people on earth.[17]

Those who agree with Hofinger's thinking, as the present writer does, must think twice before saying that intense sacramental preparation is over for the most part with the completion of first communion instruction. It is so much easier to prepare children for that event than to direct them so as to avoid routine and mechanical confessions afterwards. In fact, embodied in a reprint of the Catholic Hour broadcast, January 1961, Mother Isabel Eugenie, R.A., submits reasons for deferring the sacrament of penance until after the reception of holy communion. In preparation for the eucharist she suggests that there is no need to teach small children about sin, for confession is obligatory only where there is question of mortal sin.[18] Even after mortal sin has become a possibility, Drinkwater maintains a certain caution about misuse of the term "mortal sin." He reminds us that *three* conditions are necessary for such a transgression. Mortal sin is a psychological term and by its nature includes circumstances of mind and will. Teachers constantly forget this and use the term as an equivalent of grave matter. A little reflection on this will enable one to see the danger of engendering false consciences.[19]

As the middle-grade child is maturing, he ought to begin to be more mature in stating his sins. He can be taught to get at the underlying causes of his transgressions. He can be shown how to look for the WHY of his disobedience, the root cause of his anger,

[16] Oraison, *op. cit.*, p. 126.

[17] Hofinger, *op. cit.*, p. 524.

[18] *The Catholic Hour* (N.C.W.C.) January 22, 1961, "New Method of Teaching Catechistics."

[19] Francis H. Drinkwater, *Telling the Good News* (London: Macmillan, 1960), p. 114.

etc. Such an examination of faults ought to help the child know himself better, discipline himself more effectively, and make real progress in character formation.

A study of the personality of Christ would be appropriate to this end. It is hoped that the sacramental life will deepen, and personal intimacy with our Lord will grow with each reception of the sacraments. Jesus is God's own Word. God has told us everything in Him. To be true, our whole message must converge toward the Son of God. Exactness in presenting the divinity of Jesus demands that we emphasize that Jesus is God because He is the only Son of the Father. Neglecting this reference tends to implant in the mind of the student first the notion of the blessed Trinity, and beside it Jesus, also true God. Worse still there is the tendency so to emphasize that "Jesus is God" that complete distortion of the mystery of the three Persons results. A concomitant of this is the weakening of Catholic faith that Jesus Christ is true man. While on earth Jesus constantly called Himself the Son of Man. He is Mediator for this reason, and because it is in Him that we become children of the Father. In St. Thomas's treatment of the humanity of Christ as the "conjoined instrument" of the Eternal Word he asks if it is Jesus who redeems us or if it is properly a work of the Trinity, and answers (because he knows the terms of this Christian mystery): "He properly and immediately is our Redeemer in that He is man."[20]

Too, we must show that Jesus had a particular personality on earth, but did not allow Himself to be stamped by the individuality proper to a human person. Jesus is universal. The two things that show His humanity to us also demonstrate His divinity, namely, His free and perfect obedience and His great love.[21] Ranwez has pointed out how advantageous it may prove to the spiritual life of the child if his initial knowledge of Jesus is of someone who is *living with us,* yet "mysteriously glorious."[22] In the stage

[20] *Summa Theologiae,* III, 48, 5.
[21] Pierre Ranwez, S.J., "A Catechesis Concerning Jesus Christ," *Lumen Vitae,* 10 (October–December 1955), 528.
[22] *Ibid.,* p. 530.

of catechesis concerning Jesus Christ that dwells upon the earthly life of our Lord, we must be quite sure that it is a Christocentric approach that is made: it is not the articles of faith that deserve primacy in our catechesis, but the person and work of Christ as revealed in the New Testament.

The ten-year-old is beginning to view the catechism of faith as a systematic whole.[23] The goal of Christological instruction at this time is to inculcate a deep knowledge of the person, doctrine, and work of Christ so that a more intimate and lasting contact between Christ and the child may be established. Hence we reiterate the necessity of leading the children to a glorified Christ. He is a "Presence who acts now"; at this very moment He is "alive and doing." Clearly, the historical Christ graphically described in His workshop at Nazareth can have genuine significance for the child, but the child must never be allowed to stop at this conception. At all costs the danger of the Savior's becoming merely an historical figure functional in the past must be averted.

Children in the fifth grade can be made increasingly aware of their dignity and importance as they assist at the holy sacrifice of the Mass. These three ideas are "key concepts" at this time:

1. The Mass is our life. In every Mass we co-offer with the priest who acts for Christ; we do what Christ does; we offer ourselves through Christ to the Father and all day long live the Christ-life of obedience to the Father's will.

2. The Mass explains and is the mainspring of all dynamic liturgical worship. The other sacraments, prayer, good works are only grace-giving means because of Christ's Mass.

3. Just as Christ's earthly life is not to be dissociated from His crucifixion nor His glorification (for every moment of His life was sacrificial), so also every moment of our daily life should be formed with the spirit of our Mass, the spirit of Christ-like sacrifice.

The idea of "living the Mass" appeals strongly to children of this age. After quickly reviewing the use of vestments, altar-fur-

[23] Klemens Tilmann, "Teaching on Christ," *Lumen Vitae*, 13 (January–March 1958), 11.

nishings, etc., learned in the lower grades, work on the structure of the Mass through the missal may be begun. Owners of a missal will be anxious to use it if it will make them not merely spectators but actors in the great drama of our salvation acted in sign. It should be stressed, of course, that the missal is primarily the priest's or lector's book, not the people's, and that it is destined to obsolescence as a means to unite people and altar. With contemporary progress in the distribution of rôles, which is a part of active participation, the missal should progressively be put in context, even in children's lives.

Especially is it necessary to stress in these years the relationship between reception of the eucharist and sacrifice as a social act; to stress holy communion as the extension of the altar rather than the tabernacle, and as comprising much more than a "visit" with Jesus. This all too common mentality which starts with the true presence in the tabernacle, going from there to communion and finally to the Mass, is the reverse of eucharistic devotion set forth in *Mediator Dei:* altar, communion rail, and tabernacle. Yet this unfortunate viewpoint is still being taught.[24] Our best clue comes perhaps from the name of the sacrament itself as administered: the *body of Christ* causes a *holy communion*. This is another way of saying what Aquinas says, that the *res* or reality which the eucharistic *sacramentum* (sign) exists to achieve is the "unity of the mystical body."[25]

THE SIXTH GRADE

Age eleven has been called the "foothills of adolescence." Great social interests, outgoing friendliness, the first stirrings of restlessness characterize children of this age.[26] They have new experiences at home, in the neighborhood, with their classmates. Catechism studied in the lower grades is seen in light of this new experience and can be a great help in directing thought and action. For example, before reaching the sixth grade children have been

[24] Bernard I. Mullahy, C.S.C., "The Sacrament of Love," *Sponsa Regis,* 30 (August 1959), 308 f.
[25] *Summa Theologiae,* III, 73, 3.
[26] Gesell, Ilg, Ames, *op. cit.,* pp. 67 f.

taught something about chastity, or purity as it is commonly called. Now at the age of eleven, boys in particular show considerable interest in immodest songs and jokes. When this comes to the catechist's notice, he must not ignore the situation, but after dwelling on the sanctity of all creation, show that sex is part of a loving Father's plan for the world. Since everything God made is good, the special goodness of sex must be examined. Our bodies are important because they are "temples of the Holy Spirit." Without them we could not receive baptism, confirmation, and the holy eucharist, and the new life which these signs bring. Without sex, which transmits the gift of life, there could be no "new life."

Natural virtues must also be stressed at this time. Jungmann has noted that what we do to train children in the practice of mortification, neatness, cleanliness, obedience, and truthfulness is also the best kind of sex education. Enjoyment in little things is not to be neglected. If stories, reading, songs, games, natural beauty, walking, and a hobby occupy a child, his pleasure-seeking will be safeguarded.[27]

Above and beyond all other motivation the catechist must stress the utter reality of God. No one will want to make sacrifices unless he has the highest possible concept of the greatness of God. Time and again we must return to the two rocks on which we build: the absolute sovereignty of God and His inestimable goodness as shown forth in creation. Purity will matter tremendously when the child sees that the whole person, body and soul, is for God. In these years the idea of marriage becomes of more and more interest to some children. A good way of discussing the holiness of the body consecrated in baptism is to connect instruction on the sixth and ninth commandments with marriage.[28] The child on the brink of his teens is able to see how important is the physical and moral integrity of family life. He is well able to grasp the fact that God, wishing to protect this life, has ordained these two commandments.

[27] Jungmann, *op. cit.*, p. 347.
[28] Johannes Hofinger, S.J., *The Art of Teaching Christian Doctrine* (Notre Dame, Ind.: University of Notre Dame Press, 1962), p. 186.

A further level of mystery is the liturgy. Psychologically speaking, just because the child under consideration is at the "gang age," he is also at the liturgical age. The liturgy is the mystery of Christ lived on in the Church that we might share in it. This is what really specifies the Christian—an active participation in the salvific action of Christ. It is not the receiving of grace that should be uppermost in mind, but an efficacious will to relive the mystery of Christ in one's life. The mystery of grace, so powerful to reproduce in us what took place in Christ, is precisely what is achieved through the liturgy. We can live the same mysteries, but of course with the difference called for by the difference between Christ and ourselves.

The essence of Christ's redemptive work lies beyond the curtain of time and space, and thus is still existing. This reality made present through the medium of the liturgy unites all worshipers in the worship of Christ. The entire teaching of the Catholic Church is contained within the scope of the liturgy. The major events of the Good News file before us in the ecclesiastical year, but chiefly in the individual Sunday which contains the Nativity, Paschal and Pentecostal cycles in summary. Although the liturgy is not primarily concerned with educating us, we cannot help but cultivate that surrender which befits our creaturely condition before the majesty of God. At this level, the Christian character must emerge.[29]

The untold social solidarity which liturgical worship achieves ought surely to appeal to the child who has a new-found need to be part of a larger group. In what better way than in the investigation of the corporate worship of the mystical body can the pre-adolescent reach out to fulfillment? Socially, psychologically, spiritually, the new-found world of others, the intense need for togetherness, the autonomy developed through silent wonder can be awakened, spiritualized, and made infinitely richer for this world and the next through the unfolding of the liturgy.

The explanation of the mysteries celebrated must go hand-in-hand with active participation in the liturgy. It is the opportune time to inculcate deep, active, and vital love for the Church. Con-

[29] Jungmann, *op. cit.*, pp. 98 f.

centration on the liturgical year serves as an excellent recapitulation of the mystery of Christ. It shows how close is this divine mystery and how active a part we have in it. A presentation of the creed, not in logical but psychological order, through the medium of the liturgical year, has been outlined for the sixth grade in the proposed book of the "On Our Way" series. The topics of the individual lessons are as follows (style slightly emended):[30]

1. God's family—Mystical Body
   (Holy Mother Church)
2. Christ in His mysteries lives today
   (Meaning of liturgy)
3. Family prayer; rosary
   (Recapitulation of mysteries)
4. Christ the King
   (Kingdom on earth. Kingdom to come)
5. All Saints, All Souls
   (Communion of Saints)
6. Thanksgiving Day
   (Mass—Gratitude for natural and supernatural gifts)
7. Advent—God's actual coming
   (Correspondence to grace)
8. Immaculate Conception
   (Original sin. Sanctifying grace)
9. Advent—Preparation
   (Day of the Lord; Second Coming)
10. Christmas. "Gloria in excelsis"
    (Glory to the Heavenly Father—peace to men)
11. Epiphany—God, King, Master
    (Christian vocation. Missions)
12. Holy Family
    (Blessings of Christian families)
13. Church Unity Octave
    (One, holy, catholic Church; prayer)

[30] John Hofinger, S.J., "On Our Way," *Lumen Vitae*, 12 (July–September 1957), 531 f. The subsequently published book (1962) departs from this course.

14. Purification; "Light of the World"
    (Graces of Confirmation)
15. Lent
    (Contrition, Penance, Good Confession)
16. Lent—Passover; Old Testament
    (Need of purification)
17. Passion Time
    (Church's suffering with Christ. Way of the cross)
18. Second Passion Sunday
    (Explain ceremonies)
19. Holy Thursday, Good Friday
    (Explain ceremonies)
20. Easter Vigil, baptismal vows
    (Explain ceremonies)
21. Easter: central feast. Why?
    (Christian religion: Mystery of Christ)
22. Assumption
    (Promise of fruit of redemption. Our Resurrection)
23. Triumph of saints
    (Confessors, Martyrs, Virgins)
24. Ascension
    (Triumph of our Head, seated at the right hand of God)
25. Pentecost—Holy Ghost
    (Active Christian life)
26. Corpus Christi
    (Recapitulation of God's gifts to us. Mass)

DEVELOPING THE MATURE CHRISTIAN

Schemes for presenting the Christian message must be planned in terms of the average child's development. Yet each individual must be dealt with as far as possible in the light of his own needs. Because a secret dialogue between God and each of them is always going on, there can be no dealing with children *en masse*. One serious mistake the educator can make is to be too demanding of his charge who, like himself, is involved in the mystery of original sin. The "contradynamism" of concupiscence is a basic problem for the child. However, since psychology and theology affirm that education is a "work of guidance," becoming when necessary a work of correcting, the religious educator can help his pupil adjust and be victorious in bearing this lifelong burden.[31] In review of the situation, it would seem advisable to point out that the child is neither wholly good nor wholly bad. If rigid and negative restrictions continually bind all areas of his activities, he will turn in upon himself in a complete neurosis of failure and frustration. Confronted by constant imposition of this pessimistic attitude, the child cannot but close the door to love, gentleness, and self-sacrifice. God, who is known only as narrow, demanding, and the cause of his unhappiness, will be hated. The normal quest for Him will be smothered before it is initiated. This victim of unqualified restrictions will never know the freedom of the children of God, nor comprehend the hidden beauty of the Sermon on the Mount.

Conversely, the child who has been allowed to act without guidance, is, in common parlance, "spoiled" before he has had the opportunity to mature.[32] This child is not able to "take" the contradictions and disappointments that are a part of every man's life. His defensive reaction to whatever thwarts his desires creates a social barrier between himself and others which only heightens the problem. In the spiritual realm, a God who does not satisfy his every whim is useless. This victim of distorted giving, this "spoiled child," can never accept the fact that true joy and Christian renunciation are indissolubly wedded in this life.

Both of these types of ill-formed children are definitely handicapped by recurring narcissistic regressions. Self-love is a major obstacle to the formation of the true religious life, the Christian view of which is a progressive renewal of the spirit of sacrifice and an honest facing of reality. From babyhood to adulthood there should take place a passing from complete dependence on others to total participation in life and life's needs with others. It is the habit of spontaneous self-sacrifice that helps a man to grow in deeper communion with his brothers and paradoxically become

[31] Oraison, *op. cit.*, p. 36.
[32] Oraison, *op. cit.*, p. 38.

less dependent upon them. The more one has need of others to acquire a feeling of security or fulfillment, the more he manifests the emotional attitude of early childhood. The ideal man is not insecure because of a need for others, but finds in himself the need to be with others and to be something to others.[33]

The religious educator must have a broader view, a more life-giving and life-sustaining goal in mind than the mere presentation of the norms of morality. Above all else, he must encourage the child to form a personal relationship with Someone who is always engaged in dialogue with each man. To make children or anyone else aware of mystery, we must build on the cornerstone of faith. In his mind's eye, the teacher must see the finished structure of the living, mature Christian. Then there will be no superficial glibness of presentation, no meaningless memorization, no passing on of doctrine which is divorced from the real world of childhood. God's message must be loved and assimilated into the daily life of the student. However, it is not only to what God has revealed that the individual must assent. He must consent further to live the new life the Revealer incarnate came to share with men.[34]

Religion is a joyful, all-trusting response to God's invitation, an engagement, an affirmative reply so clearly understood and so intense as to preclude any later falling away. Basically the purpose of our presentation is to bring the pupil from acceptance of Christian revelation in faith and hope to his total commitment in the life of the Church, *Christus totus*. Cardinal Montini has well said that the Christian mission defines and puts into action the whole orientation of man toward God.[35] The Word of divine truth which enters life asks to be accepted because it is what it is, from whom it is. Our Lord's own term is Good News. God so loved the world as to send His only Son to save it; this is still Good News.

Above all else, religious educators need a true and comprehen-

[33] Oraison, *op. cit.*, pp. 26 ff.

[34] F. Somerville, S.J., "Towards a Living Faith," *The Sower*, 214A (January 1960), 10.

[35] G. B. Montini, "The Mission of the Church," *Apostolic Perspectives*, 3 (October–November 1958), 4.

sive notion of the meaning of faith. It is the anchor of moral life, not a reward of virtuous living. Faith is objective, a relationship consequent on something outside the inner world of the subject, something existing absolutely independent of the subject's knowledge of it. Since this "something" is the transcendent God, a personal relationship can be entered into which is both a mystery and a reality. The Other has become a member of the human race, and though he no longer walks on earth as man, our relationship to Him through faith, our personal commitment is the broad, deep, and only reason for undertaking all that is involved in religious education.

8 GROWING UP IN CHRIST

Religious Education in the
Seventh and Eighth Grades

Sister Mary Nona McGreal, O.P.

THE art of catechesis like the divine Word which it gives voice to is ancient and ever new. Its purpose in the twentieth century, as in the first, is not to help the pupil learn his catechism, or cover assigned material, or pass an examination, or become a well-informed Catholic. These objectives are valid but secondary. They are validated only when they serve the overwhelming purpose of helping every soul to meet God: to respond to His call and live His life, here and hereafter.

Every soul. But each person differs from all others, and in his course from birth to death is subject to multiple changes within himself. How can anyone plan to teach religion to such a variety of persons, in such a variety of developmental stages and external circumstances? This insistent question leads the catechist to a serious study of psychological traits of children and youth. It also leads him to study the society in which he and they live, seeking

to know and understand the culture that embraces them, according
to the exhortation of Pius XII:

> Look then with a sure eye to the times and the hour to learn of
> new needs and examine new remedies. Confidently fix your gaze
> on that future which you will fashion with your own hands in
> the souls of your pupils. . . .[1]

In so doing the teacher's exemplar is Christ, for the psychological
approach to teaching religion and a sympathetic understanding of
the culture and customs of the learner are marks of our Lord's own
teaching ministry. The gospel records this principle that underlay
Jesus' approach to His hearer: "He knew what was in man" (Jn
2:25).

THE CHILD GROWING UP

The stages of adolescence, spanning roughly the years from
twelve to twenty, are several and complex. The first stage ordinarily coincides with the age of children in the seventh and eighth
grades. These are boys and girls who will presently, at a time varying for either sex and for each individual, begin to grow up in the
gradual and wonderful order established by nature; for the providence of God works through the nature of things, as we are
frequently reminded by Aquinas. If the goal for each child is supernatural formation in Christ, the catechist must know thoroughly
the natural foundations on which "God's building" (1 Cor 3, 9) is to
rise.

That the adolescent is hard to understand is a truism, but one
which deserves constant reflection. Even to himself he is a
dilemma. He wishes to be mature, yet keep the fun of childhood;
to pull away from his parents, yet ask much of them; to stand alone,
yet never deviate from what the "crowd" is doing. And his marked
physical development which is only part of the wholenesss of his
human person is never separable from corresponding changes in
feelings, thoughts, ideals, and entire orientation to reality.

[1] Pope Pius XII, in *The Mind of Pius XII*, ed. Robert Pollock (New
York: Crown, 1955), p. 12.

What is there in the nature of the young adolescent that is of special interest to the teacher of religion in the Catholic school or Confraternity class? Among the key characteristics of the final years of childhood are these:

1. increasing self-concern
2. a tendency to personify ideals
3. identification with the acceptable group
4. a search for new horizons
5. cautious emergence from childhood.

Each of these will be considered briefly, together with some implications derived from them for religious instruction and formation.

Increasing Self-concern

The concern of the young adolescent with himself is not so much selfish as self-focused. His is an awakening consciousness of what is meant by person and personality, self and individual, in *him*. This is a broader meaning of "self-consciousness" than that which is identified with embarrassment. It is youth taking possession of his birthright as a human being, moving toward that full personal existence (many never reach it) which is described by Goldbrunner:

> A person does not exist like a piece of wood, a tree or a house which is determined by place, size and age. In order that a person may really speak out of itself, be present and "exist," it must do something with itself; it must acquire itself, take hold of itself, actuate itself. Only then does man "exist" in the full sense of the word. . . . In his capacity for free decision man rises above the mere state of nature and becomes the person which he is from birth.[2]

[2] Josef Goldbrunner, *Cure of Mind and Cure of Soul* (New York: Pantheon Books, 1958), pp. 18 f. Goldbrunner's exposition of depth psychology in this little book is of value for the teacher of religion, whom he addresses indirectly in several sections. A collaborator in the production of the *Katholischer Katechismus* for the dioceses of Germany, he combines psychological understanding with the experience of a catechist and pastor.

The capacity for free decision, so dear to the child growing up, is only one facet of his self-concern. By means of his new self-consciousness Providence permits fulfillment through nature's unfailing rule of growth: separation. Adulthood is entered through detachment, through putting away the things of the child. It demands independence of judgment, separation from parental control; but not suddenly, for growth is always gradual. In this separation there is anguish for both child and parent, for neither quite understands what is taking place in the slow and seemingly erratic emergence of the adult from the cocoon of childhood. Gerald Vann underscores this natural psychological reality in the supernaturally significant Finding in the Temple: the boy figure of Christ as a symbol of separation from parents; His questions, a sign of youth asking questions of life; His apparent harshness, the corollary of a child's natural directness and uncompromising candor, as well as the only way men have of driving home a hard lesson:

> So it is the Boy-Christ who teaches His mother to realize, 'This child is not mine but God's'; teaches us in turn to say of all those we love, 'These are not mine but God's.' . . . When we are babies we need other human beings all the time to look after us; and again when we are grown up we need other human beings, and know our need; it is boyhood that is independent. And so we need the lesson of Christ the Boy, not to give us back a natural independence of temperament and heart which is not proper to manhood, but to show us the supernatural counterpart of it, to touch creatures very gently lest we destroy them and ourselves.[3]

At about twelve years, then, the child manifests an increasing self-concern which, with many a turning back for help, leads to self-reliance. The sense of personal importance combined with insecurity makes him touchy, defensive, and often resistant to ideas

[3] The quotation is from Gerald Vann, O.P., *The Seven Swords* (New York: Sheed and Ward, 1953), p. 41. The preceding thoughts are taken from class notes made February 19, 1960, in the course "The Moral Virtues" at the Catholic University of America.

or actions which a year or month before—and maybe again tomorrow—he would accept without question.

What are the implications of all this for religious education?

First, the child must learn for himself, in near-adult terms, that God's concern for him is far greater than his own. This is a different concept from that of the six-year-old, whose world is relatively ordered and peaceful and who usually understands God's loving care through the medium of his parents' devotion. The adolescent is setting out on a stormy sea, no matter how close to shore he remains at first. He must be sure that God knows about, permits, and can bring to good his personal suffering (which can become extreme), the evils in the world, and the adult ways of living which he has begun to know. His patrons are the fishermen-apostles in the boat who cry out to the Master for help.

Second, the growing child should realize that adult separation from parents is one of function, not a breaking of the ties of filial relationship which reach into eternity; neither is it a withdrawal of owed honor, services, and gratitude. From God, however, there can be no separation at all, but rather a deeper reliance upon His providence, power, wisdom, mercy, and love. Perhaps, with careful guidance and prayer, this "new personality" of the adolescent can be introduced to a lifelong understanding of the role of Providence in his life:

> Providence means something great and mysterious; it means that structure of existence which comes into being around the person who makes God's concern his own. The world around such a person becomes different. The "new heaven and the new earth" begin.[4]

Whether or not the child begins to discern this meaning of Providence, his teacher of religion be he parent, priest, or classroom teacher is committed to it. His special role as mediator between this very God and His growing-up children demands the commitment. He is "charged with the duty of helping the 'children of

[4] Romano Guardini, *The Lord's Prayer* (New York: Pantheon Books, 1958), p. 46.

God' to ripen into 'sons' and 'daughters' of God." For him "the
reality, difficulty, sobriety and fulfilment" of this relationship
"should be regarded in the light of the natural, cultivated relationship between a father and his grown-up children."[5]

Finally, the teacher of religion above all others should take pains
to satisfy the psychological needs of the adolescent: respect for his
newly found dignity; reassurance in his frequent failures; tolerance
for his weathervane moods; firmness to offset his inconstancy, and
a concern for him that matches and goes beyond his own. In one
word, the teacher must give him love. Then he will reflect, at least
dimly, the attributes of the God about whom he teaches.[6]

The Tendency to Personify Ideals

The process of detachment in adolescence is inevitably accompanied by new attachments, which range from the "crush" on a
teacher or classmate to the sincere, though exaggerated, hero-
worship of some person admired from afar. This movement toward
other persons *must* take place as one steps out of the sheltered
world of parents and family. "Metaphysically, the person is related
to a Thou, its very nature is to be in dialogue."[7] Furthermore, the

[5] Goldbrunner, *op. cit.*, p. 21. In connection with this thought the author
cites Lk 15, 20. 22–24.

[6] Francis H. Drinkwater is interesting on this point, as always, in an
essay on the duties of chaplains in secondary schools. He writes in *Telling
the Good News* (New York: St. Martin's Press, 1960), pp. 106 f.: "Rightly
or wrongly, but anyhow naturally, most of these teen-agers see themselves
as struggling out of the bondage of childhood into personal independence.
Fifty per cent of them feel their home would be on their side as against
the spiritual claims of Church and school. They need to have a feeling that
they are free to stay away from Church and sacraments, that nothing is
going to happen to them at School if they do. For instance if a boy thinks
his place in the first football team depends on not missing his Easter duties,
his whole sense of justice will rise in revolt, and every other boy will agree
with him. The adolescent urge for freedom, which is not felt as a freedom
from God at all, but from the world of grown-up domination, must be
recognized and welcomed; it is the only foundation that an adult religion
can build on. The Catholic school today needs to have an outward looking,
missionary, apostolic kind of religion; and the first field for its apostolate
of love is amongst those nominal Catholics within its own walls."

[7] Goldbrunner, *op. cit.*, p. 59.

search for a friend accompanies a deepening interest in abstract ideas. Truth, beauty, goodness all beckon to the mind of the growing-up child. But he may or may not choose as ideals those persons who have true wisdom, genuine beauty, and more than superficial goodness. The child may sincerely believe he finds them in a Hollywood or TV idol, a sports hero, or paradoxically in a thoughtful grandmother who is removed enough from direct jurisdiction that she is not identified with the obnoxious "authoritarianism" of parental control.

One of the supreme privileges of the religion teacher is to reintroduce to the adolescent Christ our Lord, who can fulfill for him the role of friend, hero, guide, and exemplar. "Follow me." "Come to me." "You are my friends." He is the ultimate personification of human and divine values. His is all strength, all virtue. Other heroes may have qualifications not worthy of imitation or impossible to attain: baseball prowess, a splendid voice, physical beauty, powers of leadership. Christ can be followed by all, but each in his own way; for following Him brings to fulfillment the individual himself. He is not a static model on which one must be patterned but a living Person who brings each follower to life more fully. "I am the way, the truth, and the life" (Jn 14, 6).

Beside our Lord stands His mother, first woman of the new race of believers, who "comes forth like the dawn, as beautiful as the moon, as resplendent as the sun" (Cant 6, 9). To the adolescent some points of the theology of Mary are as yet inaccessible, but others have a strong appeal. Mary's association with her Son in His role as sole Mediator, for example, is clear to youngsters who have known the power of a parent's intercession or the sympathetic intervention of an uncle or older brother or sister in their behalf. The heart of this role of our Lady is her motherhood. To the child who is becoming an adult Mary is "Mater Amabilis," a mother lovable and understanding, strong and compassionate.[8]

The teacher may attract upper-grade boys and girls to the ideals which he himself lives. To the immature, uncertain adolescent,

[8] Cf. M. V. Bernadot, O.P., *Our Lady in Our Life* (Westminster, Md: The Newman Press, 1949), pp. 23, 38, 61.

groping for knowledge of himself and the world of adults, the teacher can offer stability and certainty, provided these are his own prerogatives. As Leeson puts it,

> Every teacher must have some central certainty in which his whole being is anchored, in which he lives and which he conceives it to be the business of his life to express. What we love to recall about the men and women who taught us is not what they told us, but what they were; there was in them a conviction about human life, human knowledge and how it should be used, which both in word and in action they desired to express; and the expression of it was often involuntary, or at least unconsidered. Without this we should not remember them as formative forces in our lives.[9]

As if to match the mixture of elements in the young adolescent, his teacher must blend the impersonal, objective approach with a highly personal one; not seeking self-gratification, but rather concentrating on the person of the pupil for his benefit. Teaching, as Pope Pius XII said, is a service, a giving, "the work of individual approach, soul to soul, everywhere, and in all circumstances."[10] To give plentifully the catechist must be developed fully as a person and be constantly developing, open on the one side to receive the action of God and on the other to give of Him to pupils hungry for life and love.

Identification with the Acceptable Group

The growing child's compelling need for security, like so much else about him, reaches in two directions: toward mature persons on the one hand, and toward the judgments and approval of his peers on the other. These latter act together like a boatload of passengers who have lost their directions. They steer this way and that, but cling together for dear life. "Older persons do not understand." (This is one of the many sweeping generalizations made by youngsters who are sharpening their powers of judgment.) There-

[9] Spencer Leeson, *Christian Education* (London: Longmans, Green, 1947), p. 3.
[10] Pollock, *op. cit.*, p. 22.

fore the "crowd" becomes the mentor and the focus of action. It is not as with the nine-year-old, who joins a team (club) to get something done, but largely for psychological support and approval. Thus the girls in a seventh or eighth grade, less interested in sports than the boys, will form a cheerleading team in order to be identified with the boys in group efforts. A wise teacher will not require too much volunteering for special assignments at an age when no one wishes to be singled out, although all will help with a group endeavor.

Leaders begin at this stage to take on new importance (what does a fourthgrader care about the functions of a class president?) and a strong personality or group can exert pressures upon the class, for good or otherwise:

> The leveling influence of "public opinion" is even evident in the classroom. If the class is left to itself the inferior elements will soon determine its tone by their greater robustness and hardly any child will be able to avoid this class spirit. Experience shows that it can suppress the expression of personal life in a class altogether. In the mass people are always below the level of their true selves. When a teacher faces a mass of children informed by the "class spirit" the children's souls are closed to him. He is confronted by a class *persona*, not by the open faces of his pupils. There is one great possibility of overcoming the class spirit: splitting the solid block by means of "functional teaching." The constant appeal to the child to cooperate with its own independent work, dividing the class into groups working at separate tables, getting the more gifted children to help the weaker ones, will gradually create an atmosphere in which it is easier to speak to the children as persons. And this is the precondition for Christian teaching. In such classes it will be possible to work with groups even in catechizing.[11]

The experienced teacher knows that this mass movement can be of positive good. The class will ordinarily respond to the challenge of a strong teacher who proposes things to be done that are recog-

---

[11] Goldbrunner, *op. cit.*, p. 113. The term *persona* (italics mine in the quotation) is used by the author, following Jung, to connote a psychological

nized as purposeful and sensible, and even magnanimous on occasion, or virtually heroic.

The obvious implication of the adolescents' "follow the crowd" psychology for religious education is to make use of it for good purposes. This can be done by: (1) using suggestions made by the class for taking certain means to an end, (2) forming small groups to carry out assignments, (3) forming a club to put into practice some aspect of Christian teachings, and (4) giving children individual roles of leadership in the school. These are extensions of Christian teaching into action, therefore a legitimate field of practice for children approaching adulthood.

More important, however, is the practice outside the classroom and school. The religion teacher will encourage children of the upper grades to move *en masse* if they must, into the life of the parish, the missions, the diocese, the whole Church.

Search for New Horizons

To offset tendencies to myopia it is not enough for the young adolescent to seek stability in a personal ideal or act with the crowd for security's sake. He must prepare for adult living in society. Even primitive tribes initiate their twelve-year-olds into tribal responsibility. How much more necessary is the gradual initiation of Christian youth into the society of the modern world, from primitive peoples to the United Nations. He must know society and its needs, for by decree of Providence he is his brother's keeper.

This broadening of horizons, necessary for the child growing up, is also sought by him as a means of orientation: Where do *I* fit— this suddenly important *I*—in the widening circles of human life that begin to come into view? What is my relationship to people and things around me? Where does God fit into the picture? The

---

parallel of the Greek actor's mask, put on by the person more or less consciously to cover his real self. Sometimes, says Goldbrunner, the teacher's personality or poor instruction encourages the adoption of a persona by the pupils: "A façade has been stuck on to them which acts as a persona and hides their own nature," p. 46.

questions are asked with a mixture of curiosity and apprehension, and sometimes with the bravado under which apprehension takes cover.

Because religious education is concerned with the answer to the last question it is also concerned with the first two. From "Who is God?" it turns to "Why did God make *you*?" By italicizing the *you* in this age-old question the teacher can show its connection with the "Where do *I* fit?" of the adult emerging from childhood, and can help him to develop the concept of a human and Christian vocation. "A man is a person called by God."[12] Every man has a vocation. Every man, woman and child is made to fulfill a certain role in the plan of the Creator. Membership in Christ brings the vocation to a new life, with the privileges of His friendship. Within this calling is another: the state of life, religious or lay, married or single, which is best suited for the individual's role in the design of Providence. Some children in the upper grades are seriously considering these choices for themselves; most are not. But all will benefit from seeing them objectively within the whole picture of Christ's work in the Mystical Body.

Every calling involves multiple human ties, and ability to respond entails responsibility. Man responds to God by living according to His law with his neighbors in the universe. If any maxim should remain to the adult from his childhood religion lessons as a corollary to Christ's law of love for neighbor, it is that "Every human relationship is an eternal responsibility."[13] And the maxim must be made specific by a study of the various relationships which involve Christians today.

A harvest of love, more than a complex of human relations, is what our Lord asks these young people to "Lift up your eyes" to: a harvest which they can sow for people everywhere by applying at home, in their own "here and now" of twentieth-century

[12] Romano Guardini, *The End of the Modern World* (New York: Sheed and Ward, 1956), p. 81.

[13] As Gerald Vann, O.P., says somewhere, possibly in *The Heart of Man* (New York: Longmans, Green, 1945).

America, the laws of justice and charity. The religious educator is obliged to encourage these personal applications by helping pupils to see them clearly, giving opportunity for their practice, and himself presenting a sincere example of love in action. The horizons of members of the body of Christ are those of the whole world, speaking not geographically but humanly and spiritually.

Cautious Emergence from Childhood

In his penetrating study of faith among adolescents Pierre Babin shows how the teacher must "come into contact with a young mind expressing itself in unpredictable rhythm."[14] Parents and teachers will find the phrasing apt. Boys and girls in the upper grades are still children, looking toward maturity with mixed feelings of joyous anticipation, fear, and caution. They are alternately child-like and childish; when least expected to, they will show signs of maturing thought or independence. But the wise teacher understands this unpredictable rhythm of development and is not deceived into thinking that the class is one of young adults. He raises the level of expectation gradually, is firm about reasonable requirements, and avoids introducing adult ideas and practices too early:

> Religious knowledge can only be realized if the problems are raised existentially. Individual instruction and religious conversation must bear this in mind and not give challenging answers before the questions themselves have been roused into life.
>
> An answer that is given too early will either not be understood at all, be felt as a burden, or lead to the formation of a persona.[15]

In these final years of childhood there is another task for the religious teacher: to review the fundamental truths of faith learned in previous years, and make new applications to prepare for the realism of adulthood. The truths of the creed, the law of love in the commandments, the life of grace in the sacramental economy

[14] Pierre Babin, O.M.I., "Rethinking the Life of Faith as A First Step Toward Stabilization," *Lumen Vitae,* 15 (June 1960), 246. The entire issue in which this portion of Père Babin's book appears is devoted to adolescence, and includes studies invaluable to the upper-grade teacher.

[15] Goldbrunner, *op. cit.,* p. 110.

of the Church—all of these gain deeper meaning with each added year of experience. The seventh commandment, for example, should be known to apply both to personal and social action: giving a full day's work for full wages, and vice versa; honesty in buying and selling, renting, and doing business.

Unfortunately, this may have to be the time for correction of some false concepts, childish or erroneous, which the child has acquired through misinterpretation or because of poor teaching. Many children grow up with ideas that should never have been introduced to their minds: that sin makes spots on the soul or makes it black; that grace is a packaged gift, rather than a life to be lived; that angels are decorative sprites—not, of course, according to the catechism definition but according to the illustrations in certain books and sometimes in the classroom. The tragedy comes when adults, waking to the foolishness of such religious concepts, equate them with the real truths of faith and turn away from them all. This kind of teaching is unintended, of course; but real teaching is always exact, always sure. Writers who give inept examples and half-true or foolish explanations are usually less ignorant of theology than of children, and believe that the latter will understand only this type of language. They do not share the insight of Chesterton:

It is the one eternal education; to be sure enough that something is true that you dare to tell it to a child.[16]

There are other concepts which children develop through the fault of no one, but as a result of their own immaturity.[17] Many of these are corrected in time; but the opportunity for quiet readjustment of ideas (which goes on with all of us until we die) should be given by review, clinching, new approaches, and exactness. The meaning of words can no more be taken for granted here than in kindergarten.

[16] G. K. Chesterton, *What's Wrong with the World* (New York: Dodd, Mead, 1910), p. 254.

[17] See, for example, the enlightening report of research by André Godin, S.J., and Sister Marthe, D.C., in "Magic Mentality and Sacramental Life in Children of 8 to 14 Years," *Lumen Vitae*, 15 (June 1960), 277–96.

For the religious educator it is not the formation of concepts alone that is at stake. Rather it is the emergence of an adult personal relationship with God, prepared for by strong ties formed in childhood. Grace builds on nature, not by a set formula $\left\{ \dfrac{\text{supernatural}}{\text{natural}} = \text{the complete Christian} \right\}$ but differently for each person through the exquisite concern of God for his needs, temperament, and circumstances. If Montessori could conclude from observation that the child has natural periods of sensitivity in growth and learning, how much more can we be sure—by observation and faith—that in every period of life God, who orders all things sweetly, reveals His face to the person in the way best suited to his insights, experience, receptiveness, and maturity. To the twelve, thirteen, and fourteen-year-old He speaks in a way suited only to them, just as He approached the men of ancient Israel with deference to their capacities as individuals and as men of their time and nation.

References to twelve-year-olds and to men of the Old Testament merge pleasantly in the figure of Anne Frank.[18] One likes to think of her as being welcomed as a daughter of Israel by the heavenly Father to whom she testified unknowingly amidst the sufferers in their Nazi concentration camp. In her daily visits to a sick, twelve-year-old boy, the girl's conversations with him were observed and bore fruit:

> David came from an orthodox family, and he and Anne always talked about God. As for God—I often thought in those days: God . . . But when I saw the two children together, I thought: No, I must not have such thoughts.[19]

[18] Any teacher of twelve- to fourteen-year-old girls will find a remarkable sourcebook of adolescent psychology in *Anne Frank: The Diary of A Young Girl* (New York: Doubleday & Company, 1952). See a critique of the book and its related play and film in Martin Dworkin, "The Vanishing Diary of Anne Frank," *The Critic*, 18 (February–March 1960), 15 ff.

[19] The words of an eyewitness, Mrs. De Wiek, quoted in Ernst Schnabel, *Anne Frank: A Portrait in Courage* (New York: Harcourt, Brace, 1958), pp. 159 f.

One can only conjecture what was in those conversations, and how many other victims of the Jewish holocaust were touched by them. This young girl, who was thrown from a normal childhood of apparently indifferent religious practice into an adulthood of inhumanity, exemplified not only a confident approach to God but other childlike features that usually mark the adolescent: simplicity, directness, and love of fun; a clinging to ideals while sharply criticizing deviations from them by herself or others. These are the characteristics that remain almost intact among seventh- and eighthgraders, and that will condition their own conversations with God or about Him.

The five characteristics reviewed here are selected from many which can be found among boys and girls of the seventh and eighth grades. They are natural, necessary, and wholly providential. Self-concern is always a part of man's turning to God: "What does it profit a man . . . ?" (Mt 16, 26). The forming of ideals is a human means of spiritual progress, carried along by grace. Conforming to the group has its proper place in all social life. Reaching for new horizons is essential for reaching toward God—again, within the moving power of grace. Slowness to leave childhood behind is a stabilizing force, conservative in the best sense. Every psychological study leads us to say, "How wonderful is God in His ways with men!" His ways are not our ways, but the best of ours are all His.

The question now is, how to apply even these few points to catechetical teaching in order that knowledge of the child will help us bring him to God.

NOTES ON THE PROGRAM OF INSTRUCTION

It is not possible here to describe and evaluate any total plan for religious instruction, as found in curricula, manuals, or textbooks. Neither is it necessary to reproduce ideas from the many excellent sources on the content or methods of religious education which are at hand today. Rather, four standards for the selection and organization of upper-grade learning experiences in religion

will be suggested: (1) freshness of approach; (2) the introduction
of certain adult elements; (3) the choice of appropriate learning
experiences, and (4) emphasis upon the individual.

Freshness of Approach

The American parish school, in contrast to the majority of public
elementary schools, normally provides an eight-year terminal program. The welcome change of pace in the seventh and eighth
grades of a junior high school must be achieved in the parish
school by other means. Sometimes this is done by departmental
teaching, but more often by giving subjects taught throughout the
earlier grades a new orientation or structure. In the religion program, of which many children can still say that they have "had the
same thing every year in the same way," it is especially necessary
that the maturing minds of boys and girls have some experiences
which differ in quality and kind from those of preceding years.

One example may be found in courses which, after emphasizing
the chief areas of doctrine together with increasing acquaintance
with the Scriptures and participation in the liturgy, center upper-
grade study about the life of Christ, first in the Bible and secondly
in the living Church.[20] The value of this arrangement, of course, is
only incidentally one of change. (It is, in fact, regrettable in the
extreme that teaching in the lower grades has been so innocent of
biblical and worship elements. But so things stand, and there is no
harm in building on the reality.) In this plan the studies of the
young adolescent parallel and benefit from the present-day revival
of studies in the two fields above mentioned, which lay bare the
roots of Christian faith. As happens in the Church itself, the study
of doctrine is given fresh insights and impetus when the "truths of
faith" are seen to center about Jesus Christ and one's relationship
to Him. The law of God is learned from His words and life, and
His continuing vitality is experienced through active membership
in His mystical body. In that body one is nourished for present

[20] Although there are several ways of providing a change of structure
in the upper grades, this pattern has been adopted by a number of diocesan
school systems and implemented by several series of textbooks.

life and prepared for eternal reunion with the risen Christ by means of the sacraments.

Children readily see these values in the study of Christ in the Scriptures and the liturgy. Here are two pupil reactions at the close of a year's study, chosen from seventh and eighth grade classes of two schools. One of them is an urban, semi-blighted area, the other in a small university city:[21]

> I think that there were many good points in the way we studied religion this year. Rather than memorize answers to questions, we used an outline form which, to begin with, acquainted us with the Bible. Secondly, we went further into the religion and as it were traveled with Christ in His building of the Church and her teachings.

> Usually, questions concerning religion come up that are not answered in the religion books. But in our study this year we used the Bible, from which the questions are made, and by doing our assignment learned the story behind the story.

> It is interesting how some children can do such surprising things. It is easy to do wrong but the more you read from the Bible the more you seem to want to do right. When you hear of how Our Lord healed the blind, cured the sick and dying, it's hard to want to do wrong.

In nearly every response children referred to knowing Christ better, getting to know and use the Bible, having personal questions answered, and—a new procedure—following an outline of the year's work. All reactions indicated a personal response to values as well as pleasure in a new approach to religious truths.

Introduction of Adult Elements

The religion teacher is obliged to look realistically into the future of his charges and introduce where feasible those applications of

[21] The program was that developed for seventh and eighth grades in the curriculum by Sister Mary Joan, O.P. and Sister Mary Nona, O.P., *Guiding Growth in Christian Social Living* (Washington, D.C.: Catholic University of America Press, 1959 rev. ed.), III, and introduced by the unit, "Through Christ our Lord: The Redemption in the Bible and the Church Year," pp. 286–302.

Christian teachings which will stand them in good stead for a long time to come. This is preventive teaching in its best sense: a going before, a constructive preparation for the fully human life ahead.

Some aspects of Christian living which will soon be making demands upon the boy and girl are personal, some social. All have supernatural importance. The personal matters will include questions of love, marriage, and vocation. The social questions will refer to a whole range of human relations, including those with classmates, the opposite sex, neighbors, the government and fellow citizens, and world humanity. All these have inherent possibilities for justice and charity, greed and materialism, cruelty or kindness. Supernatural responsibilities, springing from baptism, will always be present; but so will the encompassing graces of Christ in His Church, offering all means for practicing the faith as His members.

The religious preparation par excellence which the upper-grade child can have for a mature Christian life is to see the Church as the living Christ, teaching what each individual of our time needs to know, guiding adults in the solution of personal and social problems and calling youth to share fully in His action in the world. In this context Christ is seen giving the norms for judgment of national events, interracial action, business ethics, the work of the U.N., the struggle for peace. Religious education does not merely correlate with these topics: it *must introduce them* to show with what human issues Christ deals directly in His Church. The child's spirit of docility, or teachableness, is still present to a large degree among upper-grade children, who for some years now have been filled with the Spirit in confirmation and are ready to give witness to Christ. This is the time for absorption of certain basic teachings of the Church on adult subjects, limited of course in accord with lack of experience and interest. In a few years serious questions will arise, and greater resistance. But the mind that has glimpsed the greatness and beauty of the Church in the first years of adolescence will tend to return later to the teachings that have been reasonably and richly presented earlier.[22]

[22] A Little Sister of the Poor once gave testimony to the long-range effectiveness of Catholic schooling. "We have taken in many old men and

Christ not only teaches, but governs and sanctifies; and He does all of these things through the parish as well as the universal Church. It is a special feature of the Church in the United States that parish life is highly organized and its parishioners made especially conscious of the parish as a close-knit spiritual family by the presence—actual or hoped for—of the parish school. During their last years in this school or in their school of religion children should be reintroduced to the concept of parish life, reviewing the sacramental riches offered to people everywhere in the world from their parish altars, pulpits, and baptismal fonts. This leads immediately to consideration of the missionary apostolate of Catholics at home and in world missions, the place of various rites in the Church, and the movement toward reunion among Christians of our day. These are adult themes and adult opportunities, offering solutions to adult problems. No upper-grade pupil is going to probe deeply into them, although an individual of this age sometimes shows marked understanding of certain truths. But he can learn thoroughly the foundations on which the mystery of Christ in His Church is studied.

Appropriate Learning Experiences

As with the content, so also the ways of learning should fit the progressive development of the child, and introduce some adult features: discussion, committee work, and some modest individual or group research. Most important is learning to use the two living texts—not textbooks in the narrower sense—of Christians: the Bible and the missal. One aid to studying the Scriptures, and especially the New Testament, is a simple outline to be followed throughout the year and a personal notebook in which points can be pulled to-

---

some women who had not practiced their faith for years or decades. But of these, not one who had attended a Catholic school failed to return to the faith. They have something to return to which others have not." Interview with the writer, 1955. This welcome testimony to Catholic schooling, of course, is all tied in with testimony to good parents, and unfortunately to the level of seriousness at which many parishes have approached the problem of forming all of their children religiously.

gether and interpreted, quotations recorded, and the whole study kept for future use. As one boy put it, "You say questions once or twice and then you know them and then a couple of days later you forget, but with the notebook in your desk you take it out to look at it and you realize it's really useful." And another, "You can see what you have done and be proud of it. You also have a chance to go into the Bible and take out scriptural texts to further your knowledge of Christ and His Church. It is also easier to understand and you have more time to think about it." "The notebook is good to show to others." The principle involved is not as evident to the pupils as to the catechist:

> The working notebook has the same effect [of making the religion lesson personal]. Every child must "do" in some way or other everything that is taught in class. By transferring what has been merely heard to some practical activity *the intellect is brought into touch with the "stuff" of human nature: the power of the imagination, the will, diligence, the emotions, the creative capacity,* etc. Anyone who is required to *do* something is forced to assimilate the subject independently to a far greater extent than when he is merely required to learn it by heart.[23]

This principle can be applied fruitfully in creative activities which fit the study of Christ in the gospels and the liturgy, and likewise appeal to boys and girls of the upper grades. They like to write gospel scenes "as if I were there," skits showing some aspect of Christ-like living, personal applications of liturgical and scriptural lessons. They like to act out scenes and even do some role-playing, as of the practical problems related to religion lessons.[24] Making maps of our Lord's or St. Paul's journeys and murals of scriptural or liturgical themes, and posters of the O Antiphons, are favorite activities. The collecting instinct is utilized in gathering quotations on certain topics. Of great importance to an understanding of the sacramental idea is children's growing understand-

---

23 Goldbrunner, *op. cit.,* p. 114.
24 Rudolph Bandas, *Practical Problems in Religion* (Milwaukee: Bruce Publishers, 1934).

ing of symbols and their depth of meaning. "The making of symbols was interesting because we knew what they meant." Choral interpretation of the psalms, prophecies, and religious poetry is another worthwhile means of reviewing and vivifying the truths of man's relationship to God.[25]

Although the foregoing learning experiences appeal to children in the upper grades, there is no level at which the usual procedures of good teaching are not essential. Of these, the following are especially pertinent to the teaching of religion:

Planning, both remote and immediate, with this class and its needs especially in mind. This must include the reflection by which the teacher brings each truth to life. "In my meditation a fire shall flame out" (Ps 38, 4).

Purpose made clear to the pupils through careful orientation.

Vocabulary development. Ideas are in words; but how many ideas of religion have never been learned, though supposedly taught, because the words did not convey the meaning? Development, of course, means more than definition.[26]

Examples. The unity of truth and its shade of meaning are found in multiplicity of approach. There is no substitute for examples and parallels which fit the concept. This is the way our Lord taught.

Questioning with skill to review, clarify, stir up thought, gain attention, or test.[27]

[25] See Sister Vincent Miriam, C.S.J., "Choral Speaking with The Psalms," *Worship,* 23 (February 1959), 171–74.

[26] See Francis H. Drinkwater, "The Use of Words: A Problem of Both Content and Method," *Shaping the Christian Message,* ed. Gerard S. Sloyan (New York: Macmillan Company, 1958), pp. 263–80. Also the results of research given in David C. Fullmer, *The Vocabulary of Religion* (Washington, D.C.: The Catholic University of America Press, 1943), though the improvement in catechetical content in the intervening period has lessened the relevance of many of his findings.

[27] See the chapter on "Questioning," pp. 61–64 and other valuable procedures in Kevin Cronin, C.M., *Teaching the Religion Lesson* (London: Paternoster Publications, 1952).

Variety. Unlike the animals which, as St. Thomas never tires of remarking, do the same determinate things in the same determinate way, human nature demands variety.[28] Older persons can sometimes submit to the humdrum, but twelve- to fourteen-year-olds cannot. Neither can the ever-new truths of religion be subjected to colorless, unthinking sameness of presentation.

Illustration. With many audio-visual aids on the market it is more imperative than ever to choose wisely from among them for (a) accuracy and (b) suitability to the subject and the learner's age level. Both aspects require products of good art, right making; nothing saccharine or false.

Application to personal living. The young adolescent, oriented to himself, is quick to find applications with the encouragement of the teacher.

Conclusion. A lesson in religion, in which every minute is given to a study of eternal importance, must close with a summary of ideas, relating them to what has gone before and what is to come. The assignment, far from being routine or haphazard, should be an important part of the lesson, calling for the pupils' personal involvement. It should not be limited to a hurried "Study Lesson 14," or "Read the next three pages in in your text." One might ask, "What for?"

Emphasis on the Individual

The reasons for individualized teaching are well known and thoroughly treated in other sources. In upper-grade religious education these are accentuated by the ever-personal character of

[28] Murray McCance, a vestment-maker of Montreal, writes in his highly civilized newsletter that Aristotle argued that since man has intelligence, and intelligence means unlimited power of knowing, choosing, and so of making, man ought to be left at liberty to plan, choose, and make his own covering. So in fact he does, and woman even more so. (Though McCance wryly observes that the vestment-maker is like a man seated at a huge pipe organ with all the manuals and stops who is never asked for anything but a saccharine *Ave Maria* or *Panis Angelicus*).

religion and the need of the young adolescent for attention, support, and counseling. These can be given by the teacher without risk of stirring up self-consciousness or the unwanted notice of the class by skilful blending of counseling with individualized assignments: to look up scriptural references and report them in an interview; to write on a virtue as developed in the liturgical sources; to write a journal or "autobiography," a form which is closely related to the diary-writing interests of the adolescent. Boys and girls who want help (and many do) will take quick advantage of an assignment interview to ask questions or simply talk about problems, especially if it is scheduled on a regular basis before or after school, preferably out of the classroom. Care must be taken not to seem to be inviting too personal a discussion. The same procedure may be used to advantage by the parish priest who does not come daily to teach the class, but plans his lessons so that an interview-assignment will seem reasonable.

The interview affords opportunity for suggesting books to read, especially as an introduction—according to individual capacities —to spiritual reading. Suggestions may also take the form of bibliotherapy.[29] This is one means of fostering the practice of virtues noted as lacking in pupils. A sure sign that the teacher is following after our Lord as catechist is his own conviction that each soul is dear to him and his care that each lesson be planned to activate the natural and supernatural powers of all in the class.

FROM STUDY TO PRAYER

Religious instruction begins, not with the opening of the class, but when the teacher prays for guidance before planning the lesson or unit. It is consummated when, sooner or later, the pupil turns the truths he has learned into conversation with God. In the craft of prayer teacher and class are apprentices together, as they are in the practice of virtue. The prayer of children in the upper grades can be considered under the same four topics used for notes on religious instruction, with some variations proper to the subject.

[29] Clara Kircher, *Character Formation through Books: A Bibliography* (Washington: The Catholic University of America Press, 1952).

Change and Freshness

When one follows the prayer of the Church through feasts and seasons one wonders how the block method of class prayer could ever have originated. For example:

Morning: The Apostles' Creed, Morning Offering, Our Father, Hail Mary, Acts of Faith, Hope, and Charity,

Noon: Angelus and grace before meals; after lunch, the entire rosary, or one decade.

Dismissal: Act of Contrition, ejaculations.

The Church makes use of change and variety, as the liturgy demonstrates, because she knows man's need for it. But some seventh- and eighthgraders take part daily in "a long patter of routine prayers that may easily have as little to do with our heavenly Father as marking the register."[30] It is thirty-five years since Canon Drinkwater pointed out in sincere and humorous fashion the evils of such school prayers and gave excellent suggestions for remedy, but his words have not reached as far as would be desired. Following his admonitions, these suggestions are offered for varying and vivifying prayer in the upper-grade classes:

1. Keep prayer separate from the learning of prayers. Introduce prayer-time with recollection of the presence of God.

2. Change the choice of prayers from day to day, making use of those prayers which fit the season or feast.

3. Use fitting and varying means to compose body and soul for prayer: posture, change of location, use of picture or small altar, lighting of candle, and other such tangible helps as the liturgy of sacramentals provides for concentration and grasp of meaning.

[30] Francis H. Drinkwater, "Prayer Time," *Educational Essays* (London: Burns Oates, 1951), p. 284. Every teacher of religion would benefit from this essay, indeed from all of them, drawn from rich priestly experience in catechizing. The same author's *Telling the Good News* (see n. 6 *supra*) is doubly sprightly, if that could be, and shows an awareness of catechetical progress that one would wish to find in persons who are much closer to their own period of formation as teachers.

4. Help children to understand the communion of saints by changing the intention of class prayers; allow opportunity for secret, personal intentions as well as class ones.

5. Let one prayer of the day be a hymn, preferably with no other prayer added, lest children think it a kind of "extra," not quite valid. Let it not end abruptly with the first verse; the singing is more full with succeeding repetition.

6. Build up a repertory of hymns,[31] so that at least thirty are known before children leave the parish school or school of religion. Let hymns be learned in music class or in a practice period, sung confidently at prayer time.

7. Concentrate on one of the four ends of prayer at a time, building up an understanding of the purpose by discussing it beforehand.

8. Compose together, at the close of a certain lesson, a prayer which will summarize its points and convert them into thoughts with which to speak directly to God.

Introduction of Adult Themes

The prayer of a mature man or woman is surely different in many respects from that of a child. The prayer of a young adolescent combines some features of both. What prayers fit his needs? In addition to the Creed, the Our Father, and the Hail Mary, which belong to persons of all ages, the psalms are particularly relevant to his growing up. These are prayers composed by men of Israel, some of them simple men, some sophisticated court poets, who laid them at the feet of God much as adolescents do their joys, discouragements, aspirations, pleas for help and forgiveness. They likewise registered in terms of great poetic power their love of creation and praise of the heavenly Father. Pupils can study and discuss them with the help of the teacher. They can sing them,

[31] Among the hymnals published recently, *Our Parish Prays and Sings* (Collegeville, Minnesota: The Liturgical Press, 1959) and *Parish Mass Book* (Cinninnati: World Library of Sacred Music, 1959) are well adapted to use in the upper grades. On the subject of relating hymns to religious doctrines see Sister M. Teresine, O.S.F., "To Pray in Beauty," *Musart*, 9 (June 1957), 17–19.

chant or recite them chorally, choose certain ones for private
prayer, and compose psalm-like prayers related to their own
experiences.

The aspirations of the psalmist are seen fulfilled in the mysteries
of the rosary, the story of Christ's coming and man's salvation.
Reflection on the mysteries will become more adult with experience. But the experience will make little difference unless the
person has learned how to think about the mysteries and place
himself in the presence of Jesus and Mary rejoicing, suffering, and
completing the work of redemption. Having learned the component prayers of the rosary years before, one of the adult responsibilities which older children should take up is reflection on the
mysteries. There are innumerable source materials for the teacher
to help them do this.[32]

Helps for Learning to Pray

Two of the ways not yet mentioned for helping children to pray
are (1) building up their storehouse of prayers for various needs
and occasions, and (2) introducing them to the practice of mental
prayer.

The prayer repertory of upper-grade boys and girls can be rich
and varied, if compiled by themselves from available, approved
sources: the liturgy[33] (not forgetting prayers of the votive Masses
for special needs), the Raccolta, the prayers of the saints and the
Holy Father, those found in pamphlets or prayerbooks. Children
like to compile their own prayerbooks, selecting and copying
prayers as needed, or composing them.

As to meditation, even young children engage in a kind of
reflection which leads to resolve and action. Older ones, with
guidance, can turn reflection into meditation. Not to do so when

---

[32] For example, Maisie Ward's *Splendor of the Rosary* (New York: Sheed
and Ward, 1954) which sets forth in direct and simple language the
meaning of the rosary. "The beads are there for the sake of the prayers, and
the prayers are there for the sake of the Mysteries," p. 7.

[33] See Sister St. Thomas, S.N.D., "Prayer-Education and the Roman
Missal: the Collects of the Proper of the Time," *Lumen Vitae,* 14 (March
1959), 67–80.

they are studying the life of Christ with the Bible and liturgy as
sourcebooks would seem to be a serious omission. Many teachers
have promoted the practice of mental prayer in their classes,
especially in the secondary school; some have written of their experiences. Among the written accounts is that of a teacher who
helped seventh-grade pupils to meditate.[34] She gave the full school
year to a systematic introduction to mental prayer, in two stages:
directed (six weeks) and non-directed (six months). The first practice introduced was that of forming a resolution or "secret"—a
promise made secretly to God—following class reading and discussion of suggested resolutions. Then gospel themes were introduced,
with reflections by the teacher upon the passages assigned and
read by the children. The next step was three-minute meditations
following class discussion of gospel passages. Finally, pupils would
choose their own texts from the Gospel passages in the missal, find
them in the New Testament, write them out, and give the reason
for their choice. Next day they meditated on the chosen passage,
closing the three-minute meditation with the secret resolution.

Children carried on the practice at home and in some cases
persuaded other members of the family to do likewise. Among their
many appreciative reactions near the close of the year were these:
"Mental prayer is more satisfying because I don't just say words.
I really think." "The things I think about stay with me for a
long time." "In thinking about the life of our Lord and His
Blessed Mother, all that they did becomes part of me."[35] These
words recall the work of the Right Reverend George Johnson in
teaching twelve-year olds mental prayer, and his words of encouragement to others to do likewise:

Let it not be laid to our charge that men never rose above
mediocrity because we failed to give them, as boys, spiritual

[34] Sister Joseph Mary Miller, O.P., "An Investigation of the Possibilities of
Mental Prayer with Seventh Grade Pupils" (unpublished Master's thesis,
The Catholic University of America, 1951). An article based on this thesis
is her "Preparing Seventh Graders for Mental Prayer," *The Catholic Educator*, 24 (April 1954), 421 f.
[35] Miller, "An Investigation . . . ," p. 27.

direction. Whatever we begin, surely the Holy Spirit will complete. Through the habit of contemplation, children, unknown to themselves, build a spiritual fort which enables them to put up an effective defense against worldly suggestions.[36]

Individual and Corporate Prayer

The one and the many, the individual and the community, the person and the common good: these delicately balanced poles of human life are present in the practice of prayer as well as in other activities of the Christian. The young adolescent, aware that all prayer is a personal turning to God, learns also from the gospels that our Lord invites him to present his needs and those of others in confident petition; that all prayer is answered in the way that God knows best; that the troubles of adolescents can be brought to Him for solution by the prayer of adolescents.[37]

Balancing this individual emphasis, however, is the need to take an active, intelligent part in the corporate prayer of the Church. At this age the liturgy becomes not only a subject of study which follows necessarily from that of the Bible, but an opportunity for participation in the worship of God around the parish altar. In our day, following the mind of the Holy See, upper-grade children must sometimes play the key role within a given parish in the parishioners' transition from non-participation to participation in the liturgy:

> The Catholic school of this present time is insensitive to the demands of Holy Church if it fails to be active in preparing students to play an adult part in Catholic worship. In a sense it does not matter which group is ready first, clergy or teachers, though a mild confusion may arise if a call is issued by the one which finds no echo in the other. The people are ready now.

36 George Johnson, "Teaching Children to Meditate," *The Catholic Educational Review*, 26 (April 1928), 244.

37 On the question of "interior balance" and adolescent prayer, see Marcel Hertsens, "The Prayer of Adolescents," *Lumen Vitae*, 15 (June 1960), 297–307. See also some remarkable examples of meditation on seeking God's will in prayer in Sister Joseph Mary's "Investigation. . . ," pp. 33 f.

They are already abstaining in great numbers from meaningless Sunday Masses, and in many who are uninstructed it is doubtfully any sin. It is the teacher, whether in or out of sacred orders, who needs to worry about sin in this matter, especially that of insensitivity to the demands of the Holy See.[38]

And how does a school prepare seventh- and eighthgraders, above and beyond the preparation by daily instruction, centered in Christ, to play an adult part in Catholic worship? First by teaching the meaning of the liturgy, deepening from grade to grade the understanding of public worship "through Christ our Lord"; secondly by studying the prayers and actions which flow from the holy sacrifice of the Mass, the sacramental reality and action of Christ; and finally, by actual participation. This may mean, in some parishes, not only learning to pray and sing the Mass communally but taking special roles in a boys' choir, a schola, a group of leaders for the dialogue Mass.[39] It can mean in parish schools and graded Confraternity classes that upper-grade boys and girls assume leadership for the school by helping to explain feasts and seasons to younger children, reading lessons or leading the choral recitation of psalms at a brief feast-day assembly, and giving example by active attendance at Mass. These natural leaders of the elementary school can turn the minds of all to parish life around the parish altar by making posters, giving commentaries over the public address system, writing bulletins about the liturgy of the week. Yet none of these things, helpful as they may be, is essential. The essential practice is that of prayer with Christ, personal and communal, according to the directives of His vicar, of the local bishop, and the pastor of the living cell in the mystical body of Christ, the parish.[40]

[38] Gerard S. Sloyan, "Some Problems of Religious Formation in Our Day," *Catholic Educational Review*, 57 (April 1959), 224.

[39] See examples in "It Can Be Done," *Worship*, various issues, including Vols. 32 (May–June 1958), 370, and 33 (June–July 1959), 444: also, "Preparing Adolescents for Holy Week," *ibid.*, 33, 183 ff.

[40] For practical helps as well as inspiration see the pastoral letter of John Baptist Cardinal Montini, "Liturgical Formation," *ibid.*, 33, 136–64.

LOVE IN ACTION

Setting forth reasons for children receiving Confirmation at the age of reason, Delcuve says:

> How necessary it is that the Spirit descend upon our children in His fullness very early, and that they come to think of Him habitually as "another Friend"; come to need Him and to act with Him!

When we consider today's children, many of them cut off from religion or thoroughly disoriented by war and its effects, by family mobility and divorce, we are dismayed at the weight of their obligations if they are baptized and wish to live as Catholics. They themselves have to struggle for perseverance; no one can do it for them. They can only do it by working to alter their surroundings, their study, their leisure.[41]

Children in seventh and eighth grades have, with few exceptions, already received this fullness of the Holy Spirit. It is their reserve of spiritual strength, of truth, courage, love from which the religious educator can help them to draw in order to convert knowledge of God into loving service, to practice the truth in love. "Each Christian teacher must think of himself in relation to the priest who baptized his pupils and the bishop who confirmed them. In the classroom he helps to complete what these sacraments inaugurated."[42]

The completion of what these sacraments inaugurated is love, embracing the practice of virtue in the relation of each boy and girl to God and fellowmen. "By their fruits you shall know them" (Mt 7, 16). In the classroom the teacher can give guidance for the development and practice of virtue, translated into the practical realities of life for children growing up in our time, if he is always conscious that the task is one of disproportionate partnership: "we and the Holy Spirit."

Virtue involves strength, habit, grace, and—by its very name—

[41] George Delcuve, "Confirmation at the Age of Reason," in Sloyan, *Shaping the Christian Message*, p. 314.
[42] Sloyan, "Some Problems . . . ," p. 222.

manliness, or its counterpart in womanly stature. Furthermore, freedom of choice and fullness of responsibility are necessary to virtuous action. Young children are able to practice obedience, and other virtues to a degree limited by their lack of maturity. To adolescents, on the other hand, freedom and responsibility are given increasingly, while obedience becomes increasingly difficult as the demands of independent judgment assert themselves. During this transitional stage, how can the full range of virtues be encouraged and developed among youth? Space permits only a few notes in summary form which might be of help to the teacher of religion:

Prudence has a particular bearing upon Christian living at this age. It is the virtue of reflection before action; of taking advice; of forming judgments; of taking right means to an end; and of completing judgment by action.

Justice is a virtue which the adolescent cleaves to eagerly within the limits of his experience: fairness, honesty, no respecting of persons. But he is easily attracted to other developments of the virtue. Foremost among these is, of course, the virtue of religion —of bodily and mental homage, prayer, and worship. Filial devotion and patriotism should be shown as second only to the practice of religion in the matter of justice.

Fortitude, or courage, is a habit which the young adolescent needs to turn away from the crowd when required; to do what is right despite self-consciousness or ridicule; to accept the challenge to greatness of soul and action; to practice patience and perseverance. For the impatient, explosive teen-ager the two last-named versions of fortitude are akin to heroism![43]

Temperance, or moderation, is undeniably a matter of concern to youth, not only with regard to pleasure but in the practice of humility. But modesty and chastity are the key points here. At twelve, children will have varying needs as to sex education, and most of these should be met by parents. Unfortunately, many

[43] See Josef Pieper, *Fortitude and Temperance* (New York: Pantheon Press, 1954); also Dietrich von Hildebrand, *Fundamental Moral Attitudes* (New York: Longmans, Green, 1950).

obtain no help. Yet the religion class itself gives opportunity to present the truly Christian, positive approach to chastity:

> The true name for purity is respect for life, for the child, for the sources which give life. It does not consist of shame. The body is holy in all its parts. We must respect the gift that God has made us.[44]

This should be taught, not only in the development of the sixth commandment, but in connection with the principle that whatever is material is subordinate and important to the spiritual, acting in fact as its medium. This is the sacramental idea, the meaning of signs and symbolism. It is the key to man's total personality—"a body ensouled"[45]—and to the supernatural reality of the body as temple of the indwelling Trinity.

Faith, of course, is the key to the relationship of child and youth, man and woman, to God. It is always a mystery. "Jesus has given Himself as a mystery of faith, into which no one can enter except by a light from God."[46] But with this light from God, which is conveyed through baptism, the child is invited to enter more deeply into the mystery of faith from year to year. He must reply with his whole person to the invitation from Christ who desires to say to him at the close of life, "Your faith has made you whole." Religious education supplies the reason for the faith that is in each one. It teaches him to pray; it leads him to the altar of the Mass, the fount of grace, and to the action of Christ in the other sacraments. It makes him conscious of communal living with other members in the body of Christ. By all these means can he build up the virtue of faith.

Hope is the virtue of clinging to God and trusting in Him. It is another baptismal gift which is to be cultivated with God's grace and most fittingly in youth, which has a special affinity for it. Men

[44] Maurice Zundel, *In Search of the Unknown God* (New York: Herder and Herder, 1959), p. 170.
[45] *Ibid.*, pp. 31–33. See also Jean Mouroux, *The Meaning of Man* (New York: Sheed and Ward, 1948), chapters 3–5.
[46] Zundel, *op. cit.*, p. 111.

of hope, no matter what their age, are young in heart. Such was
Charles Péguy, who wrote of hope:

>I am, says God, the Lord of virtues.
>Faith is the sanctuary lamp
>That burns forever.
>Charity is that big, beautiful log fire
>That you light in your hearth
>So that my children the poor may come and warm them-
>   selves before it on winter evenings.
>. . . . .
>But my hope is the bloom, and the fruit, and the leaf, and
>   the limb,
>And the twig, and the shoot, and the seed, and the bud.
>Hope is the shoot, and bud of the bloom
>Of eternity itself.[47]

With what effects for eternity the teacher can lead his pupils to
the practice of the virtue of hope, particularly through simple
and sincere confidence in God on his own part, with obvious
trust in His Will under all circumstances!

Love, the virtue of time and eternity, is the beginning and end
of religious formation. Little children know love through the affection and care of their parents—through receiving; and they
understand God's love in the same way, by analogy. Youth must
come to know love as giving, so that they can find God and serve
Him through love of Him in others. But even human love requires
a "training of the heart" such as Aelred Watkin proposes.[48] Boys
and girls in the upper grades will soon be surrounded with light
and inconsequential if not actually false ideas of love. It is essential
that they be introduced to that integrity of human love in which
physical and spiritual, individual and family love have their meaning and fulfillment.

[47] Charles Péguy, God Speaks (New York: Pantheon Books, 1945), p. 70.
[48] Aelred Watkin, O.S.B., "The Training of the Heart," Life of the
Spirit, 12 (June 1958), 530–39. The article gives realistic help for teaching
adolescents the true balance and perspective in human love, oriented to
love of God.

Although human love will be accentuated in adolescent thinking, it can become the means toward that all-embracing goal of
religious formation which is the supernatural love of God. Faith
works through love, as St. Augustine reminds us, and without love
the pedagogy of faith will remain forever unfruitful.

The pedagogy is completed by instruction in the practice of
supernatural love. Such love must be universal as God's is universal, cherishing all of creation without exception and giving it
the order of values He has given it. It will be respectful toward
every person, recognizing that God dwells in him by grace.[49] It
will be courteous, self-sacrificing, and willing to serve. What better
checklist of charity can one find for upper-grade boys and girls
than St. Paul's own: charity is patient, kind, feels no envy; is never
perverse, proud, insolent; does not claim its rights, cannot be
provoked, does not brood over an injury, takes no pleasure in
wrongdoing, rejoices at the victory of truth, sustains, believes,
hopes, endures to the last.[50] It is the privilege and responsibility
of the twelve- to fourteen-year-old to translate each of these terms,
with the help of grace, into the actions of his own life.

[49] See Mary Reed Newland, "The Life of Grace Within," *Cross and
Crown*, 12 (December 1960), 464–79.
[50] See 1 Cor 13, 4–7.

9 SPECIAL PROBLEMS

OF THE FIRST TWO YEARS OF

HIGH SCHOOL

Sister Mary Virgine Pugh, M.H.S.H.

I. THE CATECHIST LEADS THE STUDENTS TO FAITH IN CHRIST

In the learning process the teacher effects a meeting between knower and known. The true teacher is concerned to be at home with both. In religious formation this meeting does not make friends of strangers but deepens friendship through fresh discoveries of God and self. If the teacher is to set the stage for this union, he must know well the nature of faith, the student, and Christ, who is the way to God.

Nature of Faith

Faith is a call from a personal God and requires a personal answer in terms of life lived. It is a life of faith "dependent on the

209

general level of maturity which the person has reached."[1] The answer to this call can be given adequately only by the mature person, whatever his age may be, who has found himself: the one who knows himself to be *this* unique existing being, aware of his individuality, of his milieu, of his ability to rise above the tide of "everyone's-doing-it" in order to take a stand—either with the crowd or against it—in pursuit of aims that have been made real to him. Such a one has achieved self-realization; he is living from within. He has the freedom and personal integrity required for the deliberate donation of self to God in a life of faith. The donation is made in accordance with his understanding of God's call to men.

The Student

The teacher will know that the teen-aged student entering the Catholic high school or the CCD high school of religion makes a fresh start. He willingly sheds the garb of an eighthgrader at the top of the student body to slip into the lowly dress of a freshman, for this beginning marks yet another step in his effort to grow into himself.[2] Yet his eagerness is tempered with a fear of the unknown. Somewhere along the line he discovers that the comfortable world of his childhood has lost its security. It is not the world that has changed, of course, but his relation to it: his relation to adults, especially parents and teachers, to upperclassmen, to his peers, and to himself. He is no longer permitted to hide within the childhood anonymity of the family, the class, or the neighborhood. He is expected to identify himself as an individual who knows where he is going, one capable of intelligently directed decision and action toward worthwhile goals. The teacher knows

[1] Josef Goldbrunner, *Cure of Mind and Cure of Soul*, trans. Stanley Godman (New York: Pantheon, 1958), p. 31.

[2] Cf. *ibid*. "The psychological steps which lead to the discovery of the self also assist the actuating of the person. And since this is a precondition of the Christian relationship to God which is called faith, it is not surprising that individuation can be regarded as a criterion for the realization of the Faith. . . . Any help that is given towards the maturing of the personality will also have a fruitful influence on the development of faith."

that such adult behavior is born of the labor pains of encounters and discoveries made during the transition period of adolescence. This birth must be self-created and self-creative, but its realization calls for adults who will assist him in it within a climate that is entirely "in Christ."

The religion teacher knows well that the trials of adolescent transition are not experienced by all at the same chronological age or with the same degree of intensity.[3] A fair sampling of the individual freshman or sophomore class, however, will testify to adolescent changes which take the form of an individual student's increased understanding of himself, his relation with his peers and with adults.

Understanding Himself

The adolescent is a puzzle to himself. "What am I really like? What do I want to be like?" are question that prod him vaguely as he senses his newly-developed powers. Unknowingly, he gropes to achieve self-realization. He looks at the world with a sense of adventure, with fear, and with emotions disproportionate to the incidents that arouse them. At one moment he is incapable of caring more, and the next, incapable of caring less—whether it be the project undertaken by the science class, work on the school paper, or the collection for the clothing drive. He does not understand this inconstancy and knows that it is not understood by others. Periods of withdrawal, introversion, and daydreaming may accompany this age of egocentrism and of high aspirations and inspiration. Most adolescents search for a personal, even heroic form of life. Yet not wanting to seem pious they may assume a mask of religious indifference and opposition.

[3] Cf. Pope John XXIII on this point: "The adolescent has his own problems, needs, and traits typical of the formative years; all of these are in urgent need of response, either from a spiritual and religious, or from an intellectual, emotional, and psychological standpoint. Every one of your students is marked by an individuality to which teaching methods must be tirelessly adapted so that your education work can consistently meet the challenges that confront it." Address to the Italian Catholic Association of High School Teachers, March 1960. An English text is provided in *The Pope Speaks*, 6 (Summer 1960), 257.

Relation with Peers

With childhood and adult behavior both closed to him, the adolescent turns to his own age group for norms of conduct. Craving peer recognition and group approval, he will be tempted to cast aside those values learned at home and school which conflict with the code of values held by the crowd.[4] If the values thus discovered seem to him to contradict the demands of Christianity, he may consider the adoption of the norms of the group as part of the growing-up process. He does not wish to revolt but feels he must if he is to "save himself," that is, establish his identity. The ardent desire for friendship and the expression of affections of his own choice manifest his striving for independence and self-assertion.

Relation with Adults

In his reach for autonomy the adolescent begins to question and seek proof for what he had formerly accepted on faith, suspecting that adults had at times taken advantage of his childhood dependence and trust. He shrinks from the adult who tries to force his confidence, who ridicules, or who even adverts to his fumbling attempts at grown-up behavior. The teen-aged boy or girl does not outgrow the need for guidance; rather he looks to adults to help him achieve the self-realization, independence, and ideals he seeks. He responds to respect shown for the dignity he has as a human person.[5]

Some drift along inertly during this period, hoping for "something to turn up" to change the current of daily sameness and thus

[4] Values dictated by society, which connote a failure to recognize the divine law as the norm upon which standards of conduct are based, are evident in the preface to a *Teens' Guide* constructed by a student committee representing four public high schools of Washington, D.C. The preface begins: "Our standards of behavior are set by the society around us and our personal desire to be a recognized and acceptable member of that society. . . ."

[5] "You must offer him [the adolescent], first of all, the delicate and charitable respect to which he is entitled as a human being, created in God's likeness. . . ." Pope John XXIII, *ibid.*, p. 258.

determine their futures. Others are up and doing, getting into everything as they expend energies they are not yet able to direct properly. All of them experience an indefinable disturbance and restlessness in face of the unknown. The adolescent needs a synthesis, a properly ordered, total view of reality which has a place for all the fragmented, conflicting experiences he has had or will have. He will not gain the needed perspective on the level of abstract ideas but on the level of persons and personal relationships. These must come to life for him. He needs to see his place in the whole and be assured of his interior continuity and identity. He must be led to discover this synthesis for himself if his actions are to flow from sincere personal conviction. Many times during the process he may find himself and God as if for the first time.

What encounters and discoveries fostered in the religion class will help the adolescent acquire this total view and identify his part in it? With an eye to the fact that "a religion too closely linked with adolescent psychology risks being completely grown out of with maturity,"[6] the catechist, nonetheless, makes good use of the adolescent need for development on the personal level, bringing him to a Person with whom he is to spend his life.

The Supreme Encounter

The teacher knows that individuals find themselves only as a result of successive personal engagements.[7] He is aware of the adolescent need for such person-to-person relationships. He is aware of his need for friendship, love, and a total view of reality. Knowing all this the teacher turns to Christ. He lets the person of Christ meet and challenge the student, stirring him to grow from

[6] "Une religion trop intimement liée à la psychologie adolescent risque d'ailleurs d'être entièrement dépassée aux approches de la maturité. . . ." R. Waelkens, "Le Mystère de Pâques et la psychologie adolescente," *Le Seigneur passe dans son peuple*. (Cahiers de la Roseraie. Bruges: Editions de L'Abbaye de Saint André), p. 85. Cited by Frère Vincent Ayel, F.S.C., "Teaching the Church to Adolescents," *Lumen Vitae*, 8 (1953), 418.

[7] "The person is actuated only by the call of other persons, in encounters, in social and communal life and in its relationship to the person of God." Goldbrunner, *op. cit.*, p. 102.

within. Christ extends His friendship, reveals the synthesis worked out in God's plan for man, shows the student his part in the whole and Himself as the way to the Father. This the teacher will do whatever the segment of God's revelation emphasized may be: faith, worship, or moral conduct; Scripture, liturgy, or Church history. No matter what content be chosen for the year's study, or within what structure, the person of Christ must shine through as the living, vital force which presents a challenge that cannot be ignored. This *must* be done; there is no other way. God acts with man—through Christ.

Christ Revealing Himself

"He who sees Me sees the Father also."[8] Christ came to reveal the Father to man and did so by revealing Himself. The person and actions of Jesus attract; man follows, going with Him to the Father. The teen-aged boy and girl need to value the interest focused on them before they will be partner to it. In what sense does Jesus attract them? How can the Master's actions with a tiny group of His fellow-nationals in the late Jewish period, half a world away, interest the tradition-scoffing lad of the modern technological West who lives for tonight's coke-bar and tomorrow's game? What great hero of the past could cope with the mentality of *our* times? Some try to hide behind such questions. A spirit-of-the-age tag can always be found to excuse failures or—worse still —the refusal even to try to achieve living contact between student and Teacher.

Yet the fact which must never be forgotten is that one who puts on the mentality of Christ can cope with the problems of any age. Christ's dealings with human nature are as timely as human nature itself. They need only be lifted out of His immediate temporal setting to match the pace of a given period. The Savior's attitude toward life with the sons of Abraham who were His brothers has its counterpart with the youth of the space age. This the modern student must discover. Telling him will not do. He must discover it for himself. The Christ who rejoiced with the merrymakers at

[8] Jn 14, 9.

Cana looks with pleasure on the fun-lovers at the school picnic. The school prom? Yes and no, for the encrustations of pseudo-adult convention have already removed it from the kind of gay family gathering we know He took part in. The Master who disdained the pharisaic washing of bowls disdains the pillars of rectitude who gasp at two-tone hair-do's and duck-tails. The Savior's gentle but uncompromising treatment of the woman taken in adultery is extended to the class-member who is an unwed mother-to-be.

The young person is on the lookout for someone who "knows his way around" and has all the answers. He finds Him in the person of the Wisdom of God in our flesh outwitting His enemies in verbal combat. The courageous Master faced His own apparent failure, not to speak of the suffering he would endure at the hands of the hate-filled mob, with a calm "Whom do you seek?" This courage will strengthen the youth who in his strivings toward an ideal falls short of the mark but does not escape ridicule from those who did not bother to try.

A person like Jesus, once known, has a chance to make of the adolescent a friend and disciple.

Christ as Friend

The adolescent has a great capacity for love and a craving for friendship. When affection is given outside the family circle, this bestowal signifies another step toward independence. The teen-aged boy or girl wants to possess and to be possessed, to give himself in devoted service—often to an ideal he has seen personified in someone. He longs for the reciprocal sharing of interests, plans, joys, and troubles, all found in the friendship he has freely chosen. The friendship may distress parents or teachers, but it has the merit of being an absolutely free choice; it has been elicited somehow, therefore it is worthy of attention and a kind of respect. For Christ to become his friend, the adolescent must be led to Jacob's well for a real encounter. He must see the Master waiting for *him*, interested in him and in the water he comes to draw, in the kind of life he is leading. The youth's acceptance of the fountain of living water is of great consequence to Christ. This the young person must know. He will respond to the respect that is shown to him in Zaccheus, the woman taken in adultery, the Roman centurion. To avoid seeming pious a student may, like Nicodemus, "come to Jesus by night"; but if like the man born blind he permits the Light of the world to render his sight open to true values he will be able to oppose the crowd—willing if need be to be cast from the synagogue of their norms of conduct. Having been with Peter on the road to Caesarea Philippi, he will confess Christ on the road to the skating rink or the drive-in. He will be ready for Christ's challenge with the answer, "Lord, to whom shall we go? You have the words of eternal life." Then will he open his heart to One who calls him a friend and not a servant.

Christ as Mediator

Becoming friends with Jesus is not enough. Friendship should lead to a clear awareness of Christ's mediatory role by which He hopes to unite men with the Father from whom sin has separated them. The redemptive work of Christ must be viewed as the return of all mankind to God accomplished in His passing to the Father. The God-man's actions, foreshadowed in the Old Testament and extended in His body the Church, retain all the force of their original occurrence in time. Christ appears as the fullness of Israel and the eternal High Priest of the New Law.

How excited can students get over Christ's announcement of the coming of the kingdom if they are unaware of their need for it? Will talk of "the sealing of the New Covenant in the blood of the Paschal Lamb" impress those who have never heard of God's loving initiative in making lovers of men? What can Christ possibly mean to young people who know nothing of the Old Covenant and man's infidelity to it, nothing of the role of the Passover lamb in bringing the Israelites from slavery to freedom? The heavenly nuptials of the New Jerusalem will be a vague figure of speech to those who have never heard of God's pledge of Himself as strong bridegroom to His beloved bride. Today's students must come to realize that Christ's sanctifying use of water, wine, and bread in dispensing saving mysteries in the twentieth century reflects His power over water, wine, and bread at Cana and the lakeshore. The Redeemer who wept over the unheeding hearts of the men of Jerusalem utters the moving cries of the Good Friday reproaches as His Church relives His Palestinian life in her worship life. Are the young open to all this? To answer this we must ask whether they are not daily creating their own heroes, making their own myths, prizing art forms that are *signs* of *things* (however this symbolism may offend the cultured eye and ear).

On balance, it appears that adolescents in our time are by all means capable of the poetry and symbol of Christian sacramentalism—if it is shared with them at full strength.

The high-school student needs to view the return of mankind to God accomplished by the death, resurrection, and ascension of Jesus as one which each member of Christ, vivified by the Spirit, achieves personally. In baptism he puts on Christ by dying and rising with Him—dying to sin and rising to the life of grace. The intention to live this "Christened" life has been expressed for the adolescent by his godparents. As an infant he knew neither himself nor the Savior. It is the task of all involved in his religious formation to lead him to a mature knowledge of Christ and of himself. Having seen the whole history of God's actions with His people summed up and continued in Jesus, having come to know himself as a unique, responsible human being, the student will be better prepared to renew the donation of self to God in a faith-filled life—the commitment made for him at baptism.

Can the adolescent who lives for the present and the future discover this total view and his part in it? The teacher leads the way to the discovery.

II. THE CATECHIST DEVELOPS HIS OWN POTENTIAL, THE CLIMATE OF HIS TEACHING, AND ITS TOOLS

The Teacher

That teacher will be able to lead the students to Christ who has already been His companion. God has always spoken to man by means of the living voice of His representative. Some like Osea and Jeremia were divinely schooled, knowing by experience the message they were to relay. Christ continues to approach men by way of the living voice of the religious educator who must likewise be divinely schooled.

The catechist who has "tasted and seen how good the Lord is"[9] will take his task seriously. He will not teach a subject. He will effect a meeting between Christ and the student. He knows when to recede into the background, but also realizes that the spontaneous answer to this message cannot always be deferred until a visit to the church or tomorrow's Mass.[10] The class hour and classroom, as well as the church or school chapel, become the setting for a prayerful reply. The proper use of the tools of instruction and a religious climate are needed to accomplish this, but the apostolic formation of the catechist is most important of all.

Teacher Preparation

To give students the total view of Christ restoring all things to the Father, the high school teacher will draw from his solid foundation in sacred doctrine, Scripture, liturgy, and catechetics. Some few high school religion departments are as serious about teacher preparation at the M.A. level as the other academic departments in the school. Others require this knowledge to be acquired progressively though in-service courses at nearby universities or summer school programs. It must be acquired somehow. The CCD lay catechist, not stopping with the minimum certification requirements, will avail himself of the opportunities for subsequent, enriched study provided by the diocesan CCD office.[11]

A lay member on the staff of a Catholic school who has the necessary academic preparation and apostolic formation should be

[9] Ps 33 [34], 9.

[10] For the mutual influence of liturgical celebration and formal classroom instruction in religious formation, cf. below pp. 231 ff., *Respective Roles* . . .

[11] In some areas these courses are offered as part of the adult education program. The offerings of Gannon College, Erie, Pennsylvania is a case in point. Hundreds of certified catechists are enrolled free of charge in the various specialized courses provided for doctrinal enrichment beyond the minimum thirty-hour requirement of the diocesan CCD office.

permitted to teach religion to his class of grade school children or to his high school homeroom section where this custom prevails for other teachers.[12] The benefits derived from this arrangement are manifold. The teacher knows his students as individual persons. He observes them during the relaxed, out-of-class moments when personality traits, attitudes, and needs are inadvertently expressed. He is the one, therefore, to assist in the Christian formation of these students. The fact that he wears neither Roman collar nor religious garb, moreover, can work in his favor. No matter how seriously a priest or religious may take his duty of acquainting himself with the milieu of his students, the boys and girls do not see him as one who is living in "their world." The impact of the layman on the students in immeasurable when his actions testify to the fact that problems related to life in Christ can be solved without compromise. Inversely, when the work of the religious formation of the lay teacher's students is reserved to another simply because the layman's dedication has not taken the form of religious habit or vow, the devaluation of his role is reflected in the attitude of teacher and student alike.

With the proper understanding of the message he is to convey, the catechist will be equipped to make Christ the Mediator live for the students in the perspective of God's salvific plan for man. The teacher who lives in the active presence of the Spirit, and by the force of his personal conviction which he puts at the Spirit's disposal, will strive to make perfect his own power to communicate, and his ability to use the tools of the trade. He will attend to both the Christ who forms (i.e., himself) and the Christ to be formed

[12] Various institutions of higher education now offer programs of study to prepare teachers of religion. The Religious Education Department of The Catholic University of America offers a program of concentration in sacred doctrine at the A.B. level, as do Dunbarton College, Washington, D.C., St. Mary's College, Notre Dame, Ind. and St. John's University, Collegeville, Minn. The Ph.D. degree is available at The Catholic University of America and St. Mary's College, Notre Dame, Ind. (women students). The M.A. degree in regular session is offered by Marquette University, the University of Notre Dame, and St. John's University (Jamaica, N.Y.) in addition to the above. More than a dozen colleges and universities award the M.A. degree through summer-session work.

(i.e., the student). In the manner of the Divine Pedagogue he will adapt the message to the level of his hearers, retaining all the while a pedagogy fitted to unite Person to person rather than truth to intellect. If he does it well he will engage in an intellectual operation worthy of a place in the best of secondary education.

The Story as a Tool

The narrative is by no means confined to the lower schools in its effectiveness. Even at the university level a teacher of physics or history will at time be praised for his lectures: "He tells it like a story." In the learning situation the story is as effective as the storyteller's art and the story told. Romance, tragedy, satire, folklore, biography, and national saga all render service in transmitting the great true story of God's love for man. At the hands of His human instruments the inspired account of God's plan is unfolded in narrative form, for "the story gets past all barriers and goes straight to that interior communication-center where mind and will and memory and feelings all meet—call it the imagination."[13] It does this if properly told!

The Israelites knew how to use the story form. Through it they handed down the inspired account known to us as sacred history. The mystery of the love their Lord bore them could never be confined solely to the past, and so their oral recital of the marvelous deeds of God enabled them to participate in these redemptive acts and to respond accordingly.[14]

[13] Francis H. Drinkwater, *Telling the Good News* (London: Macmillan & Co., 1960), p. 180.

[14] Stuhlmueller notes that the recital under religious auspices of God's redemptive acts toward Israel was the means by which the stories were lived over again. "Liturgical assemblies restored actuality to the past. Each devout worshipper felt that *he himself* was being blessed as he repeated the divine benediction upon Abraham; that *he* was being led out of an Egypt of sin, as he chanted the exodus from Egypt; that *he* was receiving the gift of the Promised Land, as the wars of Josue were liturgically represented. In order that the assembled group might experience the might of God's outstretched arms as their forefathers had done, the sacred traditions were constantly brought up to date by current religious thoughts and by present problems. . . . The accounts not only sustained the religious life

Jesus also used the story. The tales of the prodigal son, Lazarus and the rich man, the good Samaritan, and the unjust steward gave contemporary witness to His message, of love, mercy, forgiveness, and justice. Jesus continues to teach through the story of His life, an event which likewise can never be confined to the past.

The instructor will make sacred doctrine come to life for his students by going to Scripture, the source of doctrine, and to the lives of holy men, its living witness. He casts into story form the events of sacred history that foreshadow Christ in the Old Testament, present Him in the New, and continue Him in His members —the saints past and present—through the life of the Spirit. As he does this he has the opportunity to make God's call of faith real to his students. Confronted with the mystery of a love such as this, they too will experience the faith of Abraham, the love of the Magdalen, the loyalty of the disciple whom Jesus loved, the penitence of the dying thief, and the courage of Polycarp, Cyprian, and Thomas More. These events seem almost to happen for the first time in the hands of the teacher who has acquired the art of storytelling and a love for the Word of God.

Making ready for class, the religion teacher will check a reliable commentary (multiple sources if they are available) for background material on the doctrine to be taught. He will then prepare himself to relate the account spectator-fashion: setting the scene, analyzing the actions of the characters and the reactions of the onlookers. All this he will do with an eye firmly fixed on the message this segment of the whole conveys and the reply it should invite. The crowded room at Capharnaum, the dispositions of the Pharisees, the physical and spiritual state of the paralytic, his trust in this miracle-worker, the tension his entry creates, the moments of suspense following Christ's rebuke to the ill-disposed, the cure of

---

of the present moment, but also kept alive Israel's hope for the future. Past redemptive acts, living in the present, were a pledge of *the* great redemptive act of the future." J. Carroll Stuhlmueller, C.P., "Interdependence of Old Testament Liturgy and the Bible," *Proceedings of Nineteenth North American Liturgical Week* (The Liturgical Conference, Inc., 1959), pp. 141, 148.

the diseased in soul and body, the marvels of grace dispensed today in the sacrament of healing to all who have the paralytic's dispositions, and the Gospel message for ember Friday after Pentecost (Lk 5, 17–26)—all these will be grist for the mill of the catechist who relives Christ's actions with his class. Students of this teacher are prepared to recognize Jesus present in His Word proclaimed in the liturgy of the Church, and in His deeds reenacted through the medium of symbol.

Other Use of Scripture

The story of salavation via the living voice of the catechist is not enough. This narrative form enkindles the light whereby students come to "see for themselves." After the catechist has unfolded the action of Jesus at the well with the woman of no hushand, the adolescents can better trace for themselves other actions of grace recounted in the Scriptures, e.g., the story of Saul on the Damascus road. This proceeding into the heart of things will help students set aside matters of less importance, like the water jar left at the well or the food and drink Saul left untouched for three days, in their effort to make Christ known to others. In a sense the genius of high-school teaching lies in helping the students to dismiss minutiae in favor of identifying the real points at issue as the sacred texts describe them. The fingering of the sacred pages of Bible and missal in class study, home assignments, and brief mental prayer gives the students an experience with the inspired words that outlasts, but does not supplant, the oral exposition of the teacher.[15]

In treating Scripture should the catechist include the findings of

[15] The reawakened interest in the riches of the inspired word impelled Confraternity of Christian Doctrine high school students in Dallas, Texas, to select scriptural topics for themes assigned in the English class of their public high school. The intensive reading of sacred scripture and related material this selection entailed was encouraged by parents and public high school teachers alike.

Kevane advocates bringing the Bible into the academic life of students attending Catholic high schools by means of the world history course. For a discussion of this, cf. Eugene Kevane, "Sacred Scripture in the Catholic High School," *The Catholic Biblical Quarterly*, 17 (April, 1955), 136–53.

the past half-century of scholarship? Will not this matter shock the students, shake their faith, or make them question fundamental dogmas? Is it better to sit out the storm, hoping for a return to the "traditional view"? The religion teacher will realize that adolescents mastering the fundamentals of biology and geometry are aware that specialists probe into new levels of research in these sciences; these boys and girls do not find it incongruous to expect the same of biblical science. Without exposing them prematurely to theories not yet time-tested, the catechist will leave the way open to continued scholarship, for "no one foresees a return to fundamental exegesis."[16] Taking care not to teach the theoretical as certain,[17] the catechist will give principles whose specific application will be made gradually under the guidance of the teaching Church, mindful that both he and the student approach sacred Scripture as Catholics who accept the scriptural canon from the Church and believe in the inspired character of the writings. Students must be informed how little the teaching Church professes about the Old Testament beyond the fact that it is inspired in all its parts, and that in some way it all speaks to us of Christ. The difficulties that may face teachers cannot absolve them of their obligation to respect objective truth.[18]

Knowing that parts of sacred Scripture, especially of the Old Testament, are imaginative in accidentals and realistic in laying bare the heart of man as he accepts and rejects the love of his God, the Lord, the teacher will attend more to the religious truth than to the vehicle or literary device conveying this truth. Proper use of Scripture in the earlier grades precludes the necessity for

[16] John L. McKenzie, S.J., "Messianism and the College Teacher of Sacred Doctrine," *Proceedings of Sixth Annual Convention of the Society of Catholic Teachers of Sacred Doctrine* (Brookline, Mass.: Cardinal Cushing College, 1960), p. 59.

[17] Commenting on this Siegman states: "All too often the faith has suffered not so much because conflicts arose in the mind over what is actually revealed, but over mere opinions that were taught the student as revealed truth." Edward F. Siegman, C.PP.S., "The Literary Forms of the Old Testament and High School Religion Textbooks," *The Catholic Educational Review*, 54 (February, 1956), 84.

[18] *Ibid.*

unteaching what should never have been taught. If, for example, the children learn in grade school that Matthew, Mark, Luke, and John themselves actually penned the very words Jesus uttered in their exact historical context, the high school religion teacher will have to uproot this notion before speaking of such things as the apostolic oral catechesis (no less historical, or inspired, or proper to each evangelist) gradually committed to writing. If an insistence is placed on a chronological, biographical account of the life of Christ, the students will be disturbed to learn of the recorded selection of events of the Lord's earthly life determined by the needs of the growing Church.[19]

Discussion as a Tool

How is the religion teacher to respond to the indignant lad fresh from geology class who questions the location—and then the existence—of hell or heaven, as though his imagination were still playing host to the fancy of some fifth-grade teacher? Can the catechist afford to dismiss his doubt lightly, gloss over it with a dogmatic statement which compels no youthful assent by its logic, or—worse still—crush his "disrespectful outburst" with a threat of demerit? Hardly. With his newly-acquired knowledge as to what is "below" and "above," the adolescent who experiences this conflict or others like it may be tempted to consign religious belief to the realm of the Santa Claus legend in favor of a scientific view that takes nothing for granted. The teacher knows that his teen-aged boys and girls are confronting some of the great problems of life for the first time. He understands their need for a critical re-evaluation of

[19] The *Pamphlet Bible Series* published by the Paulist Press, New York, N.Y. and the *New Testament Reading Guide*, likewise in booklet form, published by The Liturgical Press, Collegeville, Minn. serve as trustworthy commentaries for the catechist. The *Religion Lessons* for the teachers of grades 1–8 done by the Mission Helpers of the Sacred Heart, Baltimore 4, Maryland and the *On Our Way* series by Sisters Maria de la Cruz and Mary Richard, H.H.S. published by W. H. Sadlier Co., New York, N.Y. are to be recommended for their use of Scripture. The *Bible Lessons* of the Mission Helpers of the Sacred Heart provide one lesson on Scripture for each grade 4 to 12 and present the conclusions of contemporary scholarship according to student level.

childhood belief and practice; hence he is not alarmed.[20] In fact he rejoices when the students express their difficulties and seek solutions to apparent conflicts, for then he has a chance to clarify the doubts inevitable for many during this period. He must therefore be ready to discuss student-raised questions concerning life in Christ in the twentieth century and to initiate such questions himself.

The believing student is the target for the scornful darts of the sophisticate who—supposedly—"knows his way around." Such a one labels religious practice "kid stuff," to be discarded with the jumping rope and the space suit. The adolescent, craving peer approval and freedom from intellectual bondage to adults, seeks answers to satisfy the crowd—and himself. He will arrive at his answer if the teacher has created a climate which invites free and open discussion.

The discussion technique benefits both teacher and taught. Attitudes, problems, conflicts, and misunderstandings which might otherwise never be revealed are inadvertently expressed by the adolescents in open exchange of opinions. None of this escapes the alert teacher who can never know his students or their milieu well enough. In the process the teen-ager acquires facility in speaking of religious truth and tolerance for the views of others. Discussion appeals to "their natural desire to find themselves, and to see themselves as persons, distinct therefore from their parents and elders."[21] Through planned discussion the high school instructor leads the students to discover for themselves what was long ago settled and thereby gain richer insights into the matter. If he indicates too hastily what *was* settled long ago, his efficacy

[20] In his discussion of the moral development in the adolescent, Smith notes that for adequate and mature religious life the adolescent must go through some process of critical reassessment of his religious beliefs and practices and moral standards to establish this area on an adult level, just as is necessary for him to evaluate critically other areas of his world, e.g., social relationships and vocational aspirations, and formulate some satisfactory solutions on the adult level of attitude, belief, and practice. Cf. Walter Smith, "Religious and Moral Development in Adolescence," *The Catholic Educational Review*, 56 (December 1958), 591–600.

[21] Drinkwater, *op. cit.*, p. 194.

may soon be at an end. He must develop a high tolerance for initial confusion and error in student discussion, relying on the
brighter ones to set matters straight. He can destroy the technique
by his impatience with wrong views that prevail for quite a while
during a class period. The force of the student's own conclusions
adds weight to their motive for deliberately giving themselves to
God according to His message. They,

> become people with settled personal convictions of their own
> . . . able to meet the difficulties of life in the modern world
> with a certain equanimity and strength because they have seen
> and examined the difficulties beforehand, and able to cling to
> their faith because they have grown into it . . . rather than
> just been told *about* it.[22]

Is religious truth matter for open discussion? Students think so,
and rightly. Not that all belief will be suspended until truth passes
the bar of adolescent scrutiny. No. The instructor must take care
that the I-won't-believe-unless-you-prove-it attitude does not prevail. Students, however, normally do not take this attitude. They
are easily satisfied—if anything too easily satisfied. They want the
respect of having their questions acknowledged, dissenting statements heard out and then refuted if need be. One student of the
writer's acquaintance objected to the "one-sided opinion of the
teacher who would not give an inch. He is right because of the way
he was taught but he can't really explain except to say the Church
says so!" The lad had asked for a "good explanation of questions
asked and not just saying, 'God said so, so do it!' "[23] Another suggested that the students "be allowed to express their ideas freely
whether all wrong or all right. Then we will be able to ask a priest

[22] Gerald L. Vann, O.P., quoted in "Jottings on the Teaching of Girls:
Replies to an Enquiry," *Lumen Vitae,* 6 (1951), 425.

[23] A catechesis on the Church which centers on an awareness of membership in the living body in which Christ lives, speaks, sanctifies, and
enlightens, rather than a catechesis emphasizing the juridic concept of the
Church, should preclude this student attitude at an age when authoritarianism repels.

or parent anything without being afraid of what the outcome may be."

The mature catechist will take measures to offset the limitatons of this technique. If he permits a dominant personality to exert an undesirable influence, if he allows the class to make a sport of drawing fine distinctions or of questioning endlessly, the discussion technique is not a good method for him. Stimulating the students to probe more deeply into the mystery of Christ by way of intellectual analysis should not have the effect of obscuring the element of mystery or the sense of the sacred. If intellectual dismemberment becomes vivisection the teaching has retrogressed. It has deteriorated to the point of engaging an intellect in an assent to a proposition instead of engaging a person in an assent to a personal God.

Climate

The discordant sounds emanating from a machine shop do not inspire musical composition. Without the proper climate the seed does not germinate, the artist does not create. Spiritual growth offers no exception to this. Life in the Spirit will thrive in those born of Him when the conditions for growth are made present. What conditions in religious education welcome the penetrating breath of the Spirit? What is needed to create a climate conducive to spiritual growth? The view the teacher has of his role, the place religious formation enjoys in parochial life and in the school curriculum largely determine the conditions.

The high school catechist stands before his class as the living witness of the message he has to convey. He does not purport to teach a subject but to make known the One his students are to follow and to show them the way to Him. His sense of mission in spreading the kingdom will not be lost on the youthful hearers, for the call to discipleship is best heard when it is being transmitted by one who has already followed.[24] Therefore the teacher's

[24] Cf. Pope Pius XII, "For a school to be Christian it is not sufficient that there be a course of religion . . . or that certain practices of piety be required; above all teachers must form spirit and character and com-

attitude toward his privilege of forming disciples of the Master is paramount in establishing the religious climate. His manner will radiate the personal interest and respect he has for each member of Christ before him. His enthusiasm, his sincerity, and his awareness of being the Christ-bearer he is will set the tone for the meeting between Redeemer and redeemed.

Educators take more than an atomistic view of the learner and the learning process. The student has no discrete mental compartments into which he stores isolated segments of truth. For this reason those engaged in curriculum planning strive to work out integrated programs of study that will provide for the organic development of the student, a development that entails the growth of the total person. Growth in knowledge for the Catholic student must involve growth in Christ. Religous instruction then must be given the place of first importance in the curriculum of the Catholic high school.

Christian formation cannot be measured in terms of semester hours, credits, or final grades. The academic status given to the religion period in Catholic high schools does, nonetheless, reflect somewhat the value administrators place on religious instruction. Proper budget balancing does not tolerate well-equipped science laboratories, art, and home ecnomics departments on the one hand, and inadequate catechetical supplies (library holdings, audiovisual aids, and textbooks) on the other. If the religion period is the one to be omitted or shortened because of an interruption—unforeseen or planned—in the daily schedule, students too will give this "subject" the status of a footnote to learning.

Special weekly instructions that supplant the lesson of the day is a matter that deserves careful consideration. The role of the priest cannot be minimized in forming adolescents in the image of Christ. This role is primarliy a sacerdotal one. Christ acts, attracts,

---

municate to their pupils the wealth of their own profound spiritual lives." "The Catholic School Today," Address to the Third General Assembly of the International Office of Catholic Teaching, 1958, *The Pope Speaks*, 5 (Summer 1959), 339.

and teaches in sacramental celebration through His human, priestly instrument. The priest is ordained to be a teacher, above all at divine service. He may also be an effective classroom teacher provided he has been trained for it. Informal activities provide him with opportunities for exerting a forceful influence on the young mind and heart. Yet taking into consideration all the pros and cons of the matter, it seems that special religious instructions given by the priest who does not conduct the daily class should be unnecessary if the brother, sister, or lay teacher has the desired preparation.[25] Such a practice often breaks the rhythm of the regular course of instruction. It gives the visitor of once a week a specious advantage that is often owing to his informality, his masculinity, or the "professionalism" of his seminary studies, more than to his priestly state or his skill as a catechist. Needless to add, the priest as full-time, skilled catechist is especially welcome in the classroom.

Knowing the students to be flesh as well as spirit, religious educators will schedule the religion period accordingly. Tired minds and late-forenoon appetites are of no help in understanding God's call or deliberately choosing to live by it. If, therefore, the religion class is scheduled when the school day and youthful energy are well spent, the religion period will not be well spent. The time for class meeting in the Catholic school presents less of a problem than that of the CCD high school of religion, where many activities vie for the adolescent's interest and time. Arrangements made with the area public high schools for one activity-free evening to be reserved for religious instruction has solved the problem for some. After-school employment makes Sunday morning classes (with time permitted in advance for a brief snack to encourage reception of the eucharist) desirable for others.

Of far greater significance in climate-setting in the CCD school is the physical set-up which conditions the learning situation. How can the import of Christ's saving actions impress freshmen who must strain to catch the teacher's words because the choir is re-

[25] Cf. above, p. 218.

hearsing in the next room? What reflective prayer can the sophomores engage in at one end of the hall while the Boy Scouts are
meeting at the other? The religion class will be little more than an
afterthought to students who must clear away the debris of last
night's rally or card party to make room for their class meeting.
The goals which even the most recently formed parish must strive
toward include the proper grading of students (with boys separate
from girls) in well-equipped classrooms; parent observation days;
examinations and report cards; student councils, student assemblies, forums, and graduation. All serve in rendering to the formation program of the CCD school of religion its proper importance.[26]

An Atmosphere of Worship

A Christian climate involves still more. Its scope extends to all
the boundaries of parochial life and all activities of the Catholic
school curriculum. Members of the People of God share life in the
Spirit, a family life of worship, and nothing in the line of Christian
instruction itself should be allowed to draw them apart.

The Son of God came to earth as one of us to effect the return of
us men to God. Although this return was accomplished in all that
He did—the saving act having begun with the Virgin's "Let it be
done" and continuing until the Son's exaltation in glory—yet it was
on the cross that the Savior's priestly function was manifest. On
Calvary Christ the priest offered Himself to God as the victim of
perfect love and adoration. Christ our elder Brother is the perfect
expression of God's love for man and the perfect expression of
man's love for God. Today Jesus invites each one of us to share in
His priesthood by entering into His act of loving God. The mystery
made present for us at the altar by which He offered His life that
men might live eternally in God is the means of entry. To introduce

---

[26] Some advocate a removal from all that suggests a formal school experience and prefer a casual discussion club approach. A particular local
problem such as that of a rural area sparsely settled or of a parish having
a disproportionate number who merely tolerate school, may warrant this
solution. Certain CCD high school programs, functioning as above described,
enroll over 90% of all public school students and have an average attendance
of over 90%.

adolescents to the person of Christ is to bring them ultimately to the "whole Christ," the eternal High Priest in union with His body the Church continuing His worship of God; it is to form worshipers fully aware of their priestly role.

The summation of God's call to man and man's reply, all expressed in the mystery of Christ, is found in the Credo. Religious formation is complete when the truths of the Credo are understood and lived—and they are lived most fully at the altar where the Credo is celebrated.[27] The catechist, then, must lead his students to the altar where the meeting between the adolescent and the Lord is most intimately found. Christ is present in His Word proclaimed and in His eucharistic celebration. He is there to be met and responded to in love. Those involved in religious formation cannot be satisfied to bring students to the threshold of a meeting with Jesus and then close the door; to introduce them but refuse to permit the warm embrace. "That the class which has listened to, studied, understood and recited Christian doctrine should become a community assembled in an act of faith expressed in the Church —is not this the sign of a catechesis that attained its properly theological dimension?"[28] The catechist's task remains incomplete if he has created in the students a mentality that is directed toward worship but left inactivated.

Respective Roles of Religion Period and Liturgy

The religion period and the official worship of the Church are mutually influential in achieving the goal of catechesis. A study of religious truth prepares students to participate more intelligently, hence more fully, in the sacred mysteries made present in worship. On the other hand fruitful participation in these mysteries should spark a desire to learn more about them. Though the learning process is of primary concern in the classroom and of secondary concern in liturgical action, to limit the class period to a didactic

[27] Cf. François Coudreau, S.S., in Martimort, et al. "The Bible and the Liturgy in Catechesis," *The Liturgy and the Word of God* (Collegeville, Minn.: Liturgical Press, 1959).

[28] *Ibid.*, p. 112.

function and the liturgical celebration to an affective role is to minimize the potential of both. Religious formation should engage the whole person in loving God. This means that the total being and not merely the intellect or will is involved in the learning situation of both class period and communal worship. No approach to the knowing person, whether outer senses, imagination, memory, or intellect, is ignored and no avenue to the affective person, whether emotions or will, is neglected in making actual God's dealings with His people and in evoking a reply.

Pius XII stated that the zeal of the teacher should apply itself to bring pupils more and more into the life of the Church, to have them take part in its liturgy.[29] How does the catechist prepare his students for Christ's act of worship in which by baptism they are invited to have a part? Indirectly by means of a catechesis essentially ordered to worship as its end, and directly by means of liturgical participation. The liturgical dimension of such a catechesis will show forth in its basic concepts, its structure, and its opportunities for living a sacramental life.

Concepts

The basic concepts of such a catechesis would include sacred history, the role of the liturgy, the Church, the redemption, and the sacraments. The progressive character of God's actions with man will identify sacred history—the object of their study—as something they are now celebrating and having a part in. They will recognize the role of liturgy as one of lifting the great deeds of God out of a constricting temporal context and making them present here and now, continuing Christ's worship of God and His saving of men. They will know the Jesus of Nazareth who in synagogal service proclaimed God's Word in Isaia as fulfilled in Himself[30] as present in the liturgy of the Word and its actualization in the realm of sign. The sense of community, of the mystery of God's boundless love, and of symbol—all fostered in the doctrinal treatment on the Church, the redemptive act, and the sacramental

29 "The Catholic School Today," *ibid.*, pp. 339 f.
30 Lk 4, 14–22.

life—will spark in students an awareness that they are God's people come together to give a Son's love to His Father and receive it in return.

Structure

The raw material of the liturgy may serve as the framework for catechesis in the religion period. The high school students learn of the great things God has done for them by following Jesus' actions through the Church year. Thus an analysis of the Easter Vigil blessings will reveal what it means to be incorporated into Christ; a closer look at the apostolic witness at Pentecost, what it means to be quickened by the Spirit in confirmation; the Advent longing for the Savior, the helplessness of fallen man steeped in sin.[31] A liturgical setting, however, is not always the point of departure for a doctrinal lesson. When a theological approach, a Scripture story, or the testimony of a saintly witness is used to expose the doctrine, the organic unity of the Christian message will still point the doctrine toward its expression at the altar. For example, the sacramental healing of penance could be taught through the story of the paralytic's cure.[32] Reference could then be made to the proclamation of this event in the Gospel for the ember Friday after Pentecost, for the placement within this setting shows penance as one of the blessings the Spirit breathed on the Church in His Pentecostal coming.

Opportunities for Living the Sacramental Life

A properly ordered catechesis of its nature flows into active liturgical participation. How would this involve the high school religious formation program? Providing opportunities for liturgical living is not a matter of multiplying extra-curricular activities.

[31] The foundation for such an approach should of course have been laid in grade school work. The developed Religion Lessons for eighth grade of the Mission Helpers of the Sacred Heart, Baltimore, Maryland use the Church year as the source for doctrinal exposition. Work for the lower grades of this series and that of Sister Maria de la Cruz, H.H.S. (New York, N.Y.: W. H. Sadlier Co.) provide a liturgical dimension.

[32] Cf. above, p. 221.

Life in Christ through worship is no liturgical afterthought to be scotch-taped to the lesson or to the day; it is rather the necessary consequence of a catechesis geared to Christian living, an integral part of religious formation.

A schedule which has the Mass at its heart invites the Holy Spirit to set the tone of the day.[33] The students (there because they choose to be) praying together, singing together, sharing Life together at the Lord's banquet table, *experience* the communal sense of union in Christ and the intuitive nature of communication through symbol that they learned about in religion class.[34] Related activities, such as choral recitation drawn from Scripture, tableau, sacramental blessing given within the framework of a Bible vigil, and timely forum discussion supply the seasonal tonic in living the mysteries of faith in the Church year. This climate favors a meeting between the Redeemer and the redeemed, for it is all done "in Christ." Such a climate should greet the freshmen arriving fresh from eighth grade.

Would a program of this sort in the school infringe upon the pastor's responsibility for the *cura animarum?* Religious formation within the CCD unit or the parish high school is the natural springboard for enriched participation in the liturgy. All activity takes place within the spirit and scope of the parish family and should emerge as a parochial project rather than a school project. The question of the central high school is somewhat different, however, for the school captures the interest, loyalty, and time of adolescents enrolling from various parishes. Will not high school students, rebelling against all who are associated with the yoke of childhood dependence and grade school days, include parish activities among their castaways—especially if the school provides opportunities for worship? Measures can be taken to offset this

[33] Some high school sophomores, attributing their boredom at Mass to their lack of knowledge, make a plea for an earlier study in the religion course of the sacred mystery and their part in it. Often what they need is merely to be *given* a part in it.

[34] For a description of a school-wide effort to launch such a project, cf. George Duritsa, "A Twelve-Day Program in High School," *Worship,* 34 (August–September 1960), 466–69.

attitude and intensify the identity of high school students with the parish. Group work in conjunction with participation at the central high school could be undertaken in parish units rather than class units. Members of a particular parish in a concerted effort could sponsor some of the activities listed above and invite their pastor and his assistants to attend. If possible the same activity could then be worked out in the parish itself by this group. Assigned projects of a parochial character which require students to become better acquainted with their respective parish programs should engender their interest and support.[35] The real question is, can we afford *not* to investigate the possibilities when the teen-aged mind, heart, and will must be won to Christ?

[35] For a treatment of this and related problems, cf. the *Proceedings of the 18th, 19th, and 20th North American Liturgical Weeks* (Washington: The Liturgical Conference), pp. 137–41; 127–35; 188–201 respectively.

10 RELIGIOUS FORMATION

IN THE LAST TWO YEARS OF

HIGH SCHOOL

James E. Kraus

SINCE the purpose of these chapters is to provide a survey of the major problems the teacher encounters on each of the levels of schooling, this essay must risk superficiality in its treatment of interesting "new" problems and "waste" valuable space on the recapitulated treatment of several "old" problems. It is hoped that teachers will find all the problems real, and that this outline will prove comprehensive, stimulating study and possibly even provide a partial solution to some of the problems raised.

First to be discussed will be a group of eight general topics: goals, teacher preparation, administration, and psychology; then liturgy, scripture, doctrine, and morality. All of these are of concern at every level of religious education, but they will be discussed here only from the point of view of the particular problem they present at this level of the sixteen- to eighteen-year-old, in the junior and senior years of high school. Three topics of special

236

concern usually assigned for study in these years will be dealt with, namely, apologetics, Church history, and the Christian vocation. Specialized problems such as a course in marriage, the matter of priestly and religious vocations, the study of the social apostolate, and the like, are simply beyond present limitations.

In the case of each of the problems, reference will first be made to what has been written by others on the subject. Most often, except in the field of adolescent psychology, the writer has found the literature to be very meager indeed. The little that has come to his notice is largely fragmentary or generalized. Quite naturally, students of religious education have begun with the elementary-school child; by the time they come to the secondary school they are usually dealing in brief generalizations or simple extensions of elementary principles. On the secondary-school level the great bulk of attention has been devoted to special areas such as the marriage course. As it happens, far more has been done in recent years on the college level than the high-school.

GOALS

Here we presuppose the distinction and the position of Coudreau in *Shaping the Christian Message,* which, very briefly, states that our goal is more than mere *instruction,* that it is *education,* without however drawing any hard line of separation between them.[1] The writer has elaborated on this difference in more concrete terms on the high-school level elsewhere, contrasting the scholastic, speculative, scientific approach with the vital, practical, poetic approach and calling for more emphasis on the latter.[2]

Against this background let us ask what specifically we should like to achieve in the high-school junior and senior. This teacher submits that it is not any one of a number of specialized things which various individuals judge to be valuable in particular future

[1] François Coudreau, P.S.S., "Introduction to a Pedagogy of the Faith," in Gerard S. Sloyan, *Shaping the Christian Message* (New York: Macmillan, 1958), pp. 131–49.

[2] James E. Kraus, "A New Approach to the Teaching of High-School Religion," in *Bulletin of the National Catholic Educational Association,* 56 (August 1959), 225 ff.

situations. For example, it is not primarily to prepare students to answer objections to their faith on a nonreligious university campus; nor to give them a summary view of the theological disciplines from Scripture to canon law; nor even to give them the type of marriage course which leaves nothing for pre-Cana or pastoral marital instructions. These not only anticipate and, to some extent, spoil the future religious development of the student, but they neglect the urgent and full-time job that is at hand.

That present task which specifically suits this age group is to make them *mature lay Catholics*. If that seems a poverty-stricken concept or one so axiomatic as to be without significance, one hopes that it shall become less so by the end of this chapter. The freshman and sophomore years are dedicated more remotely to this ideal, but they will necessarily be somewhat more negative in their specific contribution. There the students are disengaging themselves from a particular world and are somewhat preoccupied, looking inward and backward. The juniors and seniors are calmer, more positive, looking outward and forward to an engagement with a new world. This development will of course continue in college, but like it or not, in college we are dealing with a privileged few, an elite. Hence, if a mature Catholic laity is to be formed on a catholic scale, a God-given chance lies in these last two years of genuinely popular, mass education.

The Church is on the threshold of a new age in her history, an age of the laity. It is the special task of the teacher of these years to make his students aware of this and to prepare them to take their part in it. In a number of ways there is a striking parallel between the religious history of the student on this level and that of the Church herself: in their somewhat less than twenty years or twenty centuries of life, they both have passed through a precarious infancy, a dawn of reason in their lives from ages four to seven, a wondrous awakening intellectually at twelve or thirteen, and an adolescent revolt from fourteen to sixteen. Both are now in the process of emerging from that revolt. As a result, the student in our day finds himself in a peculiar harmony with the aspirations and problems of the Church of our day: it is a psychological advantage we should not fail to exploit.

Indeed, we shall need to exploit it, not just as a matter of good timing but as a practical necessity. For, this concept of the mature Catholic layman and his role is not one that has already been elaborated and needs only to be transmitted. The whole Church needs to create it, above all with the help of the layman himself. There are no pat answers to give. This may be just as well, for pat answers from a bygone day are just what have been inhibiting maturity. The Church in her lay aspect, we repeat, is coming of age, and the student of our day is in an excellent position to understand her anxieties and difficulties. Consequently, if properly prepared and guided he can be of immense value in their solution.

TEACHER PREPARATION

What kind of a teacher is required to achieve this goal of maturity? Not just anyone who needs a few hours to make up a full schedule, please. There are at least three general requirements for any teacher; each has its specific application here. First, any teacher must want to teach, and any religion teacher must possess genuine Christian charity toward his or her students. In addition, at the secondary level a special respect is in order on the teacher's part for one who is more than ever before a free and active agent in his own formation.

Second, every teacher, and therefore every religion teacher, must be a master of the matter of the course. This need not mean that the elementary-school teacher must have full-scale training in theology, but on the high-school level, he *or she* must be at least a student of theology; in other words, a real professional, a specialist in religion, both to meet the needs and to gain the respect of the more challenging students, probably of all the students. Hence the priest-teacher ordinarily has an initial advantage, though it must be emphasized that this *remote* preparation through the study of scientific theology must be complemented, especially in our day, by a constant maintenance of interest and familiarity with at least the major developments in theology[3] as they are more popularly expressed.

Third, the religion teacher, like every teacher, is concerned with the transmission of the matter, and this in turn requires both a knowledge of the students to be taught and of the methods and techniques of teaching. Concerning the former, a study of the student will be initiated under *psychology* further on; right now a few words about method and techniques, the *immediate* task of teacher preparation, are in order.

The first questions to arise at every catechetical workshop are the same: "What do you do in the classroom? How do you teach religion? What are the techniques we need to know about?" As if there were anything about it that simple! Young priests, fresh from years of hearing lectures, fall back on the lecture method for want of familiarity with anything better. Religious, fresh from courses in pedagogy, teach religion just as they would any other subject, though they suspect more and more as time goes on that religion is by definition meant to be uniquely different. The layman from a Catholic college will either be in the best position of all or be painfully philosophical in his presentation, depending on the quality of his recent experience of sacred doctrine. Yet all find the task uniquely difficult. Texts on method describe the steps of class procedure in great detail, so great in fact that the vast apparatus to be managed in a period of sometimes thirty minutes is overwhelming in its demands on teacher as well as student. Moreover, few allowances are made for differences in students, levels, teachers, or materials. The classroom texts and their teacher manuals are frequently of little help; few have a "built-in" method or are so well constructed as to "teach themselves." Frequently one has the impression that the authors themselves never really decided what they conceived the function of the text to be, or how and when it was to be used.

But enough of difficulties common to all: here again are a few

[3] Sister M. Anne Christine, B.V.M., "Suggestions from a Theologian on Improving High-School Religion," *Catholic School Journal*, 59 (January 1959), 42–44.

suggestions working toward a solution. First, *method* should be distinguished from *technique*. Method is something general and basic, a principle almost inviolable. The present writer's single principle of method is this: since teaching religion is more a matter of education than information, there must always be some proportionate response or activity on the part of the student to the material presented by the teacher. The character of that response shall be elaborated under *liturgy*, since that is its source and model.

Technique, on the other hand, is something much more concrete, for example, the manner of presentation, the steps, explanation, discussion, kinds of response, and so forth. It is highly variable from teacher to teacher, class to class, topic to topic. We cannot hope to answer this problem here, except to say that no single technique or gimmick will ever provide the answer. Above all, on the high-school level, flexibility is extremely desirable; the teacher must stay "loose," and any technique used too long becomes a strait jacket. Further, formal pedagogical training and general rules now become less important than the teacher's own study and adaptation of the material to the class.

The few special characteristics of secondary-level religious education named above are matters which demand something special in teacher education and preparation.

ADMINISTRATION

In working toward the goal we have set, even a well-prepared teacher can be stifled or else immensely aided by the conditions under which he works. This does not mean just the physical ones. Some of the problems that high-school religion teachers face can be solved by administrators. Both groups of professionals are on common ground in their general acknowledgment of two factors: first, that religion is the most important subject taught, and second, that it is the one most difficult to teach. With these in mind the following suggestions are made for those whose job it is to plan the program and to map out schedules.

First of all, the truncated period, thirty minutes or less, is almost worse than none at all; one has barely opened up a subject when the bell rings. If necessary, let there be fewer periods but full ones.[4] Lunch-hour religion periods literally "sandwiched" in have been referred to sufficiently in the preceding essay. They hardly reflect a firm principle on the importance of religion in the curriculum. Conversely, fewer than five periods a week do not reflect unimportance, if they are of full length and carefully prepared.

Second, the religion period should be divorced from both the homeroom period of school administration and activities, and the social, educational, and vocational services of the guidance course. (Note well, however, that *moral* guidance is the responsibility of the religion course primarily if not solely; its function in this regard should never be usurped.) The writer is aware of the benefits claimed for a homeroom teacher's serving as an instructor in religion because of the unique opportunities in religious education proper, available in that situation. He prefers not to argue the case, but to reiterate his stands on the well-trained religion teacher and the nonencroachment of this period by any other school function.

Third, and most important, it seems clearly desirable to arrange Mass at least once a week for the entire student body. What is meant is a well prepared and fully participated in Mass where the entire school joins in prayer. Must the only time the school comes together be for a pep rally? The activity contemplated here is in no sense a usurpation of a parochial function or a service for individuals (as, for example, the opportunity for optional daily Mass) but a school at prayer, a Catholic school performing the great act of the Church. Such an experience of community worship is vitally important to the kind of religious education we advocate. Failure to engage in it may result in the undoing of much that goes on in the classroom. Experience has shown that doing it is not impossible. Auditoriums and gymnasiums with portable altars frequently make for closer participation than churches. If parish schedules or even bination can be worked out to provide Mass once a week for

---

[4] John Hofinger, S.J., "Catechesis in the United States Today," *Lumen Vitae*, 11 (April–June 1956), 247. The analysis of the situation is excellent, though exception must be taken to the recommendation on the amount of instruction.

a convent (where the chief reason is renewal of the eucharistic species rather than the sacred action itself), it can be done for a school which has as its special need the eucharistic action. Disadvantages can be turned to actual advantages in making this primary source of Christian formation immediately accessible to teachers and students alike.

Finally, therefore, the writer (who is not without experience in making out such schedules) suggests, as a minimum, that a full period five days a week be allocated to the religion course, in some way like the following: one day a week for the Mass (fully participated in, with song and a brief homily); three days a week for religion class; and one day a week for a religious activities period (Mass preparation, demonstrations, or *pia exercitia*[5] derived from the liturgy, mission or sodality work, religious guidance, or directed reading).[6] In many instances this would provide a more workable schedule for the religion teacher, especially the priest who is also an assistant in a parish. Its chief merit, however, is that it relates truth to life. If it does not do that—if it constitutes a mere reduction of the time devoted seriously to religion without any compensatory advantage—then the writer's intention is mistaken. He envisions this schedule as more rather than less academic, since the celebration will be of the mysteries studied while the discussion will show the meaning of what is studied.

PSYCHOLOGY

That men who have no religious commitment should be the ones to have led the way in the scientific study of the student is a bit of a scandal. The Catholic respect we have for the sacred truth we transmit should not cause us to neglect the recipient of that truth. Close union in charity with the student, so characteristic of truly

[5] Cf. The Instruction on Sacred Music and Sacred Liturgy of Sept. 3, 1958, I, 1.

[6] As a supplement to the religion course, especially for superior students at this level where the span of talents and interests becomes more marked than ever, it is impossible to overestimate the importance of an individually guided supplementary reading program. By it better students can be introduced to the challenging adult considerations they are capable of, but the class as a whole is not.

Christian teaching and so necessary to the adolescent for whom personal relationships are decisive, may never be lost sight of. First of all, then, some of the useful materials to be found in standard college texts on educational psychology might be indicated;[7] then certain further precisions offered by studies in religious psychology can be considered.

Four areas commonly described in these treatises are of interest to us. The first is headed *growth*.[8] A composite picture of several standard treatments of the characteristics and needs of the adolescent in secondary school emerges somewhat as follows. *Intellectually*, such students are quite capable of abstract ideas, of analysis and synthesis; they need a philosophy, a plan of life. *Morally*, they are now capable of remoter goals and higher ideals than before; they need to be challenged and allowed to act on their own initiative. *Emotionally*, they are insecure, volatile, preoccupied with sex, rebellious to superiors, conforming to their peers; they need acceptance, and guidance, but with limits and discipline.

All three of the foregoing characteristics are found in the first two years of high school as much as the second. Is there anything genuinely proper to the latter period? While there is no fixed pattern of adolescent development, there are a number of interests or traits so characteristic of an age and a milieu that they suggest certain avenues of approach to the student.[9] Such, for example, are the junior's and senior's immense desire for self-improvement; a general lessening of the taste for things academic; considerable anxiety over the choice of a vocation; very rare fulfillment of the student's real potential. None of this is new or startling, nor does anyone claim that it should determine what we teach; but no sensitive teacher can afford to neglect the clarifications and emphases provided by studies such as these.

[7] The majority are fairly similar; we therefore cite only that of William A. Kelly, *Educational Psychology* (4th ed. rev.; Milwaukee: Bruce, 1956).
[8] *Ibid.*, pp. 202 ff.
[9] Arthur T. Jersild and Ruth J. Tasch, *Children's Interests and What They Suggest for Education* (New York: Bureau of Publications, Teachers College, Columbia University, 1949), p. 86 *et passim*.

A second area important to consider is headed *learning*.[10] A number of valuable techniques are usually offered here, along with a topic that demands our attention, motivation. The ideal of maturity we have established suggests that motivation at this level should be intrinsic rather than extrinsic. Psychologists confirm the suggestion. This means that by now such goals as passing the course, pleasing the teacher, winning out over the competition, and earning a prize (or the negative forms of any of these), should be receding into the background and be replaced by an appreciation of the value of this course in and for itself.[11] A concomitant should be an understanding of the reasonableness and goodness of what was once mere duty. This is not false idealism; such motivation is quite effective, though of course we can never stop a reasonable measure of praise and blame, grading and failing.

The challenge to the religion teacher, then, is to make the course something really worthwhile, in and of itself. There is this warning: if it is not made so, the student is just mature enough to turn his back on it in contempt. At the same time it must be said for the consolation of the teacher, if consolation it is, that even the dedicated, competent teacher must be prepared for frequent apparent failure. The sixteen- to eighteen-year-old is not a responsive, plastic child. He is largely formed. At no time of life is the battle between the world and Christ more fiercely raging. Like Christ, we shall have to watch many a rich young man, or woman, turn away.

Of lesser value is the third general area of *grading and testing*.[12] There is a passion today for objectivity and impersonality; tests and grades are true to this twofold principle, whenever the teacher can achieve it. To the extent that popular religious education goes beyond mere instruction the religion test and grade must go beyond this idea. The type of religion test given in high school can

---

[10] Kelly, *op. cit.*, pp. 280 ff.

[11] This assumes that all courses in the curriculum can be justified. For an estimate of the contemporary situation, cf. Oscar Handlin, "Live Students and Dead Education. Why the High School Must Be Revived," in *The Atlantic Monthly*, 208 (September 1961), 29–34.

[12] Kelly, *op. cit.*, pp. 353, 373.

never be entirely machine-corrected. The grade cannot be impersonal. This is especially true on this level because the goal of maturity calls for creative self-expression and value-judgments by both student and teacher. It cannot be denied that this opens the door to abuse, for whenever prudent human action is called for imprudence and partiality are possibilities. The teacher has the awful responsibility to be Christ-like: just, charitable, sensitive, and impartial, even in judging a paper. The type of test advocated here is one that calls for and emphasizes more or less equally the kind of basic instructional matter that any student can memorize and give, *along with that creative personal response which must be the fruit of reflection and even prayer, but which does not infringe upon the personal conscience of the student.* This response is easily recognized, and cannot be counterfeited. Any student should be able to pass a religion test of this kind, but in fact only one who is maturing in faith will pass it. The system of grading should somehow reflect this qualitative judgment—for the instructor in religion is charged with *forming Christians.* A merely quantitative score will not suffice.

The last area the educational psychologists take up is that of *guidance and character formation,*[13] a field requiring special training and experience. No one will deny that it has a close relation with the religion course, particularly as regards students of senior high-school age. Yet, the relation of the two has not been solved; indeed it has hardly been discussed. Until it is, the following position is submitted for consideration. Moral guidance is the proper function of the religion course; vocational (not religious), educational, and social guidance is the proper function of the guidance course. When this distinction is not observed, not only is the religion course robbed of one of its most interesting and vital functions, but these other matters take on a quasi-religious tone or force that often is not good. The legitimacy and need of the three lesser types of guidance is certainly acknowledged. But there is some controversy over their proper extent, while there can be no

[13] *Ibid.,* pp. 518 ff.

controversy about the Church's right to exercise moral guidance in her schools. Of course, it must be genuine moral guidance and not personal prejudice. This reminder is of particular importance in the guidance of high-school juniors and seniors.

We turn briefly to the findings of religious psychologists in their study of the upper-adolescent level. A certain amount of informative material has been produced by Americans both in the sociological areas of investigation and even more in the practical area of producing guidance texts.[14] But on the level of profound analysis of these conditions and difficulties, and the proposal of basic approaches and fundamental solutions, Europeans have led the way. The best of these studies have been reported on in the pages of *Lumen Vitae*. Godin gives us a small guide to such studies and a large indication of how valuable they can be.[15] Gruber describes this age level as one where conflict ends and fixation begins; he emphasizes the differences, at this age greater than ever before, between the religious evolution of boys and that of girls.[16] The boys are becoming more scientific, the girls more affective, while both are rejecting the devotions of their childhood. The obvious conclusion is that, beyond considerations of the material being studied, religious psychology demonstrates the need for separate religion classes.

Babin notes the usual characteristics mentioned above, and likewise notes in passing two points that have been found true by the writer, and valuable as information: first, the adolescent will frequently attempt to cloak a state of insecurity caused by some moral or emotional problem in the guise of an intellectual difficulty, that is, he tries to give a doubtful moral position some

---

[14] E.g., Urban Fleege, S.M., *Self-Revelation of the Adolescent Boy* (Milwaukee: Bruce, 1945); *The Insight Series* (New York: Harcourt, Brace & World, 1960–61); *Complete Group Guidance for Catholic High Schools* (Milwaukee: Bruce, 1957).

[15] André Godin, S.J., "Religious Psychology in Education," *Lumen Vitae*, 12 (January–March 1957), 20.

[16] Alois Gruber, "Differences in Religious Evolution of Adolescent Boys and Girls," *Lumen Vitae*, 12 (April–June 1957), 301 ff.

intellectual justification. We make a mistake if we are diverted by the tactic.

Again, because of his lack of ability to express himself, or because he is exploring, he will tend to shock people with some of his statements; only the unwary teacher will react quickly and adversely.[17] This is an age of questioning, even of doubt, and it is to this psychological characteristic that the study of apologetics should be directed as we shall see below.[18] In another article, Babin notes two more factors of great psychological importance in dealing with adolescents: the character of the teacher (what we today would call his "image"), and the atmosphere he creates in the class.[19] At the high-school level an air of competence and a spirit of justice and charity are equally indispensable.

An article to which attention should be called is "Christ and the Adolescent" by Van Caster.[20] This study is unique in bringing the data of psychology to bear upon a specific problem, that of teaching the life of Christ. There is need, actually, of a whole range of studies written with equal competence in every area.

LITURGY

Two of the more obvious contributions of the liturgy at this level need only be indicated and passed over rapidly. First the liturgy, here as always, is a tremendous source of doctrine, especially in view of the appropriateness of the symbolism of sacred history to this group. Thus, for example, we may develop a well-rounded and mature attitude toward the eucharist by looking at its liturgical history. Second, the liturgy is an insufficiently used structure for the plan and material of our religion courses. That is something which can be remedied only by carefully constructed course out-

[17] Pierre Babin, O.M.I., "Rethinking the Life of Faith," *Lumen Vitae*, 15 (April–June 1960), 233–46.

[18] André Godin, S.J., "Faith and the Psychological Development of Children and Adolescents," *Lumen Vitae*, 13 (April–June 1958), 299–308.

[19] Pierre Babin, O.M.I., "God's Call and Man's Response," *Lumen Vitae*, 14 (July–September 1959), 509–15.

[20] Marcel Van Caster, S.J., "Christ and the Adolescent," *Lumen Vitae*, 11 (July–September 1956), 427 ff.

lines which require for effective use student and teacher manuals
of high quality, both yet to be written.

Let us look more closely at the basic principle of method which
the liturgy follows constantly. The pattern of lesson response is
one of the most ancient and frequent features of the liturgy; it is
also the perfect model for the lesson in popular religious education.
Prayer precedes and action follows, but the core of the lesson is
listening of the most intense kind; then participation, the gift of
self in response. The lesson of the religion course always has something about it of the proclamation of the Word, of the kerygma, the
good news; its method for the faithful is never that of experiment
or discovery on their part; it is always a supernatural gift. Ample
rein, so important at this age, is given to the initiative of the student
in the response, which should be particularly free, original,
and reflective in senior high school. It may be simply contemplation of the truth, or discussion and application of the lesson, or
development of it, or even questions concerning it; but response
must be made.

Participation cannot be denied. Ideally it takes place in every
lesson; practically it takes the form of discussions, project work,
essays, quizzes, and the like, and greater participation in the Mass
itself, at least once each week. Warnings are perhaps unnecessary
to the effect that teachers must never invade the domain of conscience by demanding personal revelations or resolutions. That is
for the counselor of the individual and even then the confidences
will never comprise an "invasion." The teacher deals with groups.
The response he seeks is a more generalized one: what students
should do, and so forth. The student (and perhaps the reader) will
be confused about just what is wanted, but the task of providing
it is the very agony of the process of maturing. If the answer were
easy, if it could be set down here, tidily packaged for teacher use,
it would cease to be a response worth making to the God who first
speaks to us.

This classroom method should itself lead to something far more
important and long-lasting, namely, a genuine spirituality proper
to the layman and based on the liturgy. That this is badly needed

is a truism. How it will be achieved is an area for controversy. Some advocate theological study as the only sound basis for a layman's spirituality. The question immediately occurs, is this necessary or even possible for the majority of men? Others advocate imitating the spirituality of the religious life insofar as possible. They often do this unconsciously, through third orders and pious confraternities whose approbation by the Church is beyond question. But if history brings us knowledge of these avenues to holiness, history also shows that they have not been notably successful in producing on any scale the kind of mature Catholic layman we seek. A new generation of the pietistic is not a need of the Church at the moment. The liturgy on the other hand is the framework natural to layman and cleric alike as members of the mystical body. Using it as the basis of Catholic spirituality does not condemn us to either childishness or antiquarianism. The development of a spirituality of liturgy is not to be equated with giving a course in the Church year and the colors of vestments, nor with slavishly studying past forms, but with giving an understanding of the spirit of the liturgy as a living prayer-form. After all, the liturgy is meant to be nothing more nor less than our personal encounter with the redemptive acts and words of Christ.

Finally, a word on the importance of the Mass to the religion course. More and more the intimate connection between sacrament and Word is being realized. If we try to separate them very far, even in practice, we risk the twin abuses of sacramentalism in our Churches and verbalism in our classrooms. The one leads, at best, to an immature Catholicism that does not meet the needs of the day; the other is akin to an historic Protestantism. The Catholic needs to be as close as possible to his sources, and that more than merely academically speaking, since the religion course, again, is more than an academic matter. The Scriptures not only need to be read privately and studied in class; they must be proclaimed liturgically. The Mass is the source and climax of the religion course, the point from which it flows and to which it returns. We cannot afford to be without it; if we deprive ourselves of the Mass the religion course is then quite literally pointless. This truth is by no means peculiar to senior high-school religion courses, but it certainly applies there as elsewhere.

THE SCRIPTURES

The place and importance of the Scriptures at every level of religious education are generally acknowledged today, but there is a unique problem which probably belongs to the level of the senior high school. It is that of guiding the transition from the childlike acceptance of the Scriptures in their primary, religious meaning, to the quite mature, sophisticated study of them with their secondary questions of inspiration, literary forms, history, and so forth, without lessening appreciation of their religious meaning but rather increasing it. When the use of the Scriptures on the lower levels has been neglected, or has been fundamentalist-oriented or in some other way unwise, as is most often still the case today, this transition will be a painful experience. Many teachers experiencing this only now can testify to the fact. Even given an ideal elementary formation, there will inevitably be growing pains.

In passing, a small plea might be entered with earlier teachers not to make the problem more difficult by attempting it too soon, and so endangering the possibility of real understanding when the students are capable of seeing the problem. It is here suggested that the best time to face the properly scholarly aspects of Bible study is in senior high school when students are consciously reflective, are exploring literary form in their literature classes, when the sense of history has ripened, and when the problems of science are seen in their true dimension. It has been the experience of several well-prepared teachers that introducing the secondary questions of scriptural introduction even in the freshman year requires that the teacher create the problem in the students' minds before trying to solve it, a procedure that is hardly ever wise. Scripture scholars themselves have been naturally more concerned with problems of their own field (and often more concerned with the secondary questions outlined above) than with the whole sweep of sacred history. This leaves the high-school teacher's pedagogical problem virtually untouched by them. Popularizations of high quality such as the work of Vawter and McKenzie are valuable as background material for teachers, but are hardly classroom material even for better high-school seniors. Some persons have maintained that Scripture studies are not at a point where it is possible to make any kind of truly safe and sound synthesis for popular purposes. Outstanding work has been done on the high school level, however, by Barrosse in pamphlets, articles, and the texts of the Christian Life Series.[21]

With regard to using such material, a few suggestions are here given. First, the transition from patterns of biblical catechesis in lower schools should never be used as a deliberate "shocker," an opportunity for the teacher to startle the student with his erudition. It is sufficiently regrettable that ignorance leading to harmful presentations of the true meaning of the Bible is such that unpreparedness in students may be taken as the usual thing, without capitalizing on it. The transition should rather be made as natural as possible; it is simply growing up in our attitude toward God's Word.

Second, following this lead, as much use as possible should be made of allied literary and scientific studies; examples from secular literature should be given, instances of scientific problems in the Bible should be cited, yet always with an eye to its uniqueness as a human document.

Third, it should be made clear that the purpose of creating such a mature mentality toward the Scriptures is a positive one: the greater appreciation and use of God's word in life and prayer; and that it is never merely a defensive one, that is, to answer critics.

It is recommended that one of the chief areas in which the teacher must develop himself, and one of the principal topics he will have to introduce into present courses, is that of salvation history. Actually and ideally, the senior high-school student should have been steeped in this from his youth, but our awareness of this

---

[21] Thomas Barrosse, C.S.C., *Understanding the Bible: God Speaks to Men* (Notre Dame: Fides Publishers, 1960); with Sister Jane Marie Murray, O.P., Book 2 of *The Christian Life Series* (Chicago: Fides Publishers, 1957–60).

most important aspect of our faith has heretofore been woefully deficient. A magnificent panorama of the story of salvation, and of our place in it, should be the object of special study at least once in the course, yet a study not so extended that it will exceed the psychological grasp of the students. It should then be the object of frequent review, so that it stands always in the background. The student must be led to see that "this is our story," and that the problems of the Church and her members must be seen in this perspective to be seen truly or at all.

This is the principal contribution of the Scripture course to popular religious education. The scholar understandably cringes at the thought of high school teachers exegeting the Old Testament text and finding there literal confirmations of modern concepts of grace, spirit, future life, and so forth. The isolated, random text-jerking which is characteristic of some theological manuals of a past generation is not only a misuse of Scripture; it is poor pedagogy. The harm done to the student at the secondary level by this sort of thing is not immediate. It lies in the fact that he is led to believe that this procedure is a scientific treatment of religion, and he will end either in disillusionment or continued ignorance.

At the same time, we should not be afraid to read the Word of God itself. This is the great task. The teaching of the Scriptures in popular education must not be simply a course in scriptural introduction. It is a tragedy that the modern high-school senior probably knows more about the Bible and has read it less than any student in the Church's long history.

DOCTRINE

Among many possible considerations on the subject of doctrine, the writer offers two: one on content—what we should teach; one on form—how we should express it.

Concerning content, the first step is to settle on a core of fundamental topics or central truths around which the course is to be built. The text, the syllabus, the liturgy, our own judgment, and the like, are all factors in making the decision. But once it has been made, those aspects of the topic should be chosen which are proper to the interests, abilities, and needs of the student at this level. For example, on the sacraments: the old definitions, proofs, conditions, and so forth, which he has had in catechism class should not be repeated at length. Neither should the theology of sacramental causality be developed, nor apologetical proofs and the like, which the student neither needs, nor is capable of absorbing fully. He should be helped to form a mature attitude toward the sacraments. In the lesson this could be done by developing historically and psychologically the meaning and use of signs in general and sacred signs in particular, with emphasis on the poetic beauty and richness of the symbol. In the response this means helping students to emerge from a childish, magic sacramentalism to a real understanding and use of the sacraments, emphasizing now the *opus operantis* or role of the recipient which alone changes with maturity.[22]

A most interesting problem deals with the form in which the doctrine is expressed. It is not solely a question of the words themselves but the images and metaphors, particularly the nonscriptural ones. The problem has grown out of the desire of some to use a form of speech with students that is easily understood, that "speaks their language" or "brings it down to their level." Earlier in this volume (p. 26) Mary P. Ryan has spoken of the phenomenon: grace is "supernatural gasoline in the human engine," the priest is "God's sales representative," and so on. Such expressions seem to make their appearance on the high-school level because the teenager has his own language, and because it is so strongly desired that he understand and not merely memorize something of the truths of the faith. What is to be said of them?

Some persons whose sense of dignity has been revolted by the tasteless efforts of imprudent leaders of youth reject these expressions entirely.[23] This reaction is certainly sound enough but per-

---

[22] Josef A. Jungmann, S.J., "The Eucharist and Pastoral Practice," *Worship*, 35 (January 1961), 83–90; cf. André Godin, S.J., and Sister Marthe, "Magic Mentality and Sacramental Life," *Lumen Vitae*, 15 (April–June 1960), 277–96.

[23] E.g., Mary Perkins Ryan, *Perspective for Renewal* (Collegeville: The Liturgical Press, 1960), p. 76.

haps negative in that it does not safeguard a value particularly precious to this age group. The following positive positions are therefore put forward as a basis for discussion.

First, to express a Christian truth, to teach it or to pray it, the biblical metaphor or that expression taken from Catholic tradition has an absolute priority. After all, it contains the revelation. By the disposition of an all-wise Providence, it frequently conveys that truth in the most adequate manner. Most of the signs and images used in the New Testament, at least, have a basic natural significance or an acquired literary one that renders them almost universally understandable with little explanation. But beyond this, it must be said that the use of nonscriptural metaphors in a secondary manner is not only permitted but to an extent to be encouraged, if it is done with prudence and skill. This is permitted basically because man has a right to hear and speak to God in his own language and expression, a right confirmed by Christ when He spoke to shepherds of the good shepherd, etc. Man understands what he experiences and can re-express. This holds true above all in the religious sphere. It is the reason for the incarnation.

A number of cautions need to be lodged, however, to assure a proper, prudent use of such expressions. First, there must be careful avoidance of overextending them, pressing them, or devoting the major portion of a lesson to them. Second, the best metaphors must be carefully selected; any with unwholesome connotations should be avoided, though this is not always possible because of the nature of metaphor. Even the idea of Christians as sheep is not without its pejorative connotations, particularly one must suppose to a sheep-herder. In the Arctic Circle the symbolism is quite meaningless. A familiarity with literature is a most valuable asset in connection with apt figurative speech. Such expressions must always be subservient to the truth and secondary to the biblical and traditional formula. In all this, teachers should be above reproach themselves but they need not be too finicky with their students. These young people are not going to be terribly precise and sensitive in their expression in any case. It is far better to have them think of God than refrain out of fear of awkwardness.

MORALITY

As in the case of technique, here again the great desideratum of religion teachers seems to be a simple solution, a clear set of norms or answers which all can agree on in response to student questions on such topics as going steady, kissing, mixed marriage, occasions of sin, and the like. An immediate answer shall not be attempted on this complex question. There seem to be two quite divergent moral points of view which have their roots deep in the theologies they spring from. The one emphasizes the development of virtue in general, and prudence in particular, in the formation of conscience; this viewpoint is that of St. Thomas. It is particularly in harmony both with the psychology of the adolescent and with the liturgy and liturgical method described above.[24]

The other viewpoint is inclined to emphasize clear laws and the opinions of authorities in the formation of conscience. It is therefore more external, usually negative, impersonal, and ethical in character. It has its origin in the type of moral theology oriented toward preparing the confessor, the type which has been taught in our seminaries for several centuries. This outlook has prevailed even to our day. It is one of the primary factors in inhibiting that spiritual maturity which is our goal. The desire of teachers for clear-cut solutions springs largely from long exposure to this point of view. We repeat: falling victim to it—a quite different matter from thinking sharply and firmly about Christian morality—is a guarantee of continuing moral immaturity.

In answer to the question then, it must first be said that such a "party-line" in matters of specific detail is neither possible nor desirable. It is not possible to legislate such highly personal and circumstantial matters as hemlines, the consumption of beer, or

[24] Marc Oraison, *Love or Constraint?* (New York: Kenedy, 1959), pp. 41, 115ff. Cf. also P. Gregory Stevens, O.S.B., "Moral Theology and the Liturgy," *Yearbook of Liturgical Studies, I* (Notre Dame: Fides Publishers, 1961).

any other occasions of sin except where a clear danger exists, and then legislation is neither necessary nor effective. By all means teachers must continue to discuss their handling of these problems; they should then be free to teach what they think right, never tearing down another priest's or teacher's position (if the latter comes from students it will probably have been misrepresented anyway). They should neither encourage rigorism by imposing their own judgment in an authoritarian manner, nor encourage laxism through legalism.

Secondly, such a "code" is not desirable because it is bad psychology for this age group and poor training for maturity. The adolescent is particularly inclined to resent an authoritative solution imposed from without unless it is a confirmation or justification of his own chosen position. This state of affairs is not all bad; it is in fact a situation begging for genuine Thomistic moral training. Granted, such an approach does generate its own series of problems. The chief of these are an excessive reliance on one's own opinion and a tendency to be critical of the Church. These must be honestly faced, limits must be set, no apologies offered for the Church's doctrine or the teachings of her wisest theologians. When a clear decision on a particular case is required, and is possible, it is to be given unhesitatingly.

But this will not be often. Given freedom, adolescents are more rigorous with themselves than adults are. These very limits are a psychological necessity for them; unlimited freedom is more than they can bear. The tendency of teachers to let themselves get caught in casuistic traps and answer every question asked, not to speak of fixed answers, greatly inhibits maturity. "Father, is it a sin to . . ." is very often a plea not for information but permission. Its unheard counterpart is, "I asked Father X, and he says it's all right to. . . ." In our day we have not been notably successful in maintaining adolescent moral fiber. Maybe it is because the older moral viewpoint (meaning the solid Christian one, not without its admixture of Puritan rigor regarding everything but drink) was an adequate instrument in an unsophisticated society of another day or place. Today, however, when opportunities are unlimited, stu-

dents need to be formed from the inside rather than have temptations walled off from them by restrictions which the adult world
cannot enforce. Using a priceless metaphor Mersch has observed
that some animals need a shell because they have not got a skeleton.
In developing Catholics with real backbone we need a skeletal
rather than an exoskeletal morality.

Turning to things more positive, the present writer believes that
the Thomistic moral viewpoint offers a number of corrections to
our moral education as it stands, that is to say it broadens and
deepens it. It broadens it by taking the emphasis off sex (notice
how the "party-line" of the last one hundred years centers on it)
and giving the truly Christian dimension of charity. Social justice
and a universal charity are skimped in the preoccupation with
self in our moral education. While sex gets the headlines, outstanding violations of charity within the school or parish go unmentioned
and notable opportunities for charity are unattended to. But all
these things are prime matter for the senior high-school religion
course. One of the necessities of moral education at this level is to
bring unastisfactory moral conditions to the students' attention, in
the most concrete way possible. They need to experience the situation, see a little ugliness, feel a little pain, before they can or will
react to it. This experience is extremely difficult to bring about.
Preaching and exhortation are not the way, not with juniors and
seniors anyway, if only because they have had more than enough
of it. Providing such vicarious experience is another of the real
challenges and unsolved problems of teaching at this level.

Finally, the Thomistic moral viewpoint can also help us to
deepen immeasurably our students' moral outlook. We are not just
answering questions about duties, we are providing opportunities
to practice the Christian virtues of faith, hope, and charity, which
are the goal of the Christian life and moral education for that life.

APOLOGETICS

Surely in order are a few paragraphs dealing with several of the
specific areas usually covered during these two years, which are
under some discussion or attack. The first of these is the subject of
apologetics or "Christian evidences" as it used to be called. That

there is considerable dissatisfaction about the subject is clear. A recent study, difficult and obscure but profound, makes a new and positive approach to the problem of what apologetics on this level should be.[25] It is based on a conception of the act of faith and its motives which is controversial. But passing over that, we can for several other valid reasons welcome some of its conclusions. First, the aim of the course is not primarily to prove or to defend the faith with regard to those outside the faith, but it is to give the student a clearer understanding and a firmer grasp of his own reasons for believing. The immediate result of this is that apologetics is no longer an impersonal argument or contest, but a personal, religious exercise for the student himself. This fits in well both with our idea of religious education and the psychologist's description of this age as one in which religious doubts arise—intellectual questions which are natural and necessary for the kind of mature faith that is possible only now.

The next and most important recommendation is that the task and method of the course be primarily one of realizing and interpreting the "signs of credibility," that is, the works of Christ, and, above all, of the present Christ, the Church. The matter of presenting the philosophical and historical arguments, which apologetics has heretofore considered its greatest task, has now become secondary. Thus, in the syllabus being described, the course has two parts: one on Christ, the other on the Church. In each we consider first the "essential" motives of the "signs of faith" and then secondarily the purely scientific contributions of history, philosophy, among others. This much at least must be said for it, it does away with what must be for most a superficial, difficult, and misleading version of the course in theodicy with which the traditional apologetics begins. Once more we see that an attenuated scientific presentation of a subject does not meet the needs of the majority of the students of this level and also exceeds their capacities.

The students need to be understood and their actual problems

[25] Jacques Laforest, "The Teaching of Apologetics in the Senior School," *Lumen Vitae*, 15 (April–June; 247–63; July–September 1960), 451–66.

answered with arguments or signs that solve *these* difficulties. Because they are children of their times, this will incidentally be the best possible preparation for defending and advancing the faith among those who do not profess it. The apologetics course that fits this prescription has not yet made its appearance, surely not at the high-school level. Until it does it would seem the practical thing to suggest that the teacher not forego the values which apologetics can give, but use the traditional outline, emphasizing what he knows is of value and de-emphasizing the rest. Let him use contemporary writing as both a stimulus and a means of keeping himself in contact with real problems. Above all, let him avoid the old rigidity of the classic apologetics with its irrefragable chain of logic. This chain snaps easily in feeble hands like those of the normal teacher. Even at best, according to traditional theology, such a "preamble" never enters into the motivation of an act of faith anyway.

CHURCH HISTORY

Another victim of poor handling, misunderstanding, and consequent impatient rejection is the subject of Church history.[26] As we find it in most high-school manuals it is a simplified outline of generalizations which bears about the same vital relation and resemblance to real Church history as the catechism does to theology. Both arrived at their bloodless state by the same process. This is a tragedy, considering both the extent to which the historical viewpoint preoccupies modern man—especially the intellectual man of Europe, not to speak of the East—and the indispensable contribution it makes to our goal of maturity. A recent issue of *Lumen Vitae* and a monograph of *Vérité et Vie* have studied the matter in detail and make the following points.[27]

First, the study of Church history is essential to a mature faith,

[26] Celestine Luke (Salm), F.S.C., "The Scope and Content of the High School Religion Course," *Perspectives*, 4 (June–July 1959), 11, 14.

[27] *Lumen Vitae*, 15 (April–June 1959) esp. the articles by Georges Delcuve, S.J., and André Godin, S.J. Cf. J. Colomb, "Pourquoi et comment enseigner l'histoire de l'église," *Vérité et Vie*, Série XLVIII (Strasbourg, 1960–61).

since the object of faith is not merely a structure or synthesis but a sacred history. We must study it to know Christ, the Church, and ourselves as we really are: the products and elements of a historical process. Second, our study must be objective and religious. By an objective study is meant a completely honest and truthful one, not merely in the relating of events but also in their selection and interpretation; and by a religious study is meant one which recognizes the dominance of the supernatural factor, the theological principle of ordering all things to God. These two are perfectly compatible. Indeed it is only with a theological view of history that we can be completely honest and truthful.

In the third place, a number of suggestions concerning the teaching of this history deserve to be grouped here. One is the psychologist's assurance that the "historical function," the ability to grasp the sense of history, reaches development at about the age of fifteen and so admirably suits the senior high-school population. Another suggestion is that what is needed far more than new or separate courses is to give all our present teaching its historical—and eschatological—dimension. Thus, we should start with the present and relate to it the past and the future. This is fully possible only in the light of faith and with a theological view of history.

Still another suggestion is that we break away from the "political" type of Church history with its emphasis on diplomatic battles and the actions of the hierarchy as public men, and show how the entire Church continues the life of Christ—growing, suffering, falling, rising, ultimately conquering. Finally, we are reminded of the importance of occasional, immediate contact with the documents or sources of Church history. Even students need such concrete contacts; psychologically at least, it might be said that they need them more than does the scientific historian.

From what has been said it seems clear that the traditional type of high-school Church history which most of us are familiar with does not fill the bill.[28] The survey it attempts becomes manageable

[28] An exception is made of Joseph Colomb's Le Souffle de l'Esprit, 1. Dans l'Eglise du Christ (Tournai: Desclée, 1960); 2. Histoire de l'Eglise (ibid., 1959).

in length only by being reduced to a series of abstract generalizations which lose almost all relevance, realism, or religious significance. Moreover, it is frequently less than objective, if not consciously in its interpretation of events at least unconsciously in its omissions and isolations. Reading one such history gives the impression that all early Christians were uniformly heroic and their wicked pagan enemies constantly at their throats; that all heretics were evil or stupid men, and frequently both, who flatly denied a simple, defined truth; or that, for example, the Frankish-papal alliance under Charlemagne represented "a near ideal relation of Church and State." This is poor stuff now, and potentially dangerous for the student in the years ahead. The Church has nothing to fear from the truth, but it has much to fear from this kind of "truth." The real truth of history has the advantage of being more interesting and more practical.

Positively and specifically, what is the solution? It has been suggested by some, conscious of the values of history, that a year or even the entire course be given over to the historical approach, pursued insofar as possible according to its scientific method. We put forward a counter-suggestion here which does less violence to other legitimate approaches to the presentation of religion in the high school, such as the liturgical, the theological, or the synthetic. It also seems to preserve the true values of history even better than the direct conversion of the religion course to a history course. The proper use of history in popular religious education is far more akin to the concept of historical writing in the ancient period than it is to modern German, nineteenth-century scientific history which often borders on historicism. In fact, its proper use is just that, a *use* of history rather than a study of history for its own sake.

The ancients used history to teach a doctrine. They selected incidents, rearranged them—not always chronologically—and interpreted them to suit their purpose. Some who misunderstand this use call it an abuse, even in the gospels; it hardly meets the canon of objectivity, they say. But the mistake here lies in seeking something that is not there, and in misunderstanding what comprises objectivity. Objectivity is not neutrality. It requires only that our criterion be truth viewed in the large. We are not advocating a departure from the truth in any way. In fact, by means of history we seek to get at the true nature of the Church. We watch the evolution of those characteristics and positions that are so explicit today but were only implicit in the little group on Pentecost. A partial and it seems very promising beginning has been made in the revision of the *Living with Christ* series of texts.[29]

History then, the historical dimension, must constantly reappear in teaching the Church, her works, the sacraments, and many other doctrines, even though these topics may be arranged according to an entirely different principle than the chronological one. A broad survey of a period or of the whole might also be given, if it were to teach some truth such as apostolicity or God's providence. Even then, the treatment must be just long enough to serve the purpose of conveying this truth. Would it not be meaningless to provide so many partial pictures, so much splintering without a panorama of the whole? Yes, but the giving of that panorama in any explicit, extended, formal way is the function of the world history course, where the Church is shown in proper relation to the world of her times. It might be added here that a popular panorama of the Church's history of the symbolic, ancient type, which still can contribute much in the way of an historical dimension, is ever-present implicitly in the structure of the Church's year. It should be clear by this time that the writer favors the annual cycle as the basic plan of the high-school religion course.

By way of conclusion to this section, it should at least be mentioned that a mature formation in the area of religion cannot be attained independent of a mature formation in other areas, notably history, literature, and to some extent science.

THE CHRISTIAN VOCATION

To return to our initial goal—forming the mature Catholic layman—there are many dedicated to this ideal who speak of it and write of it and work for it, who condemn that Victorian compromise

[29] *Course 4*, High-School Religion Series by the Christian Brothers (Winona: St. Mary's College Press, 1958).

which makes religion a negative, compartmented, individual ethic, and who work for the full participation of the laity in the life and work of the Church. But it does seem that of all of those who work for the various specialized forms of this or that apostolate, relatively few concern themselves with the formation of the apostolic spirit in every layman, in other words with the formation of the apostle as such. Endless talk goes on about "vocations," but little is said of the primary and common vocation of all to the work of the Church: the Christian vocation as such. What is badly needed is a theology of life and a layman's spirituality to direct and to sustain the apostolate of Catholic action. Such a theology and spirituality could be the invaluable contribution of the junior and senior year of high school to our students. A few remarks are in order, in extension of the significant work of people like Congar, Putz, Greeley, and M. P. Ryan.[30]

The phrases "theology of life" and "lay spirituality" may be as much clichés as is "maturity"; it all depends on the content one gives to these expressions. The theology of life refers to the ideal and plan which orders all our life to God as to our final end; the spirituality consists of those practices by which we implement that theology in our daily life. The important thing is what we mean by life. The thirteenth century saw a flowering of Catholic life that is the admiration of the ages; yet, though lay in its origins, it was a profoundly clerical life that flourished then in government, in the universities, almost everywhere that religion really flourished. The theology that was created was a professional one, a science; the spirituality was one based primarily on the exaltation of the supernatural and the rejection of human values as such: sanctity lay in poverty, and the like. It was simply too much for man to turn the world into a mendicant order. Apart from all the aggravating abuses on either side, the reaction of the renaissance, which at its best exalted human values, was in part the layman's answer to the preponderance of the clerical.

We have now passed through the Church's natural and neces-

[30] Cf. especially Yves Congar, O.P., *Laity, Church and World*, tr. Donald Attwater (Baltimore: Helicon Press, 1960).

sary, but rather negative, reaction to the layman's riposte, and are witnessing in our own day another age of glory for the Church. The theology of life and the spirituality we envisage as the work of this age have about them nothing that is really inimical to the thirteenth century; indeed they look to it and spring from it. But they do invade new areas, and these areas are chiefly those of the human values that play so great a part in the life of the lay members of the Church. The theology of life that is suited to our day must speak of work, of family life, of politics and business life, of recreation especially, and must integrate them all into the plan of life for God. Nothing is alien to it, no value is rejected. Whatever we do in word or work is to be offered up, in, with, and through Christ to the Father, in the Holy Spirit, for God has made all these things good.

This theological view of the world will include two inseparable steps: first, it will respect and exploit the natural goodness of things, of every human value; and second it will offer and relate all to God. The first step was neglected by the Church of the Middle Ages; the second was ignored by the pagan renaissance. The Christian renaissance had the vision, but any execution was made impossible by the rupture in Christendom. Only the Church in our day can do both and thereby retain all the "middle-class" human values produced by the last five hundred years, some of them very good indeed: representative government, general education, higher standards of living, social welfare. These must all be incorporated into the supernatural plan, in a sense consecrated, given an eternal function and dimension. They must be made part of that great restoration of man and all things to God which began with the fact of God's becoming man.

The formulation of this work and its execution are not the work of the cleric. His is a work of formation and service to the laity who will be paramount in its execution. The concept of the layman as a mere instrument of the clergy, or as simply and solely an executor of plans and actions handed down by them, is the result of an inadequate theology. The ultimate authority of course remains where Christ put it, in the hierarchy, but the areas spoken of above are specifically lay areas, known and understood at first hand only by laymen and subject only to their influence. Without this theology of life the layman in the apostolate will risk either becoming an activist or never achieving his proper stature and function.

This theology of life requires a spirituality and a form of asceticism based not on the rejection of human values but on their use and purification. All the strife and tension, all the disorder and dissension that pervade these areas is the object of a lay asceticism that is not merely individual but social. Each man by his work in the world is not just saving his soul or creating a purely natural and temporal social order. He is helping to establish a climate for the exercise of charity by the entire Christian community. The cross he must bear is that all imperfection must be burnt away, so that this area, this facet of life too may be dedicated and incorporated into the plan of salvation. Surely only this goal can give religious significance to much of the drudgery of daily life in the world, and make it all worthwhile. This is not the asceticism of another day, of the thirteenth century. In a sense it is not as lofty. But it is ours of the twentieth century and right for the layman of the contemporary world.

How and when does one teach this sense of Christian vocation? It is first of all a tone that should color and direct all teaching, especially on such topics as the sacraments and the apostolate. Beyond that, these ideas can be directly planned and taught at the close of the school year when the Pentecostal season makes them liturgically appropriate; also at the time of retreat. The closed retreat is a spiritual exercise that is lay as well as clerical in character. It should be repeated annually, and thus become a basic of a lifetime's spirituality.

Beyond this, the sensitive teacher must be ever ready to cooperate with the Holy Spirit, in the classroom or in an individual conference, in taking advantage of one of those crucial, sensitive moments, one of those golden moments, when the time is ripe and the soil is fertile for the planting of the seed that is the vocation to Christian maturity.

11 THE PROBLEM OF SACRED

DOCTRINE IN THE COLLEGE

Bernard Cooke, S.J.

ONE of the most promising aspects of Catholic life in the United States is the large number of young men and women graduated each year from Catholic colleges and universities, and from those in which Newman membership has meant apostolic action and a Christian intellectual formation. If one views this situation against the background of the worldwide condition of the Church, or views it in the light of the Church's history over the centuries, he begins to realize that the American Church possesses a unique potential that gives ground for great hope for the future. If Christianity has been able to struggle through so many ages when great numbers of Christians were inadequately informed about their faith, developing her intellectual edifice all the while, what will be the spiritual strength of the Church at a time when she has at her disposal the educated faith of thousands of college graduates?

Undue optimism is checked, however, by one searching question that has been raised by a number of contemporary Catholic educators: though these young people are educated in Catholic institutions of higher learning, how deep and mature is their faith?[1] Have not the Church's undergraduate colleges, perhaps, in the midst of raising and maintaining intellectual standards in literature, natural sciences, and the like, neglected higher religious formation? In many institutions faculties have succeeded in rehabilitating philosophy so that it holds a respected place among the other academic disciplines; but can assurance be given by and large that theology is not the academic stepchild, deprived of the role of queenship that is properly hers? To the present writer it seems not.

Scarcely anyone who is intimately connected with the work of teaching sacred doctrine on the college level would argue that the situation should remain as it is. Not a few would hold that a rather thorough rethinking and reworking of the college religion course is in order.[2] Considerable ferment has been at work among college teachers of this discipline. This has manifested itself in the past ten years in a growing body of literature and in the rapidly expanding influence of the Society of Catholic College Teachers of

[1] In addition to the current scrutiny of United States Catholic intellectualism, triggered by books like those of John Tracy Ellis, Thomas O'Dea, Justus George Lawler and Walter Ong, there has been much questioning of religious education as such. Frank Sheed's *Are We Really Teaching Religion?* (New York: Sheed and Ward, 1953) represents an early and more general presentation of the problems; for the specific posing of the college level question, one can consult the annual *Proceedings of the Society of Catholic College Teachers of Sacred Doctrine.*

[2] One of the earlier confrontations of this problem can be found in the article of John Courtney Murray, "Towards a Theology for the Layman: The Problem of Its Finality; The Pedagogical Problem," *Theological Studies,* 5 (1944), 43–75; 340–76. Since that time, a number of other suggested revisions have appeared: an approach based upon the "Thomistic synthesis" can be found in Thomas Donlan, *Theology and Education* (Dubuque: William Brown, 1952); and in *Theology in the Catholic College* (Dubuque: Priory Press, 1961); a somewhat different orientation is represented by the article of Christopher Mooney, "College Theology and Liberal Education," *Thought,* 34 (Autumn 1959), 325–46 or the essay of Gustave Weigel, "The Meaning of Sacred Doctrine in the College," in *Shaping the Christian Message,* ed. Gerard S. Sloyan (New York: Macmillan, 1958), pp. 170–82.

Sacred Doctrine.[3] Since much has already been written by way of analysis of the existent state of sacred doctrine teaching in the colleges of the United States and Canada, the present essay does not attempt to examine current practice critically; instead, it proposes to look ahead to some of the things that must be done if improvement is to continue.

What steps must be taken in bettering sacred doctrine courses if the college educator is to exploit the challenging opportunity that is his? What must the teaching of Christian revelation be in Catholic colleges and universities and in other faculties where there are chairs of Roman Catholic thought, if it is to lead to intellectual deepening of faith? Four characteristics would seem to provide convenient headings under which to group a discussion of these questions: the instruction provided in sacred doctrine must be *scientific, integrated, contemporary,* and *vital.*

TRULY SCIENTIFIC

There are some who in the past have argued against the use of the word "theology" to denominate courses of religious instruction in the college, but no serious development of this theme has been made in the past eight or nine years. Regardless of how these courses are entitled—and often the proximity of a theological college where convictions are strongly held will be an influential factor in this—what the college student needs is theology, that is to say, the application of genuine theological method to the understanding of supernatural revelation. Granted that the purpose is not to form professional theologians of college students, an aim entertained by no undergraduate department in any field, there should still be the attempt to present as scientifically controlled an understanding of faith as students are given in other areas of

[3] Founded in 1953, this organization is now operating in twenty regions throughout the country. Its 770 members represent 287 Catholic colleges and universities, that is, all but 16 of such institutions. For an account of the beginnings of this group, cf. Cyril M. Vollert, "The Origin, Development, and Purpose of the Society of Catholic College Teachers of Sacred Doctrine," *Bulletin: National Catholic Educational Association,* 51 (1954), 250.

knowledge.[4] Neither the good of the individual student nor the good of the Church allows the college to send students forth at graduation with an intellectual approach to Christianity that does not match their intellectual approach to the remainder of life.

Higher education today is the heir of the critical spirit that has always marked university circles, but has been notably prominent during the past century or so. This questioning attitude has been strongly felt in the areas of literary and historical studies; from these it has passed into the field of what is sometimes called "history of religions." Along with this there has been the application of sociology and anthropology to the study of religious phenomena, and certain efforts to form a philosophy of religion.[5] Much good is to be derived from such studies; but the general spirit of investigation has been quite naturalistic, because of the philosophical backgrounds of the men engaged in these studies and the lack of Catholic and other Christian scholars in these fields. Catholic college students come into constant contact with these more or less agnostic currents of thought; any attempt to isolate them from such ideas is undertaken at the price of putting them out of touch with their times.

College students wonder, and rightly so, about the precise historical roots of Christianity; they ask whether the facts of Christianity's origins can stand strict historical appraisal; they question the claim that Catholicity is a unique form of Christianity, or that

[4] An increasing amount of current writing on the subject seems to recognize the possibility and need of teaching theology to college students. Cf. the article of Mooney (cited above), Gerald Van Ackeren, "Reflections on the Relation between Philosophy and Theology," *Theological Studies,* 14 (Dec. 1953), 527–50; John L. McKenzie, "Theology in Jesuit Education," *Thought,* 34, (Autumn 1959), 347–57: Vincent Edward Smith, "Sacred Doctrine or Christian Education," in *The School Examined: Its Aim and Content* (Milwaukee: Bruce, 1960), pp. 259–90.

[5] To use the word "scientific" of theology is not to oppose those who would argue for a more "humanistic" approach in our college teaching of theology. Cf. Murray, *op. cit.,* "The Pedagogical Problem," pp. 34–76, Van Ackeren, in his study *Sacra Doctrina* (Rome: Catholic Book Agency, 1952), opens up a dynamic notion of sacred doctrine which throws considerable light on the relation between revelation and the developing process of history and human culture.

Christianity is so uniquely different from the other great world religions.[6] For the majority of these young people such questions are not strict religious doubt; but there is in the spirits of most of them a deeply felt need to rest their fear that their Catholic education has "brain-washed" them in the area of religious knowledge.

That there have been advances in biblical studies has become a matter of common knowledge among the Catholic laity; but the exact nature of these advances is not too well known, and there is rather widespread uncertainty as to where we Catholics stand with respect to the understanding of the Bible. Actually, classroom experience shows that there is little problem involved in presenting college students with a reverent yet up-to-date understanding of the sacred texts. They do not expect nor welcome an iconoclastic and completely secular explanation of the Scriptures, but they do want an honest and straightforward presentation of the scholarly understanding of the Bible. For the most part, the college instructor cannot hope to give them any firsthand experience of the methods of contemporary exegesis, since they lack the linguistic tools to appreciate this; but they can and should be given a scholarly distillation of the results of contemporary biblical research.[7] What applies to the Bible is equally true with regard to the historical evaluation and understanding of the writings of the Fathers of the Church and of the decrees of the Church's magisterium.

What is needed for college students is, in brief, a clarification regarding *why* and *what* they believe—a clarification that is effected by utilizing history, anthropology, archaeology, textual criticism, etc., according to the scientific procedures proper to each of

[6] Cf. Mircea Eliade and Joseph Kitagawa (eds.), *The History of Religions* (Chicago: University of Chicago Press, 1959); this is a more recent discussion of methodological questions raised by Joachim Wach in his *Sociology of Religion* (Chicago: University of Chicago Press, 1945).

[7] For this, there now exists a considerable body of non-technical literature by means of which the educated layman can inform himself of these biblical advances. Besides the books of McKenzie, Vawter, Charlier, Gelin and others, there are the periodicals *Catholic Biblical Quarterly, Worship, Theology Digest,* and *The Bible Today* which make it possible to follow the present trends.

these disciplines. As the college curriculum is now set up in most places, such study of the factual aspects of revelation would seem to fit quite well into the early portion of the college course, at a time when the student does not yet have the philosophical background required for a more speculative approach to theologizing. To have adverted to the *need* (as we have just done) of solid historical and textual approaches to the study of revelation is in no way to have solved the problems as to how this can be done—and these problems remain very real and sizable.

During the latter half of their college careers, students are generally introduced to areas of study that are more analytic. Here, as their powers of appraisal and philosophical thinking develop, students take on a cast of thought that is more critical, that tends if kept within bounds to analyze whatever evidence is a necessary part of intellectual maturation. It is inevitable that in this stage of intellectual development the more intelligent college students will begin to subject what they know of their faith to the same critical appraisal to which they subject all else in their world. They will want to apply the insights gained from philosophy, from psychology, history, literature, to a deeper understanding of what they are told by revelation about man and his life on this planet.[8]

It is absolutely essential for the intellectual peace as well as for the intellectual deepening of Catholic college students that they be given, in the light of philosophy, psychology, and other knowledges, a truly scholarly analysis of the object of faith. The college cannot be content to impose upon them, for memorization rather than for understanding, a body of formulas which have achieved the status of pat answers, especially when these formulas have the appearance of theological reasoning. Not only are students justified in being curious about the meaning of revelation; those who teach them must stimulate that curiosity, for it is a necessary prelude to their investigating the deep meaning of revelation.

---

[8] Cf. Carroll Stuhlmueller, "Catholic Biblical Scholarship and College Theology," *The Thomist*, 23 (October 1960), 533–63; also, the September–October 1960, issue of *Perspectives*, which has three articles devoted to the teaching of Scripture in college.

Revelation is not a sterile body of truth; it is a vital truth given by God to direct and shape human life and human thinking. This revelation must be presented to college students in a form that explores the profound depths of the truth it contains, a form moreover that is ordered according to the scientific methodology proper to theology, so that this knowledge can genuinely nourish and mold the whole of their thinking.[9]

Catholic theology lays claim to being a scientific discipline, that is, a body of truth ordered in a way in which human reason can proceed with clarity and conviction from principles to conclusions.[10] It would be a tragedy in the intellectual life of college students if the theology that is presented to them in their formative college years were to fail to represent such a scientific approach. Obviously, there are serious limits to what one can do with undergraduates and in a very limited time; these limitations are greater still when all of the theology courses are required courses, or when few students concentrate in the field; but if college courses in sacred doctrine are little more than a higher level of the same kind of catechetics which students have experienced in earlier years,

[9] It is by such a process—applying natural knowledges to deeper understanding of revelation—that theology itself advances. This would seem to indicate that our Catholic universities have a most important role to play in the intrinsic growth of theology. The words of George Shuster seem quite pertinent here: "It is not too much to say that the immaturity, or it might be better to say the incompleteness, of American culture manifests itself at no point so clearly as it does when religious issues are under discussion. There are many reasons why this is so, but the principal one undoubtedly is that theology has been studied so far away from the main stream of university life," "What is Education?" *Daedalus*, 88 (Winter 1955), 38.

[10] "What the undergraduate needs and seeks for most is some ultimate frame of reference for the countless intellectual and emotional stimuli involved in the maturing process called college, some subjective integration of all those vital forces which the development of his natural powers has suddenly released within him. This theology must give. It must show him that Truth is Life, and therefore *evangelium*, a message of joy, for joy is the sentiment of fullness of life. Hence on the college level the Church will present her intellectual discipline humanistically, as an abiding vision of human life and work, so that the student will have a rational basis for reacting in a Christian fashion to the society in which he finds himself." Mooney, *op. cit.*, p. 329.

then they cannot take seriously the claim that theology is the highest form of human knowing. On the other hand, if a genuinely scholarly approach be employed in the college instruction of faith, students will not have to be reminded that theology is a scientific discipline; they will themselves experience it.

In providing an analytic approach to the study of revelation, there are undoubtedly many problems. It is in this area that theology is necessarily and intrinsically dependent upon knowledge of other disciplines such as philosophy, because this kind of theologizing can take place only by applying these human disciplines to the understanding of revelation.[11] This creates a serious curriculum problem: one must await a certain development in the student's grasp of philosophy before the student can be introduced with profit into systematic theology courses that are truly such. Again, to propose the need for genuine theology on the college level is not to solve the problems, but to point to the fact that some solution must be essayed even if it be only partial. It would be ideal if the college could keep the student beyond his present four years of college and in the later years teach him his theology; but such is not the case, and the best must be done in the time provided to furnish the students with at least a sampling of that kind of theology that deserves the name.

INTEGRATED THEOLOGICAL KNOWLEDGE

As the need for more specialized knowledges grows, the problem of integrating knowledges in the educational process becomes more acute; this problem is particularly pertinent to theological knowledge. Theology is not just an ordered investigation of a certain area of truth; it is a wisdom, a knowledge which acts as an ordering principle for all other knowledges.[12] Moreover, theology investi-

[11] Cf. Yves M. J. Congar, "Théologie," DTC, vol. 15, cols., 459–561 also, Charles Journet, The Wisdom of Faith (Westminster, Md.: Newman Press, 1952), pp. 64 ff.

[12] Speaking of the flowering of theology in the Middle Ages, McKenzie says: ". . . theology received the results of all other sciences and combined them into an organic whole. Theology was creative to the highest degree

gates the mysteries that God has revealed to man, mysteries that are inseparably intertwined and unified. To understand any one area of revelation involves a knowledge of all other areas. Hence, to be a genuine theologian, one must study, grasp, and then unify an impressively large body of knowledge.

Even in the case of one who can devote years to the pursuit of theological knowledge, there is considerable problem in finding that principle or principles of integration which can make of his theological knowledge a unity rather than an accumulation of facts. In the case of the college student this problem is much more acute: as is all too clear, he has a very limited amount of time in which to acquire some experience of theology. He himself cannot work through any sizable portion of theological knowledge and form his own synthesis; this must be done for him in terms of some principle so clearly integrating that it can function in simple yet effective fashion to form a unified vision of faith. Let us not underestimate the dimensions of the problem: there is no question of giving to the student a statement about his faith that is formulated in scientific terminology, so that he can learn it by rote and repeat it somewhat intelligently; there must be a process of *thinking*, in which some integrating insight will function in the student's own thought processes to relate to revelation all other knowledges and so integrate them.[13]

Theology is not meant to develop as a discipline in isolation; as a matter of fact, it is impossible to do the work of theology without constant dependence upon the other disciplines of knowledge. Theology advances precisely by applying these knowledges to the fuller understanding of revelation. It follows that college teaching of theology cannot avoid the need to integrate instruction in sacred doctrine with the teaching being given in other areas of the college curriculum. This is at once a problem and a challenge: how make

---

when it was most receptive. . . . If we wonder why theology lost its eminence, we cannot help but notice that after the fifteenth century theology became isolated and self-centered, no longer willing to receive therefore unable to give," *op. cit.*, p. 350.

[13] Cf. Congar, *op. cit.*, cols. 486–87; *Summa theologiae* I, q. 1, a. 6.

the truths of faith meaningful to young people in terms of those insights and values which they obtain from their studies of the social sciences, philosophy, natural sciences, and literature? The teacher must be able to grasp those genuine problems concerning human life and its meaning and conduct to which natural disciplines of knowledge draw attention; and he must be able to show that in theology one can at least approximate an ultimate answer to these questions. Theology, if it be taught genuinely for what it is, cannot but be unified in itself and related to other areas of human knowing. Herein lies a difficult task for one who would teach sacred doctrine in the college or university situation.

CONTACT WITH CONTEMPORARY THOUGHT

Most college students or graduates have encountered those courses which have a title indicating that they are meant to treat of the modern scene but which actually begin with the late Middle Ages and end with Napoleon. Such a lack of connection with the contemporary situation is characteristic of many courses in Catholic colleges; instead there seems to be a tendency to emphasize the classic and the traditional. In sacred doctrine teaching we can notice on many Catholic campuses a definite lack of contact with contemporary theological thought, whether it be Catholic or non-Catholic. Yet, there is on the part of students a great interest in the thought and life patterns of the world in which they find themselves. And there is on the part of Catholic theology itself an important need to encounter contemporary thought currents as found in university circles.

There is an amazing amount of activity in Catholic theological circles today.[14] We are breaking out of the post-Tridentine era of

[14] Considerable variety of opinion can be found as to the way in which theology should function in the college experience as an integrating principle. For somewhat differing opinions, one might consult the article of Mooney quoted above (which is representative of the more "humanistic" approach) and the talk of James V. Mullaney, "The General Principles of Integration of the Curriculum" in *Proceedings of the Society of Catholic College Teachers of Sacred Doctrine*, 3 (1957), 9–19, which develops the notion of sacred doctrine as a normative principle of integration.

theological discussion, and we are already into a much more positive and pioneering epoch. Many areas of theological investigation —biblical, liturgical, historical—have burst into full bloom within the past quarter century, and their growth is so rapid that it is impossible to keep informed about even one area. Somehow during the four years of college, Catholic students of theology today must be made aware—at least in a general way—of that body of knowledge which the Church guards and transmits as her sacred trust and which she is clarifying in the light of the contemporary world, its problems, and its advances. Young people are always attracted by the up-to-date, by the new; the college student is done a disservice if the truths of theology are presented to him as something static, outmoded, and out of contact with reality.

What is taking place in theology at present is extremely interesting; it will interest students if they come to know of it. The very questions that theologians are investigating are the questions that students are asking themselves at different levels in other areas of their educational formation.[15] Why, then, should they be deprived of the knowledge about what is actually happening in the Church, when this would help them toward an intellectual approach to faith? Why should they be given the impression that natural science, psychology, etc., are going ahead into areas of new understanding and new vision which promise a better and richer and more personal life, and not be informed that that which holds the greatest promise both for understanding and for shaping the future is theology?[16]

Students would be receiving an inadequate orientation, however, if they were being informed about contemporary develop-

[15] One need only read, in magazines like *Theological Studies* or *Revue des Sciences Philosophiques et Théologiques*, the summaries of current developments to discover how vast is this modern development. For a short introduction, one might consult the August–September 1959 issue of *Perspectives*, which contains reviews of contemporary developments in Scripture, Dogma, Moral, and Liturgy. Another valuable introductory work is R. Aubert's, *Théologie catholique au milieu du XXᵉ siècle* (Tournai: Casterman, 1954).

[16] The writings of Charles Moeller are quite interesting in this regard, particularly his *Littérature du XXᵉ siècle et christianisme* (Tournai: Casterman), a multivolumed work that is still incomplete.

ments in Catholic religious thought alone. They are going out into a world of ideas that is largely non-Catholic. They will encounter many intellectuals deeply committed to truth who hold religious positions other than that of the Catholic Church. The young Catholic must be prepared to appraise, criticize, and learn from the religious thought of others in a sympathetic spirit, and to explain his own faith in terms that are meaningful to those outside the Catholic tradition almost as a condition of making it meaningful to himself. Preparing him simply to defend and guard his own position will end in not even achieving that much.

In the years ahead college graduates will be living in a world marked by a great merging of cultures. The people whom they will encounter from these other cultures will come with quite different religious backgrounds and traditions. For the most part these people will have many valid natural insights into religious areas; the Catholic student must be taught how the revealed truths they believe as Catholics are related to these natural religious insights, how they build upon them, how they transcend them. There is going to devolve upon Catholic graduates a large part of that delicate process of adaptation which comes with expressing God's revelation in terms that are intelligible to the men of our age. In order to do this, college graduates will have to possess two things: a deep grasp in its essentials of the faith that is their heritage, and a clear understanding of the contemporary mind and the language in which it expresses itself. If they understand their faith and their age, they will be able to transmit intelligently and accurately the Christian revelation which is meant to transform the thinking and the lives of men. If the graduates of Catholic institutions of higher learning or formative Newman situations are unable to do this, the task will not be done.

VITAL UNDERSTANDING OF REVELATION

When one approaches the revelation given by God and attempts to systematize and make it more explicit in scholarly fashion, there is always the danger that the end result will be an abstract formula at least one step removed from reality. The history of the development of theology in the Church gives adequate witness to the presence of this danger.[17] Not a few of the difficulties that beset religious education in our day find their roots in the fact that theology itself was often developed in an atmosphere of scholarly speculation somewhat apart from the concerns of concrete daily life. Fortunately, this is changing in most heartening fashion, and in college teaching the Catholic theologian's concern with life should be exploited.

In the last few years, theologians have given a great deal of their attention to a study of the mystery of sanctifying grace; these investigations owe much to the advance in biblical studies, particularly to important though pioneering efforts in biblical theology.[18] As one goes back to the Old Testament and examines the main current of God's revelation to the people of Israel, one cannot escape the conclusion that God is presenting to man a *way of life*.

Even at the origin of Israel in the Exodus experience the lesson is present for those who will see the events with faith: Yahweh guards the life of his people from the enslaving influence of Egypt, from the engulfing power of the waters, from the threat of death by famine or thirst—even when this requires some special intervention. So, too, when they enter into the land of promise, it is this God who provides the rain for their crops and in many other ways provides for their livelihood. Yet the people tend to fall in with the thinking of their Canaanite neighbors and attribute the success of the crops to vegetation divinities; and the prophets must insist again and again that the gods of these surrounding peoples are incapable of giving life. These false gods are not themselves living; they are but lifeless idols; the God of Israel is, on the other hand, a living and life-giving divinity. No attribute of God is more

[17] On the influence that the Church should play in contemporary thought, cf. Yves Congar's *Lay People in the Church* (Westminster, Md.: Newman, 1957), pp. 258 ff.

[18] Cf. P. Vignaux, *Nominalisme au XIVᵉ siècle* (Montréal: Institut d'études médiévales, 1948); Louis Bouyer brings out this same point in sketching the thought background of the Reformation in his *The Spirit and Forms of Protestantism* (Westminster, Md.: Newman, 1956).

fundamental in Old Testament thought; Yahweh is the living God, and he is the source of all life.[19]

Associated with the notion of God as source of life is the notion of God's Word; it is the Word of God that is the bearer of life.[20] Through the words of the Law, through the oracles of the prophets, Yahweh's Word is a force transmitting life to his people. One must listen to the word of Yahweh in order to have life. If one would be wise and learn the secret of life, he must pay attention to Yahweh's Word. For one who closes his ear to this Word the result is inevitable: death.

Christ comes to be our way, our truth, our life. His task is one of giving life, "I came that they may have life, and have it more abundantly" (Jn 10, 10). He is the fulfillment of the entire Old Testament revelation regarding Yahweh as the source of life, regarding Yahweh's Word as the bearer of life; for Christ is Himself the life-bearing Word. He is the light come into the world, a light that is the life of men. He is the true bread come down from heaven; unless a man eat this bread he cannot have life in him. He is also Yahweh feeding his people with manna; the description of the multiplication of the loaves points to this. All this reaches a climactic fulfillment in the supreme transforming action of the Cenacle in which Christ, having transformed bread into Himself, can literally give Himself as source of man's life.

We know, in the light of later clarification, that the life of which Christ spoke is above all that transformation of man which we call sanctifying grace. This is a life that is highly personal, since it enables us to enter into personal communion with the three Persons in God; it is, somehow, a participating in that life which is proper to them. It is a life whose very causing in us makes the divine Persons present to us in a special way which Christ Himself describes as an indwelling. We know that this life constitutes a

[19] As examples, one might instance Viktor Warnach's *Agape* (Düsseldorf: Patmos Verlag, 1951), and Jacques Guillet's *Themes of the Bible* (Notre Dame: Fides, 1961).

[20] Cf. E. Jacob, *Theology of the Old Testament* (New York: Harper, 1958), pp. 37 ff.

veritable divinization of man; it is a life that is meant to transform and vitalize everything else in his being. The mystery of this life as it perfects and transforms us will culminate in the mystery of our resurrection when the full power of the risen life of Christ will manifest itself in us unendingly.[21]

Such is the emphasis on *life* that is to be found in theological thought today; and it is important that theologians teaching in college present the message of revelation in this fashion to college students. In our day, there are so many influences in men's lives that hold out false promise of furnishing fullness of life. The values that guide the majority of mankind in their search for happiness and peace and personal fulfillment are values that are illusory, values that in large part are contrary to the values of Christ. What must be emphasized in the teaching of sacred doctrine is that true personal development can come only with the acquisition and growth of grace. This means that in the theology class santifying grace cannot be described in vague, general, and abstract terms. The instructor must enter profoundly into the transformation that grace effects in the human person and his powers of action. Students must come to understand that when divine life enters into human life, what results is not a destruction but a greater fulfillment of the human in us.

But the grace that we possess is grace coming from Christ. We are Christians, which means that we are the continuation of the mystery of Christ in the present day. Again, college men and women must learn to see the influence of Christ as a vital force; they must realize that the reign of Christ through the power of grace and faith and charity is the most profound and ultimate reality in today's world, that what is shaping history more conclusively than diplomatic arrangements and the fighting of wars and the development of economic power blocs is the influence of Christ.

St. Paul tells us (in Ephesians) that the mystery of Christ work-

---

[21] Cf. John L. McKenzie, "The Word of God in the Old Testament," *Theological Studies*, 21 (June 1960), 183–206.

ing in his Church is the great mystery, that Christ's redemptive work in the Church is the final cause of God's creative action. To realize that one is involved in this work of Christ as a participant, as an active contributor, is something that can give meaning and depth and stimulation to the living of Christians of college age. Not only that, but to understand and to adopt the values and mind of Christ is to acquire simultaneously great maturity and great sanctity.[22] Students must come to see that there is in their lives a process of acquiring insights, of developing attitudes, of making decisions; and that the only ultimate framework in which these insights, attitudes, and decisions can be meaningful is the reality of the Christian mystery.

At the mention of sanctity, an idea is introduced that must be understood in new dimensions by young people of today. For them there is little appeal in a concept of sanctity which is one of mild self-destruction, a negation of the genuine values of their world; but no such concept need be given them. The fact that there is no Christian sanctity without the mystery of the cross does not make sanctity essentially negative. Rather, revelation's record is that sanctity is fullness of life; it comes with maturity of choice; it centers around the virtue of prudence[23]—these are the things that the college student of today must be told. His is a challenging world, a world in which he wishes to make his place, a world in which he wishes to help men, a world that he sees as being good for the most part. He is willing to sacrifice what is needed to bring a good world into being; he may even be willing to die in order that the world become more Christian. But he does not wish to enter that world as a child, nor to be considered as a child by those who are shaping that world. If Christianity is presented to him in any terms but those which see it as a mature and decisive grasp-

[22] Cf. F. X. Durrwell, *The Resurrection* (New York: Sheed and Ward, 1960), pp. 349 ff. Cf. also the Spring 1960 issue of *Theology Digest*, which was devoted to articles dealing with the resurrection.

[23] Cf. A. Wikenhauser, *The Mystical Theology of St. Paul* (New York: Herder and Herder, 1960) and J. Goldbrunner, *Holiness is Wholeness* (New York: Pantheon, 1955).

ing of life's possibilities, then the faith will not enter into the actual conduct of his life.

Again, it is essential that there be impressed upon students the fact that intellectual clarification of faith contributes to, and does not hinder, true holiness. Too often, a certain opposition has developed in people's minds between sanctity and an intellectual approach to God. Somehow, there is the lurking suspicion that to understand, to appraise, to construct a theology upon the data of revelation will draw men away from a deeply reverent attitude toward God. Such is not the case; the Church has always fought for the position that faith is essentially an intellectual assent, and she does so in modern times.[24] Today, when old and young are fascinated and concerned by the discoveries of psychology and the resultant insistence on the need for personal integration and clarity, revelation must enter into men's conscious living. The correct understanding of the healing and integrating aspects of sanctifying grace, faith, hope, and charity can bring great insight into the function God's grace has in our lives, and at the same time bring great peace to those who possess the gift of faith.

Contemporary teaching of sacred doctrine must vitalize not just the individual lives of our students but the society into which they will move as graduates. Man is a social being by nature, a fact which revelation has always insisted upon. As far back as we can go in the record of God's manifesting Himself in the Old Testament dispensation, God has always acted in terms of a social group. If an individual was singled out for special calling, as was Abraham or Moses or David, this individual calling was itself subordinate to the calling of the people. God called and formed *Israel;* God gave his Law to a chosen *People.* As the Old Testament period progresses, there is increasing emphasis on the role and responsibility of the individual; but throughout those centuries the social dimen-

---

[24] There is a conjunction of scholastic and biblical theology that would make an interesting study: scholastic theology in analyzing the morality of the human act places the virtue of prudence in a focal position: in biblical thought, the quest and possession of wisdom is highlighted (particularly in the later centuries of the Old Testament period), a wisdom which is not a speculative but a practical wisdom, i.e., prudence.

sion holds the primacy. One sometimes hears that the revelation of
man's obligation to his fellow man, obligation in justice and charity,
is something that comes only with the Christian era. Yet, as far back
as the beginnings of the prophetic movement we can find strong
expression of God's interest in justice among men; and the notion
of brotherly love is found in not a few passages.

This emphasis in Israel's Scriptures on the social dimension of
human life and human salvation finds its fulfillment in the revelation of Christ's living on in the mystery of the mystical body. Along
with the recent return to stressing the vital nature of the Church,
there has come a wider awareness that salvation and sanctity are
impossible in isolation.[25] No man can reach his destiny by himself.
Above all, if he is baptized into the Church, he is meant to live
out his life as a Christian, as a member of Christ linked to the other
members by bonds of faith and love. Christ described his Church
as a leaven, an element placed in the midst of the world to give
movement, even more to give a life which the world does not
possess. Christianity is essentially active and apostolic, and the
mystery of the Church is the mystery of Christ working in the
world throughout human history, in order to transform and to
redeem the world.

It is this challenging and dynamic approach to the understanding of the Church that must be transmitted to students as they are
taught sacred doctrine. It is not the function of the college teacher
as such to train apostles; yet college education in the faith can
never be something separate from this, for the very truth that the
college professor conveys is a truth oriented to the apostolate and
to the sanctity of the students who are in the classrooms. The
Church exists to transform the society of every age, including this
one. Students who take our courses in sacred doctrine will move as
graduates into contemporary society; they are meant in God's
providence to possess the truth in such a way that it can become a
transforming force in the modern world. Somehow—and this is a
gravest problem in college teaching—they must be given that

[25] Cf. the decree of the Vatican Council on faith, John Clarkson *et al.*
(eds.), *The Church Teaches* (St. Louis: Herder, 1955); Denz., 1789.

understanding of revelation which will be the principle of their own sanctified living as persons and of their participation in the apostolic mission of the Church.

Difficult as the task may seem, well-nigh impossible at times, there is one element in Christ's institution of the Church that gives both hope and the means of accomplishing the task which confronts us: the sacramental system.[26] The sacraments are at once *vital actions*, the proper life-actions of Christ working in his Church, and one of the principal channels for the transmission of revelation.[27] If the college professor will but estimate this situation correctly and give to students a deep and accurate and personal understanding of the sacraments, they will have an indispensable insight into the nature of Christianity and be prepared for an intelligent and adult participation in the life process of the Church. To be able to live the sacraments is to be able to enter into Christ's redemptive acts; to know that one is part of the sacramental life of the Church is to begin to understand what it means to be a Christian; to order one's actions and one's life around the sacrifice of the Mass is to enter upon a deeply apostolic approach to human living.

Sacramental life in the Church must become that which polarizes all college teaching of sacred doctrine. Classroom instruction must necessarily terminate in an intelligent participation in the eucharist. But such a manner of teaching supposes a rather radical reexamination of the presentation of the Church, sanctifying grace, and the sacraments themselves, as it is now being carried on. In the light of what seems unmistakably to be the Holy Spirit's effective working in the Church, the present-day teacher of sacred doctrine

[26] Cf. E. Mersch, *Theology of the Mystical Body* (St. Louis; Herder, 1952), chaps. 19, 20 (on sanctifying and actual grace), pp. 594 ff.; H. de Lubac, *Catholicism* (2d rev. ed.; New York: Sheed and Ward, 1957), pp. 177 ff.; L. Lochet, *Son of the Church* (Chicago: Fides Publishers, 1956), particularly chap. 6, pp. 149 ff.

[27] An interesting collection of essays on the relation between the sacraments and religious instruction, specifically on the connection of Bible to liturgy, is *Liturgy and the Word of God* (Collegeville, Minn.: Liturgical Press, 1960).

has no choice but to concentrate on making the sacramental life of his students a more intelligent, more mature, more profoundly Christian reality. He must prepare his students to *live in Christian fashion*.

CONCRETE NEEDS IN THE PRESENT SITUATION

Such, then, seems to be the problem facing those who wish to give an adequate formation in sacred doctrine to college students. If those engaged in the work are to meet the challenge that confronts them, there are several concrete steps that must be taken. If their teaching is to be vital, scientific, contemporary, and integrated, they must move with courage and decision in four areas.

1. There must be a training of teachers, thought through in the light of the present-day situation, and aimed precisely at training people for *college and university* teaching of sacred doctrine. Happily, there is in progress a rapid recovery from the illusion that anyone who has had the regular seminary course in theology is prepared to teach theology on the college level. As one can see from what we have said about the urgent problems facing college teachers of revelation, it requires a highly specialized and specifically oriented training to enable a teacher to provide that kind of intellectual formation of faith which college students need.

Teaching in college is more difficult than teaching in a seminary because of the variety of disciplines and professions represented there. College teachers of sacred doctrine must have a clear, scientific, and penetrating grasp of theology; but they must also have a fairly wide knowledge, general though it be, of other areas of investigation, particularly those which impinge upon theological advance today. At least some acquaintance with the questions being asked by sociology, psychology, philosophy, history, and literary criticism must be possessed by the college teacher; this will enable him to fit the teaching of revelation into the intellectual life of the young people who attend institutions of higher learning. Without such an acquaintance, the college teacher of theology is doomed to an academic isolationism that will make his classes less interesting, and that will render his words sterile as far as the practical living of his students is concerned.

Here we face a major problem: there are very few doctorally trained theologians teaching sacred doctrine in Catholic colleges or Newman foundations at the present moment; and extremely few who have been specially trained for the apostolate of college teaching of sacred doctrine.[28] Even if it were possible to free large numbers of teachers for such training—and it is not—the question arises: where could they obtain the training requisite for their important role? Here is one of the greatest needs in the American Catholic college situation. It is being filled in one or two American faculties at most. Unless it be filled on the large scale—since the problem is a large one and can only grow—all other speculation and effort in the area of improving Catholic college teaching of sacred doctrine will be inadequate and ultimately ineffective.

2. Conjoined with, and acting as a guiding principle for, the desired training program for teachers, there must be a theology worked out for the precise needs of Catholic college students and graduates—there must be a theology oriented toward the life of the laity. This will not be a new theology, but the points of emphasis and the principles of integration and orientation will be selected from the precise viewpoint of the layman—his needs, his opportunities, his apostolate in the Church at the present time and in the foreseeable future.[29] The fact must be faced by all Catholics, but especially by the clergy, that theology is not a clerical preserve, that it is something that belongs by rights to every intelligent and educated Christian. The faith that is in him is pointed toward growth, and this growth of faith can only come through an active process of engaging in theology.

[28] For an accurate, detailed estimate of the contemporary situation, cf. Sister Mary Francis Regis Carton, S.S.N.D., *An Inquiry into the Study of Sacred Doctrine and Faculty Preparation in Sixty-Three Catholic Colleges* (microfilm; Washington: The Catholic University of America, 1963).

[29] Cf. the encyclical letter of Pius XII, *Mediator Dei*, "On the Sacred Liturgy" (New York: America Press, 1954), paragraphs 3, 17, 20, 47–50.

Professional theologians have set themselves the task of examining the way in which contemporary advances in natural knowledges can be brought to bear on the understanding of revelation, so that the inexhaustible riches of the Word of God can be exploited. Pioneering work is being done by a number of theologians in the Church—men like Congar, Journet, Murray, de Lubac, Durrwell; yet in many respects the modern Church is only making a start. An immense and fascinating task lies ahead if the theologians of our time are to work out a theology that fits the present and the future. Only if this promising development of theology takes place will there result that profound doctrinal synthesis which college teachers need to teach sacred doctrine adequately.

3. Any teacher of sacred doctrine in the college or university can testify to the third key need: there is a sad lack of adequate textbooks and reading matter in English. No one would wish to disparage the important contribution made by the LeMoyne College series, that of the Priory Press, or the texts published by the University of Notre Dame; yet the editors and authors of these text series would be the first to admit that the country is only in the first generation of college textbooks. These books have filled the present gap; their use has helped clarify the precise type of textbook needed. Now the task remains to refine and improve these initial efforts. At this writing two publishers, Prentice-Hall and Bruce, have in prospect extended series in the newer mold. Without good textbooks there is no external norm for teacher and student alike as to what comprises scientific excellence in theological study.

In addition to adequate textbooks in numbers, there is great need also of collateral reading material for college theology classes. During the past few years there has been a marked progress here: a large number of the better European books have been translated, more and more things of merit are being written in English, the spectacular advent of paperbacks has brought many things within the range of the student's financial means. Moreover, the publication of magazines like *Theology Digest, New Testament Abstracts,*

Cross Currents, Downside Review and *Worship* have made much of the best contemporary theological thought available to students. However, there are still great lacks—for example, there is no up-to-date history of dogmas done by a Catholic hand, much less a competent history of theology.[30]

4. Finally, college teaching of sacred doctrine must receive the support of the bishops of the country, of college administrators, of parish priests. As is proper, Catholic people look to their bishops for direction in matters of faith; if these members of the Church's hierarchy take not just a permissive but an encouraging attitude toward the deeper theological training of lay people, this will do much to stimulate young Catholics to a serious intellectual investigation of their faith. It will also help to ensure the bishops a learned clergy, for part of theology's current problem is that it is engaged in largely by clerics for the immediate end of a priestly ministry. A possible result of this is that this most liberalizing of disciplines may tend to become professional and sterile. The things of the mind are best savored by the best minds; cleric or lay is no true distinction in the aristocracy of intellect. The whole Church will know the salutary difference when the seminary or "theological college" is no longer the court of last appeal.

College administrators, for their part, can do much by their practical decisions to situate sacred doctrine as a serious and respected academic discipline. If theological thinking is so vitally important in the intellectual formation of collegians, administrators must be courageous in resisting those pragmatic pressures that would tend to reduce sacred doctrine teaching to a secondary position in our colleges.

Lastly, the college teacher of sacred doctrine is dependent upon the parish priest to complete what has been begun in the college classroom; for, as we have seen, the final step in the intellectual formation of faith can only come in a vital sacramental life. Parish

[30] Cf. the presidential address given by Brother Alban of Mary, F.S.C. at the 1960 national convention of the SCCTSD (published in the *Proceedings*, pp. 7–18).

celebration of the eucharistic liturgy is meant to be a constantly deepening experience, in which college graduates probe ever more deeply into that process of grace and redemption which our college courses have tried to explain.

12 SEMINARY TRAINING

AND RELIGIOUS EDUCATION

Gerard S. Sloyan

THE American Catholic has a high stake in the education available to his clergy, whether secular or regular. Yet it may be observed in passing that just as the Harvard, William and Mary, and Yale of today (the three oldest colleges in the United States) were not achieved in three or even five decades, so good seminaries can not be had merely for the asking, no matter how zealous the clergy nor generous the faithful. Numerous theological colleges exist that are more than one hundred years old. Others far less venerable are able to rival them in excellence because they are conducted on a good educational principle. The important matter for the American Catholic is that the educational principle at work in his seminaries, both in sacred and profane studies, be such that his Church will have the caliber of priestly leadership it deserves.

The modern seminary system dates to legislation enacted at the Council of Trent (1563).[1] The patron of these clerical institutions

[1] Cf. James A. O'Donohue, *Tridentine Seminary Legislation, Its Sources and Its Formation* (Louvain: Publications Universitaires de Louvain, 1957), pp. 121–67. The 18th canon of the 23d Session (July 15, 1563) is patterned largely on the seminary legislation enacted by Reginald Cardinal Pole of England in the Legatine Synod of 1556 (London).

is St. Charles Borromeo, who came to be the chief executor of the legislation, and who died as Archbishop of Milano in 1584. Up until Trent the pattern had been one of private study in the residences of bishops and other clergy, with some attendance at university faculties of theology.[2] In monasteries and friaries the cause of priestly formation was served by conferences and occasional theological lectures. The contrast between the serious studies in the humanities and law engaged in by clerics at the universities and the rather casual sandwiching in of theological instruction in preparation for the priesthood was considerable.

The Western Church has never departed substantially from the terms of the Borromean reform. Although cultural and scholastic patterns differ in the East, the program of priestly preparation is basically very similar there. Recent popes have discoursed upon seminary education, among them Leo XIII in his restoration of Thomistic studies, chiefly philosophical, in the encyclical letter *Aeterni Patris* (1879). Pius XI issued the apostolic constitution *Deus Scientiarum Dominus* (1931) which regulates the course of studies for the priesthood and higher theological degrees quite specifically. The present pope has given much attention in public utterances to the sanctification of priests and priestly candidates, but he has not dealt specifically and at length with seminary education apart from his insistence in *Veterum Sapientia* (1962) that the instruction be in Latin.

According to modern legislation, applicants for seminary entrance must first complete a classical course. In the United States that means that after high school, aspirants have two years of college in a liberal arts sequence that includes the study of Latin. Paradoxically, there is no strict requirement of theological study at the college level in order to prepare for higher theological study. This means, among other things, that at age twenty-one the priestly candidate can be seriously deficient intellectually in relation to his laymen counterparts in the area of his primary concern, and that he may lose a year on the way to a college

2 *Ibid.*, pp. 1–16.

degree for lack of these studies, if he retires from a college-level seminary.

There exist in the United States numerous "minor" or "junior" seminaries. They frequently bear the name of college, though many include four years of high school as well as two years of college. Most congregations of regular clergy conduct these seminaries for their own candidates; the Jesuits and Dominicans are notable exceptions. Numerous dioceses or ecclesiastical provinces (i.e., the territory associated with the nearest archbishop) do the same. In the past and even until now, attendance at the college department of the minor seminary is a condition of entrance into the major seminary of some dioceses.

The major seminary (*grand séminaire*, say the French) is normally a six-year foundation which provides two years of philosophy study and four of theology. The two religious orders mentioned above and certain other secular and religious clergy give three years of philosophical training. Some groups, like the Jesuits and Marianists, interrupt or defer the course of priestly studies for profane study, or teaching, thereby putting off the ordination date.

It is a much argued question whether the minor seminary serves a constructive purpose in the scheme of clerical education. In Europe and Latin America it can have the important function of shielding boys from an actively nonreligious state schooling and certain of the harsher realities of life. The dangers in this country are somewhat different but by no means nonexistent.

In many cases, however, the most that their proponents claim for these seminaries is that they assure a serious secondary education under Church auspices. Some also say that they provide the adolescent with a unique opportunity for the election of the priesthood uncomplicated by premature assaults on his passionate nature. His "still fragile will requires the prudence and respect . . . which experienced and attentive counselors are able to give," in the words of Pope Pius XII. Despite this strong affirmation (which all Catholic educators make, though not with respect to the minor seminary exclusively), no one who knows priests in numbers will care to generalize on the graduate of the one type of collegiate institute or the other. As for identifying them later on, it is impossible.

In an interesting address to some members of the French "Young Seminarian Movement" on September 4, 1957, the same pope remarked that the Church had not regretted setting up special schools for candidates for the ecclesiastical life (i.e., minor seminaries).[3] Touching on their studies, he singled out history as providing the opportunity for penetration of judgment, broadmindedness, and skill at analysis; Latin and Greek as making available a part of the Scriptures and many monuments of Christian literature in their original languages. These two disciplines are the backbone of the classical course. An insistence upon social studies and the sciences is part of the educational outlook of the modern world. Bishops and administrators in this country who know the picture best are quick to praise the regional accrediting agencies for raising seminary standards in these and other respects. Library holdings increase, science courses improve from lecture operations by untrained and at times unsympathetic teachers to careful laboratory studies, and the social and behavioral sciences receive serious attention, all as a result of these external agencies. The priesthood benefits greatly thereby, since aprioristic thinking is the hallmark of a "clerical" mentality and empirical study one of the best assurances that the clergy will see the world as it actually is.

Papal directives state clearly that the best men in the diocese or province of religious should be put in the seminaries. The faculty members are invariably that: good students who edify by their fidelity to priestly ideals. Their great contribution, perhaps even beyond that of learning or piety, is the balance and prudence they provide for idealistic young men of varying temperaments and intelligences. If their seeming prudence should be at root imprudence, that is to say timidity or mere caution, they would make no contribution. Over the years there have been professors who acted prudently in their rejection of unimaginative means suggested to them as best suited to attain the end of a learned and pious clergy. They possessed at times a little too much awareness of the problem;

[3] Pope Pius XII, "The Minor Seminary" (*C'est une grande*), in *The Pope Speaks*, 6 (Winter 1959–60), 101–04. French text in *L'Osservatore Romano*, Sept. 6, 1957.

they did some salutary truth-telling to persons who were not ready for it. The way of such ecclesiastics has never been easy, but the vitality of the seminary system lies in men of this type. Despite their own daily routine and the changes of fortune all around them, some of them stay on and influence whole generations of priestly leaders.

More than one hundred years ago Newman wrote to his friend Dalgairns from Rome: "For there seems to be something of an iron form here, though I may be wrong; but I mean, people are at no trouble to deepen their views." The graduate of a really fine American college is likely to have a similar impression of the major seminary upon his first introduction to it. Why should this be? Why should the observations of a distinguished member of the New York clergy, John Talbot Smith, made in 1905, still have a familiar ring in every quarter of the United States: "As a body the New York clergy are too wedded to routine to be original. They prefer the well-trodden ways to the new path, although the city conditions demand new methods every year. . . . Clerical shyness is strong in New York, where a singular appearance on so great a stage causes widespread comment."[4]

The answer lies in the training available to the men who became seminary professors and the terms on which they must operate. Those who are chosen for the work are generally solid performers in the sacred sciences, though these may have been indifferently taught in the first instance. They are given further theological training but little encouragement to refashion the educational scheme they will be a part of. The mentality of *nihil innovetur* is likely to be assumed as that which best befits their new responsibilities. As a result of this situation some of the best apostolic types, men of intelligence, express impatience with the seminary system on their way through it. They make it clear that they are not keen on spending a lifetime in circumstances where they can not effect change, and their mentors understandably concur in the view.

The second difficulty is even graver. It is that the higher theo-

[4] John Talbot Smith, *The Catholic Church in New York*, I (New York, 1905), 592 f.

logical faculties around the world that are thoroughly alive both pastorally and intellectually are not very many. This makes preparation for really effective seminary teaching an uncertain matter. Private initiative more than anything else resolves the problem.

Complications regarding the seminarians themselves are numerous. They have been brought together by a common desire to serve the Church in her ministry, a calling which is apostolic primarily and a "learned profession" secondarily. The ambivalence between a high scholarly ideal and a minimally decent one is known to all concerned. Resistance to serious learning may be symptomatic of an individual's unfitness for the priesthood, or it may merely be his sound instinct that the divine call he experiences is not to a life of scholarship. Yet if his resistance to learning runs high, or if it is dealt with too understandingly by his teachers, he will be showing signs of unfitness for the priesthood which the normal operation of the seminary system may miss. A greater danger than either of the aforementioned lies in a seminary's earnest fidelity to a bad educational ideal and its tacit or expressed suspicion of a good one.

Another important factor is that major seminaries are usually closed communities. The men who teach in them pass judgment on the fitness of students for an office which they desire more than anything else in life. It does not take the candidates long to assay this situation. Anything like a genuine intellectual interplay, the give and take in which sparks fly, is largely absent from the lecture hall. Very few seminarians care to take the risk of winning in such an encounter because the stakes are in an entirely different order—priesthood itself. Their response to all this is a lively dialogue outside the lecture hall but a near-complete silence within it which is often hard to distinguish from passivity. Paradoxically, attempts by professors to pierce this wall often make the communication they seek more elusive still. They confess defeat, and give up discouraged.

A major difficulty exists in the lecture method itself. Seminary classes are numerous: five or six meetings a week in the major subjects with twenty-five or six hours of total attendance. This tends to give the impression that the essence of teaching is getting everything said once. The faculty cannot in conscience assign extended readings or papers to students whose major expenditure of energy is devoted to so much listening. Because of certain understandings in seminaries on the relative importance of the disciplines, a professor whose course meets only twice or three times weekly may be nudged by his colleagues or rector if he approaches matters as he might in a course of equal scope in a graduate school.

Most seminaries see to it that there are opportunities for apostolic activity: the catechizing of children, visits to hospitals or jails, census-taking, and the like. This service program is frequently under the direction of upperclassmen and there is everything to be said in its favor. The absence of it in institutions isolated either geographically or otherwise is a serious loss, rivaled only by having seminarians spend summer after summer with their fellows at make-work in which they have no experience of the problems real people face. One needs a very good memory to keep the image of lay life clear for four or six years, especially in prosperous times.

The pattern of interaction between apostolic endeavor and classroom study is extremely varied. In some seminaries the labors will be under the guidance of faculty members; in others they are viewed chiefly as having power to distract from the obligations of study. The concrete and immediate can draw many minds away from speculation if they are not fully at ease in it. Since most of the human race, including the clergy, is governed by the concrete and immediate even in divine things, it would seem that the best solution to this problem ought to lie in wholehearted sponsorship of apostolic works on the best terms. This would mean eliminating any conflict or overlap between study and practice, in the interests of both. If any single factor in priestly training other than the quality of academic life itself needs serious study, it is the Church's approach to internship for the priestly ministry.

Most of the problems outlined above are capable of solution by grace and human insight. Great strides have been made since

World War II by bishops and seminary authorities, and greater still are in prospect as the two work closely together. There remains one question larger than any of those touched on, a solution to which, while far from easy, is essential. It is the shape of the seminary curriculum. At present the "big four" in studies are dogmatic theology, moral theology, canon law, and Scripture. The fourth is subject to various fates in various faculties because of the diverse training of the men who profess this fast-developing science and the strong views held by those who have not had the opportunity to keep abreast. After the major studies there come, in importance, Church history, homiletics, catechetics, pastoral theology, liturgiology, and music. Religious sociology is not taught as a part of the theology course. Questions from the social order are dealt with in special moral theology, in the sense that all professors enunciate the relevant principles, though not all have been trained to analyze the social order as such. Many who are conscious of their limitations attend to these questions very little.

To improve clerical education it is not necessary to tamper with the existing curriculum formula so much as to provide the whole program with new directions. Reducing lecture hours and substituting a certain number of papers and seminars all round would undoubtedly help, but this is not as essential as giving a pastoral-liturgical orientation to all sacred science. This proposal is made with respect to the seminary because of the type of theological institute it is, not by any means to all theological study. It would be a mistake to identify the suggestion as a move away from the scientific in the direction of the practical. There are researches and researches, speculations and speculations. The inquiry into divine things which befits candidates for a sacramental ministry most is one which first examines all that God has done for His people, and then how they may be made recipients of His loving gifts. The heart of the message to Israel His beloved, the heart of the Gospel, the celebration of the redemptive mystery in life-giving sign—these are the matters that vitally concern the candidate for orders. He must know what factors in human life interfere with faith, what factors contribute to it, how by human fault the unity of faith has been lost, how in the Spirit it may be regained. The science of theology is the perfect vehicle for this presentation. It must be in many respects a richer theology than has been available up to now. There are signs from numerous American seminaries that such a theology is being made available.

Pastoral theology, understood as the study of the care of souls according to sound evangelical and doctrinal principles, is an infant science in this country. The only serious higher study of its problems being done at the moment in the United States is through faculties of sociology or psychology and psychiatry. Workshops and institutes in these auxiliary sciences are beginning to be available to the clergy, but not yet the theological discipline itself. Catechetics and homiletics are in only slightly better condition, though stirrings there are noticeable in a number of seminaries. Of the three, liturgy seems to be exhibiting the most life of all. An important development is that liturgiology or the history and practice of worship is being viewed more and more in the total context of its theology and spirit. Once real progress begins in these so-called auxiliary sacred sciences, social awareness inevitably sets in by a law of nature.

It comes as a surprise to the Catholic laity to discover how earnest the Church is in conveying theological learning to her priests without apparently having an equal concern for the way they transmit the message of salvation to the people. The form in which theology has been cast since the period of Trent has much to do with this. For it has not been simply a case of passing along pure doctrine in the seminaries, in aid of which an adult catchesis has been developed with a puzzling slowness. Rather it is a case of a need of inner renewal by all the sacred sciences; this they have been experiencing since the turn of the century at the urging and with the encouragement of the Holy See. A necessary consequence of this revivification of theology is improvement in the way in which God's truth is brought alive into the human heart.

Anyone who looks for signs of hope in clerical education should examine the journals produced by a variety of United States seminaries and theologates—unfortunately not widely available beyond alumni circulation and library use. Sitting in on the question period after a guest lecture on art, the population problem, or urban renewal would provide encouragement; so would a catechetical day put on by students or a Cana meeting by guests. But the real test of excellence is the day-to-day lecture by the resident professor during which the air is crisp with biblical faith, theological precision, and pastoral concern. The multiplication of these hours of teaching is *the* seminary problem

Whenever priest-catechists gather in international congress, invariably their chief resolution is that catechetical formation in the seminaries must improve if anything lasting is to be achieved on any level. Whenever major seminary professors gather they are prone to discuss psychological testing, standards of admission, or norms for judging the fitness of candidates for orders. They discuss other things as well, but on such occasions as they do are usually gathered as theologians or philosophers rather than as the directors of priestly candidates. Even in the latter case, it is surprising how infrequently catechetics, preaching, or pastoral care is the subject of consideration. The Catholic Theological Society of America, for example, has not had a major paper on the catechetical formation of adults and children or on pastoral liturgy in the more than fifteen years of its existence. Yet the Society is constantly trying to be relevant, in the sense of dealing with what are thought to be the people's deepest needs.

This condition is symptomatic of the entire state of clerical education. The interesting fact is that genuine relevance is likely to flourish in evening seminars of the students' devising—in itself a good tendency, but with the paradoxical situation obtaining whereby students note with delighted surprise any approbation from the professor's dais of what seem to them pastoral imperatives. This initiative of the candidates for priesthood is wholly to be praised, but there is a point at which their need to exercise it is regrettable.

On December 21, 1944, there was a directive issued by Cardinal Pizzardo in his role as prefect of the Sacred Congregation of Seminaries and Universities with respect to seminary courses in pedagogy and catchetics.[5] Although written in Italian there is every indication it was meant for the universal Church. It recommends a course in what we should call education (its history, philosophy, and practice), to be given once a week during the two years of the study of philosophy. There is a forthright declaration in the document about the course of theological study: not only is it to comprise "teaching the noblest of sciences, but also the transmission of *that word which is life;* it is not an exercise in doctrine . . . but an apostolate." The papal instruction is introduced by a paragraph that distinguishes between a priest's role as liturgical celebrant and as "educator, instructor, and former of minds and consciences." Since the rest of the message is concerned with his role as a classroom person the distinction is understandable, though one might wish that his function as catechist within the ambit of the liturgy had been underscored rather than assumed.

The instruction asks for the "validation and specification of the catechetics course already provided as part of pastoral theology," particularly in the form of lessons prepared and taught by the seminarians on the basis of the theological theses. They are to give classes either to each other or in real-life situations, on those "arguments of theology which bear some relation to [*hanno attinenza con*] catechetics." The problem is evident. If the *tesi* or the *argomenti* are the right ones, the directive is simplicity itself. If not, that is to say if the shape of the theological course has been non-"proclamational," then an insupportable burden has been laid on the shoulders of professor of catechetics and students alike.

Theoretical approval for lectures delivered in Latin would much more readily be given, provided that works of pastoral-theological significance begin to be written in that tongue. Student manuals for the courses in theology must themselves integrate biblical, patristic, liturgical, and historical data in such a way that this science comes to the student as a living word. The presumption that it must be transmitted in static condition, to be enlivened by courses in pedagogy, catechetics, or homiletics, is one that all pro-

[5] [Istruzione] "Agli Eccmi Ordinari sull' Importanza dello Studio della Pedagogia nei Seminarii," *AAS*, 37 (1945), 173–76.

fessors of theology will resist. They find themselves, however, constantly having to draw from works in the living languages to frame a theology of relevance.

Here, perhaps, is the crux of the problem. The theologians who have something of genuine significance to say to seminary students have not seen the importance of saying it in Latin textbooks. Yet they must, or else the unbreachable chasm between pastoral needs and attempts at theological fulfillment of those needs will continue. A factor that confuses the issue considerably is the rudimentary financial one. Publishers—and authors—have come to learn that there is a much broader market for theological literature than that comprised by a Latin readership. Conversely, they are withheld from the costly venture of seeking to produce manuals of genuine theological worth in Latin when there are numerous signs that these might not be adopted on the wide scale, given the overall state of seminary education. At the moment the impasse seems complete. Apparently we have in prospect some decades of split-level theological study in the seminaries. Possibly the need to translate the content of theology into terms of modern life has a certain advantage—*per aspera ad astra,* so to say. Still, one cannot but think that the inner reorientation of the discipline along lines proposed by K. Rahner, Flick and Alszeghy, or the Feiner-Böckle-Trütsch team at the seminary in Chur, Switzerland, might be a more direct approach to the question. The fact is that Catholic theological writing in the modern tongues enjoys a market that the Latin manuals in translation could never count on, precisely *because* it speaks to the needs of real people: a parable to learn wisdom from. Catechetics and preaching will flourish in the Church when the theology through which the sources of faith are mediated runs pure and free, *saliens in vitam.*

A final word might be devoted to a particularly complex aspect of the question of educational patterns in general. Seminary faculties (or rectors) do not feel fully free to experiment with excellence unless they have been given the mandate to attempt drastic change. Similarly, bishops and provincial superiors (many of whom have been seminary rectors) are hesitant to demand change now that they are free to do so lest it appear they do not have full confidence in the men on whom they rely so much. The result can be a static human situation desired by neither side, in which each is unwilling, for lack of certitude as to the mind of the other, to cut the knot. What is indicated is some conferring at the highest level and in considerable numbers by those who have the responsibilities in these affairs. Written studies by experts are not numerous. Experience is manifold but elusive. The problems that face the Church in the present age seem to make a thorough review of the terms of clerical education mandatory.

APPENDIXES

APPENDIX A

BRINGING CHRIST

TO PUBLIC SCHOOL YOUTH

Theodore C. Stone

ASSISTANT DIRECTOR
CONFRATERNITY OF CHRISTIAN DOCTRINE
ARCHDIOCESE OF CHICAGO

INTRODUCTION

"WHICH of you, intending to build a tower, will not first sit down and calculate the cost, to see whether he has the wherewithal to finish it? Otherwise, if after laying a foundation he has not means enough to complete the work, the curious crowd will indulge in mockery at his expense. 'Here is a fellow,' they will say, 'who began building without having means enough to finish!' " (Lk 14, 28–30).

In building a program of religious instruction, it is important to plan wisely. The purpose of this chapter is to offer suggestions on the organization of religious instruction programs. It will deal especially with the problem of bringing the Christian message to

Catholic youth attending public schools, and with the use of the laity in instructing these students.

It is estimated that 50 per cent of all elementary-school children in the United States and 70 per cent of high-school youth attend schools not conducted by the Church. Each year their numbers increase. These young people must be fired with the same love of Christ and His truth as those receiving a Catholic school education. There are not two types of religious education; there is one. To a great extent the Church is as strong as the family life of her members. Since the majority of Catholic mothers and fathers of the future are now attending public schools, something effective and realistic must be done to instill Christ's message into their hearts.

In setting up a parish elementary or high school of religion it is first suggested that there be three distinct departments in the school: one for home-visiting; another for teaching; and still another made up of helpers in the work. The role of each department will be studied in the following pages. It is presupposed, as suggestions are put forth, that various points will need greater or less stress depending on the parish and the special circumstances found therein. The writer's hope is that thoughts will be stimulated and avenues of procedure opened that will prove beneficial to the present and future religious educator. With this in mind, the *organization* of parish schools of religion is the first topic to be treated.

HOME-VISITING DEPARTMENT

One of the great problems in dealing with public school students is trying to get all of them to attend the parish school of religion regularly. Specific plans must be formulated to deal with this problem. Ordinarily, it is unrealistic to seek students through pulpit announcements alone. Some argue that parents have an obligation to cooperate and that the responsibility before God to send their children is on them. All this is true, but it usually will not bring the youth to religious instruction. Some additional moral pressure must be brought to bear on parents, though once it is recognized as pressure its usefulness is at an end. It is more realistic to say that parents must be helped to acquire the personal conviction that regular attendance at the school of religion is a good thing. In most parishes there are large numbers of Catholics who are indifferent, lazy, or simply unwilling to understand their obligations in these matters. What is earnestly suggested is a home-visiting department to create this climate of conviction through firm but inoffensive moral suasion.

If the problem of attendance is to be met successfully it will be given over exclusively to home visitors. Home-visiting has everywhere shown itself to be the most important factor in maintaining good attendance. The visitors link the home with the school, but they cannot do this unless they know that their authority will not under any circumstances be undercut, and that the school of religion cannot succeed without them. On the high-school level it is suggested that men do the home-visiting. Women may do it on the elementary-school level without loss of effectiveness.

Finding Out Who's Who

The first step in setting up an effective home-visiting system is to determine, as accurately as possible, who the children in the parish are who are attending public or other non-Church schools. In rural areas where everyone is known, this may not be a problem. Owing to changing population in cities and suburbs, however, unless there has been a very recent census parish records will not give a total picture. Let us suppose that a parish is establishing a school of religion for its members who attend high school. The first step in supplementing the parish census is to go over the lists of graduates from the parish elementary school of the previous four years. The help of several high school students should be enlisted in crossing off the names of those who have moved or who attend Catholic high schools. In case of doubt, the presupposition must be that they attend public school. Subsequent contacts with the students in question will eliminate any errors that have been made. The same can be done with the lists of those who have attended CCD elementary school instructions. In addition, it is sug-

gested that for several weeks in succession a teenage "data card"
be distributed at all Sunday Masses. In issuing a data card, one
should not disclose its specific purpose. Those parishioners who
have high-school youth in their homes or on their blocks should
simply be asked to fill out a card so that the names of all the young
people in this group, whether they attend public, Catholic, or any
other high school, may be known. On the data card spaces should
be provided for the young person's name and address, the name
of his school and his year in school, and a question inquiring about
his favorite sport or interest. By not explaining the full purpose of
the data card the parish school of religion will have a better chance
of receiving initial cooperation.

Making Districts

After the number of students has been determined, they should
be divided into districts according to residence. No more than
ten students should compose a home-visiting district, and each
district ought to have either one or two adults permanently assigned to it as home visitors. This means that if there are ten
districts, between ten and twenty visitors are needed. In making
districts it is strongly recommended that elementary and high
school students be separated. It is usually more workable to have
two distinct home-visiting departments, one for the elementary
school of religion and another for the high school of religion.

Key parishioners, known as captains, should be put in charge
of the districts in the two departments, one for each five or six
districts. Each captain supervises the home visitors under his
charge, helping them with their problems and checking to see that
the visitors are doing their work properly and faithfully, and re-
visiting difficult cases.

Home Visitors' Work

A home visitor is a personal representative of Christ. He does
not stand for "religious instruction for young Catholics" so much
as for the Master himself. Those whom he visits include all sorts,
just as in Jesus' day: parents and students who wish to meet the

Son of Man and hear His message, those who emphatically do not, and those who do not care one way or the other. A home visitor takes up the challenge of presenting a person to all three of the above groups. In representing Christ on the doorstep and in the living room there is no substitute remotely acceptable for absolute certainty in the visitor that he comes as an ambassador from Heaven to men. "He who receives you receives me; and he who receives me receives him who sent me" (Mt 10, 40).

Persistence, joined with sincere friendliness, is the key to effective home-visiting. In many instances, the parents do not practice the faith they profess. The young person in turn may be going through a period in life in which he feels little need for God. The grace of Christ given in the Spirit is really the only thing that will move parent and youth to cooperate. That is why one of the home visitor's primary tasks is to pray and sacrifice that the parents and children committed to his care will be open to God's gift. The home visitor's persistence and Christlike concern may easily be the last contact a youth will have with someone who is sincerely interested in leading him to God.

The main work of a home visitor is to keep in contact with parents. Whenever a student is absent, the visitor should take the child's textbook to the parents and point out to them the pages to be studied and the assignment to be completed. He should drop in on the home at regular intervals to give a report of the child's progress. He must make repeated visits to the homes of the students who fail to register, even when parents say they are not interested. Like Christ, he will "go in search of the sheep that is lost until he finds it."

It is important that the home visitor develop the same spirit of generosity and dedication that Christ possesses. The dogmatic foundation for expecting such dedication in lay people is the great gifts which God gives them in baptism and confirmation. United to Christ and to their fellow members in His body, Catholics are called to be those in whom Christ lives in a special way in their community. They are invited by God to become apostles—ambassadors of the Lord who strive in every way possible to lead those about them to closer union with God. One of the chief tasks of the parish priest is to help deepen the home visitors' realization of their unique partnership with Christ. A home visitor must grow in his awareness that he is an instrument through whom Jesus Christ Himself is coming to the people he visits. Once he begins to realize that he is an extension of Christ, he will be the kind of home visitor who does not give up in the face of opposition and indifference. He will more readily make sacrifices for his students, pray for them, and try to find a way to win them over.

Getting Home Visitors

When trying to get parishioners to volunteer as home visitors, general appeals should be avoided. A personal request by a priest of the parish is the proper procedure. It is suggested that the priest and two or three parishioners take the following steps in establishing the home-visiting department:

1. make a map of the parish and pinpoint the home of each Catholic youth attending public school;
2. divide the parish into home-visiting districts with about ten students to a district;
3. examine the districts and pick out several parishioners living in each district;
4. after having compiled a sufficient list of prospective visitors, make personal contact with the prospects and ask them to help in the program; this is ideally a work of the priest himself.

When asking a parishioner to be a home visitor, the pastor or assistant ought to propose the proper motivations, e.g., "Would you be willing to spend one hour a week for Christ . . . in thanksgiving for your faith . . . in reparation for past sins . . . in the spread of the Gospel?" The priest may also stress the following points: the ordinary home visitor averages one hour of work per week, if he proceeds efficiently; arrangements can be made so that the home visitor can put in his hour when it is convenient for him; it will be as beneficial to him in gaining insight into the faith he lives by as to the children and parents he serves.

Values of Home Visiting

The effort expended in seeking out parishioners to be home visitors and in developing a solid foundation for the home-visiting department is well worth the effort. It tends to strengthen the entire parish. Through the men and women who visit the homes, the indifferent and careless come to know that the members of the parish care about them. Besides this, those who do the home-visiting become a bulwark of faith. For as they grow in their awareness that they are the extension of Christ in their community, they tend to radiate Him more completely and thus build up the mystical body.

There is an added reason for using a complete home-visiting system: home visitors are concrete witnesses to the fact that God really counts in life. When people see respected members of the community going out after the youth of the neighborhood to bring them closer to Christ in the parish, they themselves become more aware of the Church and are sometimes led to follow Christ. The easy way out is to let two or three workers do all the visiting, or to resort to phone calls when students are absent. When this is done, the "witness" value created by the full complement of home visitors is lost. Ordinarily, attendance at the school of religion suffers as a result of such attractive short-cuts.

The establishment of a home-visiting department is strongly suggested even in those places where schools of religion are conducted on released-time. Visitors are invaluable for getting the parents more involved in the religious education of their children.

TEACHING DEPARTMENT

St. Paul once wrote: "We have been called to the apostolate and set apart to proclaim the good news now made known by God, as he had promised it of old through his prophets in Holy Writ. This good news concerns his Son . . . Jesus Christ our Lord" (Romans 1, 1–4). A teacher of religion is set apart for the same purpose. He is to be a herald of the eternal King proclaiming God's message of love and forgiveness. In ancient times a herald held a position of trust in the community. He was the one who brought messages of public importance from the sovereign. Jesus Christ, the chief herald, brought from the Father the life-giving news that God, through His only-begotten Son, invites mankind to enjoy an intimate and everlasting union with Himself. Grafted to Christ and forming His body in the modern world, Catholics are called by God to be instruments whereby Jesus Christ can continue to lead the people of today to His heavenly Father. The teacher of religion, like the Lord Jesus, is a herald of the great King. He is to transmit the message of salvation in such a way that students are disposed to follow Christ in their daily lives. He is to lay the groundwork, so that the Holy Spirit may lead students to a profoundly personal encounter with God within the framework of the body of Christ.

Goal

A school of religion will take a particular shape depending on what goal is set for it. If it is established merely to impart religious information, it will differ radically from a school whose goal is to direct the student toward a personal and intimate friendship with God and Christ in the Spirit. What ought to be the goal of a school of religion? The basis for favoring an educational program aimed at leading students to embrace the Christ-life in its totality is the personal nature of religious faith. Although faith is essentially an intellectual action, it is much more than this. A person may know the whole rational foundation of Christian belief, and still not possess supernatural faith. This is because faith is a free act, as the Vatican Council has stated explicitly (*Sessio* III, 24 April, 1870; D1814).

It involves a choice. Consequently, an act of supernatural faith is at one and the same time an intellectual assent to truth and a practical, personal acceptance of that truth. This personal acceptance of God's teachings is necessary because His truth is of a peculiar kind. The truth of God involves a person, who is Jesus Christ. One does not accept a person with sheer intellectual assent, as he would the conclusions of a mathematical problem. Close friends know each other with a kind of knowledge that is quite different from the knowledge of mathematics. It is a knowing that involves one's whole affective life. If one would know a person deeply, he must love that person. As his knowledge grows, his love increases; conversely, as love increases, insights and understanding grow.

Now this is the kind of knowledge which is involved in knowing God through supernatural faith. It is a profoundly personal kind of knowing, involving love and choice. Because mere intellectual assent is not enough for supernatural faith, the educational process in religion ought to be so oriented that it leads to a deeply personal commitment to God on the part of the student. For this reason, religious formation rather than mere information is the proper goal of a school of religion. Even the person whose task seems the humblest in the parish operation must know that a personal encounter of the students with God is the end toward which his energies are directed. He may be a member of a transportation committee or the custodian of the building during class time in the school of religion, but he no less than the teachers must know the core of the Christian message and discover how the truths of faith are centered on the mystery of Christ. During the long course of sacred history God has involved Himself in the affairs of men. He sent His Son to earth so that men might be led back to Him to possess Him. The student can be disposed toward a profound and personal acceptance of God and of all that this acceptance implies if everyone concerned with God's action in history, *now, in this parish*, is aware of the full implications of his mission. It is for this reason that salvation-history and the sacred dealings of God— recorded in the Bible and celebrated at altar, pulpit, font, and confessional—have such a key place in the educational framework of a school of religion.

Using Lay Teachers

In setting up a teaching department, serious consideration must be given to the use of lay parishioners as teachers. As long as lay people have been duly enrolled in the Confraternity of Christian Doctrine, they are given some responsibility by their bishop to assist in the teaching mission of the Church. Too often young people think it is the "job" of the priest or religious to teach about

God. When they observe a lay person from the parish however—someone like themselves—speaking about God and what He means in the religious, family, and business life of the teacher, students begin to grasp the importance of God in their own lives. The testimony of the Christian life as exemplified in the lay teacher can leave a lasting impression on youth.

A mighty, untapped reservoir of Christian laity stands ready to assist in the teaching mission of the mystical body. In most parishes there are men and women with attractive personalities who, because of their loyalty to Christ and their strong personal convictions, are fitting witnesses to the mystery of God's life-giving love for man. These are the people to seek as teachers in a school of religion. They do not have to be professional teachers, though normally these are well worth seeking out. The most important qualifications to look for are attractive, winning personalities, native intelligence, and deep loyalty to Christ and the Church. Such people can be trained to be excellent teachers of religion; but they must be trained, and over a period of years.

Establishing the Teaching Department

The first step in setting up the teaching department is to select a key parishioner as principal. If both an elementary and a high school of religion are established, a separate principal should be appointed for each. If possible the principal should have teaching experience, since he or she will be in charge of the teaching staff. The principal ought to be free of any other regular assignment in the school of religion (e.g., teaching a regular class) during the term of office, so that he can spend all his time directing school activities. Christ's success in accomplishing His mission toward the students and workers in the school of religion depends to a great extent on the quality of leadership displayed by the principal.

Several main ideas have contributed to the success of schools of religion. These should be carefully considered:

1. in its structure the school of religion ought to be a real school: it may not become in the minds of students or parents a

social activity or "just another parish activity"; it is the school where Christ prepares His followers;

2. classrooms ought to be used; if this is impossible, separate meeting-halls or even classes in homes should be worked out, so that students can be divided into small groups according to their grade level;

3. one or two of the regular teachers should be assigned as teacher-representatives, from week to week sounding out the problems, needs, and suggestions of the other teachers and making a report to the principal; with the principal they form the committee which is responsible for directing the teaching phase of the school;

4. the principal is to visit several classes each week, observe the teaching situation, and report to the parish priest on the enrichment of teaching, i.e., whether any depth is being plumbed in the teaching, who needs help, whether visual aids are being used properly and effectively, etc.

Check-List

The following is a sample guide of duties to be carried out by principals and teacher-representatives if there is to be a well-run school.

———— Prepare *calendar* of the school year.
It should include such things as the dates of class, dates of meeting between parents and teachers, graduation, etc.

———— Have secretarial staff make enough copies of the calendar so that all workers will have a copy. (It might be well to make enough copies so that each parent will receive one too).

———— Prepare *schedule* of workers' meetings.
Establish definite dates for meetings of key personnel, for the monthly meetings of teachers, evening of recollection for working staff, etc.

———— Have secretarial staff make enough copies of the meeting schedule so that all workers will have one.

———— See that the *letter to parents* announcing the opening date of school is prepared and mailed about ten days prior to the opening date.

———— Prepare *class lists*.
Arrange students according to the class they will attend, and assign teachers to their proper class.

———— Have secretarial staff make three copies of each classroom list.
One list is for the teacher, one for the secretarial office, and one for the principal.

———— Determine what *books and supplies* will be needed, and arrange to get them.

———— Check with priest-director concerning the amount of the *student registration fee*.

———— Compile a *list* of all workers.
This list should contain the name, address, phone, and position of each worker in the school of religion.

———— Have secretarial staff make enough copies for all workers.

———— Compile a list of *directives* for the teachers.
This should include such things as:
(1) name, address, telephone number of principal and teacher-representatives;
(2) attendance-taking procedure;
(3) particular regulations; e.g., reporting to secretarial office before and after each class session; conferring with teacher-representatives concerning problems, supplies, etc.;
(4) school policy concerning late-comers, problem students, homework, etc.;

    (5) report card procedure;

    (6) procedure for getting a substitute teacher;

    (7) procedure for notifying teachers if classes are called off.

_____ Have secretarial staff make enough copies of these for all teachers.

_____ Compile a list of school regulations which will be given to students at opening of the school year.

_____ Have secretarial staff make enough copies for all students and workers.

HELPERS' DEPARTMENT

The third section of a school of religion is the helpers' department. The helpers are often divided into monitors and secretaries.

Monitors

The monitors or hall guards have an important role to perform in the operation of a school of religion. They are to take care of its physical needs. For instance, they open and close the school, see that the lights are on, ring the bells for the beginning and end of class, supervise the corridors and keep general order. A few minutes after school begins, they collect the teachers' attendance charts and the books of those who are absent. These they bring to the secretarial staff, who in turn prepare the books of absentees so that home visitors may take them to the homes. During the class period a monitor should be stationed on each floor where classes are in progress. If a youth is dismissed from the classroom, the monitor attempts to get his cooperation. If a student repeatedly disturbs the class, the monitor is to arrange that the student be taken to his parents. The presence of monitors in a school of religion usually helps to avoid trouble before it begins.

Secretaries

A secretarial staff is necessary for the efficient operation of a school of religion. The secretaries prepare lists, address envelopes, make copies of necessary materials, and coordinate the work of the home visitors and teachers. A key woman should be put in charge of the secretarial staff, one who is able to get enough helpers to accomplish the clerical work involved in conducting a school of religion. At each school session members of the secretarial staff are to be present. Their main task is to prepare materials which the home visitors bring to the parents of absentees.

Home visitors, teachers, monitors, and secretaries are all required if a successful school of religion is to be conducted. These groups are like links of a chain; if any link is broken the chain falls apart. Another link in this chain is the priest-director of the school of religion. He is the last link with his bishop, who in turn is joined to Christ in the succession of the apostles.

THE PRIEST-DIRECTOR

Lay workers usually succeed in their task in proportion to the interest and zeal of pastor and priest-director. If workers sense that the pastor and other priests consider the school of religion very necessary and important, they will do everything possible to make it a success. Consequently, parish priests should frequently remind workers how important they are to this apostolate. They should build up their spirit of dedication, and urge them to make sacrifices for the young people entrusted to their care.

Suggestions for the Guidance of the Priest-Director:

Show an Interest

1. The priest-director of the school of religion ought to work in close collaboration with the staff. He should instill in them a keen sense of the importance of this work, so that they in turn will be a source of encouragement to the other workers.

Give Workers Responsibility

2. He should help workers develop a sense of responsibility, let them solve problems, formulate plans, and determine policy. Many workers lose interest and feel they are not really needed when the priest makes all the decisions and plans everything by himself or with merely one or two workers.

Keep Free

3. The priest-director should not tie himself down to a particular classroom or task. He is advised to keep free to direct the overall program, to give help when it is needed, and to counsel students.

Give Recognition

4. Occasionally, the names of the workers should be printed in the parish bulletin.

Make Visits

5. If a home visitor does not succeed after at least four visits, the captains should take their turns visiting the parents. If this does not work, the priest-director or the pastor should call on the parents. Only by persistent visiting will the wall of indifference break down.

Help Teachers

6. Finally, the priest-director is encouraged to spend a short time after class with the teachers, to help them with their problems, and to give suggestions and background for next week's lessons.

SPIRITUAL GROWTH

A school of religion succeeds in proportion to the spiritual growth of those conducting the school. If workers do not strive to become more fitting instruments through whom Christ can carry out His Father's mission, the effort expended in developing a school of religion will bear little lasting fruit. Christian spirituality springs from the bond which the Holy Spirit establishes between Christ and the members of the Church. Because we are the extension of Christ, our spiritual life consists in becoming more fitting instruments for Christ's manifestation of His Father's truth and love. Those who labor in a school of religion are encouraged to grow in the Christ-life, so that all they do contributes to spreading God's kingdom upon earth. They are to live out in daily life what they hold by faith, namely that only through Christ and in union with His Sacrifice can they reach the Father in the Holy Spirit.

Through a more active participation in Mass and greater generosity in the work of the apostolate, workers of the schools of religion are transformed into heralds of the eternal King. The more they enter into the mystery of the Mass and into the work of their school of religion, the more their hearts begin to beat in harmony with the desires of Christ and His Father. The eucharist and the apostolate are the two great means of transformation into the likeness of Christ.

Establishing a school of religion along the lines indicated in this chapter takes labor and dedication. Through it, however, Christ can more effectively reach out to bring the good news of salvation to Catholic youth who need Him so desperately. The silences imposed by constitutional principle, and the simple fact that religious faith is not professed by teachers and students in particular school situations, combine to indicate how greatly a concentration of temperate zeal is needed in this incomparable apostolic labor, the parish school of religion.

APPENDIX B

CHRIST'S PEDAGOGY

IN THE GOSPEL

Brother Philippe André, F.S.C.

The normal class hour of religious instruction is not especially alive, nor adapted to the mentality of the child, hence it is not very effective. It does not overflow into authentic Christian life because it is such a cut-and-dried affair. To remedy the shortcoming treatises on the pedagogy of catechetics are multiplied; most of them go out of their way to attend carefully to the laws of child psychology, while respecting the sacred character of the message to be got across. It should be worthwhile, however, in a matter such as this, to "go back to sources"; to put ourselves in the school of Jesus, in other words—to study His teaching methods as He presented the "good tidings." After all, the catechist is sent by the Master Himself for the sole purpose of performing the task described in the charge: "Go and make disciples of all nations . . . teaching them to observe all the commandments I have given you."[1]

[1] Mt 28, 19 f.

In speaking of the catechesis, that is to say, the actual teaching done by Christ and all who teach in His name, three elements are supposed:

—a matter to teach or *message* to communicate: in this case, the "good news";

—a *mentality* to overcome: at times a series of long-ingrained habits or prejudices to master, so that those depths of spirit may be reached where the message will germinate and ultimately bear fruit;

—finally a *pedagogy*, that is an intelligent approach calculated to bring the message deep into the hearts of the hearers despite their confused outlook or their wrong preconceptions.

What is the message? To what mentality is it directed?

Answers to these two preliminary questions will shed some light on the problem. But the core question that should hold our attention longest is, what was the pedagogy of Christ? We are going to attack this problem with those young people chiefly in mind whom the Church seems to exercise the least influence over: not the girls in neat school uniforms nor the boys whose parents see to it that they get to the Confraternity class regularly, but the ones who are not there most of the time; the ones the priests lose track of between confirmation class and the police court or the request for validation of an early marriage.

THE MESSAGE

Jesus comes from God. He is the Son of God. The teaching is not His, we learn, not that of the human Jesus who speaks, but of His Father who sent Him. He preaches the tidings that the kingdom has arrived: that kingdom of God predicted by the prophets and awaited by all the people. No, not all. An exception must be made of those loaded down with riches and prestige like the Sadducees, or with a sense of their own learning and importance like some of the Pharisees.

The reality of the kingdom, when it arrives, far exceeds in splendor what was expected. It is of another order, rather, being wholly of the Spirit. The message of Christ is a message of truth and of life.

"I have come to bear witness to the truth."[2]

"Whoever belongs to the truth hears my voice."[3]

"I have come so that my sheep may have life."[4]

"And eternal life is this, that they may know you, Father, and Him whom you have sent, Jesus Christ."[5]

A prophet sent from God was awaited. It is the Son of God, very truth and life, who has come, making Himself the way to God. This message is not so much a doctrine as a person; an epiphany of God.

This living, personal message demands an adherence of the same order. Jesus does not say, "Follow my reasoning processes," but, "Be converted. Change your whole way of seeing and judging. Believe in me. Follow me. Be poor, be gentle, be single-minded. Let your hunger and thirst be for holiness and the kingdom of God is yours. The kingdom is 'within you'; it depends upon you for its coming."

If the gospel contains a dogma and a "moral" it is that God is a Father who watches over us. To love Him and to love one's neighbor for His sake is the sum of moral teaching.

What is the message of those who catechize? What do they bring to learners who aspire, despite all their scatterbrained performance, to the truth and life of God? A series of irksome lessons added to their other schoolwork? Or genuine "good tidings" such as the angels proclaimed on the day of Christ's birth? The news that is shared with them must be a cause of great joy. It has to convince them that they are children of God, brothers of Christ, redeemed by Him and called to have a part in His kingdom; better than that, it must convey that they are called to bring it about.[6] Surely this is the sublimest venture anyone could propose to them.

[2] Jn 18, 37.
[3] *Ibid.*
[4] Jn 10, 10.
[5] Jn 17, 3.
[6] "We are charged to announce the gospel, a word that means 'good news.' While we have preserved the word 'gospel,' it is not true that we have so organized our mental categories that it no longer signifies 'good

MENTALITY

Such in broad outline is the message.

What is the state of mind of those who hear it? Are they ready for it?

If the leaders of the Jews had had less carnal hearts, if they had grasped the teaching of all their great religious geniuses from Moses down to the last of the prophets and the Book of Wisdom, this message would not have scandalized them. It would have filled them with wonder and more than satisfied their hopes by corresponding to the deepest aspirations of a people gradually educated by the Lord.[7] The kingdom of God which the new prophet Jesus speaks about all await, all that is except the skeptics and the sensualists.

The great commandments about the love of God and neighbor are in the Law, of course (Dt 6, 4f.; Lv 19, 18). They are read in the synagogues; the first is recited in daily prayer.

There is widespread belief in the resurrection of the body, except among the Sadducees who find satisfaction in the life of this world. A slow, providential education has refined the ancient Israelite concepts of a purely temporal justice and retribution. The wicked may prosper but they will yet have their punishment. The just may be condemned and persecuted (what prophet has not been?) but "they are in the hand of God"; such men are truly wise. This is what the contemporaries of Jesus read in their holy writings.

These people are very religious, taken as a whole. They venerate

---

news'? Listen to catechists or to preachers. Do you get the impression from hearing them that what they have to say is *news*? In the first place doesn't their tone convey the impression that it is a sad tale they are communicating rather than a good report? One needs to be an incurable optimist to hear 'good news' in our parishes at the Sunday Masses. It is more realistic to call it stale news, dated—'old stuff.' You get the idea that everything about it is stereotyped, dull, has been trotted out hundreds and hundreds of times; has been endlessly repeated, endlessly listened to, endlessly ignored." J. Michonneau and H. Chéry, O.P., *La Paroisse, communauté missionnaire* (Paris: Eds. du Cerf, 1946), p. 138.

[7] Cf. A. Gelin, "God's Design in Mankind," in *The Key Concepts of the Old Testament* (New York: Sheed and Ward, 1955), pp. 36–63.

the Law, observe it scrupulously. Bloody victims continue to be offered, morning and evening, in the temple at Jerusalem.

But if one examines more closely, he quickly sees that the teachings of the prophets are not grasped. Except for the insights proper to a "little remnant," there is evidence that these beliefs are superficial and exterior among the great majority. They await the kingdom of God and the Messia but what kingdom, what Messia? A realm of glory like David's? A national Messia, powerful, warlike, who will reestablish independence and put the Romans to rout? The Messia who in fact comes is the Son of God in the strict sense. He preaches an interior and spiritual kingdom, a universal one in which the title "son of Abraham" counts for nothing when it comes to disposition of the heart. "Many will come from the east and from the west, and will take their places in the kingdom of God with Abraham . . . while that kingdom's own sons are cast into the darkness without . . ."[8] Had they but recognized him, the Messia could have been for them a king of peace reigning over faithful souls; but by their hardness of heart and their spirit of hate they will make him a suffering Messia.[9]

What has been made of the twofold commandment of love which the Law contains? The postexilic scribes have abandoned it to follow their traditions. Their religion is formalistic and external, a matter of homage with the lips while the heart is far from God. The things that count for them are blood sacrifices and the minute observance of the Sabbath rather than charity; ritual purifications and repeated ablutions of body rather than interior freedom from stain; prayers, fasts, and almsdeeds in preference to the purity of intention of works done secretly before the Lord. Such is the

[8] Mt 8, 11 f.

[9] "The Messiah is there, but the form his mission will be allowed to take depends on the readiness of the people. The coldness and reserve with which he is received do not permit him to become the Prince of Peace he should have become in the immeasurable abundance of the prophecies. . . . His intrinsic sacrifice is turned outward, and the solemn revelation of his identity is linked with the dark annunciation of the coming agony, death and resurrection (Matt 16, 21)." Romano Guardini, *The Lord* (Chicago: Henry Regnery, 1954), p. 222.

mentality of the leading classes, of those "who sit in Moses' seat." The "man in the street" is influenced to think in this vein because he knows no better. He follows what he sees done higher up.

These are not a few obstacles to overcome, and they are not small ones. Apathy, torpor, inveterate habits in some; incomprehension and resistance in others; perhaps violent opposition in a few. Conflict is inevitable. The message will not easily gain a hearing. Nonetheless it is required of Jesus "to bear witness to the truth."

How does he go about things, in light of all this? The heart of the catechist's problem lies in the answer.

Nowadays serious efforts are being made to ascertain the degree to which young people are impregnated by the mentality of the age. Unprotected, they are left to the formative influences of companions, the street, even the family, of television, movies, and comic books. Their minds are drenched with images. Youth dreams of unbridled freedom, thrilling adventure in fast cars, the adulation that crowds give to sports stars and "sex-kittens." In short, everything draws them away from the religion teacher, who by definition represents the humdrum, the "square." Youth seems so out of harmony with the message the catechist wants to transmit. The trip to a supernatural world must represent a terrible wrench of displacement to the young. The teacher looks for points of contact, chinks in the façade, through which to introduce a little truth. He does not find any and he gets discouraged.

As a matter of simple fact, could it be today's youth are more fixed and hostile in their attitudes than the Pharisees—assuming of course that their culture has conditioned them? Not a bit of it! They are surely better off than the doctors in Israel and their self-sufficient virtue. "Upright men of that type do not grow moist at the dew of grace," as Péguy puts it. No, our failure to "get through to youth" is chiefly owing to our not putting the Master's pedagogy to use. He never had a failure to record. His most noteworthy successes, in fact, were the victims of poverty and passion rather than pride. Suppose we examine his pedagogy to determine whether that statement is justified.

TRADITION AND
INNOVATION IN PEDAGOGY

The first point to be made about the pedagogy of Christ is that it is traditional and within the reach of all. He does not break with authentic tradition. Even when He seems to run against Pharisaic observances head-on He is in the purest tradition of the prophets of Israel. Resolutely He goes ahead.

He has no desire to abolish the edifice which Moses and the prophets have raised; He is their continuer. They laid stones in preparation. He is the chief stone at the corner. He venerates the Scriptures and considers it a duty to fulfill them scrupulously, that is to prove that in reality they are oriented toward Him. He respects the temple. In a holy wrath He makes clear the reverence that is due the sacred area. He shows respect for the Law by submitting to its least prescriptions, announcing solemnly that there is not a letter "i"—the smallest in the alphabet—nor a brush-stroke that will not be accomplished.

All the while, however, He is thundering against constricting and mean formalism. "Man is not made for the Sabbath, but the Sabbath for man." He shows that ultimately it is love which sends forth its beams from the center of the Law, summing it up and making every other prescription subordinate. It is better far to do an act of charity (and He bases His words on example by the cure of the man with a withered hand) than to observe the letter of the Sabbath. It profits one more to come to the aid of parents than to make a symbolic temple offering by way of compensation. Sacrifices offered to God are unacceptable unless one first is reconciled with his brother.

There is nothing revolutionary here. All of that teaching is founded on the authentic spirit of the Law. Even the scribes who were in good faith came to recognize this, like the one St. Mark tells of (12, 32 f.): "Truly, Master, you have answered well. . . . To love Him with one's whole heart, and with one's whole mind, and with one's whole strength, and to love one's neighbor as oneself, is more precious than all burnt offerings and sacrifices." These truths had come to be almost forgotten, however. For one loyal scribe there were many who remained obstinate in their blindness.

The chief result of the primacy Jesus conferred upon love was a teaching invitingly open to the breath of the Spirit—not imprisoned stiffly in the letter.

The case is similar with the relative position He accorded to interior dispositions and exterior acts. Religion is primarily an interior matter. "God wills to have adorers in spirit and in truth." He never looked for any other sort under the Law. Never could He be satisfied with a purely exterior worship. In Heli's time, the Israelites thought they had transformed the holy ark into a magic talisman, brought it to their camp to win a victory over the Philistines. They were defeated and the ark captured (1 Sm 4, 3–11). At the time of Jerusalem's siege in 587, Jeremia, in the name of Yahweh, fulminated against those who cried "The temple of the Lord! The temple of the Lord!" instead of changing their ways. Now Jesus says, "It is not those who cry 'Lord, Lord,' who will enter into the kingdom of heaven." He applies to himself the severe warning of Isaia with respect to the Lord: "This people honors me with its lips, but its heart is far from me." Religion from the heart is the only sort that honors God: the prayer, fasting, almsgiving done for him, not so as to be seen by men. Conversely, evil thoughts are what defile a man—murderous thoughts, adulterous desires.

There is no sharp break with tradition in this teaching, therefore; but with what force and insistence it sets the living spirit free from the time-hardened letter. No baffling language is used here. Every sincere Jew can understand it if he has ears to hear. The new light shines so suddenly, however, that eyes accustomed to semi-darkness or the protective shades of night will not be able to bear it. "They flee the light because their works are evil."

The teaching of the catechist must of course be rigorously traditional. But tradition is a life which one receives and then transmits enriched. It is not a human way of doing things no more than a few hundred years old. It was that for the Pharisees.

The catechist must ask himself if he has given free play, so to say, to this life-principle, not imprisoning it in molds, formulas, or attitudes that remain such and nothing more. He must try to bring everything to life by charity, to make all interior, to present the Christian law with all its duties and demands in a liberating way as the response of man's love to God's call. The sacraments must be shown as fountains of life constantly welling up from which children may draw in a spirit of faith.

The Christ-like teacher will try to promote a conscious and intense liturgical life, teaching the young through actual participation what the Mass really is. This assembly in unity around the victim Christ, in which one takes his part in the sacramental action by means of dialogue, song, attitudes, and gestures, by the offering of self, by communion, is the epitome or great sacrament of Christian life. Nothing less than an invitation to take part in the Church's worship can ever make the young feel at home in "the temple of the Lord," which under the New Covenant is the glorious body of Christ.

The young require a taste for prayer, the kind that is intimate, personal, independent of formulas and unrelated to stipulated times. Young people must be allowed to pray freely to achieve that. Relaxing the rigidity and sameness of formulas by varying and adapting them can help in that. A spirit of the need for prayer must be brought to birth; it will be a spirit of recollection and intimacy with God through Christ, and in turn His virgin Mother. There is no requirement to teach actions or formulas; there is one to form children of the living God "in spirit and in truth."

This means that the stilted speech patterns that mark the religious approach to adults and children alike will have to be jettisoned: the adjective "divine" used endlessly, "soul" never employed except in company of "immortal"; indeed the very summit of meaningless phrasing to moderns: "to save our souls." It is needless to say that the alternative proposed is not colloquial speech nor journalese, but the crisp clear speech that is able to determine whether the doctrine is understood or not.

SENSE OF PROGRESSION

A second characteristic of the pedagogy of Christ is that it is prudent and progressive. It therefore leaves no truth obscured.

Jesus has a sense of what is opportune and assimilable: "I still have much to say to you," he confides to his apostles on a certain occasion, "but it is beyond your reach as yet."[10] In this His pedagogy is no different from that of the Lord God all through the history of Israel, with the variation that now "the fullness of time is accomplished" and the supreme revelation is being given. He takes numerous precautions, though, to prepare minds for this shattering new knowledge. He does not cast His pearls before swine. There is an "economy" or careful plan in Jesus' message, especially in what concerns the revelation of His status as the Son of God. Exegetes observe it everywhere, even in St. John's gospel. There is good reason to speak of the "messianic secret" in St. Mark, guarded jealously by Jesus as if He were fearful to disclose before the appointed time His messiaship and divinity. He is prudent about transitions, sheds light in careful measure, frequently avoids those challenges of His enemies which are too specific or which categorically put Him "on the spot." "Why do you keep us in suspense? If you are the Christ, tell us openly."[11] He prefers to respond indirectly by His works; they are sufficiently of God for those who wish to see.

Once the proper moment has come, however, He does not hesitate to make those revelations which circumstances demand, or to tell the whole truth even at the risk of scandalizing and precipitating defections. "Blessed is he who does not lose confidence in me."[12] A certain amount of scandal over Him is inevitable, He will later teach. Despite it, men will be obliged to make a choice. Truths hard to accept, even though received confidently enough ("To whom shall we go? You have the words of eternal life . . ."[13]), are not grasped immediately by even the best listeners. What does

[10] Jn 16, 12.
[11] Jn 10, 24.
[12] Mt 11, 6.
[13] Jn 6, 69.

it matter? The truth has been sown like seed at the opportune time. It will germinate if the soil is good.

Jesus reckons in the factors of time, of repetition, of the lesson taught by events such as His death and resurrection. He counts especially on the coming of the Holy Spirit. Jesus proceeds somewhat like a farmer who knows that whether he sleeps or wakes the seed continues its process unseen but nevertheless uninterruptedly.[14]

To be prudent and progressive with children means that certain truths will always be in process of being prepared for; they will be adapted to the children's capacities, but never minimized. Pupils must be introduced to the heart of the sacred mysteries, however taxing the effort. They may not be familiarized with them at the threshold, so to say. God expects man to go beyond bare minimums, to seek perfection and die to self. Hence all the "hard sayings" must be revealed to the child: the need to carry one's cross, renounce self, do penance, lose one's life, forgive everyone from the bottom of one's heart. The Christian is a person who makes a place in his life for the cross because it is the sole way to life, the unique means of redemption by Christ. ("If the seed die not . . .") Yet the cross will always be a folly and a scandal. ("Let him who can take this in, take it . . .") Not to lead young people in that direction—prudently, progressively, going at their pace, taking them as they are—would simply be to keep them busy while leaving aside the essential problem.

The normal hardships of the poor will be ascetical program enough for them, but as in Jesus' day they must be taught how these should be accepted and why others must alleviate them. A greater problem for our day is the right attitude toward a comfortable existence. The voluntary poverty of religious should not be normative for layfolk, least of all for children. Ascetical practices injurious to bodily or mental health may never be prescribed. What must be taught is a love for things and a disinterest in possessions, a respect for conveniences and an un-

14 Mk 4, 26 f.

concern for comforts. Paradoxically, economic status has not got a great bearing on the question. Except for the destitute it is largely a matter of outlook.

CATECHESIS OF INITIATION

With these last remarks we touch on another characteristic of the instructional plan of Christ, namely that it is what one might call a preparatory catechesis, a catechesis of initiation or testing. It is not a life itself so much as a catechumenate preceding the authentic life of real importance. The catechesis of Christ was intended to clear away the underbrush, set boundary markers, and open up the spirit rather than fill it with definitive teaching. It was in short an approach to hearers that derived from their actual needs. Our aim is to create in hearts those conditions favorable to acceptance of the message. Fruition will come only if good soil is prepared for the seed of the Word to grow in. The catechesis of Jesus tries to beget in souls those simple, elementary dispositions which will open them up to the kingdom of God.

a. One negative disposition is that of liberty of spirit sometimes erroneously called "detachment." "Where your treasure is, there also is your heart."[15] If the heart is possessed by "goods and services," ambitions, the heat of passion, it is not free to receive the message of Christ. Even if the heart should receive it, all these brambles as they proliferate will stifle it. If the heart is too given over to endless acquisition—toys, guns, furniture, furs, "which rust and moth consume"—it will not suspect the existence of the hidden treasure for which it should sell all. It is closed to the message.

b. A no less indispensable disposition is a hunger and thirst for holiness. Not a vague desire, platonic, sterile, but a dynamic love —what St. John forcefully describes as "doing the truth." "He whose life is true (*qui facit veritatem*) comes to the light," presents himself to its rays, while "he who acts shamefully hates the light, will not come into the light, for fear that his doings will be found out."[16] Every adult is in some measure a prisoner of his own past; he has

[15] Mt 6, 21.
[16] Jn 3, 20 f.

created himself in an image which he does not care to disavow. There are actually few who love "justice." There is need of the simplicity of outlook and purpose that is proper to the small child. He does not have the complete faith in his own insights that is the canker of adulthood. The sufficiency which catches the Pharisees in the trap of their own excellence needs to be dislodged. They are too wise, too knowing; they see much too clearly.[17] They are altogether too virtuous, too just, and Jesus "did not come for the just, but for sinners." "Father, I give you praise that you have hidden all this from the wise and the prudent, and revealed it to little children!"[18]

c. Once the light of Christ is admitted into hearts in virtue of this liberation and desire, once men are open to His unimpeded activity, only one thing may be expected to follow: their irrevocable attachment to His person in full confidence and faith. Even the most shattering revelations (like the passion) and lost illusions (like that of the earthly kingdom) will be neutralized by this strong attachment.

In concluding His catechesis to the apostles, Jesus opens their souls to the light; He binds them to Himself and insists that there is no turning back. Despite this, they are still far from realizing the demands laid on the perfect disciple. In a sense it does not matter. What remains to be done is the work of the Holy Spirit in the souls of those who live in the faith and love of Christ. Jesus has been but

[17] "Upright men, or at least those who call themselves such and like to be so described, have no chinks in their armor. You can not wound them. Their forever intact moral pelt is a breastplate and a hide free of any flaw. They present no opening that might lead to a grievous wound, an unforgettable distress, a regret beyond overcoming, a sutured spot forever botched, an imperceptible backward look of anxiety, a scar ill-healed for all time. They do not present that entry to grace which is, essentially, sin. Because they lack nothing, that which is all can not be brought to them. Even the charity of God can not dress those who have no wounds. Righteous living has the power to clothe a man against grace. Morality makes us the proprietors of our poor virtues. Grace makes of us a single family, one race of men. Grace makes us sons of God and brothers of Jesus Christ." Charles Péguy, *La note conjointe sur M. Descartes et la philosophie cartésienne* (Paris, 1924), pp. 101–103.

[18] Mt 11, 25.

the *preparatory* catechist for the true interior Master to whom the disciples were entrusted with the words, "He will recall to your minds everything I have said to you."[19]

Is the contemporary catechetical effort patient enough? Is it humble enough? Are its laborers satisfied to be merely modest precursors of the only true Catechist, that Master of the interior life, the Holy Spirit? It would certainly be vanity to pretend to do better than Christ in this matter.

The adult tends to stuff youngsters with all the religious knowledge possible, on the false assumption that if they do not learn these things in school they will never have the time nor taste to learn them in life. At all costs they must be encased in the armor of good habits, made to conform to a pattern of virtuous behavior. A certain measure of conformity is doubtless necessary, but careful attention must be paid to the vocations of children as individuals.

If a taste for God has been awakened in their souls, a desire for him, "a famine and a thirst not of bread and water only but for hearing the words of the Lord";[20] if their gaze has been turned toward invisible reality because the teacher's gaze—and this they can mark easily enough—is directed there, but without contempt for this world; if they have been launched on the great adventure of search for the hidden pearl and treasure; if, through a catechist's voice, they have met Christ and are attached to Him because He has the words of eternal life,[21] then a task has been accomplished in depth far more effective than any scheme of guaranteed behavior within school hours.

The habits that take such pains to inculcate and consume so much time, they will probably lose soon enough. Their surroundings will see to that. But a need within their beings, a sense of unrest, a hunger, these are things that will carry them through the most treacherous eddies of life. And the interior Master, the

19 Jn 14, 26.
20 Am 8, 11.
21 Cf. Mt 16, 16; Jn 6, 69.

Holy Spirit, what do we make of Him? Do we believe in the efficacy of His action more than in our own? If we do, we should make our modest work one of preparation. We must be convinced we have done enough if we have taught them to listen for His inspirations and to pray to the heavenly Father under His guidance.

APPEAL TO PERSONAL LIBERTY

With Christ it comes down to a single thing: one must pronounce freely that decisive choice which will bind him to his eternal destiny. "He who believes will be saved . . . he who refuses belief will be condemned."[22] Christ's is a catechesis sensitive to human liberty, but it is also a pressing appeal to this liberty to commit itself. The divine principle remains unchanged. Christ proposes, He does not impose, Himself. He plays the great game of freedom to the hilt. He accepts all its risks and knows that it can result in the apparent failure of His action. The same seed tiny as the mustard falls on all sorts of ground. Whether received, rejected, or trampled on along the public roads, it is this Word that will pass judgment on souls.[23]

The supernatural which Christ comes to reveal does not win its victories through intellect alone but through the whole being, by means of symbols. Jesus presents himself both to the crowds and to His apostles by way of signs. He employs the whole gamut from the most visible to the most interior and spiritual. Once the soul discerns the first type—miracles for example—it goes on to higher things like the sublimity of Christ's doctrine and His holiness. All His signs, even the most obscure ones like the parables, are graces. All serve as tests devised to elicit decisions from every kind of hearer. There is an ambiguity about every sign that enables it to shed light or to blind according to individual prejudice or desire. Viewers will see in the signs the finger of God, marvel at them and be aroused to the supernatural, or else they will attribute them to the devil and shut out the light, according to the inclinations of

22 Mk 16, 16.
23 Jn 12, 48.

their hearts. Men judge themselves in all they do according to their natures.

Two specific examples should illustrate this method of Christ's, the one of miracles and the other of parables.

Miracles are visible signs of the supernatural truth or fact proposed. They teach by action. Their purpose is to jolt, to astonish, to force attention on souls enmeshed in the material. In the face of miracles three attitudes come to the fore:

Some see them, express amazement at them as they would at anything out of the ordinary, but put no questions to themselves.

Others take scandal at them and make a show of challenging the Wonder-worker on His credentials. They have experienced the supernatural but it sets them off balance because it threatens to dim their star.

Lastly, there are those who ask themselves the question that Jesus sought, the one that comprised His whole appeal to men and His will with respect to them; it disturbed them in a way that was good for them, put indifference to flight and replaced it with "metaphysical unrest." "Who is this, that even the winds and the sea obey him?"[24] Or, "'A great prophet has risen among us,' and 'God has visited his people.' . . ."[25]

In a word, as a result of miracles some begin to be enlightened and to approach the kingdom of God. They are direct, simple. They hunger and thirst after justice. Others quibble, finding highly theological reasons to establish that Jesus is a sinner. They attribute this sign to Beelzebub, and since the common herd is naïve enough not to be satisfied with this, after the raising of Lazarus they decide to destroy Him.

Each individual reacts in accord with his deepest-seated views. His heart makes the difference. The sign acts as a judge of men. It was Pascal who wrote: "Jesus Christ came to blind those who

24 Mk 4, 40.
25 Lk 7, 16.

saw clearly and to give sight to the blind."[26] He appeared open
to those who sought Him with all their hearts and hidden to those
who fled Him with all their hearts. There was light enough for
those whose only desire was to see Him, darkness enough for
those who wanted it otherwise.

As to the parables, undoubtedly they employ a concrete language adapted to the popular mind, but one must also recognize
in them signs of a supernatural order that is proposed without
being imposed. They have about them a quality of half-light
which respects individual freedom.

One must dissociate from Jesus any designedly esoteric approach; speaking so as not to be understood, in other words, or
even in order to blind and pass sentence. It is true that He refers
to the prophecy of Isaia 6, 9 ff. when He says, "It is granted to
you to understand the secret of God's kingdom; for those others,
who stand outside, all is parable; they must keep watching and
never see, keep listening and never understand, nor turn about
and have their sins forgiven them."[27] De Grandmaison explains
these harsh expressions, which catch us up short by seeming to
attribute to God the will to blind men, by pointing out the nature
of Semitic speech. It is unable to convey nuances as between
what God formally wills and what He permits. Christ's mission is
to seek and save what is lost. He does not go against His own
mission any more than the prophets of old did.

The parables are a great grace but one which the hearers can
abuse. Like all graces they can be a two-edged sword to wound
or heal, to accomplish a cleavage between the seeing and the
blind. "Given a certain degree of ill-will, which only God knows,
the light has the morally inevitable effect of blinding those whom
it does not enlighten."[28] Grace is like the sun in that it gives light
to eyes that see and damages the blind even further. The mercy of
Jesus is thereby contrasted with the malice in certain hearts.

26 *Pensées*, 770.
27 Mk 4, 11 f.
28 Léonce de Grandmaison, *Jesus Christ, His Person—His Message—His
Credentials* (New York: Sheed and Ward, 1934), II, 40.

The catechist needs to ask himself whether, like Christ, he knows how to reconcile his strong desire to attract souls to God and respect their liberty? Can we speak with authority and conviction as Christ did, but stop short before the mystery of the human spirit to which no violence may be done? Christ wants to appeal to souls through the voice of the teacher; it should be a warm and vibrant one, and persuasive, but the catechist must have a horror of whatever smacks of charlatanism or propaganda. Any inquisition technique or disciplinary pressure with regard to prayer and the sacraments is absolutely out of order.

If the Christian's speech comes from Christ, it is evident from the start that it must clash with indifference or hostility, for it forces people to look within themselves and take a stand. In this sense the words of the teacher burn and smart. ("This is strange talk; who can be expected to listen to it?")[29] Easy victories should put him on his guard, indicating that perhaps he has not been in at the heart of the problem. The pious or denunciatory literature of the Church does not make souls ask themselves questions or spur them to any personal decision. The catechist does well to distinguish between the immediate and visible results of his action (easy solutions, such as a gentle intimidation that encounters no resistance, blazes of sentiment, the smooth workings of school routine) and its more lasting and interior fruits, the only ones that count for anything in the long run.

FROM THE
CONCRETE TO THE SPIRITUAL

Lastly, we need to examine some of the concrete means employed by Jesus in His teaching. They were well adapted to the kind of listener He had and designed to engrave the teaching in memory.

Christ's word is the ally of memory. In accord with the genius of His people and the customs of the time, He uses parallel sen-

[29] Jn 6, 61.

tences in symmetrical or antithetical expressions. Thus, he speaks of the house built on sand and that built on rock; the two sentences of judgment—"Come you blessed. . . . Depart you cursed"; the three parallel responses of the servants in the parable of the talents; the eye that must be gouged out or the foot that needs cutting off; the two ways, broad and narrow, etc. He unhesitatingly has recourse to hyperbolic turns of phrase, familiar in all the Semitic literatures. Generally the expressions are striking: the scandal-monger who must be thrown into the sea with a millstone around his neck; the outer darkness where there is weeping and the gnashing of teeth; the gnawing worm which dies not; the speck and the beam; the right cheek offered to him who strikes the left; the whited sepulchers; the camel passing through a needle's eye more readily than a rich man entering the kingdom, and so on.

He displays great force in his sentences which are delivered in sovereign tones ("with authority"): "Give back to Caesar what is Caesar's. . . . Unless you do penance you will all perish. . . . No man can serve God and money. . . . He who listens to you, listens to me; he who despises you, despises me. . . . The man who would save his life must lose it. . . . How is a man the better for it, if he gains the whole world at the cost of losing his own soul? . . . Though heaven and earth should pass away, my words will stand," etc.

His comparisons have a richness and variety, whether they are simply formulated or developed into allegories: the good shepherd, the vine and branches, the barren fig-tree. His parables are always evocative and realistic; all Palestinian life is mirrored in them. The grazing industry and agriculture have their place there (the lost sheep, the mustard seed, the sower, the seed growing silently, the weeds and the wheat, the murderous tenders of the vineyard); the rough life of fishermen on Tiberias (the net with its catch of all sorts); business (the crooked general manager, the treasure, the pearl); homelife (the lost coin, the yeast in the batches of dough).

These tales of His reflect effortlessly the hearers' preoccupations, their familiar way of life, the things they see, do, love, what they have had personal experience of. It is a great grace of God that Jesus spoke in a language so simple, so thought-provoking yet easy to grasp. The catechist may not rest at admiration. He must try to place himself in the innermost world of the young or he does not teach like Jesus.

The Gospels are likewise rich in object lessons. No incident is without its use for an opportune and direct application. There is the widow's mite, the lesson at Jacob's well on living water, that given to the apostles when they want to dismiss the children. At other times there are symbolic actions in the manner of the prophets: the withered fig-tree, the washing of feet and its immediate application to charity, the child whom Jesus put in the midst of his disciples as an example.

In the fourth Gospel certain miracles are used as symbolic and concrete lessons. There is the miracle of the loaves followed by the discourse on the bread of life; the cure of the man born blind, so obviously didactic, accompanied by the notice served on the Pharisees, "I have come into this world so that a sentence may fall upon it, that those who are blind should see, and those who see should become blind";[30] the raising of Lazarus in which Jesus is seen more clearly still as resurrection and life. All these miracles are strictly linked to the teachings of Jesus who is presented by St. John as "light and life."

Such is the whole range of means Christ employs to adapt Himself to his hearers. It seems needless to indicate in precise detail pedagogic applications to particular catechetical situations. All teaching must look to the mentality and needs of the times, and be rooted in the daily preoccupations of students in their social setting. At times the application of doctrine to life will suggest itself; when it does not immediately do so it must be worked on diligently.

One important observation needs to be made in conclusion. That is that Jesus never stops with means. He constantly insures the

[30] Jn 9, 39.

transition from the concrete to the more deeply meaningful, from the symbol to the reality signified. He sees to it that the attention is not hypnotized by the exterior device but that this always leads into the supernatural, the sacred, whether it be a question of prayer, adoration, or personal act of faith.

Even those means best adapted to the psychology of the young, the most ingenious explanations, telling comparisons, and graphic illustrations, conceal their danger. They can enlist the mind's whole attention on the side of their "materiality" and make the mystery disappear. Explanations that are too facile give the child the illusion that he has understood the mystery: he will lump it in with secular learnings under the same heading. Concrete means such as comparisons and word-pictures can hold the attention by their inherent interest without sufficiently letting the child's soul fall in with the supernatural plan. There is a real danger here. It exists in the classroom story hour and in colorful speech, but most of all in film strips and in pictures. Often these are very graphic without having a shred of the theology of mystery behind them.

Jesus himself was never taken in by quick, external results or by the enthusiasm of crowds after His miracles. Their marvelling at His discourses did not affect Him, nor any of their immediate reactions except genuine faith. At the risk of disappointing them and bringing on defections He deliberately accentuated the deeper significance of His deeds. The hearers who were too material and earthly-minded retired in disappointment or disgust, but others crowded around him more faithful than ever: "To whom shall we go? You have the words of eternal life!"[31] The general attitude after the multiplication of loaves, which was followed by the discourse on the bread of life, was typical. Jesus did not care. The catechist must not care. There is a sense in which he must fear an easy and popular acceptance.

CONCLUSION

This then is the way Christ's message and his way of presenting it must appear to the catechist. His pedagogy is an inexhaustible

[31] Jn 6, 69.

source of meditation on method for the religion teacher because the lessons come from heaven.

Let us recapitulate quickly some of the more important and too little recognized aspects of the pedagogy of Christ which must be put into practice.

First, there is the traditional aspect: Christ does not disavow the past but completes and crowns it. He proposes himself as the focal point of the Scriptures. For us that means that Christ must be made the central figure in the broad sweep of catechetical presentation. The whole story of salvation looks toward Him, either making ready for Him, living according to His sacrifice and example, or carrying His work forward through the ages in His mystical body. There is no sharp break in continuity between the two Testaments; there is only an ascent toward Christ and with Him a fulfillment, as when flower is fulfilled in fruit and the child in the man.

Most of all there has to be a profound knowledge of what is meant by the "good news," not just a mouthing of the term as a watchword. God has addressed incomparably good tidings to each of us. He requires of the individual an inner conversion to the kingdom of God. This good news should interest the learner supremely since his own happiness is at stake. Good news is not such unless it makes an appeal to the liberty of youth and solicits a response. This response can only be a fervent, unconditioned adherence to Christ. Young people learn more about making this response by contact with Christ in prayer at Mass, during which they do their part, or in the exercise of love of neighbor who is Christ, than by systematic, intellectually-oriented lessons. Nothing in the line of achievement is quite comparable to bringing the young into contact with Christ and making them enthusiastic over Him in a personal union that will develop shortly into a social one: Christ as the company of believers rather than as the isolated Son of God.

The light of the truth of Christ is not shed by books, though they may serve as a medium. It makes its way into the soul by a process of vital osmosis. The final object of all instruction in catechetical theory must be to establish a personal and living contact with Christ, a fervent attachment to His person. Otherwise the catechist simply engages in a succession of lost opportunities. All their lives long the young will strengthen the bonds of faith and charity by openness to the Holy Spirit, but these bonds cannot be strengthened unless they are properly forged in the first instance.

The divine teaching plan of the Old Testament is continued and completed by Christ's pedagogy in the Gospel. Neglect of one or the other is deeply injurious to Christian faith. If the teacher does not employ the dew and refreshment available to his teaching from the two sources, he runs the risk of that insensitivity to inspiration from God that Jesus taxed His contemporaries with so vehemently.

APPENDIX C

SOME LIGHT FROM

DEPTH PSYCHOLOGY

ON ADOLESCENCE

Marc Oraison, S.T.D., M.D.

THE integration of the data of depth psychology with the study of the life situation of the child as he enters puberty can be very rewarding, and help us understand better what is going on at this critical point of the child's evolution. Before expounding the problem briefly in its general lines, it will be well to make two observations.

First we must not confuse depth psychology with pathology. It is not our intention in this essay to study unnatural types or deviates but rather a dramatic moment in the history of personality.

On the other hand, it seems useful to underline that the experimental data from this modern study of psychology are such as to make us recognize the dynamic character of creation, of Christian life, of the human condition, of salvation. These data put us face to face with the practical consequences of the primordial mystery of the fall of man. Human nature is seen to be profoundly disturbed in the harmony of its positive dynamism. Man discovers that in the last analysis he cannot save himself. He requires the intervention of God.

After these introductory remarks let us recall rather summarily a few characteristics of the psychological transformation which puberty initiates, seen in light of these new data.

The onset of adolescence is marked initially by a reexperiencing of the evolutionary stages of earliest childhood with a new intensity and awareness. The fact is that there is a real, vital continuity between the newborn child and the adult; this continuity takes the form of development. Virtually speaking, the child is conscious and rational from his conception, but he achieves a real entry into the world of the spirit only around his sixth or seventh year. Up to that point his evolution has been carried on in an essentially affective mode. He reacts out of instinct. Being a conflict situation, this reaction can be momentous in its consequences. In man instinct is not an infallible dynamic life-force, only an impulse.

As he approaches the seventh or eighth year—the onset of Freud's "period of latency"—the chaotic debates of the world of instinct are regulated, to some degree. He learns to live according to the rhythm of reason. This is the age of school attendance; it is likewise the age aptly termed by certain authors that of the "child-adult." The subject adapts well to the world in which he lives. He finds himself in a temporary, satisfying state of balance. His various dynamisms—whether instinctive or cognitive—are resolved in the context of family and school with something resembling harmony.

But the child must enlarge his adaptation to the quasi-unlimited world of the adult no matter what it costs him; in other words, he must somehow face the world as it is. Something of his childhood security will be demolished in the interests of achieving a new equilibrium. The biological role of puberty on the physiological plane brings about complete transformation of the definitive functions of the adult. On the psychological plane, the rational world of the child must receive a violent thrust from the forces of instinct which he is to some degree conscious of, at least in their effects. These forces have already had a history in him, so this reexamination will take place in accord with an already constituted living physiognomy. Quite simply, these are the dramas of his early childhood. The subject will relive them with conscious intensity. If these primitive dramas have been badly resolved their traces can disturb, retard, or even—in pathological cases—block, the harmony of the unfolding process. This new perspective issues from certain scientific works of Freud which put us forcibly in the presence of an elementary truth too often forgotten.[1] The psychology of a living human being is not reducible to general principles, however exact they may be on the theoretical level. It represents a *personal, experienced history* from birth.

We must take former episodes in this history into account if we wish to understand what is going on at the moment we are considering. But it should not be forgotten—a logical consequence of what has just been said—that the general descriptions we provide will have value as a schema (or hypothesis) only. They are meant merely to help clarify the exposition.

In the first stages of life, all the affective areas react together in a vague and confused way, centered around the satisfaction or frustration experienced at the higher extremity of the digestive tube. This is called the oral stage. In matters such as this we must use a vocabulary analogous to that of adulthood to describe, however inadequately, the affective reactions of early infancy. It is evident of course that these terms will have a merely suggestive value. In a sense the nursing baby looks for satisfaction and finds it only in connection with eating. One may say that his mother represents warmth, security, solicitude, and nourishment to him, and also stands in the place of the first woman he meets. (The "sexuality of nourishment," an idea that has shocked many

---

[1] It is evident that we are leaving to one side the philosophical reflections of this author, derived from his doctrinaire outlook.

right-thinking persons, consists in certain vague and confused reactions that are nonetheless real.) The affective evolution of the first years consists essentially in this, that in his reactions and then in his conscious awareness the child is going to distinguish, to individualize, the different elements of instinctive and affective life. This is done in successive stages which are progressive discoveries; their importance is considerable for subsequent equilibrium in psychological life. There is no need to describe all of them. We shall give only three examples destined to convey this evolutional continuity.

Weaning is a real disturbance in the affective habits of the nursing baby. He passes from a total alimentary dependence to an autonomy of sorts. The oral aspect of his life tends to lose importance, in the sense that it is no longer going to take the lead in his emotional life. Set free from this primitive attachment to his mother, the child is susceptible to a widened interest that will include other things. This comprises an evolutionary law of growth, but it can also be a regressive attachment to primitive satisfactions. Patterns such as these can render the adaptation dramatic if external conditions are not favorable (weaning too late or too roughly, an unstable family situation, and so on). Persistent traces of a badly accomplished weaning are by no means rare in the psychology of the adult.

Another stage is that in which the subject affectively takes cognizance of his individual powers. This corresponds to the education of sphincters, that is to say the period when the child learns to eliminate voluntarily. That is why this stage is called in technical language the anal stage. At it the child experiences genuine and considerable satisfaction in imposing form on something that goes out of him. This is somehow—in an embryonic and analogous way, obviously—the instinctive root of what will later be the joy of personal creative action at the level of the spirit. So that this aggressive component may be distinguished harmoniously from the rest, and integrated into a new synthesis of affective life, the conditions in which this stage is reached must likewise be favorable.

It is customary to give the name "Oedipus complex" to the stage we shall speak of next, certainly one of the most important for later harmonious development. To understand this notion and situate it properly, it is important to rid it of all literary associations and recall that here again vocabulary borrows adult language; it can only be analogous, if not indeed symbolic. We shall describe rapidly the scheme of unfolding history in the reactions of a boy between four and six years, which in some way obliges him to depart from his primitive infantile state. For the girl the same general scheme is valid, but it admits of certain nuances.

Up to this time the little boy has heard everything from his mother, chiefly. He is still totally dependent on her and instinctively demands in return a sort of exclusivism. We might say that up until this point his mother is for him an animated object entirely at his service. Now, progressively, the person of the father takes on an outline he had never had before in the boy's eyes; his presence appears continual to him, though he is seen only periodically during the day. He evidently occupies a place in the thought and the life of the mother the boy had never suspected. The child then experiences vividly, although confusedly, a reaction of abandon, frustration, even protest against this father who thus "steals" his mother's affection. This sentiment is conveyed in amusing exchanges like the following, a dialogue between a six-year-old boy and his mother:

"When I'm grown up you and I will get married!"

"But dearest, how about Daddy?"

"Oh, he'll be dead a long time by then!"

This transitional stage is unbearable. The father does not disappear. The child's maneuver to recover his past circumstances of primitive passivity are to no avail, or else they pass unperceived (return of "babyish" behavior). In a word the child needs to go out of himself. Regarding this transition, we observe that it is the child's first true *experience of solitude:* he *feels* himself abandoned, dispossessed, when faced with a permanent dialogue of two *persons* who have vital demands and reciprocal relations. He will have to adapt himself positively to this aspect of the world he has just discovered. This he will be able to do only by following the main lines of a personal conduct that will make him enter the complex society of the family at his own level, and with a new sense of stability. The social aspect of the Oedipus is at least as important as its sexual aspect. There should be no need for insistence here on harmony and love in the family as essential factors in the normal psychical development of a child. This truth cannot be sufficiently emphasized.

The child has only one positive avenue of escape from his dramatic position: to cease experiencing his father as a rival and take him progressively as a model. This process can be translated by the phrase, "to become a little man like daddy." In technical language it is called father-identification. It will orient the child definitively toward affective reactions masculine in type (if the father is a real man, that is!) and lay a foundation for the sexual instinct. One can imagine the difficulties that arise when the father does not totally assume his male role in the family, especially when the mother has a tendency to be masculine. Unfortunately this is all too often the case.

These are not the only aspects of affective evolution during the first years of life, but they are doubtless the most important ones and those most apt to convey the dynamic conception of modern psychology. The unfolding of adolescence will be conditioned in part in its affective substrata by these early details, concluding around the seventh or eighth year. Experience shows that in general this unfolding takes place without too much difficulty when the critical points of childhood have been successfully got past. But this again will depend in good part on the affective climate of early childhood. There is nothing surprising in the fact that this early evolution almost never takes place in *absolutely* ideal fashion. There always persist what can be called "traces of non-fulfillment" which slow down or impede adaptation to the adult world in the course of adolescence.

We must distinguish carefully here. Certain unresolved conflicts concerning one or other primitive stage can cause true neuroses in adolescence, which will manifest themselves according to their proper modes at different periods. Most of the time, however, these conflicts will not have been very serious, and the normal educative climate helps sufficiently to resolve them. The subject will be able to relive them, sometimes tormentedly, it is true, on the occasion of puberty, without their greatly impeding his adjustment to adult life. This is the most frequent case. But it seems imperative to avoid falling into the contrary excess, namely supposing that every adolescent will get past this difficult stage without genuine neurotic symptoms that are accidental and transient. In this phase of his development the subject is actually torn by two opposing interior forces. On the one hand, he discovers by the very thrust of his own affective dynamism the interest and attraction of life outside the family—the almost limitless world which for all practical purposes he will be living in tomorrow; on the other hand, he retains a certain nostalgia for the childhood in which he found stability, satisfaction, a life without major problems. It is inevitable that, for a while at least, he will make certain untimely, retrograde steps in which he will be the chief sufferer, steps which will at times render his conduct incoherent and baffle him in his exercise of will. Neurosis may be described as a fixation in the adult of infantile patterns of reaction, and the resulting interior conflict. These adventures of adolescence are neurotic in the sense that they are retrograde steps; despite this they are not neuroses because they do not constitute true fixations. The conditions of everyday life make these little difficulties inevitable. Traces of primitive conflicts can never be avoided totally. Such is the fact of day-to-day experience. The only exhaustive explanation that can be given is not in the psychological order. It is one that corresponds to universal human anguish and the enigma of suffering: the revealed notion of original sin. From this point of view, the only human person in history who was adult in the fullest sense was the virgin Mary.

SOME PARTICULAR ASPECTS

Frustration

According to the evolutive schema of Nuttin, we can say that the psychic growth of the self consists in passing harmoniously from primitive needs, vegetative for example and quite uncomplicated (like the need for nourishment and security in nourishment), to needs that are broader and more specifically human—spiritual needs, that is. Primitive needs should have been satisfied properly if this transition is to take place positively and successfully; otherwise the subject will nourish a sense of unfulfillment, of lack, of *frustration*, to use the proper term, and will reply instinctively at the level of his "earlier self" in the measure of this frustration. A part of his affective dynamism—varying in accordance with the importance and precocity of this earlier self—will be unavailable for progress. What happens is that the essence of the dynamic "I" is not achieved because of this reflex of *narcissism*. In other words the subject must learn to overcome unavoidable frustrations and absorb setbacks. From a religious point of view this is of prime importance: after all, is not life itself terminated by the fatal defeat of death, and is Christ the Victor through anything but accepting and rising above this very defeat?

The period of adolescence is the last stage of *instinctive* rising above a barrier in this sense, that the subject must, in order to adapt himself to the life that will soon be his, relinquish a certain infantile security in which he is at ease because of his restricted circumstances. The unfolding within him of impulses in an adult key urges him on almost in spite of himself. His great hardship consists in taking on this blossoming process harmoniously so as to enter on adult or oblative behavior, as Freud would say, in a positive way. The adolescent often reacts to this interior impulse which baffles him and shatters his whole equilibrium by stiffening his defenses: processes such as moral response, ascesis, thirst for the Absolute. Anna Freud brings this out well in *The Ego and Its Defense Mechanisms*.

Refuge in an excessive and hypersensitive idealism is another way of inner withdrawal. Here the subject discovers himself faced with the discovery of the real and the actual, with an ambivalent world made up of good and evil. The discovery may be a progressive one or it may be harsh. He will come to know the struggle of life at the level of what until now has represented a certain degree of security to him: the family. If the shock is too strong or the ego too weak as a result of previous conflicts, the subject runs the serious risk of taking refuge in a lasting dream; to be more exact, in a compromise between dream and reality, seeking *passionately* to make his impossible dream and reality coincide. The typical expression of this attitude is the "flight from reality," which pursues the realization of some "kingdom of heaven" upon earth with complete single-mindedness. It is needless to demonstrate further the importance of the stage we are here considering.

Aggressiveness

At least as important as sexuality is the aggressive urge. This basic drive of the psychic make-up translates, on a psychological plane, the need each person has to maintain, ensure, consolidate, and defend his own existence. One can say without qualification that the child's aggressiveness, like his sexuality in a broader sense, is in the order of enticement. In other words, he perceives objects and persons around him according as they may represent an advantage or threat to his own existence. The psychic state of the adult is quite different: the relational sense (roughly outlined in the Oedipus conflict) develops, and the subject normally places himself at the same level as others in the depths of his being, finding security and love in an exchange. On the social level he discovers security, both communal and reciprocal. At the level of personal engagement he discovers the unity of a couple.

Adolescence comprises the last instinctive transition (or its last instinctive step), sketched out roughly in the early affective conflicts. On this score too, the boy is going to find himself a temporary victim of an inevitable pulling apart, a paradoxical ambivalence. It would be a mistake to look for conduct in an adolescent that is fully in equilibrium. On the one hand an almost irresistible force presses him to shatter the family tie, if need be intemperately and brutally. On the other he is incapable of rising above a certain softness or ease of childhood. He opposes his father violently, for example, but is still very dependent on his mother with an egoism which often takes the form of a repulsive cynicism.

From the religious point of view there is a most important matter here. The first notions of God the child can have are strictly tied in with the idea of his father, e.g., in the sign of the cross, the Our Father. At this period his affective reactions to the reality of fatherhood are completely conditioned by the relation in which he stands to his own father. In the course of growing up, he must somehow disentangle his theological awareness, if one may so describe it, from these affective reactions. He must put aside these reactions to his father, not only to isolate an idea of God that is as non-anthropomorphic as possible, but also to cease viewing his father as a kind of demigod and begin to see him as a human being like himself, his equal in the face of destiny.

Here again the adolescent stage can be decisive for the normal subject. It may even be the only point at which he can be helped. There inevitably remain traces in him of an infantile guilt—that is to say, fear of paternal sanction when he has done something stupid, not repentance in any strict sense. In this case the subject must be helped to pass from an emotional reaction of childhood to a genuine, consciously religious attitude. Traces of this confusion in affectivity between God and the human father—although inevitable at the outset—can linger on. Surely a solid and positive theological formation is preferable to an apodictic morality which seems to be conceived negatively much of the time.

The adolescent does not yet know how to make the distinction between respect and dependence as regards his father. Too often, family education is of no help here. The boy will have a tendency to show opposition—harshly, often enough—without anyone's realizing that this is still an aspect of dependence more than a mark of disrespect. From this stage, a transfer of attitude to God—not yet disengaged from anthropomorphic affective states—is only a step. For this reason it seems unnecessary and even unwise to get too excited over crises of non-conformism in adolescence. Such a response by the adult may easily have the opposite effect from the one intended.

Sexuality

The instinct of sexuality presents two components, both of them important but quite different from each other: eroticism and sentiment. To be more exact and in accord with the expression used by those expert in the study of sex, sentiment should be called "tender emotion." Anything like the aggressive instinct, and in strict relation with it the sexual instinct itself, undergoes a development at puberty which is accompanied by new, sensible manifestations. It becomes necessary for the adolescent to achieve integrity in his conscious and voluntary behavior as harmoniously as he can. Given the normal intensity of his discovery of sex (and the too-frequent ignorance of parents who, despite their serious responsibility, often fail their children on this point), this aspect of puberty takes on an importance that is potentially the greatest of all in the area of conscience. In its wake comes an affective burden of guilt much more intense than the individual concerned ever experienced before.

Normally, the synthesis of the two components of the sexual instinct must be achieved between ages fifteen and twenty, in such a way that eroticism fits into a pattern of dependence upon the sentimental element. In other words, in a well-developed adult eroticism loses the preponderant and often autonomous place it tended to have during the crisis, so as to be oriented properly toward sentiment. Thus it is that very often a boy who has contracted an auto-erotic habit of masturbation will see it disappear almost without effort the day he comes to *love* a girl. A woman then ceases to be for him a sexual *object* (in the precise expression of a young man of twenty who once consulted me), and becomes a person or *subject*. But at the age that interests us here, namely that of the psychological onset of puberty, the major risk and one rarely avoided—in virtue of the failure of parental education especially—is that of the masturbation habit.

First there is the fateful discovery of sexual pleasure, whether by accident or through initiation by others. Since the subject is still very much a prey to narcissistic relapses from a childhood he has not yet put aside, he finds in this pleasure instinctive compensation in his solitude, his black moments, or his temporary failure to adapt to the need for activity he experiences. It seems that whenever he experiences a mute unrest in the face of life, his sexual instinct returns to plague him. The vague anxiety which this practice instinctively begets will be compounded by moral anxiety. The subject habitually experiences all sort of difficulties in extricating himself. The physical consequences are negligible, but from the psychological point of view this constitutes an aberrant eroticism which is more or less obsessive for a time. It hampers the further normal evolution of the sex instinct, its proper setting in the ensemble of psychic life, and the beginnings of the synthesis spoken of above.

Masturbation in the adolescent, contrary to what can be called the pleasures of discovery at ages five or six, represents a real neurotic manifestation, in the sense that it immobilizes the normal evolution of the affective dynamism by constricting it. Without doubt the greatest risk lies in the potential contribution to fixing an attitude, or better a whole outlook, with respect to the spontaneous psychic structure of the future adult. This outlook is largely egocentric and is very badly adapted to the psychological requirements of that life with a partner in marriage which the subject is destined for.

On the other hand, since the synthesis of the two elements of the sexual instinct has not yet taken place, there is the risk that another phenomenon will arise. This is especially the case in circumstances where, practically speaking, the subject has only companions of the same sex as himself, for example in boarding school, under religious auspices or otherwise. This is the affective crisis known as "particular friendship." Often this situation is less disturbing than the description of it in certain circles would lead us to expect. It by no means indicates an ulterior homosexual orientation. The problem of homosexuality is infinitely more complicated, and besides, it throws down its roots much sooner in the course of psychic evolution. Particular friendships ensue when the emotion of tenderness, wishing to express itself, finds no other nourishment than the environmental context. A certain temporary shyness hinders the boy from envisaging any other situation than the present one, and so he seeks satisfaction of his need for tenderness here and now.

There are other cases in which erotic life will develop in a normal line but be reduced temporarily to a world of phantasms, or find expression in examining questionable picture magazines. If a person knows how to take advantage of such a crisis it can be an extremely fruitful aid in the discovery of a realistic giving of self.

True chastity—which is the contrary of ignorance or repression —requires a long educative process and a constant clarification. Prescinding from moral values, for the moment, it represents the ideal of psychic equilibration before the pairing off with another that is the normal conclusion of growth. This will even more be the case when an adolescent's orientation is in the direction of religious or priestly commitment, where the tendency is not to contradict nature but to rise above it.

Transference

This is a common phenomenon and one by no means confined to cases of psychoanalytic cure. In the latter the phenomenon of transference is intense, being a function of the patient's neurosis. It can help the analyst greatly in his work of drawing the subject out. But transference marks every human being to a different degree, particularly during adolescence. It consists in an emotional reaction produced during infancy before reason has set in, which if it has not been totally liquidated in the evolution of the affective process, tends to sink to the depths of the unconscious. Much later, on the occasion of an event which presents some hidden or apparent analogy with what produced the first emotional shock, it is translated onto the level of consciousness by a movement of the affective self disproportionate to the circumstances that elicit it, the affective burden of which often surprises the subject himself. Consciousness is stirred by something objective, but it is so upset that while it recognizes this intensely it cannot make any connection with the primitive emotional shock that escapes direct investigation.

In this understanding of the term "transference," one frequently observes in a child the welling-forth of an entire emotional world in depth, upon contact with a teacher or a "spiritual director." Affective relations with his father pass through a difficult liquidation-phase; then all forgotten conflicts with respect to this person who is inevitably clothed in the habit of authority or prestige tend to reappear in the form of transference. It becomes positive if the person to whom the subject transfers constitutes for him what is called in analytic language a "father image." He can be utilized very profitably in helping the adolescent grow into an attitude of adult autonomy. The transference will on the contrary be negative if the subject relives, through this father substitute, the conflicts of opposition which he experienced with his own father without knowing exactly what they consisted in. Here too the phenomenon can be very useful in achieving a destruction of the traces of infantile conflict. It is needless to insist on the key importance of the attitude of the educator on this occasion. Any "paternalism" is to be proscribed, since it is precisely a matter of the subject's passing *from* his father psychologically speaking. It should be realized that often such a "shedding" or violent opposition is not properly addressed to the educator but to a phantom of the past which the subject carries around with him. This notion, acquired through the clinical experiences of many over a long period, can help educators better acquire the virtue essential to their state: indifference to attachment.

* * * * *

The period examined in the foregoing remarks is the inauguration of a profound drama for the child who is becoming a man: a questioning of his whole self. He must emerge from this drama to a positive commitment in which he will construct a personal synthesis and exercise autonomy. The fact may never be lost sight of that his synthesis and autonomy are in good part a function of what has already happened, that is to say, of the patterns of affective evolution between birth and the age of around seven.

In a sense, one can do almost nothing during this drama, from the educative point of view. One can only follow it closely with care and discernment, at the same time guarding against certain errors which can only complicate the situation. From the religious point of view, for example, whatever could resurrect conflicts or give a place to infantile notions should obviously be avoided in teaching. This is very much a question of vocabulary; truth does not change, so long as teaching does not distort it in some legalistic or sentimental way.

Depth psychology makes good use of the demands that arise in family life which contribute to the evolution of a child. In a sense, if parents are resolutely decided to surpass each other in the basic quest for understanding and love, and if on the other hand they are penetrated by the elementary but too often forgotten truth that children are not created and put into the world for *their* personal satisfaction, there will be a minimum of havoc worked. This basic truth cannot be insisted on enough. The adolescent period, with its characteristics sketched rapidly above, is primarily an opening out of someone who has been readied for it long before. It is essential that the educator—completely beholden to parents at this stage—should realize that he is assisting in the making of a human person who is charged with a distinctive character fraught with mystery. On the educator's part the only thing that can contribute to encouraging the child is an attitude of respect, patience, and openness. To cultivate such an attitude is simply to develop the autonomy and the freedom of a child of God.

SELECTED BIBLIOGRAPHY

Books

ADAM, KARL. *Christ Our Brother.* (1931) New York: Collier Books, 1962. Pp. 128.

———. *The Spirit of Catholicism.* (1935) Garden City, N.Y.: Double-day Image Books, 1954. Pp. xiii + 260.

———. *The Christ of Faith.* (1957). New York: Mentor Omega Books, 1962. Pp. 408.

AHERN, BARNABAS, C.P., SULLIVAN, KATHRYN, R.S.C.J., and HEIDT, WILLIAM, O.S.B. (eds.) "New Testament Reading Guide." (A series of fourteen pamphlet titles). Collegeville, Minn.: The Liturgical Press, 1960.

ATHILL, MOTHER EMMANUEL, S.S.A. *Teaching Liturgy in Schools.* Chicago: Fides, 1958. Pp. 101.

BERON, RICHARD, O.S.B. *With the Bible through the Church Year.* New York: Pantheon Books, 1953. Pp. 243.

BOUYER, LOUIS. *Liturgical Piety.* Notre Dame, Ind.: University of Notre Dame Press, 1955. Pp. x + 284.

CARTER, G. E. and REEDY, W. J. *The Modern Challenge to Religious Education.* New York: W. H. Sadlier Inc., 1961. Pp. xvi + 422. This book contains an extended bibliography of specific articles from catechetical journals.

CASEL, ODO, O.S.B. *The Mystery of Christian Worship and Other Writings.* Westminster, Md.: Newman Press, 1962. Pp. xvii + 212.

Catholic Catechism, A (tr. of *Katholischer Katechismus der Bistümer Deutschlands*). New York: Herder and Herder, 1959. Pp. 448.

CULLY, IRIS V. *The Dynamics of Christian Education.* Philadelphia: Westminster Press, 1958. Pp. 205. This volume shows the progress of kerygmatic teaching in the Protestant communions.

DANIÉLOU, JEAN. *The Advent of Salvation.* (1951) New York: Paulist Deus Books, 1962. Pp. 192.

———. *The Bible and the Liturgy.* Notre Dame, Ind.: University of Notre Dame Press, 1956. Pp. x + 372.

———. *God and the Ways of Knowing.* (1957) New York: Meridian Books, 1960. Pp. 249.

361

————. *From Shadows to Reality.* Westminster, Md.: Newman Press, 1960. Pp. viii + 296.

————. *Christ and Us.* New York: Sheed and Ward, 1961. Pp. xii + 236.

DANNEMILLER, LAURENCE, S.S. *Reading the Word of God.* Baltimore: Helicon Press, 1960. Pp. xiv + 201.

DAVIS, CHARLES. *Liturgy and Doctrine.* New York: Sheed and Ward, 1960. Pp. 123.

DELCUVE, G., S.J. and GODIN, A., S.J. *Readings in European Catechetics.* Brussels: Lumen Vitae Press, 1962. Pp. 194.

DIEKMANN, G. L., O.S.B. *Come Let Us Worship.* Baltimore: Helicon Press, 1961. Pp. 180.

"Doctrinal Pamphlet Series." New York: Paulist Press, 1962–63.

DODD, C. H. *The Apostolic Preaching and Its Developments.* (1936) New York: Harper and Brothers, 1962. Pp. 96.

DRINKWATER, F. H. *Educational Essays.* London: Burns Oates, 1951. Pp. 412.

————. *Telling the Good News.* New York: St. Martin's Press, 1960. Pp. 228.

DURRWELL, F. X., C.SS.R. *The Resurrection. A Biblical Study.* New York: Sheed and Ward, 1960. Pp. xxvi + 371.

FARGUES, MARIE. *The Old Testament. Selections, Narrative, and Commentary.* London: Darton, Longman and Todd, 1960. Pp. 341.

FISCHER, HUBERT. (ed.) *An Introduction to A Catholic Catechism.* New York: Herder and Herder, 1960. Pp. xiv + 169.

GOLDBRUNNER, JOSEF. *Holiness Is Wholeness.* New York: Pantheon Books, 1955. Pp. 63.

————. *Cure of Mind and Cure of Soul.* New York: Pantheon Books, 1958. Pp. 127.

————. *Teaching the Catholic Catechism,* 3 vols.; *Teaching the Sacraments.* New York: Herder and Herder, 1959–61.

GUARDINI, ROMANO. *The Lord.* Chicago: Henry Regnery Co., 1954. Pp. xi + 535.

————. *Sacred Signs.* St. Louis: Pio Decimo Press, 1956. Pp. 106.

————. *The Lord's Prayer.* New York: Pantheon Books, 1958. Pp. 124.

HÄRING, BERNARD, C.SS.R. *The Law of Christ,* 3 vols. Westminster, Md.: Newman Press, 1961.

HOFINGER, JOHANNES, S.J. and HOWELL, CLIFFORD, S.J. (eds.) *Teaching All Nations.* New York: Herder and Herder, 1961. Pp. xvi + 421.

————. *The ABC's of Modern Catechetics.* New York: W. H. Sadlier, Inc., 1962. Pp. 119.

————. *The Art of Teaching Christian Doctrine* (2d rev. ed.) Notre Dame, Ind.: University of Notre Dame Press, 1962. Pp. 290.

HORNEY, KAREN. *Neurosis and Human Growth: The Struggle toward Self-realization.* New York: W. W. Norton and Co., 1950. Pp. 391.
———. *Our Inner Conflicts. Ibid.,* 1945. Pp. 250.

JOAN, SISTER MARY, O.P. and NONA, SISTER MARY, O.P. *Guiding Growth in Christian Social Living,* 3 vols. (1944–46) Washington: The Catholic University of America Press, 1957–59.

JUNGMANN, J. A., S.J. *Public Worship. A Survey.* Collegeville, Minn.: The Liturgical Press, 1957. Pp. vii + 249.
———. *Handing On the Faith. A Manual of Catechetics.* New York: Herder and Herder, 1959. Pp. xiv + 445.
———. *The Good News Yesterday and Today.* New York: W. H. Sadlier, Inc., 1963. Pp. 228.
———. *Pastoral Liturgy.* New York: Herder and Herder, 1962. Pp. 430.

KILGALLON, J. and WEBER, G. *Life in Christ.* Chicago: 720 N. Rush St., 1958. Pp. 286.

LEESON, SPENCER. *Christian Education.* New York: Longmans, Green and Co., 1947. Pp. xvi + 258.

LUBIENSKA DE LENVAL, HÉLÈNE. *The Whole Man at Worship.* New York: Desclée, 1961. Pp. 86.

LUPTON, DANIEL E. *A Guide to Reading the Bible* (in four parts). Chicago: ACTA Publications, 1959–62. Pp. 95 each.

MARIA DE LA CRUZ, SISTER, H.H.S., RICHARD, SISTER MARY, H.H.S. and LEONARD, SISTER MARY, S.H.F. "On Our Way Series." New York: W. H. Sadlier Inc., 1957–.

MARTIMORT, A. G., *et al. The Liturgy and the Word of God.* Collegeville, Minn.: The Liturgical Press, 1959. Pp. xv + 183.

MARX, PAUL, O.S.B. *Virgil Michel and the Liturgical Movement.* Collegeville, Minn.: The Liturgical Press, 1957. Pp. ix + 466.

MC ELENEY, NEIL J., C.S.P. (gen. ed.) "Pamphlet Bible Series." New York: Paulist Press, 1960–.

MÉNASCE, C. G. DE. *The Dynamics of Morality.* New York: Sheed and Ward, 1961. Pp. 353.

MERSCH, EMILE, S.J. *The Theology of the Mystical Body.* St. Louis: B. Herder Co., 1952. Pp. xviii + 663.

MILLER, RANDOLPH C. *The Clue to Christian Education.* New York: Charles Scribner's Sons, 1950. Pp. xi + 211. This and the following titles represent some of the best in Protestant catechetical thought.
———. *Biblical Theology and Christian Education. Ibid.,* 1956. Pp. xiv + 226.
———. *Christian Nurture and the Church. Ibid.,* 1961. Pp. xiv + 208.
———. *Education for Christian Living* (1956) Englewood Cliffs, N.J.: Prentice-Hall, Inc., 2d rev. ed., 1963. Pp. 448.

MOUROUX, JEAN. *The Meaning of Man.* (1948) Garden City, N.Y.: Doubleday Image Books, 1961. Pp. 278.

––––––. *The Christian Experience.* New York: Sheed and Ward, 1954. Pp. xi + 370.

––––––. *I Believe. The Personal Structure of Faith.* New York: Sheed and Ward, 1959. Pp. 109.

NORRIS, FRANK B., S.S. *God's Own People.* Baltimore: Helicon Press, 1962. Pp. vi + 122.

ODENWALD, ROBERT P. *Your Child's World from Infancy through Adolescence.* New York: Random House, 1958. Pp. viii + 211.

ORAISON, MARC. *Love or Constraint? Some Psychological Aspects of Religious Training.* (1959) New York: Paulist Deus Books, 1961. Pp. 160.

PIEPER, JOSEF. *Fortitude and Temperance.* New York: Pantheon Books, 1954. Pp. 128.

––––––. *Justice.* New York: Pantheon Books, 1955. Pp. 121.

––––––. *Prudence.* New York: Pantheon Books, 1959. Pp. 95.

REINHOLD, H. A. *The American Parish and the Roman Liturgy.* New York: The Macmillan Co., 1958. Pp. ix + 148.

––––––. *Bringing the Mass to the People.* Baltimore: Helicon Press, 1960. Pp. 114.

––––––. *The Dynamics of the Liturgy.* New York: The Macmillan Co., 1960. Pp. xii + 146.

RYAN, MARY PERKINS. *Perspective for Renewal.* Collegeville, Minn.: The Liturgical Press, 1960. Pp. v + 94.

SCHEEBEN, MATTHIAS J. *The Mysteries of Christianity.* St. Louis: B. Herder Co., 1946. Pp. ix + 834.

SLOYAN, GERARD S. (ed.) *Shaping the Christian Message.* New York: The Macmillan Co., 1958. Pp. ix + 327.

––––––. *Christ the Lord.* New York: Herder and Herder. 1962. Pp. 238.

––––––. *Vocabulary for the Roman Catholic Faith.* Flushing, N. Y.: Data-Guide Inc., 1963.

––––––. (ed.) *Foundations of Catholic Theology* (twelve volumes). Englewood Cliffs, N. J.: Prentice-Hall, 1963.

TERRUWE, A. A. A. *The Neurosis in the Light of Rational Psychology.* New York: P. J. Kenedy and Sons, 1960. Pp. xxi + 200.

VAGAGGINI, CYPRIAN. O.S.B. *Theological Dimensions of the Liturgy.* Collegeville, Minn.: The Liturgical Press, 1959. Pp. xii + 242.

VAN DER MEER, F. *Augustine the Bishop.* New York: Sheed and Ward, 1962. Pp. xxiii + 679.

VANN, GERALD, O.P. *The Heart of Man* (1945) Garden City, N. Y.: Doubleday Image Books, 1960. Pp. 190.

––––––. *The Paradise Tree.* New York: Sheed and Ward, 1959. Pp. 320.

VON HILDEBRAND, DIETRICH. *Transformation in Christ*. (1948) Baltimore: Helicon Press, 1960. Pp. ix + 406.

———. *Fundamental Moral Attitudes*. New York: Longmans, Green and Co., 1950. Pp. 72.

———. (with ALICE JOURDAIN) *True Morality and Its Counterfeits*. New York: David McKay, 1955. Pp. ix + 179.

ZUNDEL, MAURICE. *In Search of the Unknown God*. New York: Herder and Herder, 1959. Pp. 194.

Some Foreign Language Titles

ARNOLD, FRANZ X. *Dienst am Glauben*. Freiburg: Herder, 1948. Pp. 91.

———. *Glaubensverkündigung und Glaubensgemeinschaft*. Düsseldorf: Patmos, 1955. Pp. 141.

BABIN, P., O.M.I. *Les jeunes et la foi*. Lyon: Éds. du Chalet, 1961. Pp. 279.

BERGMANN, P., KARRER, O., GUARDINI, R. *Katholische Schulbibel*. München: Verlag Ars Sacra Josef Müller, 1958. Pp. 341.

BOYER. A. (dir.) *Enseignement religieux du secondaire* (10 Vols.) Paris: Éds. de l'École, 1954–60.

COLOMB, JOSEPH. *Pour un catéchisme efficace*. Paris: E. Vitte, 1956. Pp. 193.

———. *Aux catholiques: plaie ouverte au flanc de l'Église*. Paris: E. Vitte, 1954. Pp. 153.

———. *Aux sources du catéchisme*. I. Au temps de l'Avent: la Promesse (1946). II. De Noël a Pâques: la vie de Jésus (1947). III. De Pâques a l'Avent: le Christ glorieux et l'histoire de l'église (1948). Tournai: Desclée, 3d ed. This and the following title are resource books for teachers.

———. *La Doctrine de vie au catéchisme*. I. Vie nouvelle et nouveau royaume (1952). II. Combat spirituelle et soucis de l'église (1953). III. Portrait du Chrétien et loi de charité (1954). *Ibid*.

———. "Le Souffle de l'Esprit," 1. *Dans l'Église du Christ* (1960). 2. *Histoire de l'Église* (1959). *Ibid*. A secondary school textbook.

———. 1. *Parlez, Seigneur!* (ages 7–9). 2. *Dieu parmi nous* (9–11). 3. *Avec le Christ Jésus* (11–13). An elementary school catechism; with teacher's guides. 2d rev. ed.; Lyon: E. Vitte, 1960.

COUDREAU, FRANÇOIS (pour le Bureau Internationale Catholique de l'Enfance). *Dix années de travail catéchétique dans le monde*. Paris: Éds. Fleurus, 1960. Pp. 501.

ELCHINGER, A. avec DHEILLY, J. *Lectures bibliques, "L'histoire du Salut."* Colmar: Éds. Alsatia, 1951. Pp. 385.

FARGUES, MARIE. *Nos enfants devant Dieu*. Tours: Mame, 1959. Pp. 269.

FILTHAUT, THEODOR. *Das Reich Gottes in der katechetischen Unterweisung.* Freiburg: Herder, 1958. Pp. 224.

————, und JUNGMANN, J. A., S.J. *Verkündigung und Glaube. Festgabe für Franz X. Arnold.* Freiburg: Herder, 1958. Pp. 359.

FOURNIER, NORBERT, C.S.V. *Exigences actuelles de la catéchèse.* Montréal. Les Clercs de Saint-Viateur, 1960. Pp. 285.

GRELOT, PIERRE. *Pages bibliques.* (1954). 2e éd.; Paris: E. Belin, 1957. Pp. 386.

Glaubensbüchlein für das 2. Schuljahr. München: Deutscher Katecheten-Verein, 1962. Pp. 81.

Glaubensbuch für die 3. und 4. Klasse der Volksschule. Ibid. Pp. 223.

HITZ, PAUL, C.SS.R. *L'annonce missionnaire de l'évangile.* Paris: Éds. du Cerf, 1954. Pp. 267.

KRÄMER, KARL. *Gott unser Heil. 1. Altes Testament. 2. Neues Testament.* Freiburg: Herder, 1960–61.

KREUTZWALD, HEINRICH. *Zur Geschichte des Biblischen Unterrichts.* Freiburg: Herder, 1957. Pp. 305.

LENTNER, L., FISCHER, G., BÜRKLI, F. (eds.) *Katechetisches Wörterbuch.* Freiburg: Herder, 1961. Pp. xvi + 831 + 17.

MARTIMORT, A. G. *Les signes de la nouvelle alliance.* Paris: Éds. Ligal, 1959. Pp. 405.

MERLAUD, ANDRÉ. *Jalons pour une pastorale de l'enfance.* Paris: Éds. Fleurus, 1957. Pp. 205.

PESCH, CHRISTIAN. *Das Bild in der katechetischen Unterweisung.* Düsseldorf: Patmos, 1957. Pp. 198.

Pratique du catéchisme, La. Plan de travail pour former les catéchistes. Supplément à *La Documentation Catéchistique.* Paris: 1960. Pp. 131.

SCHREYER, LOTHAR. *Schaubuch zum Katechismus, eine Bilderverkündigung.* Freiburg: Herder, 1957. Pp. 160.

VAN CASTER, MARCEL. *IV. L'homme en face de Dieu.* Brussels: Aux Éds. "Erasme," 1958. Pp. 95.

————. *II. L'homme dans la communauté humaine. Ibid.,* 1959. Pp. 127.

————. *Dieu nous parle.* Bruges: Desclée de Brouwer, 1962. Pp. 120.

Periodicals

Bible Today, The. The Liturgical Press (Collegeville, Minn.), $5 per year, 6 issues.

Bulletin, Grail Council of Religious Education (Grailville, Loveland, O.), $1 per year.

Catéchèse. Centre Nationale de l'Enseignement Religieux (19, rue de Varenne, Paris 7e), 13 NF per year, 4 issues.

Catéchistes. Frères des École Chrétiennes (78, rue de Sèvres, Paris 7e), 9 NF per year, 4 issues.

Christlich-pädagogische Blatter. Katechetische Institut (Stephansplatz 3/IV, Wien I), S 42 per year, 9 issues.

*Clergy Monthly, The. Catholic Press (Ranchi, Bihar, India), $2.50 per year, 12 issues.

*Clergy Review, The. (14 Howick Place, London SW. 1), 40s per year, 12 issues.

*Furrow, The. (St. Patrick's College, Maynooth, Ireland), $4.50 per year, 12 issues.

Good Tidings. East Asian Pastoral Institute (Box 1171, Manila, P. I.), $.60 per year, 6 issues.

Guide. Paulist Institute for Religious Research (411 W. 59th St., New York 19), $1 per year, 10 issues.

Katechetische Blätter. Deutscher Katechetenverein (Kösel-Verlag, Kaiser Ludwigs-Platz 6, München 15), 15 DM per year, 12 issues.

Learning for Living. A Journal of Christian Education. SCM Press (56 Bloomsbury St., London WC. 1), 9s per year, 5 issues.

Lumen Vitae. International Centre for Studies in Religious Education (184, rue Washington, Brussels), $6 per year, 4 issues.

*Lumière et Vie. Pères Dominicains (2, Place Gailleton, Lyon), 18 NF per year, 4 issues.

*Maison-Dieu, La. Éditions du Cerf (29, Boulevard Latour-Maubourg, Paris 7e), 14 NF per year, 4 issues.

*Orientamenti Pedagogici. Società Editrice Internazionale (Corso Regina Margherita, 176, Torino), L. 2.500 per year, 6 issues.

Our Apostolate. De la Salle College (Castle Hill, N.S.W., Australia), $1.50 per year, 3 issues.

Religious Education. The Religious Education Association (545 W. 111th St., New York 25), $5 per year, 6 issues.

Sinite. Estudios Lasalianos (Tejares, Salamanca, Spain), 80 pesetas per year, 4 issues.

Sower, The. National Catechetical Centre (11 Cavendish Square, London, W. 1), 8s per year, 4 issues.

*Theology Digest. St. Mary's College (St. Mary's, Kansas), $2 per year, 4 issues.

Vérité et Vie. Centre de Pédagogie Chrétienne (1, rue de la Comédie, Strasbourg, France), 13.50 NF per year, 4 issues.

*Worship. The Liturgical Press (Collegeville, Minn.) $4 per year, 10 issues.

* An asterisk indicates that a journal, while not professedly catechetical, has a view of the pastoral task that makes it especially suitable for catechists.

INDEX

NOTES ON THE CONTRIBUTORS

Reverend Gerard S. Sloyan is the Head of the Department of Religious Education at the Catholic University of America, and the editor of *Shaping the Christian Message*. He is a priest of the Diocese of Trenton.

Reverend Joseph Colomb, P.S.S., is the Director of Religious Education in the diocese of Strasbourg, France.

Mary Perkins Ryan, author of *Perspective for Renewal* and *A Key to the Psalms* is also a well-known translator of religious works.

Reverend Franz Schreibmayr of the Munich Oratory is the co-author of the *Teacher's Manual* for *Katholischer Katechismus*.

Mother Maria de la Cruz Aymes-Coucke, H.H.S., co-author of the *On Our Way* series, is an Archdiocesan Supervisor for the Confraternity of Christian Doctrine in San Francisco.

Eva Fleischner is the Director of the Department of Religious Education at the Grail in Loveland, Ohio.

Sister Anne Norpel, S.N.D., is on the staff of the Lieutenant Joseph P. Kennedy Jr. Institute in Washington, D.C.

Sister Mary Nona McGreal, O.P., President of Edgewood College of the Sacred Heart in Madison, Wisconsin, is co-author of *Guiding Growth in Christian Social Living*.

Sister Mary Virgine Pugh, M.H.S.H., is a teacher of catechists in Boston and has been a lecturer in catechetics at the Catholic University of America.

Reverend James E. Kraus, S.T.D., author of *O Give Thanks to the Lord*, teaches at St. Charles Seminary in Columbus, Ohio, and is Diocesan Director of the Confraternity of Christian Doctrine there.

Reverend Bernard J. Cooke, S.J., is Chairman of the Department of Theology at Marquette University, and a contributor to many theological periodicals.

Reverend Theodore C. Stone, Assistant Director at the Confraternity of Christian Doctrine of the Archdiocese of Chicago is the author of a number of high school religion texts for public school use.

Brother Philippe André, F.S.C., is a secondary-school teacher in Lyon, France.

Abbé Marc Oraison, S.T.D., M.D., an eminent French priest-psychiatrist is the author of *Love or Constraint?*, *Union in Marital Love,* and the forthcoming *Illusion and Anxiety*.